More Praise for *Inrushes of the Heart*

"ʿAyn al-Quḍāt's scintillating spiritual prose is brought to life in this brilliant anthology by Mohammed Rustom. Rustom's impeccable historical and philological scholarship creates a conductor for ʿAyn al-Quḍāt's lightning-like flashes of insights on the nature of reality, humanity, intellect, ethics, and revelation. *Inrushes of the Heart* is a veritable defibrillator, shocking our spiritual hearts back to life."

—Oludamini Ogunnaike, Associate Professor of African Religious Thought and Democracy, University of Virginia

"Bringing to light the full spectrum of ʿAyn al-Quḍāt's bold and creative writings for the first time in modern scholarship, *Inrushes of the Heart* shows with blinding clarity why ʿAyn al-Quḍāt is to be seen as one of the most luminous stars in the night sky of Islamic spirituality and intellectuality."

—Omid Safi, Professor of Islamic Studies, Duke University

"The lucid translations and painstaking historical research on display in *Inrushes of the Heart* can serve as a model for scholars of religion and philosophy in general, and Islamic thought in particular. This definitive book on one of premodern Islam's most significant thinkers will be an indispensable resource for students and researchers for decades to come."

—Cyrus Ali Zargar, Al-Ghazali Distinguished Professor of Islamic Studies, University of Central Florida

Inrushes of the Heart

SUNY series in Islam

Seyyed Hossein Nasr, editor

Inrushes of the Heart

The Sufi Philosophy of ʿAyn al-Quḍāt

MOHAMMED RUSTOM

SUNY
PRESS

Cover Art by Seyit Ahmet Bursalı

Published by State University of New York Press, Albany

Printed in the United States of America

For information, contact State University of New York Press, Albany, NY
www.sunypress.edu

Library of Congress Cataloging-in-Publication Data

Name: Rustom, Mohammed, author.
Title: Inrushes of the heart : the Sufi philosophy of ʿAyn al-Quḍāt / Mohammed Rustom.
Description: Albany : State University of New York Press, [2023]. | Includes bibliographical references and index.
Identifiers: LCCN 2022053657 | ISBN 9781438494296 (hardcover : alk. paper) | ISBN 9781438494302 (ebook) | ISBN 9781438494289 (pbk. : alk. paper)
Subjects: LCSH: ʿAyn al-Quḍāh al-Hamadhānī, ʿAbd Allāh ibn Muḥammad, –1131. | Muslim philosophers—Iran—Biography. | Sufis—Iran—Biography. | Sufism—Iran—History.
Classification: LCC B752.A964 R875 2023 | DDC 297.4092—dc23/eng/20230424
LC record available at https://lccn.loc.gov/2022053657

10 9 8 7 6 5 4 3 2 1

In memory of Leonard Lewisohn

Contents

Detailed List of Figures xi / Acknowledgments xiii / Preface xvii / Format and Style xix / Sourcing Hadiths and Sayings xxi / Abbreviations xxiii

Introduction: A Sage in Exile
Life 1 / Execution 4 / Writings 7 / Reception 18 / The Present Book 21

1. Autobiography
Discovery 23 / Helplessness 26 / Tasting 28 / Charismatic Gifts 29 / Apparitions 31 / Muhammadan Encounters 32

2. Counsel and Confession
Advice and Admonition 37 / Criticism 41 / Sandal-Service 44 / Two Defenses 47 / Divine Jealousy 49

3. Heavenly Matters
The Essence 55 / Rational Proof 58 / Withness 60 / Divine Names and Attributes 61 / Oneness of Existence 66 / Levels of Light 68 / The Goal of Creation 70

4. Earthly Concerns
Good and Evil 75 / Cosmic Well-Being 77 / Against Dualism 80 / Bad Transmitters 81 / Compulsion and Freedom 83 / Guidance and Misguidance 86

5. Inside Out, Outside In
Intention and Sincerity 89 / Assent 91 / Purity and Prayer 94 / Fasting 96 / Pilgrimage and Alms Tax 98 / Praise and Gratitude 100 / Imaginalization 102 / Death before Death 108

6. Wayfarers and Masters
Habit-Worship 111 / Body and Soul 115 / The Heart 117 / The Spirit 123 / Wayfaring and Seeking 127 / Renunciation 131 / The Ripened Master 132

7. Knowledge Transcendent
Brothers and Mirrors 141 / Knowers and Recognizers 144 / The Scale of the Intellect 147 / Beyond the Intellect 149 / Self-Recognition 153 / Self-Perception 158

8. Quranic Origins
Paradise Found 161 / Vastness and Worthiness 162 / Knowing and Hearing 166 / The Imprint of Letters 173 / Letters and Dots 175 / Dots, Nothingness, Subsistence 182

9. Muhammad and Iblis
Periphery to Center 187 / Muhammadan Light 194 / The Black Light of Iblis 198 / Face, Mole, Tresses 202 / Faith and Unbelief 205 / Two Commands 210 / An Ideal Lover 214

10. Love Transcendent
Love as Guide 221 / Love and Loverhood 224 / Trial and Tribulation 228 / Madness and Burning 231 / The Religion of Love 236 / Levels of Unbelief 239 / Self-Love 248 / In the I of the Beholder 252

Notes 263

Bibliography
Works by ʿAyn al-Quḍāt (Editions, Manuscripts, Translations) 311 / Works Misattributed to ʿAyn al-Quḍāt 312 / Scholarship

Detailed List of Figures

Figure 1	Statue of ʿAyn al-Quḍāt (Hamadan, Iran); photographed by Omid Bayati	xxvi
Figure 2	Page from a manuscript of ʿAyn al-Quḍāt, *Tamhīdāt*; Süleymaniye Kütüphanesi, MS Ayasofya 1839, fol. 3	22
Figure 3	ʿAyn al-Quḍāt Artistic and Cultural Center (Hamadan, Iran); photographed by Omid Bayati	36
Figure 4	The symbolic tomb of ʿAyn al-Quḍāt (Hamadan, Iran); photographed by Habib Sharafi Safa	54
Figure 5	The tomb of Avicenna (Hamadan, Iran); photographed by Mohammed Rustom	74
Figure 6	ʿAyn al-Quḍāt's spiritual network; designed by Jeremy Farrell	88
Figure 7	Page from a manuscript of ʿAyn al-Quḍāt, *Zubdat al-ḥaqāʾiq*; Kitābkhāna-yi Dānishgāh-i Tihrān, MS 1047–1048, fol. 66	110
Figure 8	ʿAyn al-Quḍāt Square (Hamadan, Iran); photographed by Omid Bayati	140
Figure 9	Aḥmad Ghazālī imparting spiritual instruction to a student, possibly ʿAyn al-Quḍāt; Kamāl al-Dīn Gāzurgāhī, *Majālis al-ʿushshāq*; Bodleian Library, MS Ouseley Add., 24, fol. 42r	160
Figure 10	From conjoined letters to a dot/dots; designed by Khalil Andani	181

Figure 11	From conjoined letters to obliteration; designed by Khalil Andani	183
Figure 12	From black words to white parchment; designed by Mohammed Rustom	184
Figure 13	From whiteness to whiteness; designed by Mohammed Rustom	185
Figure 14	The tomb of Bābā Ṭāhir (Hamadan, Iran); photographed by Mohammed Rustom	186
Figure 15	From "No god" to "God"; designed by Oludamini Ogunnaike and Syed A. H. Zaidi	189
Figure 16	Mount Alvand (Hamadan, Iran); photographed by Mohammed Rustom	220
Figure 17	Levels of unbelief; designed by Jeremy Farrell	248
Figure 18	Imaginalizations of reality into metaphor; designed by Jeremy Farrell	259
Figure 19	Page from a manuscript of ʿAyn al-Quḍāt, *Nāma-hā*; Süleymaniye Kütüphanesi, MS Carullah 1100, fol. 135	262

Acknowledgments

This book would never have materialized without the help of a good number of individuals and institutions. First and foremost, thanks go to my beloved wife Nosheen and our children, Isa, Suhayla, and Sophia. I am grateful to each of them for being such wonderful travel companions in ʿAyn al-Quḍāt's world, and along the journey of life itself.

A research grant administered by Carleton University's Faculty of Arts and Social Sciences allowed me to get started on this project, and an Annemarie Schimmel Fellowship courtesy of The Institute of Ismaili Studies was instrumental in helping me to finish it. Much of the research and writing was done during the years I spent as a Senior Fellow in the New York University Abu Dhabi Institute's Library of Arabic Literature and Humanities Research Fellowship programs.

It gives me great pleasure to thank Reindert Falkenburg, Martin Klimke, Taneli Kukkonen, Alexandra Sandu, Philip Kennedy, Shawkat Toorawa, James Montgomery, and Amani Alzoubi. Not only did they help make the fellowships at New York University Abu Dhabi possible, but they also pulled out all stops to facilitate a most congenial environment in which I could carry out my research.

I am deeply indebted to Seyyed Hossein Nasr for his many years of mentorship and guidance, and for accepting *Inrushes of the Heart* into his esteemed book series.

Isabelle Mook-Jodouin, James Morris, Oludamini Ogunnaike, Yusuf Samara, and the late Arthur Buehler read various versions of this book from beginning to end. I am grateful to them and to State University of New York Press' two anonymous reviewers for providing me with very sound suggestions on how to make the work more accessible.

I had the fortunate pleasure of reading ʿAyn al-Quḍāt with Farhang Rajaee, while Abdul Hayy Darr and Nasrin Askari offered much help when I first tried to translate our author's tantalizing Persian prose into readable English. William Chittick took me through the most difficult passages in ʿAyn al-Quḍāt's writings, correcting my translations and saving me from all kinds of errors along the way. Words cannot convey my appreciation to all of them for their help, but I will at least try: *sipās guzāram*!

Many friends and scholars offered excellent advice on the content of this study and/or helped me to refine my thinking on a wide variety of issues taken up in it. Particular thanks in these regards go to Rodrigo Adem, Christopher Ahn, Nicholas Boylston, Ryan Brizendine, Davlat Dadikhuda, Justin Cancelliere, Yousef Casewit, Annabel Keeler, Atif Khalil, Hermann Landolt, Todd Lawson, Joseph Lumbard, Salimeh Maghsoudlou, Rostam Mehdipour, Matthew Melvin-Koushki, Daryoush Mohammad Poor, Reza Pourjavady, Lloyd Ridgeon, Omid Safi, Ayman Shihadeh, Shafique Virani, and Cyrus Ali Zargar.

An even greater number of colleagues provided me with all kinds of useful references, supplied manuscripts, and sent along summaries of articles in languages that I do not read. At the risk of conflating these favors, I mention all of their names here with gratitude: Taha Abdollahi, Amílcar Aldama Cruz, Hassan Ansari, Alireza Asghari, Amir Hossein Asghari, Ahab Bdaiwi, Andrew Bush, Faheem Chishti, Jonathan Dubé, Michael Ebstein, Sebastian Günther, Shigeru Kamada, Christian Lange, Mohammad Amin Mansouri, Sayeh Meisami, Sayyed Mohsen Mousawi, Fujii Morio, Abolfazl Moshiri, Jane Lewisohn, Bilal Orfali, Alexandre Papas, Alireza Pharaa, Maurice Pomerantz, Nasrollah Pourjavady, Enrico Raffaelli, Mehran Rahbari, Sajjad Rizvi, Renata Rusek, Soroosh Shahriari, Shahram Sharaei, Reza Tabandeh, John Walbridge, Saeed Zarrabi-Zadeh, and the late Zailan Moris.

At various stages, I was able to bring on board Shuaib Ally, Hassan Arif, Jeremy Farrell, Muhammad Faruque, Shiraz Sheikh, and Ramzi Taleb as research assistants. Their heroic efforts in tracing a wide variety of primary and secondary textual materials saved me a great deal of time and energy.

The contemporary Turkish calligrapher Seyit Ahmet Bursalı granted me permission to use his artwork for the front cover, while many of the images that are scattered throughout the book were shared with me, and in some cases designed upon request, by Khalil

Andani, Omid Bayati, Jeremy Farrell, Oludamini Ogunnaike, Habib Sharafi Safa, and Syed A. H. Zaidi. Moreover, a grant administered by the New York University Abu Dhabi Institute's Humanities Research Fellowship program allowed for these images to be printed in color.

Respective thanks are due to Brill and Routledge for granting me permission to incorporate two of my previously published articles (in the *Journal of Sufi Studies* and the *Routledge Handbook on Sufism*) into the introduction, chapter 2, and chapter 8.

As I was finalizing this project, I received the sad news of the passing of Leonard Lewisohn. A serious reader and admirer of ʿAyn al-Quḍāt, Lenny selflessly spent hours on end commenting on an earlier iteration of *Inrushes of the Heart* and offering many helpful insights on how to improve its presentation. His presence thus looms large in this book, which is lovingly dedicated to his memory.

Preface

My interest in ʿAyn al-Quḍāt was first piqued in 2007, when I was a doctoral student at the University of Toronto. Captivated by ʿAyn al-Quḍāt's unique manner of expression, I began to think that his writings would make for an ideal PhD dissertation topic. Given my inexperience and naïveté, my academic advisory committee gently pointed to greener pastures. Their advice could not have been better. After graduating in 2009, it would take me another five years of training to be able to step into ʿAyn al-Quḍāt's world.

Thanks to a series of grants and fellowships (see acknowledgments), I was freed from teaching and administrative responsibilities for several academic years. This large block of study time gave me the opportunity to carefully read and take copious notes on all of ʿAyn al-Quḍāt's writings, work out a translation method that would allow his style to faithfully come across in English, and translate and explain the most interesting passages. The result of these labors is the present book, which serves as an introduction to ʿAyn al-Quḍāt's spiritual and intellectual teachings. Having put aside my interpretations of his ideas for other studies (see bibliography), in this book I have tried to let him speak for himself as much as possible.

If *Inrushes of the Heart* has been able to communicate something of ʿAyn al-Quḍāt's originality and depth of insight, it would surely not be due to any merit of its author. As ʿAyn al-Quḍāt himself puts it, it would be by virtue of *his* understanding—an understanding that peers through, however imperfectly, the pages to follow.

Mohammed Rustom
December 2022
Saadiyat Island

Format and Style

Translations

In his Persian writings, ʿAyn al-Quḍāt often provides Persian translations or paraphrases of the Arabic sayings he cites. In cases where these renderings do not add anything new, I have excluded them in translation. Needless to say, all translations from ʿAyn al-Quḍāt's writings are my own. Translations from his *Zubdat al-ḥaqāʾiq* are derived and occasionally modified from my published translation of this work, while translations from the Quran are mostly adapted from Nasr et al., eds., *The Study Quran* (henceforth, "*SQ*").

Transliterations

Arabic and Persian terms have been transliterated in accordance with the rules devised by the *International Journal of Middle East Studies*, with the following major exceptions: (1) no distinction is made in transliterating consonants shared between Arabic and Persian; (2) following Steingass' *A Comprehensive Persian-English Dictionary*, the Persian prepositions به and بـ are transliterated as *ba-* and not *bi*, which is reserved for their Arabic equivalent; (3) Arabic and Persian book, journal, and article titles retain their diacritical marks and do not necessarily follow English capitalization rules; (4) the names of authors who have published in European languages in addition to Arabic and/or Persian have not been transliterated. Also, for purposes of consistency, names and technical terms that appear in passages cited from scholarship have been standardized accordingly.

Throughout the book, the designation "P." comes before the transliterations of singular terms and constructions that are unique to Persian. So, for example, the Persian term *pust* features in transliteration as "(P. *pust*)" and the Persianized version of the Arabic *maʿrifa* as "(P. *maʿrifat*)." At the same time, the Persian plural *sālikān*, which consists of the Persian plural ending *ān* appended to the Arabic singular *sālik*, features as "(P. *sālikān*)." In every other instance, transliterations of terms, complementary word pairs, and constructions can be assumed to be of Arabic origin even if they are also used in Persian. Thus, for example, although the Arabic Sufi term *kashf* is common in Persian Sufi literature, it appears in transliteration as simply "(*kashf*)."

Referencing

The referencing format in this book generally follows *The Chicago Manual of Style* (17th ed.), but with three important modifications: (1) a shorthand citation method has been employed throughout the notes for books, articles, and the like, thus reserving their complete bibliographic details for the bibliography only; (2) works published in multiple volumes have not been indicated as such; (3) book and article titles in the bibliography do not necessarily include their subtitles, especially when these titles are well known or can stand on their own without them.

Sourcing Hadiths and Sayings

ʿAyn al-Quḍāt has an endless repertoire of Hadiths and sayings at his disposal, and he does not shy away from making full use of these materials in his writings. In this book, great pains have been taken to track down his sources in this regard. In order to avoid excessive and unnecessary documentation, where a given Hadith or saying is to be found in multiple sources, only one of these sources is cited.

The IHSAN database (http://www.ihsanetwork.org/about_en.aspx) has of course proven to be particularly helpful with respect to tracing Hadiths in the most important Sunni collections. On occasion, other important Hadith works—both Sunni and Shiʿi—have been employed to locate Hadiths not featured in this database. In the vast majority of such cases, however, the Hadiths are traced back to such indispensable sources as ʿAjlūnī's *Kashf al-khafāʾ* and Ḥaddād's superlative *Takhrīj Iḥyāʾ ʿulūm al-dīn*; these works are particularly useful since they often provide a wealth of information on obscure narrations and the like.

In a handful of instances with respect to Hadiths, and in the majority of cases with respect to statements made by earlier Sufis, references go back to those Sufi works with which ʿAyn al-Quḍāt was intimately familiar (i.e., Makkī's *Qūt*, Qushayrī's *Risāla*, Ghazālī's *Iḥyāʾ*, etc.), and from which he likely derived the materials in question.

Other sayings that are not easily traceable to a single source have been referenced vis-à-vis any given authoritative text in the Sufi tradition on the one hand, and reliable, modern scholarship on the other. The dozen or so sayings that were untraceable to written sources have been passed over in silence.

Abbreviations

Abbreviations for ʿAyn al-Quḍāt's works refer to the titles of the Arabic and Persian texts; for information on the editions used, see bibliography, s.v. "Works by ʿAyn al-Quḍāt (Editions, Manuscripts, Translations)." As is customary, the bibliographic details for reference works are given here, but are excluded from the bibliography. Lastly, abbreviations for book titles are indicated after the first instance in which the work's title has been provided.

ʿAyn al-Quḍāt's Writings

N: *Nāma-hā* (*The Letters*); referenced by volume, page, and section numbers (e.g., *N* I, 401, §607 = *Nāma-hā*, volume 1, page 401, section 607).

NU: *Nuzhat al-ʿushshāq* (*The Lovers' Excursion*); referenced by MS folio and line numbers (e.g., *NU* 245.2 = *Nuzhat al-ʿushshāq*, folio 245, line 2).

RJ: *Risāla-yi Jamālī* (*Treatise Dedicated to Jamāl al-Dawla*); referenced by page number (e.g., *RJ* 2 = *Risāla-yi Jamālī*, page 2).

Sh: *Shakwā'l-gharīb* (*The Exile's Complaint*); referenced by page number (e.g., *Sh* 2 = *Shakwā'l-gharīb*, page 2).

T: *Tamhīdāt* (*Paving the Path*); referenced by page and section numbers (e.g., *T* 207, §266 = *Tamhīdāt*, page 207, section 266).

W: [*Wāqiʿa-hā*] [*Apparitions*]; referenced by page number (e.g., *W* 3 = [*Wāqiʿa-hā*], page 3).

Z: *Zubdat al-ḥaqāʾiq* (*The Essence of Reality*); referenced by section number (e.g., *Z* §14 = *Zubdat al-ḥaqāʾiq*, section 14).

Reference Works

BEIP: *The Biographical Encyclopaedia of Islamic Philosophy*, edited by Oliver Leaman. London: Thoemmes Continuum, 2006.

DZAF: *Dānishnāma-yi zabān wa-adab-i fārsī*, edited by Ismāʿīl Saʿādat. Tehran: Farhangistān-i Zabān wa-Adab-i Fārsī, 2012.

EI2: *Encyclopaedia of Islam*, 2nd edition, edited by H. A. R. Gibb et al. Leiden: Brill, 1960–2004.

EI3: *Encyclopaedia of Islam*, 3rd edition, edited by Gudrun Krämer et al. Leiden: Brill, 2007–.

EIr: *Encyclopaedia Iranica* (founding editor, Ehsan Yarshater). New York: Encyclopaedia Iranica Foundation, 1982–.

EIs: *Encyclopaedia Islamica*, edited by Wilferd Madelung and Farhad Daftary. Leiden: Brill in association with The Institute of Ismaili Studies, 2008–.

LN: ʿAlī Akbar Dikhudā, *Lughat-nāma*. Online: https://dehkhoda.ut.ac.ir/fa/dictionary.

REP: *Routledge Encyclopedia of Philosophy*, edited by Edward Craig. New York: Routledge, 1998.

SEP: *Stanford Encyclopedia of Philosophy*, edited by Edward Zalta. http://plato.stanford.edu.

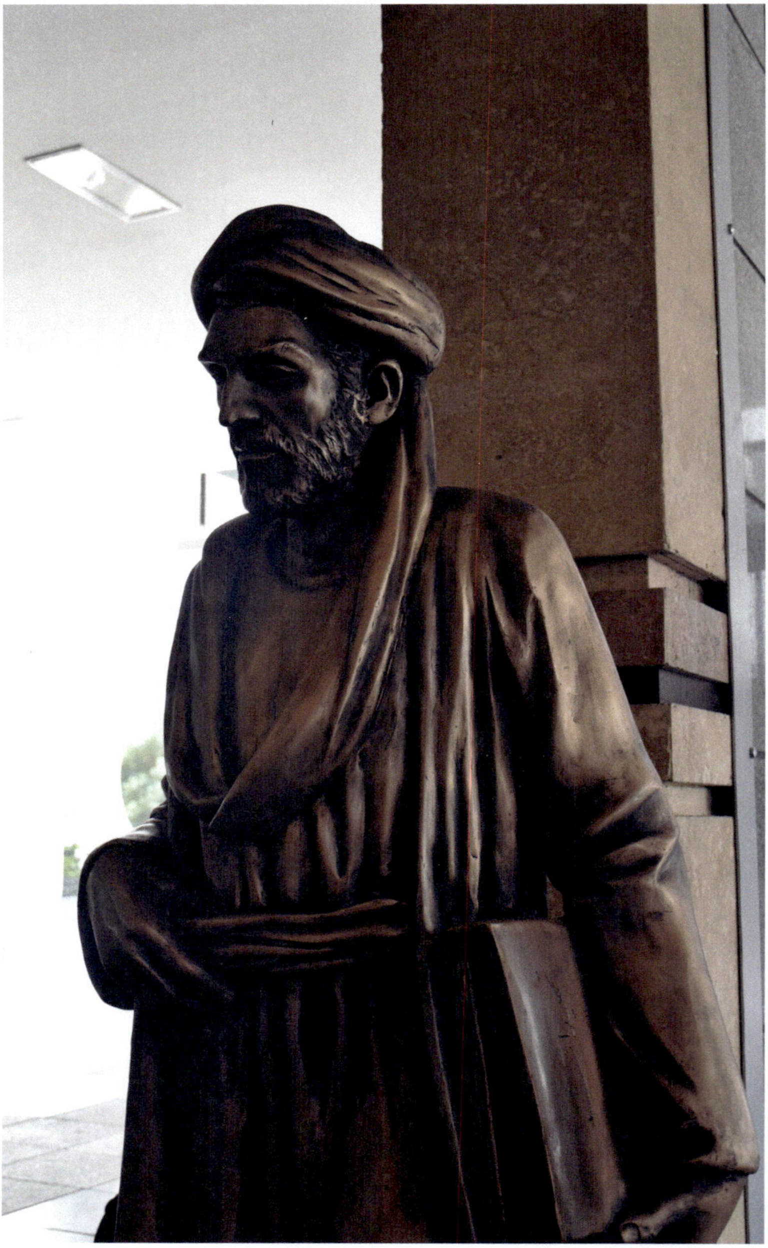

Figure 1. Statue of ʿAyn al-Quḍāt (Hamadan, Iran)

Introduction

A Sage in Exile

هو

Life

Abū'l-Maʿālī Muḥammad[1] b. Abī Bakr Muḥammad al-Miyānajī al-Hamadānī, more commonly known as ʿAyn al-Quḍāt Hamadānī, was born in the western Iranian city of Hamadan in 490/1097.[2] His family originally hailed from Miyana, which is in present-day Iran's province of East Azerbaijan. The sources all point out that ʿAyn al-Quḍāt was born into a family of learning. His grandfather Abū'l-Ḥasan b. ʿAlī (d. 471/1079) was a well-known scholar and judge in Hamadan who was executed in Baghdad for reasons that are not entirely known.[3] ʿAyn al-Quḍāt's father Abū Bakr Muḥammad was also a judge in Hamadan, and by his son's own testimony was a practicing Sufi.[4] ʿAyn al-Quḍāt may have had a son named Aḥmad.[5] If this was the case, we do not have any information concerning his son's whereabouts after the demise of his father.

ʿAyn al-Quḍāt received his legal education in the Shāfiʿī tradition and his training in theology in what was by his time the most widely available form of rational theology (*kalām*), namely Ashʿarism. It is clear from his writings that ʿAyn al-Quḍāt excelled in all of the Islamic sciences, along with mathematics, and had an especially strong attachment to Arabic language, poetry, and literary culture. Some sources mention that ʿAyn al-Quḍāt had studied with the great philosopher and mathematician ʿUmar Khayyām (d. ca. 517/1124).[6] This is plausible,[7] although Najib Mayel Heravi rejects this claim on account of the fact that ʿAyn al-Quḍāt does not mention Khayyām in his writings.[8]

We are not sure when ʿAyn al-Quḍāt received his title of distinction (ʿAyn al-Quḍāt means "the most eminent of judges"), although it indicates that he rose to a considerable level of prominence in his function as a judge and religious figure at some point in his short life and career. It can fairly be surmised that this must have been when ʿAyn al-Quḍāt was still a young man, perhaps before he was twenty, since he had already begun writing books in the Islamic intellectual sciences at around that age.[9]

We know from an autobiographical note in his Arabic work *Zubdat al-ḥaqāʾiq* (*The Essence of Reality*,[10] written in 514/1120) that ʿAyn al-Quḍāt had gone through a period of intellectual crisis in roughly 506/1112 on account of his preoccupation with rational theology.[11] He credits a close to four year period of immersion in the writings of Abū Ḥāmid al-Ghazālī (d. 505/1111)—presumably his monumental *Iḥyāʾ ʿulūm al-dīn* (*The Revival of the Religious Sciences*)—as having rescued him from his predicament and for compelling him to turn more fully to Sufism.

ʿAyn al-Quḍāt dictated the text of the *Essence* to scribes while he was under the palpable spiritual influence of a certain Shaykh Baraka Hamadānī.[12] He kept this master's company for seven years and had the utmost reverence for him.[13] Shaykh Baraka could barely recite the Quran and had no formal learning, but he was very advanced along the Sufi path. He died in around 520/1126 at the age of eighty.[14]

ʿAyn al-Quḍāt also speaks admiringly of two other teachers: Muḥammad b. Ḥamūya al-Juwaynī (d. 530/1137)[15] and Shaykh Fatḥa. The latter was the spiritual master of Shaykh Baraka[16] and someone whom ʿAyn al-Quḍāt did not meet in the flesh.[17] Nevertheless, he tells us that Shaykh Baraka sent him on his first visit (*ziyāra*) to Shaykh Fatḥa's tomb—a pilgrimage that proved to be of great benefit for ʿAyn al-Quḍāt.[18] We know from one of ʿAyn al-Quḍāt's letters that this was a practice he himself encouraged a student to habitually perform in order to thwart worldly afflictions. And, in a different letter, ʿAyn al-Quḍāt admonishes his student not to deem the two nights that he had spent at Shaykh Fatḥa's tomb to be an insignificant matter.[19] So spiritually efficacious was the tomb of Shaykh Fatḥa that ʿAyn al-Quḍāt would write some of his letters to his disciples both during and after pilgrimages to it.[20] Furthermore, ʿAyn al-Quḍāt was also inspired to write letters after visiting the grave of the great Persian Sufi poet of Hamadan Bābā Ṭāhir ʿUryān (d. 418/1028),[21] who himself was the master of Shaykh Fatḥa.[22] It is clear that ʿAyn al-Quḍāt placed a great deal of emphasis—both for himself and his students—upon making regular pilgrimage to the tombs of Bābā Ṭāhir and Shaykh Fatḥa, so long as these weighty undertakings were accompanied by the right kind of intention.[23]

In 513/1119[24] ʿAyn al-Quḍāt became the disciple of Ghazālī's younger brother and foremost Sufi master of his day, Aḥmad Ghazālī (d. 520/1126), during one of the latter's visits to Hamadan.[25] Aḥmad Ghazālī had some formal tie to Hamadan, perhaps even having had a Sufi lodge (P. *khānaqāh*) or at least a gathering place of sorts in the city. Having spent less than three weeks in his master's company, ʿAyn al-Quḍāt received a great spiritual opening that left an indelible mark upon his soul.[26]

ʿAyn al-Quḍāt continued to receive instruction from Aḥmad Ghazālī even after he left Hamadan. This is evidenced by a treatise that the master dedicated to his disciple,[27] as well as a series of correspondences between them that exhibit their mutual love and affection for one another.[28] On account of ʿAyn al-Quḍāt's significant accomplishments on the Sufi path under the formal guidance of Aḥmad Ghazālī and through his association with the likes of Shaykh Baraka, he was appointed by Aḥmad Ghazālī as one of his spiritual successors. Given the fact that Aḥmad Ghazālī died in 520/1126, and assuming that ʿAyn al-Quḍāt took up his assigned function after the death of his master, he would have been roughly twenty-nine years old when he himself became a Sufi shaykh.

While still earning his livelihood as a judge, ʿAyn al-Quḍāt operated a Sufi lodge where he trained his disciples.[29] He also taught daily classes in the Islamic sciences to a wider audience; at times, he tells us, these classes numbered seven to eight a day.[30] Another means through which ʿAyn al-Quḍāt trained his disciples was by way of formal correspondence. Among his writings are a precious collection of nearly 160 letters, to which we have already alluded. Commonly referred to by the Persian title *Nāma-hā* (*The Letters*), these letters by ʿAyn al-Quḍāt to his disciples and students were often written in response to their spiritual and intellectual questions. They offer us a wealth of autobiographical and biographical information and give us a rare glimpse into ʿAyn al-Quḍāt's social and political context, both of which are essential to coming away with a clearer picture of the circumstances surrounding his death.

Execution

In around 522/1128 certain accusations were made against ʿAyn al-Quḍāt in Hamadan, likely at the instigation of a local scholar or group of scholars. In a passage in his magnum opus the *Tamhīdāt* (*Paving the Path*), ʿAyn al-Quḍāt notes that his close friend and student Kāmil al-Dawla[31] wrote to him and told him that the specific accusation leveled against him had to do with his supposed claim to divine status.[32] Although the people in Hamadan had a fatwa or legal edict issued against him with this specific charge in view, ʿAyn al-Quḍāt notes in his *Letters* that he was also accused of styling himself as a Prophet.[33]

Anyone familiar with ʿAyn al-Quḍāt's writings and persona would clearly understand why some may have been put off by his words and manner of being. For starters, he was an unapologetic follower of the great Sufi martyr Ḥallāj (d. 309/922), which would have troubled not a few scholars.[34] ʿAyn al-Quḍāt would also have been viewed as arrogant or as a person who makes grandiose spiritual claims (something not unrelated to the charge of his so-called claims to divinity). To be sure, Ayn al-Quḍāt's mode of oral and written communication is best characterized as "drunken," and his own writings show that he had been endowed with the ability to perform miracles. The best example of this power involves a story, told by ʿAyn al-Quḍāt on two separate occasions, in which he brings a dead person back to life.[35] These two considerations would explain why a number of people came to regard him as a kind of sorcerer or magician.[36]

Speculating over the accusations against ʿAyn al-Quḍāt, his consequent imprisonment in Baghdad, and his eventual execution would take us down an all-too-familiar path in the secondary literature (which derives in part from medieval hagiographic sources[37]): ʿAyn al-Quḍāt, like Ḥallāj, was a heterodox thinker who had to pay for his nonconformist views by being killed. The details of his death then take on a proportionately exaggerated form: ʿAyn al-Quḍāt was imprisoned and eventually brought back to his homeland of Hamadan only to be flogged, doused in oil, and then burned alive, or skinned alive, or symbolically hung in front of the very school in which he taught his "dangerous" ideas.[38] Taking these kinds of accounts at face value does a gross injustice to the other factors that were at work in bringing ʿAyn al-Quḍāt to his demise—factors that are corroborated by external historical sources and ʿAyn al-Quḍāt's own writings.

There is no doubt that ʿAyn al-Quḍāt was accused of heresy and that this was the ostensible means on account of which he was killed. But what was so heretical about his views? Not surprisingly, the charges laid against him had nothing to do with what would seem like the more eyebrow-raising aspects of his mystical theology, such as his exalted view of Satan or his open support of such controversial Sufi figures as Ḥallāj and Abū Yazīd Basṭāmī (d. ca. 260/874).[39] Even the aforementioned accusations to the effect that ʿAyn al-Quḍāt was claiming divinity, or that he was a sorcerer, were not brought forth as the reasons justifying his execution. The explicit charges laid against ʿAyn al-Quḍāt had to do with some statements that he had made in the *Essence*. Yet of all of ʿAyn al-Quḍāt's writings, this would be the one book that one would *not* want to cite in an attempt to build a convincing case against its author in support of the charge of heresy.

The only contemporaneous public record that we have of the kinds of accusations leveled at ʿAyn al-Quḍāt are featured in his *Shakwā'l-gharīb* (*The Exile's Complaint*), which he wrote in prison in defense of these charges.[40] These accusations by those who wanted to see ʿAyn al-Quḍāt executed were clearly haphazard. For one thing, and somewhat ironically, the ideas in the *Essence* are in line with statements made by Ghazālī, who was championed by the very state that had ʿAyn al-Quḍāt killed. This is precisely the same point that ʿAyn al-Quḍāt makes in *Exile's Complaint*.[41]

According to ʿAyn al-Quḍāt, the accusers said that he (1) upheld some kind of belief in the eternity of the world that is related to (2) his view concerning God's being the Source of existence (*maṣdar al-wujūd*) while also (3) not knowing particulars (*juzʾiyyāt*) but only universals (*kulliyyāt*). A related charge to (2) was that (4) ʿAyn al-Quḍāt (a Sunni) approved of Ismaili teachings, which was reflected in his emphasis on the absolute dedication of the Sufi disciple to his spiritual master. Finally, ʿAyn al-Quḍāt was accused of (5) proclaiming himself to be a Prophet[42] and also (6) asserting that the Friends of God (*awliyāʾ Allāh*) are above the Prophets and Messengers, and this because he believed that there was a certain epistemic standpoint to which the Friends of God were exclusively privy.[43]

In *Exile's Complaint* ʿAyn al-Quḍāt presents a very convincing case in refutation of these claims, often citing the *Essence* itself.[44] And his

Letters also reveal a number of instances in which these charges are shown to be completely untenable. At the same time, in *Exile's Complaint* ʿAyn al-Quḍāt provides us with an inventory of his writings[45] but suppresses any mention of *Paving the Path* and the *Letters*, from whose contents an accusation of "heresy" could much more easily have been constructed. In their case against ʿAyn al-Quḍāt the Seljuq government's assembly (*maḥḍar*) likewise did not mention these works.[46]

Grounding his inquiry in a thorough study of the *Letters*, Omid Safi has convincingly argued that the cause of ʿAyn al-Quḍāt's death was intimately bound up with his unrelenting critique of the Seljuq regime's corrupt administrative practices.[47] After all, it would have been one thing had he been a sideline critic of the Seljuq regime. But he was a man with significant social standing and, as his *Letters* demonstrate, many of his own disciples occupied very high positions at the Seljuq court.[48] ʿAyn al-Quḍāt often uses harsh language to characterize their relationship with the Seljuq authorities, particularly the young Sultan Maḥmūd b. Muḥammad b. Malikshāh (d. 525/1131), more commonly known as Sultan Maḥmūd II.

On one level, ʿAyn al-Quḍāt's concerns are consistently straightforward in his *Letters*: the Seljuqs in general and Sultan Maḥmūd II in particular are not really defenders of Islam and are morally corrupt.[49] No matter how financially lucrative service at the Seljuq court may be, working there is not an option for those on the Sufi path. In one letter to a disciple who worked for the Seljuqs in some capacity, ʿAyn al-Quḍāt voices his disappointment with this student, severely chastising him for what he took to be open excesses and even affronts to the spiritual pact he had taken with him.[50]

Alongside ʿAyn al-Quḍāt's criticisms of his students' mistaken view that they will financially benefit from service at the Seljuq court, his position against the Seljuqs is informed by another financially informed perspective: in contrast to ʿAyn al-Quḍāt's emphasis on the merits of charity[51] stood the Seljuqs' open hoarding of people's wealth and property.[52] This was particularly true of the ruthless Seljuq vizier Qawwām al-Dīn Abū'l-Qāsim Dargazīnī (d. 527/1133).[53]

Among all of ʿAyn al-Quḍāt's disciples who worked for the Seljuq state, a finance officer (*mustawfī*) by the name of ʿAzīz al-Dīn (d. 527/1133) was a bitter foe of Dargazīnī.[54] It was thus in the best interest of Dargazīnī to discredit ʿAzīz al-Dīn's teacher who was already critical of the Seljuqs and was undoubtedly seen as a corrupting influence upon ʿAzīz al-Dīn, a Seljuq state employee. This was a carefully thought-out strategy that, as Safi explains, had a "double effect": (1) if ʿAyn al-Quḍāt was accused of heresy, his disciple ʿAzīz al-Dīn would have been further discredited; and (2) the death of ʿAyn al-Quḍāt, who was an influential public figure insofar as he was a judge and religious teacher in Hamadan, meant that ʿAzīz al-Dīn would have been all the more vulnerable.[55] Dargazīnī successfully had his enemy imprisoned and put to death two years after the execution of ʿAyn al-Quḍāt.[56] Ironically, shortly thereafter Dargazīnī was himself brutally put to death by the Seljuq ruler Tughril of Azerbaijan on concocted charges of Ismaili affiliations.[57]

Following a brief period of imprisonment in Baghdad in 523/1129, where ʿAyn al-Quḍāt wrote the *Exile's Complaint* and a private letter to one of his disciples,[58] he was returned to his native Hamadan, still as a prisoner of the state. He was publicly executed on the order of Sultan Maḥmūd II on the evening of the 6th/7th of Jumādā Thānī 525 AH, which corresponds to the 6th/7th of May 1131 CE.[59] He was aged thirty-five lunar years or thirty-four solar years at the time of his execution. The historian Ibn al-Fuwaṭī (d. 723/1323), to whom we are indebted for dating ʿAyn al-Quḍāt's birth, mentions that he made a pilgrimage to ʿAyn al-Quḍāt's grave in Hamadan and that it was commonly visited by others.[60] Although ʿAyn al-Quḍāt's tomb was destroyed in the Safavid period,[61] today Hamadan hosts a large cultural center established in his honor that contains, among other things, his symbolic tomb.[62]

Writings

Having lived such a short life, ʿAyn al-Quḍāt was nevertheless an extremely prolific author in a variety of subjects. By his own testimony in *Exile's Complaint*, he wrote a total of eleven works in such fields as scriptural exegesis, rational and creedal theology, mathematics, Arabic prosody and grammar, and Sufism.[63] Most of these works have not survived. If we add these to the other books that he wrote but did not mention in *Exile's Complaint*, the total list of his writings (excluding *Exile's Complaint*) would be closer to fifteen titles.

There are also a number of works that ʿAyn al-Quḍāt certainly did not author but that have been wrongly attributed to him for one reason or another.[64] Chief among these is the *Lawāʾiḥ* (*Flashes*), which is inspired by Aḥmad Ghazālī's *Sawāniḥ al-ʿushshāq* (*Incidents of the*

Lovers) and parts of ʿAyn al-Quḍāt's *Paving the Path*. It therefore certainly belongs to the Persianate "School of Love" (P. *madhhab-i ʿishq*).[65] Having said that, there are many internal textual and stylistic reasons why ʿAyn al-Quḍāt could not have been the author of this treatise.[66] And then there is the manuscript evidence that, beginning with Hellmut Ritter,[67] has led some scholars to leave the question of authorship open or ascribe it to a Sufi figure other than ʿAyn al-Quḍāt.[68] A number of scholars, particularly Nasrollah Pourjavady, have maintained that the real author of *Flashes* was an Indian disciple of Muʿīn al-Dīn Chishtī (d. 633/1236), Ḥamīd al-Dīn Nāgawrī (d. 641/1244).[69] Thanks to the conclusive findings of Muḥammad Shādruymanish, we can now be certain of this ascription.[70]

ʿAyn al-Quḍāt's extant books number seven in total and would run to just over 1,700 pages in modern print. These works are mostly in Persian, with three shorter titles in Arabic. At any rate, ʿAyn al-Quḍāt's Persian writings are heavily filled with Arabic passages, consisting mainly of citations from the Quran and Hadith, the words of the great Sufi masters of the past, Arabic poetry, technical philosophical discussions,[71] and even verses from the Bible.[72]

ʿAyn al-Quḍāt had a great mastery of Arabic and his mother tongue Persian. Many of his own poems, commonly in the form of quatrains (*rubāʿiyyāt*) when they are in Persian, are peppered throughout his writings. He also cites various past and contemporary poets in both the Arabic and Persian poetic traditions.[73] In total, ʿAyn al-Quḍāt cites about 695 poems in all of his writings. 475 of these poems are in Persian,[74] and the rest are in Arabic. One of these Arabic poems is a thousand lines long and accounts for a small fraction of our author's extant literary corpus (see section 7).[75] ʿAyn al-Quḍāt often cites the verse of a famous contemporary who lived on the opposite end of the Persian-speaking world: the great Sufi poet Sanāʾī (d. 525/1131) whom he mentions by name in one of his letters.[76] Incidentally, Sanāʾī's work was patronized by the same Dargazīnī who was responsible for ʿAyn al-Quḍāt's execution.[77]

1. *Tamhīdāt* (*Paving the Path*)

ʿAyn al-Quḍāt's Persian prose style is very unique. It is at once poetic, multilayered, and exhilarating, carrying with it a strong sense of profound learning, wit, lyricism, irony, symbolism, and spiritual and intellectual rigor. Leonard Lewisohn has described it very well: "ʿAyn al-Quḍāt's prose is intimate and spontaneous, while also quite complex, combining oracular utterance, passionate rapture and the weighty symbolic diction of poetic inspiration, with philosophical depth, prolix theological lore and rich mystical anagogy."[78] This characterization is particularly apt for ʿAyn al-Quḍāt's masterpiece *Paving the Path,* which was written almost entirely in Persian and completed on the 9th of Rajab 521 AH / July 21st, 1127 CE.[79] According to Fritz Meier, most manuscript sources give the title of the work as *Zubdat al-ḥaqāʾiq fi kashf al-khalāʾiq* (*The Essence of Reality: On Unveiling Created Beings*).[80] The term in the subtitle, *khalāʾiq* or "created beings," is clearly a misreading. In ʿAfīf ʿUsayrān's edition of *Paving the Path,* which is not without its errors,[81] ʿAyn al-Quḍāt introduces the book by the same title but with the more sensible *daqāʾiq* or "subtleties" in place of *khalāʾiq*:

> A group of friends requested that some words be put together for them so that it may benefit their days. Their request has been granted. This book, *The Essence of Reality: On Unveiling Subtleties,* has been completed in ten chapters so that it may benefit its readers. (*T* 1, §1)

We are fortunate that the work came to be known as *Tamhīdāt* since *Zubdat al-ḥaqāʾiq* is, as we have seen, also the title of ʿAyn al-Quḍāt's major work in Arabic. In its printed edition, *Paving the Path* is 354 pages long and consists of 470 sections. These sections are spread out over ten chapters that collectively provide foundational sets of insights that help "pave the path" (*tamhīd*) for spiritual adepts. A careful study of *Paving the Path* reveals the profound manner in which much of it is concerned with the theme of self-recognition (P. *khwud-shināsī; maʿrifat-i nafs*) and nonduality at the highest level.

ʿAyn al-Quḍāt states that the book represents the essence (*zubda*) of the inspirations he receives as they come to him in real time; consequently, it is not arranged according to any particular order,[82] although the author undoubtedly edited the final draft of the work. This is clear on account of the internal references in parts of *Paving the Path* to other parts. Hence at the beginning of the fourth chapter of *Paving the Path,* which is on self-recognition, ʿAyn al-Quḍāt notes that the topic's most complete exposition is to be found in the book's tenth and final chapter.[83] It can easily be argued that the tenth chapter serves as the axis around which the other chapters revolve, which is perhaps why ʿAyn al-Quḍāt singles it out with these words:

> Alas! What do you know? In this section that paves the path, I have left behind several thousand diverse stations. From all of these worlds, I have brought an essence in the cloak of symbols to the world of writing. (*T* 309, §406)

The distinct chapter titles and divisions that were inserted by ʿUsayrān into his edition of *Paving the Path*[84] can at times be misleading. As the manuscript tradition of *Paving the Path* indicates, ʿAyn al-Quḍāt did not title the book's chapters and may not have even divided the work into chapters per se.[85] This possibility is perfectly sensible, given that the ideas in the text flow in a way that defies easy categorization. At every turn of the page, the reader gets the clear sense that he must somehow be "like" the author in order to understand the import of his statements. ʿAyn al-Quḍāt says as much in the book's very last paragraph:

> Wait until you arrive at my world, where the torment of humanness does not interfere and where I myself can speak to you about what is being spoken. In the world of letters, more than this cannot fit into expressions. (*T* 354, §470)

Nevertheless, ʿAyn al-Quḍāt only writes under "inspiration." The net effect is that he says things at the beginning of the book that are not entirely clear until pages later. There are also indications in *Paving the Path* that ʿAyn al-Quḍāt composed the work by penning it himself and having others write down his oral discourses.[86]

Without doubt, ʿAyn al-Quḍāt follows his master Aḥmad Ghazālī's *Incidents* on several key points related to the fundamental doctrine of love. This is hardly surprising since *Incidents* is in many ways the foundational work on the metaphysics of love and loverhood in the School of Love. However, *Paving the Path* is an entirely unique composition and thus is quite different from *Incidents* in terms of form, content, style, and length. The foundational text for the defense of Iblis in the Sufi tradition, namely Ḥallāj's *Ṭawāsīn*, is cited by ʿAyn al-Quḍāt in *Paving the Path*, but not by name.[87] At any rate, there is no doubt that Ḥallāj's defense of Satan, along with that of Aḥmad Ghazālī, shaped ʿAyn al-Quḍāt's Satanology. Yet even here ʿAyn al-Quḍāt offers a much more nuanced view of Satan that is deeply connected to his formal theology on the one hand, and his mystical theology on the other.[88]

Paving the Path contains almost every major aspect of ʿAyn al-Quḍāt's Sufi teachings in its fully developed form. In this text we are given the author's mature expositions on such matters as the nature of the master-disciple relationship, the role of the Prophet Muhammad in the spiritual life, the true meaning of knowledge and the various psychological faculties involved in its reception, "esoteric" interpretations of the rites and pillars of Islam, Satanology, a highly developed and stylized understanding of beauty, and a profound doctrine of love. The only major idea in ʿAyn al-Quḍāt's Sufi worldview that does not receive as extensive a treatment in *Paving the Path* as it does in another of his works is his original understanding of the Quran. For this, one would have to turn to the *Letters*.

2. *Nāma-hā* (*The Letters*)

The *Letters* represent ʿAyn al-Quḍāt's most extensive body of writing, and he refers to them in passing at one place in *Paving the Path*.[89] Many scholars have noted the similarities between passages in *Paving the Path* and the *Letters*.[90] A close analysis of both texts shows that at least fifteen percent of the *Letters* contain materials that are also found, in one form or another, in *Paving the Path*.[91] It would be impossible to derive a hard-and-fast formula for the carryover of passages from one text to another since *Paving the Path* was written concurrently with at least some parts of the *Letters*. At times, the *Letters* contain expanded discussions or slightly altered points that are found in *Paving the Path*, and in such cases the texts from *Paving the Path* seem like more primitive forms of the corresponding sections in the *Letters*. In these instances, it can safely be assumed that the respective texts from *Paving the Path* precede the corresponding texts in the *Letters*.

There are other technical cues that can give one subtle and at times overt indications as to when a particular letter was written, and this can at times lead to ultimately trivial points of observation concerning which text preceded which in time. What is more interesting is the manner in which *Paving the Path* and the *Letters* complement one another, with the latter shedding light on the political and historical context that is normally absent from the former. The *Letters* are also an incredible source for ʿAyn al-Quḍāt's ideas if only for the fact that they highlight a dimension of their author that is not easily discernable in *Paving the Path,* namely his concrete spiritual advice to disciples and his candid solutions to their many problems.

The modern edition of the *Letters* is in three sizeable volumes and amounts to 1,136 printed pages. There are 159 letters in total, all of which but the last two are written in Persian.[92] Assuming that ʿAyn al-Quḍāt began to write them when he became a Sufi master, we can be fairly confident in stating that most of the *Letters,* with the exception of one in particular (see section 3), were written between 520/1126 and 525/1131. The last of them, as already mentioned, was penned while ʿAyn al-Quḍāt was imprisoned in Baghdad.

Like *Paving the Path,* the *Letters* are written under inspiration, which is a point ʿAyn al-Quḍāt makes throughout the work. Often, a letter will end abruptly since its author has run out of paper. Thus, it is common to find such statements as "Alas! The paper is full!," or "Bring paper right now!," and "Right now, there is no more paper!"[93] At times, the requested paper gets to the writer, but his task is already complete: "The paper has arrived, but this is sufficient!"[94]

ʿAyn al-Quḍāt knew the value of each of his *Letters,* which is why he tells one recipient, "Read this letter every day for blessings—God willing, each word will do its work at the right moment."[95] He instructs a different student, "Read these *Letters* attentively, and ask about whatever is obscure."[96] Beyond his students, ʿAyn al-Quḍāt declares his inspired correspondences to quite literally contain something for everyone:

> In these *Letters* of mine are so many wonders that, were the first and last generations of people to have been alive, they would have taken nourishment from them! (*N* II, 206, §304)

Even under inspiration ʿAyn al-Quḍāt is careful to refine his words in his *Letters* and add important clarifications along the way. This explains why, as he states, a letter of typical length (about ten pages) takes him from about an hour after the late afternoon prayer (*ʿaṣr*) to just before the sunset prayer (*maghrib*) to compose,[97] which would amount to something like two and a half to three hours per letter.

The *Letters* are not as haphazard to the naked eye as is *Paving the Path.* This is partly because ʿAyn al-Quḍāt wrote much of the *Letters* in clusters, and over closely related periods of time, often in response to a particular question that was addressed to him by one of his disciples. Thus, *Letters* 1–9 are generally on the topic of intention (*niyya*), dealing with both its inward and outward manifestations and its relationship to the pillars of Muslim practice.[98] *Letters* 10–27 form a commentary on the exclamatory phrase *Allāhu akbar* ("God is the Greatest!").[99] This cluster of the *Letters* generally have to do with an extended discussion of the divine Essence, names, and attributes as they relate to the divine name *Allāh*, with the last of this portion of the *Letters* comprising a commentary on the phrase *akbar*. *Letters* 25 and 26 clearly state that the theology and technical discussions in *Letters* 10–24 deal with the outward nature of things, and that *Letters* 25 and 26 address their inner reality. This is a clear indication, if there was ever any doubt, that ʿAyn al-Quḍāt saw his rational theology as profoundly subordinate to his mystical theology.

When viewed as a whole, the *Letters* are often quite theological in nature. In *Letter* 75, for example, ʿAyn al-Quḍāt engages in a critique of Ismailism, and *Letters* 92–95 deal with the manner in which the teachings of previous religions have been altered (*taḥrīf*).[100] Other parts of the *Letters* point to ʿAyn al-Quḍāt's specific concerns in rational theology, taking in such topics as proofs for the existence of God, how it is that human beings are both free and constrained in the realm of action, and why in the final analysis one should never uphold a view that imputes injustice to God for what may seem like wrongs that occur in the world.[101] That ʿAyn al-Quḍāt would dedicate so much time to matters of formal theology indicates that at least some of his students were neophytes who were still concerned with matters of theological doctrine, which, as ʿAyn al-Quḍāt's writings on love reveal, he would sufficiently problematize for all of those closer to the end of the Sufi path.

As we have seen already, ʿAyn al-Quḍāt is particularly critical of the Seljuq state in a number of his *Letters*. When we bring all of these passages together, a rather coherent picture emerges with respect to his concern and care for his students, as well as his unrelenting stance against political and social injustice.

Other features of the *Letters* that merit close study are ʿAyn al-Quḍāt's many interpretations of particular Quranic verses[102] that are found throughout the collection. A particularly rewarding area of investigation here would be the many instances in which ʿAyn al-Quḍāt offers interpretations of the opening chapter of the Quran, the Fātiḥa.[103]

3. [*Wāqiʿa-hā*] ([*Apparitions*])

In at least two concrete cases the *Letters* incorporate entire Persian texts that were previously written by ʿAyn al-Quḍāt. As already pointed out, we have a handy set of correspondences that took place between ʿAyn al-Quḍāt and Aḥmad Ghazālī. In actuality, they are almost all in the form of letters written by Aḥmad Ghazālī to ʿAyn al-Quḍāt, with references that clearly indicate earlier conversations and non-written modes of communication to which ʿAyn al-Quḍāt's master was responding. In only one instance in these correspondences does the teacher directly address a letter by his student.

This letter by ʿAyn al-Quḍāt, which we will refer to with the Persian title *Wāqiʿa-hā* (*Apparitions*), can be found in the printed edition of Aḥmad Ghazālī's letters to ʿAyn al-Quḍāt.[104] It is also available, in the exact same form, in ʿAyn al-Quḍāt's *Letters*, namely *Letter* 148.[105] In his letter, ʿAyn al-Quḍāt comes as a disciple, seeking to verify the truth of some of his visions and seeking answers to a few of his questions.[106] *Apparitions* therefore represents the only instance in all of the *Letters* wherein the author is himself a student who poses questions to his teacher.

4. *Risāla-yi Jamālī* (*Treatise Dedicated to Jamāl al-Dawla*)

The second concrete case in which an entire text written by ʿAyn al-Quḍāt refigures in the *Letters* is that of his treatise on theology, the *Risāla-yi Jamālī* (*Treatise Dedicated to Jamāl al-Dawla*), which accounts for *Letter* 127.[107] At the beginning of this treatise, ʿAyn al-Quḍāt mentions a no-longer-extant Arabic treatise that he wrote in order to refute misguidance in matters of creed: the *Risālat al-ʿAlāʾī*.[108] This text was dedicated to a certain Tāj al-Dīn[109] of the ʿAlā al-Dawla family who had been ruling over Hamadan since 450/1058.[110] In all likelihood, Tāj al-Dīn would have been a friend of ʿAyn al-Quḍāt, but not a disciple per se.

The *Treatise Dedicated to Jamāl al-Dawla* was written in Persian and dedicated to the Hamadānī prince Jamāl al-Dīn Sharaf al-Dawla.[111] This work is divided into three parts and addresses two main points:

(1) The Prophets are like physicians, people are like patients, and the Quran is like the medicine cabinet. Some people follow the physicians in this life and others do not—the latter resultantly increase

in illness. For the people in this world, the illness they increase in when not following the Prophets is spiritual illness and heartsickness. Likewise, the believers benefit from their physicians. Ultimately, different people receive different medicines from their doctors—some receive more and some less, some bitter medicine and some sweet. So the Quran gives different prescriptions to each type of person in accordance with what their souls require in order to improve their spiritual condition.[112]

(2) The Prophets and the religious scholars (*ʿulamāʾ*) must administer medicine to the community; this also explains why, when innovation (*bidʿa*) and misguidance entered into the religion, many of the vanguards of Islam had to resort to unusual means to assuage these difficulties. The argument here is a justification for the use of rational theology, but not for the masses, which is in line with Ghazālī's emphasis on the utility of rational theology for scholars and its danger for lay people.[113] With this in mind, the study of rational theology is legitimate and helpful for a person whose faith in God and His Messenger has been shaken by religious innovators and cannot be helped by a preacher or teacher.[114]

5. *Zubdat al-ḥaqāʾiq* (*The Essence of Reality*)

ʿAyn al-Quḍāt's mastery of rational theology is on full display in the *Essence*. This work of one hundred short chapters also fuses rational inquiry with "tasting" (*dhawq*), thereby bringing its findings more in line with what is now commonly referred to as "philosophical Sufism."[115] ʿAyn al-Quḍāt completed the *Essence* at the age of twenty-four[116] in a matter of two or three days.[117] This is rather remarkable, given the density of this Arabic work. The work is essentially concerned with the three principles of religion, that is, the oneness of God (*tawḥīd*), prophecy (*nubuwwa*), and eschatology (*maʿād*).[118] In the introduction, ʿAyn al-Quḍāt describes it as follows:

> It is a complete provision for seekers and an ample means for the aims of those traveling to *the knowledge of certainty*.[119] (Z §2)

ʿAyn al-Quḍāt also notes that the book was written primarily for people who have already attained a high level of theoretical knowledge of God by way of rational theology; unlike most intellectually inclined theologians, however, they do not merely wish to know God with their minds.

> Their bewilderment in knowledge of God only increases their resolve to pursue this knowledge, their longing to augment their insight, and their quest for what lies beyond knowledge and the intellect. (Z §28)

In the *Essence*, our author takes a position against the notion that the divine names and attributes are superadded to God's Essence. He makes the familiar argument that they inhere in God's Essence but in a way that does not make God more than one. The names and attributes are thus not God, but they are not not God. ʿAyn al-Quḍāt also displays his deep indebtedness to Ghazālī when he argues against the Avicennan notion of God's inability to know particulars (*juzʾiyyāt*) except in a universal way, and the idea that the universe is eternal (*qadīm*). Concerning the latter, ʿAyn al-Quḍāt states in his *Letters*, "In *The Essence of Reality* I have given a complete exposition of this point that I had not seen anywhere, and which I had not heard from anyone."[120]

A key philosophical position in the *Essence* has to do with God's "withness" (*maʿiyya*), which is to say that He is with things but that nothing is with Him. This discussion gives a greater context for the more mystically oriented ideas in the book, particularly that creation is in a perpetual state of renewal (*tajdīd*) and that there is, in reality, nothing in existence but God.

The *Essence*'s single most important teaching has to do with the nature of the intellect and its limitations in knowing God, prophecy, and particularly what comes after death. The doctrine alluded to in the passage from the *Essence* just cited, namely that there is something "beyond the stage of the intellect" (*warāʾ ṭawr al-ʿaql*), finds its most sustained exposition in this work.[121] Since the intellect can affirm eschatological realities but not grasp them in any real and concrete way, ʿAyn al-Quḍāt maintains that we can only witness them if we transcend the intellect, since the afterlife corresponds to a realm that is itself beyond our ken and imagination.

6. *Shakwā'l-gharīb* (*The Exile's Complaint*)

We have already had occasion to discuss this short Arabic work of less than fifty pages, as well as its date of composition. Here, it is worth citing ʿAyn al-Quḍāt's justification for why he took up the pen in defense of himself:

> Since not a single one of the scholars or Sufis responded to these accusatory statements—on account of an excuse of theirs that I accept, but that I cannot mention because it would be too long-winded—I myself have taken hold of the pen—upon which I rely—and have responded to the statements of my critics, defending myself before them in this treatise. (*Sh* 31)

This was a self-defense that was to fall upon deaf ears, and the tone of the work from the very beginning is one of a clear recognition of this fact on the part of the author. He nevertheless writes, and by all accounts the degree of eloquence of this work, in terms of both its Arabic prose and poetry, ranks it as among the great masterpieces of Arabic literature.

Exile's Complaint is characterized by the aforementioned "sanitized" inventory of ʿAyn al-Quḍāt's writings to be found in it, as well its author's attempts to explain how some of his statements in the *Essence* match up with a number of enigmatic Sufi sayings and some statements made by the Prophet's Companions. These, ʿAyn al-Quḍāt argues, cannot be understood without recourse to Sufism, which has its own terminology and technical vocabulary.[122]

As a historical document, *Exile's Complaint* provides us with a window into how a major Sufi author understood the history of Sufism and its relationship to the other Islamic sciences, while also painting a picture of something like a "who's who" of the Sufi tradition. It is particularly interesting to note in this context that ʿAyn al-Quḍāt lists no less than six Sufi women as among the foremost guides of the path, beginning with the famous Rābiʿa al-ʿAdawiyya (d. 185/801)[123] and ending with Fāṭima b. Abī Bakr al-Kattānī, who famously died in front of the great Sumnūn al-Muḥibb (d. 287/900) as he was discoursing on love.[124]

7. *Nuzhat al-ʿushshāq* (*The Lovers' Excursion*)

In *Exile's Complaint* ʿAyn al-Quḍāt states that he wrote a one-thousand-line poem over the span of ten days under the complete title *Nuzhat al-ʿushshāq wa-nuhzat al-mushtāq* (*The Lovers' Excursion, and the*

Beloved's Chance).[125] Also referred to as the *Wajdiyyāt* (*Poems of Ecstatic Love*), ʿAyn al-Quḍāt penned this collection of Arabic love poetry at the instigation of his companions. Their specific request was that he muster his talents and put together "verses that would cause the one who relates them to quiver, constantly turning his gaze upon them."[126] It is generally believed that ʿAyn al-Quḍāt wrote *Lovers' Excursion* in his youth. This would put the date of this work's composition to some point before or even during his intellectual crisis in 506/1112, when he was roughly sixteen years old. Casting aside an argument in favor of the early authorship of *Lovers' Excursion* because it is based on several calculation errors and some unsound speculation,[127] we do have a very good reason to infer that this book goes back to an earlier period in its author's life. And that is his own testimony in *Exile's Complaint*, where he states that his youthful immersion in belles lettres was permanently replaced by his preoccupation with a much more serious and all-consuming science: traveling the Sufi path. As we will see in chapter 10, it is the inner life that allows ʿAyn al-Quḍāt to take the amorous and sensual discourse in a work like *Lovers' Excursion* to an entirely new level, allowing him to ground every kind of experience in God, the supreme Lover and Beloved.[128]

Reception

The fourteenth/twentieth-century Niʿmatullāhī Sufi hagiographer Maʿṣūm ʿAlī Shāh Shīrāzī (d. 1344/1926) aptly characterized ʿAyn al-Quḍāt as being "Christ-like in perspective and Ḥallājian in approach" (*ʿĪsawī al-mashhad wa-Manṣūrī al-maslak*).[129] Despite this exalted image of ʿAyn al-Quḍāt nearly eight hundred years after his death, it is rather difficult to textually trace his influence upon writers contemporaneous with him. This is why we find no mention of him in the Persian Sufi works of Rashīd al-Dīn Maybudī (d. ca. 520/1126), Sanāʾī, and Aḥmad Samʿānī (d. 534/1140).[130]

It has been argued that ʿAyn al-Quḍāt's Persian writings were first drawn upon by the Kubrawī author Najm al-Dīn Rāzī (d. 654/1256) in his famous Persian book on Sufism, *Mirṣād al-ʿibād* (*The Servants' Lookout*).[131] But this claim does not stand to scrutiny because ʿAyn al-Quḍāt is never mentioned by Rāzī in this text. Indeed, the one instance in which Rāzī cites a poem that is identical to what is to be found in ʿAyn al-Quḍāt's writings does not originate with ʿAyn al-Quḍāt but with another well-known figure who preceded him and is linked to his spiritual network;[132] thus, both ʿAyn al-Quḍāt and Rāzī were drawing on common (and likely oral) sources.[133] Most importantly, there is nothing in *Servants' Lookout* that clearly resonates with ʿAyn al-Quḍāt's ideas, neither in form nor in content. Be that as it may, one aspect of ʿAyn al-Quḍāt's teachings that could have been influential upon a different Kubrawī figure is his highly original explanations of the nature of the Quranic detached letters (*al-ḥurūf al-muqaṭṭaʿa*) and primordial dots. They may have been drawn upon by the founder of the Kubrawī order Najm al-Dīn Kubrā (d. 618/1221) in expounding his profound synesthetic teachings.[134]

ʿAyn al-Quḍāt does appear in other medieval Persian Sufi texts in more concrete ways. There are, for example, references to him by such major figures as Shams al-Dīn Tabrīzī (d. 643/1246), who in the *Maqālāt* (*Discourses*) seems to take issue with him on at least one of his statements.[135] ʿAzīz al-Dīn Nasafī (d. before 699/1300) discusses ʿAyn al-Quḍāt's treatment of the soul in one of his treatises[136] and was probably the first person to refer to him with the title *sulṭān al-ʿushshāq* or "Sultan of the lovers,"[137] a different form of which is commonly reserved for the famous Arab Sufi poet Ibn al-Fāriḍ (d. 632/1235).[138] And, in his Sufi hagiography *Nafaḥāt al-uns* (*Breaths of Intimacy*), ʿAbd al-Raḥmān Jāmī (d. 898/1492) extols ʿAyn al-Quḍāt's spiritual status, approvingly citing the account of his raising a dead person back to life.[139]

Among later, premodern authors, the great Safavid philosopher Mullā Ṣadrā (d. 1040/1640) often drew on ʿAyn al-Quḍāt in his Arabic writings, and in one important instance reworked his exposition of the detached letters into his main theoretical book on the Quran, but without citing his source.[140] ʿAyn al-Quḍāt was also being read in Ottoman Turkish, with *Paving the Path* having been translated twice into that language by the tenth/sixteenth century.[141] It is thus not surprising to learn that in his Sufi Quran commentary, the Ottoman spiritual master Ismāʿīl Ḥaqqī Burūsawī (d. 1137/1725) praised ʿAyn al-Quḍāt's understanding of the detached letters and sought to defend it from any charge of unbelief.[142]

On a more speculative level, arguments can be made for some form of engagement with ʿAyn al-Quḍāt's Persian Sufi writings in the works of such major medieval authors as Ruzbihān Baqlī (d.

606/1209), Farīd al-Dīn ʿAṭṭār (d. 618/1221), Jalāl al-Dīn Rūmī (d. 672/1273), Fakhr al-Dīn ʿIrāqī (d. 688/1289), and, most significantly, Maḥmūd Shabistarī (d. ca. 720/1320).[143] Among Rūmī's followers in Konya, it is said that they used to read ʿAyn al-Quḍāt's *Paving the Path* alongside a commentary upon the *Mathnawī* by Ḥusayn-i Khwārazmī (d. 840/1436).[144] Interestingly, Khwārazmī refers to ʿAyn al-Quḍāt as being "Christ-like in doctrine" (P. *ʿĪsawī-yi mashrab*),[145] which is a clear precedent to Maʿṣūm ʿAlī Shāh's characterization cited earlier.

We can trace ʿAyn al-Quḍat's influence upon the Arabic literary tradition more concretely. This is because of the fact that in the late sixth/twelfth century, the *Essence* was naturalized into the curriculum of the Madrasa Mujāhidiyya in Maragha. At this important school, it was included in and taught as part of a philosophical anthology comprised of several major works in philosophy, logic, philosophical theology, and philosophical mysticism. Among the students who studied at the Madrasa Mujāhidiyya, and who likely read these works, were such luminaries as Shihāb al-Dīn al-Suhrawardī (d. 587/1191) and Fakhr al-Dīn al-Rāzī (d. 606/1210).[146] Given the theoretical sophistication of the *Essence*, it is rather natural that the polymath Naṣīr al-Dīn Ṭūsī (d. 672/1274) would have undertaken to translate it into Persian, likely during the time he spent in Maragha at the court of Hülegü Khan.[147] Unfortunately, this translation has not survived. The *Essence*'s cogent case for the superiority of the Sufi approach to problems in metaphysics and epistemology drew the attention of Saʿīd al-Dīn Farghānī (d. 699/1300)[148] and especially Jāmī, who made good use of its arguments in his famous *Durrat al-fākhira* (*The Precious Pearl*) and in his own glosses upon it.[149]

Indeed, the *Essence* was known to intellectual and spiritual circles throughout the Muslim east. In a work that dates to the time he had settled in Damascus, for example, Ibn ʿArabī (d. 638/1240) makes a passing reference to ʿAyn al-Quḍāt that at least indicates his familiarity with the *Essence*'s underlying argument.[150] However, a later Arab follower of Ibn ʿArabī and contemporary of Burūsawī, the theologian and mystic ʿAbd al-Ghanī al-Nābulusī (d. 1143/1731), does refer to the *Essence*'s Sufi epistemology with particular approval.[151] We also find the *Essence* cited in a treatise on Sufi metaphysics by Faḍl-i Ḥaqq Khayrābādī (d. 1277/1861), a major philosopher and mystic active in British India.[152]

The one place where ʿAyn al-Quḍāt's Persian writings took firm root was in premodern India, particularly among Sufis in the Chishtī order.[153] He is thus cited by the likes of such great Sufi teachers as Niẓām al-Dīn Awliyāʾ (d. 725/1325), Rukn al-Dīn Kāshānī (d. after 738/1337), Naṣīr al-Dīn Chirāgh Dihlawī (d. 757/1356), and Masʿūd Bakk (d. 789/1387).[154] In his oral discourses (*malfūẓāt*), Sharaf al-Dīn Manīrī (d. 782/1380) also draws on ʿAyn al-Quḍāt's words, reverentially weaving them into his popular doctrinal and practical teachings.[155] ʿAyn al-Quḍāt's influence on Indian Sufi circles would reach new heights with the Persian commentary upon *Paving the Path* penned by Sayyid Muḥammad Gīsūdarāz (d. 825/1422).[156] This commentary itself was translated into Dakhini by the Chishtī master Mīrān Jī Ḥusayn Khudānamā (d. 1078/1668) during the Mughal period.[157]

The Present Book

What follows are ten chapters that collectively contain nearly eight hundred passages from ʿAyn al-Quḍāt's corpus in translation. These texts—the vast majority of which appear here for the first time in English—have been carefully organized in accordance with the major themes that guide our author's thought. For the most part, I have avoided translating the poems found in ʿAyn al-Quḍāt's oeuvre. This is because a good deal of textual work still needs to be done on many of these poems in order to determine which of them originate with him and which of them belong to other poets.[158] Moreover, ʿUsayrān's readings of some of the poems in his edition of *Paving the Path* are in need of correcting.[159]

A facilitating commentary accompanies the passages found in each chapter. I have taken as my inspiration William Chittick's exegetical approach in his two landmarks of scholarship in Sufi studies, *The Sufi Path of Love* and *The Sufi Path of Knowledge* (henceforth, "Chittick, *SPL*" and "Chittick, *SPK*" respectively). As such, my commentary has been crafted so as to allow readers to better understand key concepts, ideas, and terms, while also giving them the opportunity to make broader connections between pertinent texts and sections throughout the book. Among other things, the notes to each chapter explain unclear references, trace the various scriptural passages and sayings ʿAyn al-Quḍāt cites, and point to relevant leads in his writings and essential secondary literature.[160]

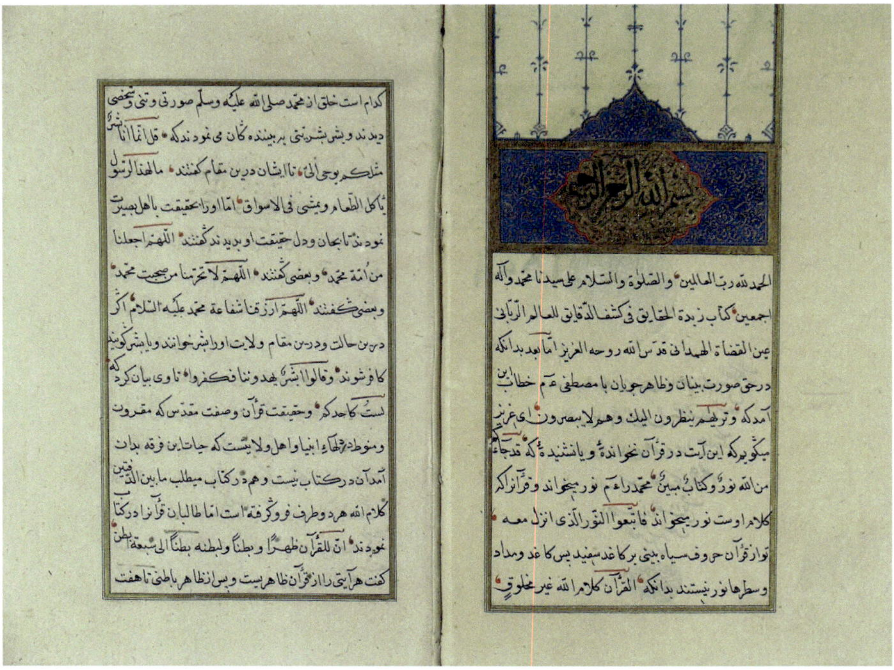

Figure 2. Page from a manuscript of ʿAyn al-Quḍāt, *Tamhīdāt*

1

Autobiography

ʿAyn al-Quḍāt's works are peppered with autobiographical remarks that give us a window into his intellectual trajectory and magnetizing personality, as well as the unfolding of his spiritual life.

هو

Discovery

ʿAyn al-Quḍāt tells us that, in his youth, his cerebral and dry approach to religion and immersion in rational theology eventually presented him with some unresolvable intellectual and possibly spiritual dilemmas. It is only after prolonged engagement with the writings of Ghazālī[1] that he finds himself freed from his existential predicament.

> My excuse for diving into every aspect of knowledge is clear: the drowning man clutches at straws, hoping for salvation. Had God in His bounty and generosity not delivered me from it, I would have been *on the brink of a pit of fire*.[2] This is because I would study the books of rational theology, seeking to raise myself from the depths of blind imitation to the summit of insight. But I did not get what I sought from these books. In fact, the foundations of the schools of rational theology so confounded me that I encountered all sorts of predicaments that cannot be recounted. . . .

> I was totally bewildered about my situation. On top of that, it ruined my life—until the "Guide of the bewildered"[3] gave me guidance and extended His generosity toward me, bestowing aid and success. In short, after God's bounty, nothing other than a study of the books of the Proof of Islam Abū Ḥāmid Muḥammad al-Ghazālī revived me from my wretched state. For almost four years I studied his books. During this period when I was occupied with true knowledge, I beheld many wonders that steered me away from bewilderment, blindness, error, and unbelief. Explaining this will not do it justice, for it is beyond the confines of analysis and calculation, nor is there any hope in even trying to come to terms with it. (Z §§13–14)

The incredible spiritual state (*ḥāl*) that results from ʿAyn al-Quḍāt's period of self-discovery eventually leads his inner, spiritual eye to be opened. Seeing more clearly than ever before, the hands of destiny bring him face to face with Abū Ḥāmid's younger brother, Shaykh Aḥmad Ghazālī. Under the guidance of this great Sufi master, ʿAyn al-Quḍāt's spiritual journey takes on an entirely new meaning.

> Suddenly, the eye of my insight began to open. Do not be deluded in your thinking: I do not mean the insight of the intellect. The eye of insight opened, little by little. I stood there, marveling at the obstacles that nearly barred me from the path of pursuing what lies beyond rational theology. I remained like this for almost a year without fully comprehending the reality of the situation I was in during that year until destiny brought my master Shaykh Abū'l-Futūḥ Aḥmad al-Ghazālī, that most illustrious leader, the sultan of the path and the interpreter of reality, to Hamadan, my birthplace. In his service, the veil of bewilderment was removed from my situation in under twenty days, and in that period I bore witness to an unmistakable spiritual state. (Z §14)
>
> Had I not persisted at the door of this master, for the rest of my life my heart would have accumulated blameworthy

> attributes, the escape from which is hopeless and impossible. (Z §134)

This spiritual state to which ʿAyn al-Quḍāt refers results in the disclosure of a certain "thing" that consumes him entirely.[4] What, exactly, is this "thing"? Simply put, it is the all-embracing presence of God. In another context, the Shaykh explains how, while in the act of writing, he is overcome by God's presence or what he calls the "splendor of majestic Beginninglessness." "Beginninglessness" translates a word that derives from one of ʿAyn al-Quḍāt's favorite terms, the Arabic noun *azal*. In strictly speaking theological and philosophical contexts, *azal* denotes "eternity without beginning." It is often paired with *abad*, which denotes "eternity without end."[5] Despite the fact that these terms denote different senses of eternity, when the divine floodgates open for ʿAyn al-Quḍāt they take on a temporal coloring, causing him to ebb back from time to the Timeless.

> The splendor of majestic Beginninglessness shone forth: knowledge and intellect became naught, and there remained only the writer, but without himself. Rather, the Real Identity[6] enveloped me and drowned my metaphorical identity. (Z §160)

So long as ʿAyn al-Quḍāt is an embodied subject bound by temporality, he must resurface from the Beginningless. At times, he will share the precious jewels that he has discovered, and at times he will conceal them.

> When the Beginningless beauty returned my intellect, knowledge, and self, my tongue began to ring with the words of the poet:
>
> What happened, I will not mention.
> Think well, and ask no more![7] (Z §160)

The poet cited by ʿAyn al-Quḍāt is Ibn al-Muʿtazz (d. 296/908). Unlike most other bards in the annals of history, Ibn al-Muʿtazz is famous for his verse and his short-lived career in politics: he reigned as Abbasid Caliph for but a day, only to be murdered shortly thereafter by forces conspiring in his very midst. As we have seen, ʿAyn al-Quḍāt's career was also cut short, and he was on one level also the victim of political subterfuge and intrigue. In other words, both Ibn al-Muʿtazz and ʿAyn al-Quḍāt were helpless against the causes at work around them. Even during his life, ʿAyn al-Quḍāt was very much a pawn in the hands of the Divine Chess Player, rendering him helpless not only at the time of his death but also at key moments throughout his life.

Helplessness

It is quite common to find ʿAyn al-Quḍāt intending to write on a particular topic in the *Letters* only to be sidetracked by his having fallen into "a different world"[8] and "landing far" from his goal "once again."[9] This is because, in the course of writing, he has already "flown to and wandered in hundreds of thousands of worlds."[10] Readers of ʿAyn al-Quḍāt are thus struck by the degree of emphasis he places on the lack of agency involved in his teachings, be they in the form of writing or speaking.[11] When he does not want to write, he is forced to do so and cannot but put pen to paper.

> Whenever I write something, writing comes before me and overpowers me until I write. It is as if I do not want to write, but cannot do otherwise. (*N* II, 308, §465)

> The fear is that if the reins of the pen are let loose, all that would not have been written will be written! (*N* I, 370, §617)

> Alas! As much as I want to flee from the world of writing, writing seizes me by the hand and does not let go. (*T* 323–324, §424)

> I know that you are saying, "These words should not be said." But these words that explain the exalted ranks—namely aspiration—are being spoken! (*T* 310, §407)

All of this is to say that ʿAyn al-Quḍāt's words proceed from the spiritual world and are the result of what are known in Sufi literature as *wāridāt* or "inrushes." When written down, in the first instance these inrushes pose serious obstacles for the uninitiated or those referred to by ʿAyn al-Quḍāt as "strangers" (to whom we will return in chapter 8).

> The more I write, the more difficulties there are for strangers! (*N* I, 280, §466)

> Alas! The more I write, the more difficulties that come! (*T* 196, §254)

> The more I write on these pages, the more difficulties there are! (*N* I, 270, §448)

What characterizes these strangers is that they have not conquered their lower selves and thus cannot hear the Shaykh's words. He conveys his teachings through the tongue of his spiritual state (P. *zabān-i ḥāl*),[12] but they hear these words' outward sounds only, that is, with the ear of conventional speech (P. *gūsh-i qāl*).[13] ʿAyn al-Quḍāt's inspired words also throw him into a perplexed state, resulting in some rather paradoxical statements as far as both the speaker/writer and listener/reader are concerned.

> Whatever I write is unfitting, but if I write nothing, it is also unfitting. If I speak, it is unfitting, but when I remain silent, it is also unfitting. If I hold back these words, it is unfitting, but if I do not hold them back, it is also unfitting! (*N* II, 199, §293)

> Where is this meddling judge of Hamadan from? Where are these words of mysteries from? The speaker does not know what he is saying, so how can the hearer know what he is hearing?! (*T* 15, §22)

> I am an unbeliever if I know what I am saying! Alas! Since the speaker does not know what he is saying, how can the hearer know what he is hearing?" (*T* 249, §327)

Tasting

Paralleling the inrushes to which ʿAyn al-Quḍāt is privy is his tasting (*dhawq*) of God, a Quranic verse, the reality of prophecy, a certain doctrinal point, the nature of existence, a spiritual teaching, and so on. Tasting is particularly meaningful when it comes to knowledge of what lies beyond our normal faculties of sense perception. This is why ʿAyn al-Quḍāt tells us that the certainty he has in the four elements (air, earth, fire, and water) is not by way of tasting but simply by way of his senses. As for those worlds that lie beyond that of the four elements, they cannot be got at through ordinary human means and are the exclusive purview of tasting.[14]

In its widest technical usage, "tasting" is a Sufi term that was made popular by Ghazālī.[15] It conveys the direct and unmediated nature of one's encounter with God in particular, and "divine matters" in general. When it comes to the question of the acquisition of true knowledge, Sufis always contrast tasting with more conventional forms of learning, pointing up the futility of the latter and the superiority of the former. This is to say that if one has tasting he has true knowledge, but if he does not have it, he has no real knowledge at all. Nothing illustrates this point as succinctly as the famous Arabic proverb "He who does not taste, does not know." As someone who does know, ʿAyn al-Quḍāt insists that his writings are almost entirely based on tasting, which explains the strong sense of certainty conveyed through them.

> O friend! Speaking about honey is one thing, and seeing it is one thing. But eating honey is quite another thing! (*T* 235, §305)

> I write out of tasting, not out of having read or heard. (*N* III, 278, §3)

> Whatever I have written in this letter[16] and the other letters, I have done it all out of tasting. In my *Letters* only a few examples are derived from what is transmitted and heard. (*N* II, 308, §465)

> O dear friend! On the path to God, I have seen it all. . . . Without doubt, you do not know because you have not arrived. I know, because I have arrived. (*N* II, 25, §34)

> Alas! Whoever wants to hear the divine mysteries without an intermediary, say, "Listen to ʿAyn al-Quḍāt Hamadānī!" This is, "The Real speaks on the tongue of ʿUmar."[17] (*T* 300, §394)

Charismatic Gifts

This tasting is the result of any given station on the Sufi path or the necessary complement to or antecedent of a particularly significant spiritual state. At the height of the latter, ʿAyn al-Quḍāt is able to freely produce what the Sufis refer to as "charismatic gifts" or "miracles" (*karāmāt*).[18] In the following passage, he makes the usual distinction between a miracle given by God to a Prophet (*muʿjiza*) and a charismatic gift given by God to one of His Friends. In doing so, our author also sidelines the accusation leveled against him (encountered in the introduction) to the effect that he is a sorcerer.

> People do not listen to me and call me a sorcerer. Just as Jesus had been given miracles . . . so too is it with the Friend of God—but they are charismatic gifts. And so too is it with this helpless one. (*T* 250, §327)

In an incident recorded in *Paving the Path* and the *Letters*, ʿAyn al-Quḍāt reports that he, his father, and some dignitaries had attended a Sufi gathering in Hamadan. As is customary in such contexts, those present began to partake in the ritual Sufi dance (*samāʿ*). During the dance, ʿAyn al-Quḍāt's father reports an apparition in which he sees Aḥmad Ghazālī—who was not physically present and possibly no longer alive at the time of this incident—dancing with them. The lead singer (*munshid*) expresses his astonishment and perhaps even disgust over the vision, and exclaims that he wishes he were dead. It is at this moment that ʿAyn al-Quḍāt intervenes and gives the man what he had wished for. Then, true to his Jesus-like (*ʿĪsawī*) nature, ʿAyn al-Quḍāt brings the man back to life.

> I know that you have heard this story:[19] One night, me, my father, and a group of leaders from our city were in the house of a certain Sufi leader.[20] We then began to dance while Abū Saʿīd Tirmidhī was reciting a few verses. My father carefully looked and said, "I saw Khwāja Imām Aḥmad Ghazālī dancing with us. His garment was like this and like that." And he made some gestures. Shaykh Bū Saʿīd said, "I cannot recite. I wish I were dead!" I said, "O Bū Saʿīd, die!" Immediately, he lost consciousness and died. A local mufti—you know who he is—said, "Just as you caused the living to die, so too bring the dead back to life." I said, "Who is dead?" He replied, "Maḥmūd, the jurist."[21] I said, "O God! Bring Maḥmūd the jurist back to life!" Immediately, he came back to life.[22] (*T* 250–251, §328)

Another one of ʿAyn al-Quḍāt's charismatic gifts is his ability to step outside of the normal flow of corporeal existence and serial time. In one of these "out-of-body experiences" ʿAyn al-Quḍāt leaves his body and can see his companions in the room, but he is hidden from their sight. He remains in this state, entirely unnoticed by those around him, for an entire month. This charismatic gift, too, is Jesus-like in nature since the Quran reports that Jesus was also snatched away from the order of space and time. When God took Jesus back to Himself, that is when he was seen by others.

> If you want to know, ask Nāṣir al-Dīn. There was a time when he came in with a group of friends. In the state that I was in,[23] they themselves had nothing to do with me—they were veiled from me. They came in, but did not see me. I remained in this station for a month such that nobody perceived me.
>
> Wait until this verse concerning Jesus is shown to you! *And they did not slay him, nor did they crucify him, but it appeared so to them.*[24] Given everything, how was he found?

He was found when he was raised up. This is, *But God raised him up to Himself.*[25] (*T* 247–248, §325)

Apparitions

ʿAyn al-Quḍāt does not hide the fact that he lives an intense religious life, which is regularly punctuated by what we would call "spiritual experiences" in modern parlance. These are undoubtedly normal states for our author, and he would probably even say that the so-called regular waking moments that we experience are rather abnormal in comparison. When the Shaykh returns to the world of form and writing, he attempts to express his visions, often with some degree of ambiguity.

> O chevalier![26] Eighteen thousand worlds have been created, and the lowest of them all is the world of bodies. These other worlds are not bodies at all. By the majesty and worth of the Beginningless, I have had this apparition many times! How are bodies worthy of existence? The men[27] have come from another path, but you are knocking at a different door! Do you not know, *Come into houses by their doors*[28]? (*N* I, 88, §120)

> Everyone is not ʿAyn al-Quḍāt, who is drowned in the exaltedness of the circle of "He."[29] Robes are bestowed upon the world through the protection of the sanctuary of self-sufficiency after this helpless one became a madman in the protection of its exaltedness, for "children are throwing stones at him."[30] (*T* 348–349, §462)

> I heard it said to me that the secret of destiny, the Supreme Name,[31] and the Trust—all of these go together.[32] (W 2)

> One time, before a sickness, I became absent to myself. Someone asked me, "What does '*Ḥāʾ, Mīm,*[33] ʿAyn, Sīn, Qāf'[34] mean?" I said, "A land in Makka." I had never seen or heard this explanation.[35] (W 2)

> Alas! That night, namely Friday night, I was writing these words. I reached a place where I saw that whatever was and is in the Beginningless and the Endless is in the letter *alif*.[36] Alas! One needs to understand what I am saying! (*T* 347, §459)

On another Friday night, ʿAyn al-Quḍāt tells us that the identity of a certain mystery man had been disclosed to him. Up to this point, the Shaykh had confirmed that there were nine people who belong to that distinguished group of knowers referred to in the Quran as those who are *firmly rooted in knowledge*.[37] But who was the tenth? While preparing to write or perhaps even busy in the act of writing, the answer came to him.

> O friend! For quite some time nine of the firmly rooted knowers were known to me. But tonight, namely Friday night—which are nights devoted to writing—the tenth of them became known to me. He is Khwāja Imām Muḥammad Ghazālī. I knew that Aḥmad was one of them but did not know that Muḥammad was—he also belongs to us.[38] (*T* 280–281, §366)

Muhammadan Encounters

By this point it should be apparent that ʿAyn al-Quḍāt's words are often shrouded in mystery. What is clear is that, for all of his experiences, his encounters with and direct guidance from the person of the Prophet are essential. This point ties into a major aspect of ʿAyn al-Quḍāt's thought, namely his Muhammadology.

One of the themes that will emerge later in this book is the degree of emphasis ʿAyn al-Quḍāt places on the Muhammadan light as a cosmogenic principle. But it is also a palpable reality that ʿAyn al-Quḍāt encounters in his waking state and through the dreams of his companions. In the following passage we encounter ʿAyn al-Quḍāt enraptured in an exalted spiritual station. He encounters the light of the Prophet as utterly detached and disembodied,[39] and this light then merges with a light that comes from within himself.

> In this station that I ʿAyn al-Quḍāt was in, I saw a light separated from him and a light that came from me. Both lights came forth and connected, and a beautiful form appeared, leaving me bewildered in this state for some time. (*T* 303, §397)

In an apparition of the end of time and the Resurrection (*qiyāma*) of all creatures before God, ʿAyn al-Quḍāt sees the various religious communities, each raised up with their respective Prophet. The Prophet Muhammad appears in a luminous form that is different than the other Prophets, as does his community of followers. ʿAyn al-Quḍāt then communicates his vision to a local Rabbi in Hamadan[40] who affirms it based on a teaching in the Torah.

> Alas! In this Resurrection the Prophets were displayed to me with the members of their communities. Each Prophet had two lights, and his community had one. But I saw Muhammad, who was all light, from head to toe: *and those who follow the light that has been sent down with him*.[41] And I saw that the members of his community had two lights. . . .
>
> Alas! What do you know about what you will hear? I saw one of the Rabbis and asked him about this apparition. He said, "In the Torah I also have read this description about the ranks of the wayfaring of the Prophets. They have spoken in this way to the members of their communities, and God has spoken in this way to Moses."[42] (*T* 322, §422)

Given the profound connection ʿAyn al-Quḍāt had with his companions and disciples, it is not surprising to find references in his writings to their dreams that in some way or another involve him. In one such instance, the Prophet counsels ʿAyn al-Quḍāt through the dream of his friend Shaykh Siyāwish. This then leads to ʿAyn al-Quḍāt's waking encounter with the Prophet (Muṣṭafā), followed by a second incident that would cause many people to think that the sage of Hamadan was actually a wizard.

> Shaykh Siyāwish said to me: "This evening, I saw Muṣṭafā in a dream. He came in from the door and said, 'ʿAyn

> al-Quḍāt, you tell me, 'I still have not become a resident of the abode of divine stillness.' Be patient for a while, and come along with patience, until that moment when all will be proximity to us without distance, and all will be union without separation.' "
>
> When Shaykh Siyāwish related this dream to me, I let out a patient lament and my entirety became immersed in reciting these lines. When I looked, I saw Muṣṭafā, who came in from the door and said, "What I had said to Shaykh Siyāwish, he could not handle in his waking state." Some flames raged from the light of Muṣṭafā. A small speck landed on Shaykh Siyāwish and he burned up immediately. But people imagine this to be sorcery and magic. (*T* 234, §304)

Another dream reported by ʿAyn al-Quḍāt by his companion Abū ʿAlī Āmulī marks the end of *Paving the Path*. In Shaykh Āmulī's dream, the Prophet requests from ʿAyn al-Quḍāt that he hand over to him his copy of *Paving the Path*. Then follows the story's highly instructive climax.

> Tonight, which is Friday night, the ninth of Rajab, Shaykh Abū ʿAlī Āmulī said, "This evening I saw Muṣṭafā in a dream: You, ʿAyn al-Quḍāt, and I came before him and you had this book with you. Muṣṭafā said to you, 'Show me this book.' You showed him the book. He took it and said to you, 'Leave it with me,' so you left it with him. Then he said, 'O ʿAyn al-Quḍāt, do not reveal any more mysteries than these!' " May my spirit be sacrificed upon the dust of his feet! When he said, "do not reveal any more mysteries than these!," I accepted it and immediately desisted from speaking. I have become entirely occupied with him until the next time he gives me an order. (*T* 353–354, §469)

Shortly after the words just cited, *Paving the Path* abruptly comes to an end. Not only does this show us to what extent ʿAyn al-Quḍāt was an obedient follower and ardent lover of the Prophet; it also offers us another window into the intricate internal workings that inform ʿAyn al-Quḍāt's function as author and orator.

Now, to what is the Prophet referring when he tells ʿAyn al-Quḍāt that he should not reveal any more mysteries? As we will see in chapter 2, the Prophet's admonishment is based on the knowledge of a particular danger lying in wait for the Shaykh, amounting to nothing less than the vertical cause of his eventual demise.

Figure 3. ʿAyn al-Quḍāt Artistic and Cultural Center (Hamadan, Iran)

2

Counsel and Confession

In addition to leading a profound devotional and visionary life, ʿAyn al-Quḍāt is also a spiritual advisor, critic of the government, lover of his native Hamadan, and prognosticator of his own death.

هو

Advice and Admonition

ʿAyn al-Quḍāt's writings—particularly his *Letters*—reveal the concrete manner in which he serves as a spiritual guide (*murshid*; P. *pīr*) for his disciples. They thus receive theoretical and practical advice on all aspects of their inner lives from an accomplished master whose words always come across as clear, concise, and comforting. The Shaykh's most straightforward words of instruction are for his students to never forget their sole purpose in life, and for them to listen to their master.

> Do not imagine that being an aspirant[1] is easy work! (*N* I, 274, §454)

> Since death is inevitable and you do not know when it will be—for it is possible at any moment and might happen at any moment—the prudence of the men[2] entails that the intelligent person not be heedless of it. (*N* III 433, §272)

> Seek well, find, keep watch, and listen to me until you know. (*T* 64, §87)

> Do not be heedless of your duty, for heedlessness is not the work of the men. (*N* II, 469, §730)

By "duty" the Shaykh is of course referring to immersion in the act of invoking and remembering (*dhikr*) the name of God. He also calls this task meditation (*fikr*), which is not to be confused with reflective thinking (*tafakkur*).

> Recognition of God is only obtained through correct meditation. I am speaking about meditation, not reflective thinking. (*N* II, 153, §225)

> Correct meditation is only obtained by a limpid heart that is pure from worldly occupations and bodily attachments. (*N* II, 153, §225)

The Shaykh tells one student that the state of meditation and invocation should be so total and all-consuming as to involve his entirety (P. *hamagī*), namely his body, mind, soul, and everything in between.

> Of what concern is the entirety of the Sun to you? Your share from the Sun is for your home to be illuminated in its entirety. (*T* 132, §182)

> *Frequent invocation*[3] is for you to invoke with your entirety—not a single speck of your makeup should be left out. *Remember Me*[4] is here. (*N* II, 433, §683)

A life in which one is absorbed in the remembrance of the divine does not entail neglect for one's neighbors. Quite the contrary: the more characterized one becomes by proximity to God, the more does his concern for all sentient beings increase. For ʿAyn al-Quḍāt the best way to show and address concern for others is through charity (*ṣadaqa*). As a form of spiritual discipline, he requires his students to distribute some of their own wealth on a daily basis. And if they are remiss in doing so on any day, they have to make up for it the following day.[5]

In addition to feeding the poor, by charity the Shaykh also has in mind spreading peace and mercy among people, and bringing joy to everyone's heart. Just as one must give himself to the invocation of God with all that he has and is, so too must he give himself to others with all that he has and is.

> Obey God, as much as you can. And charity is the best form of your obedience: *and they spend from that which We have provided them*.[6] You have wealth, fame, power, the pen, and speech. "Have mercy on those below you, and the One above you will have mercy on you."[7] Spend whatever you have so that what you do not have will be spent on you. "A pleasant word is charity"[8] and "Affability with people is charity."[9] (*N* II, 211, §314)

There is a famous story that tells of a companion of ʿAlī b. Abī Ṭālib (d. 40/661) who came to him complaining about the wrongs that another person had committed against him. After hearing of his friend's plight, ʿAlī replied, "You must have done a lot of good for him." In other words, while a person must have concern for people and be good to them, he should never expect anything from them in return. This explains why ʿAyn al-Quḍāt ties the condition of not expecting anything in return from others to the very act of charitable giving. After all, if one's giving is for the sake of God, it will not matter whether he is thanked for it by others or not.

> Every day, set aside some of your wealth. Give it away for the sake of God, and know that this is for the sake of God. (*N* I, 114, §165)

> O friend! I have written a piece of advice, namely that you give something in charity every day—not by way of habit,[10] but from a place where questions are not asked and a gift is not expected in return. (*N* I, 106, §149)

On the one hand, expecting something in return from people compromises the sincerity of one's kindness toward them. On the other hand, it causes the giver to assign worth and agency to "his" actions and to ultimately expect things not only from people, but also from God. At the highest level, one should simply do his duty and only want God Himself.

If a person is to assign no worth to the effects of his actions in the form of expected rewards in a deferred future, he should assign even less worth to the opinions people have of him, be they positive or negative. As ʿAyn al-Quḍāt is quick to point out, this is because concern with what people think will take one away from his fundamental task, which is to always remember God and to only be concerned about what He "thinks" of him. Whatever views people may have of a person ultimately have no bearing upon the destiny of his soul, whereas the converse is the case with respect to God.

> What benefit is there in people's praise, or what harm in their blame? If someone habitually suffers on account of people's statements, he will have nothing but sorrow, night and day. Watch out for God, and that's it! (*N* II, 438, §689)

> The fear of God is reality, and the fear of people metaphor. If you are occupied with God, He will suffice you. But if you are occupied with people, He will leave you to yourself. "He who works for the next world, God shall put his affairs in order in this world."[11] *Those to whom the people say, "Surely people have gathered against you, so fear them." But it increases them in faith, and they say, "God suffices us; an excellent guardian is He!"*[12] (*N* II, 438, §689)

With God as one's sole concern in life, it is not only what may or may not come from people that is ultimately irrelevant. It also applies to the world and all that happens to a person while living in it. Whatever her lot in life, she need not grieve over it. But if she faces danger in the next life, then that is a call for grave concern.

> Why should a person sorrow over his lot in life in this abode of evanescence? Why do you not sorrow over what will be said to you after you die? (*N* II, 438, §689)

One should not assume that ʿAyn al-Quḍāt is somehow a pessimist. On the contrary: he has a rather optimistic view of the future and of the ability for many human beings to realize their spiritual potential. This is why the Shaykh sees an opportunity for a person to receive God's mercy even in the face of what are known in the Islamic tradition as major sins (*kabāʾir*). For the spiritual aspirant, these and all other forms of disobedience toward God must be avoided to the greatest extent possible. If one should happen to fall into them, he should never despair—God's mercy is ever near. As for a person's obedient deeds (*ṭāʿāt*), the judge of Hamadan reminds us that they are very significant with respect to the divine equilibrium, which puts everything in its proper place.

> If you have major sins that fill the heavens and the earth, God's mercy is more than them. And if you have obedient deeds that fill the heavens and the earth, do not deem them to be specks, thanks to His justice. (*N* I, 114, §164)

The only way a person can begin to put God at the center of his concerns is to take the spiritual or inner journey. This demands that he relinquish the world and cease to journey within it, for such a journey is the antipode of the inner journey.

> So long as you do not arrive, how will you know? Right now, you reside in the house of human mortal nature—*whosoever forsakes his home*[13] is a condition for the task, not going from Hamadan to Tabriz, for nothing will come of this. Listen to the Quran: *Let it not delude thee that those who disbelieve are free to come and go in the land.*[14] (*N* II, 433, §683)

> What will come of the outward journey? *"Paltry is the enjoyment of this world"*[15]—the entirety of this world is paltry. But something will come of walking in that land: *"God's earth is vast."*[16] (*N* II, 433–434, §683)

> As long as you do not abandon creation, you will not reach the Creator. This is, *Whosoever emigrates in the way of God will find upon the earth many a refuge and abundance, and whosoever forsakes his home, emigrating unto God and His Messenger, and death overtakes him, his wage will fall upon God.*[17] But where are you? (*T* 207, §266)

Criticism

For the one who is undertaking the inner journey, she must choose her friends wisely. After all, the great Sufi master Dhū'l-Nūn al-Miṣrī

(d. ca. 245/859)[18] once said, "There is no good for you in keeping the company of someone who likes to regard you as sinless."[19] As a spiritual guide for his disciples and as their loving friend, ʿAyn al-Quḍāt understands the meaning of this statement all too well.

> O chevalier! Were one of the deniers to keep my company, there is no doubt that, after ten days, his denying would disappear. Since the Companions used to keep the company of Muṣṭafā, see what their state was like! Over the last two years, have you not sat in twenty sessions with me? Look at how your faith is now, and how it was before. So you should know how it is with my noble companions, each of whom has kept my company for ten years. The first time you saw me, you were not as you are today, and were you to keep my company for ten years, your state would not be as it is right now. (*N* I, 52, §62)

The Shaykh does not shy away from criticizing his students when circumstances call for it and when his words of rebuke will aid them along the way.

> You never know what I am saying! Wait until you arrive and see. You still reside in the house of human mortal nature and are captured by the hands of caprice and the ego.[20] (*T* 247, §324)

In its most extreme form, he chastises some of his students in response to their queries. Rather than answer their questions, he simply observes that they are unworthy of meriting a response from their master, and this because of their own shortcomings.

> The smell of milk still comes from your mouth, so what can one say to you? (*N* I, 209, §335)

> What should I write? You do not deserve that I should write something to you! (*N* II, 374–375, §583)

> What do you hear? Alas! You do not have the strength! And I do not know who will have the strength! (*N* I, 270–271, §449)

> How much should I write and how long do I have to repeat that your faith is by way of habit? (*N* I, 182, §281)

> You say, "You have written nothing." What should I write? I have written to you about whatever is useful on the path to God concerning wayfaring, subtleties, and arriving. But what have you done with that?! (*N* III 406, §234)

When it comes to the fundamental act of the remembrance of God, ʿAyn al-Quḍāt makes no concessions for his students. If they fail to uphold their pact with him and undertake the essential practice of the inner life, they can rest assured that they will be hearing about it. In one letter to a disciple, the Shaykh identifies the root cause of this particular student's inability to remember God, namely his having a sinful and dark heart.

> I take it that you do not remember God because your heart has become blackened by darkness. Is there a moment when you can forget death? Do you imagine that, of all people, you have some special attribute so that the angel of death will not come upon you? (*N* III, 410, §238)

In a different letter to a student, ʿAyn al-Quḍāt bluntly tells him that if he fails to regularly perform the special litany (*wird*) that he has given to him, he can almost be certain that he will be unsuccessful on the spiritual path.

> The first night we met, I offered you advice and gave you a litany. I do not know whether you have been persevering with that litany or not. If it happens to be that you have not been persevering with it, then most likely nothing will come of you. (*N* I, 114–115, §166)

At times, we find ʿAyn al-Quḍāt reviling his students because of some mistaken view on their part that requires immediate and decisive correction. In one instance, a certain disciple of his tells him how, after so many years of failing to understand the meanings of his master's letters, he now understands them. Rather than congratulate the student, the Shaykh reprimands him, reminding him that even his so-called "understanding" comes from his teacher and not from himself. If a disciple imagines that he has been successful in any matter by virtue of his own efforts, he will open himself up to the dangers of pride and egotistical self-congratulation.[21] Thankfully for this student, he is put in his proper place before it is too late.

> You write that you now better understand the letters that have been written? Where have you reached by this point? You should keep my company for ten or twenty years—then you will know what color knowing has, and you will know that you have never known! What do you think my letters are? Whatever you can understand of them does not belong to you—indeed, it is not your understanding. It is my understanding. If it is not my understanding, then what do you think it is?! May God cause you to arrive at the realities of these matters by His mercy and help.[22] (*N* III, 302, §42)

Sandal-Service

ʿAyn al-Quḍāt's wrath is also unleashed upon those of his disciples who serve at the court of the corrupt Seljuqs, and that in accordance with the degree to which this service interferes with their spiritual lives.

> Hypocrites are one thing, and lovers are quite another thing! To which group do you belong? *Wavering between this [and that], being neither for one group nor for the other.*[23] O chevalier! If you fear the sultan more than you fear the master, then you are still a hypocrite. Listen to the Quran: *Surely you incite more intense dread in their breasts than God. That is because they are a people who comprehend not.*[24] (*N* I, 46–47, §54)

This above passage illustrates an important element in ʿAyn al-Quḍāt's criticisms of his students' service at the Seljuq court. Not only does the company of kings and worldly court officials corrupt the students' souls, but their reason for working at the court is itself based on a major ethical and spiritual shortcoming, namely their view that service to the Seljuq sultan will provide them with financial security. Such a view in ʿAyn al-Quḍāt's eyes is false because it stems from what the Sufis call "worrying over one's sustenance" (*hamm al-rizq*), which is informed by and itself weakens the supreme virtue of trust in God (*tawakkul*).

> Are you not ashamed that you are spending your precious life in pursuit of fulfilling appetites? *They enjoy themselves and eat as cattle eat.*[25] What virtue is there in being like beasts? *Worship your Lord, who created you.*[26] He Himself sends sustenance, but you do not rely on Him! He says, *There is no creature that crawls upon the earth but that its provision lies with God.*[27] Have shame! You rely on the assurance of someone who was created from a filthy fluid,[28] but you do not rely on the assurance of the Lord of lords, the Causer of causes, and the Creator of the earth and the heavens! Why do you not leave your ignorance behind?[29] (*N* III, 412, §243)

> O chevalier! How long will you be in the service of the king? Why do you not serve God, who created you and the king from a drop of fluid?[30] *"Surely those whom you worship apart from God have no power over what provision may come to you. So seek your provision with God."*[31] *Surely those whom you call upon apart from God are servants like you.*[32] Do you imagine that there is something in the king's hands? *"They have no power over what benefit or harm may come to themselves."*[33] What can he do with you? (*N* III, 412, §242)

Since in the spiritual life concern with anything other than God is tantamount to associating other people and/or orders of reality with God (*shirk*), a fortiori, seeing one's daily bread as coming from other than God is even more problematic for those on the Sufi path, who are often referred to as wayfarers (P. *sālikān*). The judge of Hamadan addresses one such wayfarer in the following passage.

> O chevalier! You fancy being the king and having a kingdom, and that withholding and bestowing should be yours? . . . In the view of the recognizer,[34] this fancy is all associationism because only He is the bestower, only He is the withholder, and only He is the existent. This is why in the Quran He says, *And most of them believe not in God, save that they are associators.*[35] (*N* I, 233–234, §385)

> What do you see and know? "The search for knowledge is an obligation upon every Muslim man and woman."[36] You have gone thousands of parasangs[37] in service of the sultan. But then you say, "I have faith in Muhammad's statement,[38] 'Seek knowledge, even to China.'" "Modesty is a part of faith."[39] I am ashamed to say that you follow a person who says, "Seek the world, even to China"! If even today the sultan says to you, "Go to Marv" and, "O so-and-so, do such-and-such," you would not dare offer any excuse![40] (*N* I, 157, §232)

> What virtue is there in boasting about serving a sinful administrator, a human satan, and an enemy of God and the Messenger? Dust upon the heads of the server and the served! *Surely God is beyond need of the worlds.*[41] I mean, what pleasure do you get from this service? What do you lack by way of daily bread or clothing? Even if you were to live a hundred years—what a thought!—you have more than enough for you and your children. (*N* II, 375, §584)

Serving the Seljuqs is a dead end for ʿAyn al-Quḍāt's students. They should give themselves to the spiritual path and cultivating their relationship not with the sultan, but the Sultan.

> If the present-day sultan were to spend one night alone with you, you would probably die out of joy! Why do you not seek the one who is the Sultan of sultans and King of kings, who speaks and listens to you every night? (*N* III, 413, §245)

The surest way for ʿAyn al-Quḍāt's disciples to receive unveiling (*kashf*) is for them to dedicate themselves and their energies to being in the company of and in converse with their spiritual master. Serving the master (P. *khidmat*) was how ʿAyn al-Quḍāt himself received spiritual illumination,[42] and he invites his disciples to do the same. The term the Shaykh tellingly reserves for this single-minded devotion is "sandal-service" (P. *khidmat-i kafshī*).[43]

> Why not do sandal-service? It just might deliver you from the flood of destruction. You should be ashamed at what

> you are doing! . . . I advise you as befits your intelligence, or, rather, your unintelligence! (*N* II, 375, §584)

> If you come out of your shell before death, you will see everything. But if not, then at its proper time—at the time of death—you will know: *"Now We have removed from you your cover; so today your sight is piercing!"*[44] One must have the attribute of ʿAlī so that he can say, "Were the cover lifted, I would not increase in certainty."[45] Unveiling comes about through sandal-service to the men, not from service at the sultan's court![46] (*N* II, 388–389, §609)

Since ʿAyn al-Quḍāt was in many ways a public intellectual in Hamadan, his condemnatory remarks about the Seljuqs would have made a real impression on the great numbers of audiences drawn to him. But before the Seljuqs would have him killed on account of this, ʿAyn al-Quḍāt had the opportunity to defend himself not once, but twice.

Two Defenses

In the introduction we outlined the nature and content of *Exile's Complaint*, which ʿAyn al-Quḍāt wrote while imprisoned in Baghdad and awaiting his trial and execution. On the face of it, the treatise amounts to a futile defense of the trumped-up charges of heresy leveled against its author.

What is particularly striking about *Exile's Complaint* is the degree to which the Shaykh expresses his longing for his native Hamadan. The notion of longing for one's homeland is a standard trope in classical Arabic literature,[47] and ʿAyn al-Quḍāt develops it to great rhetorical effect. He describes himself as someone who is

> an exile from his homeland, afflicted by the passage of time and its trials. With eyes transfixed out of sleeplessness, constant disquiet, weeping, prolonged wailing, and sighing, worry seizes his whole heart and augments his distress. . . . The fires of separation set his heart ablaze as he ardently longs for his beloveds and brothers. Fire from the heat of anguish burns his insides, while its traces are on display with the passing of each day. (*Sh* 1)

But such statements are not to be understood as mere literary artifice. ʿAyn al-Quḍāt defends his longing for his homeland, arguing that it is in accordance with a Prophetic saying. After all, the love of where one comes from is an aspect of one's primordial disposition (*fiṭra*).

> How can I forget my brothers and not long for my homeland when the Messenger of God said, "Love for one's homeland is a part of faith"?[48] It is evident that love for the homeland is kneaded into man's primordial disposition. (*Sh* 5)

While in prison, ʿAyn al-Quḍāt also writes a final letter to one of his disciples.[49] In this letter, he addresses several important points related to the sloppy charges leveled against him. For example, he makes it very clear that he in no way deems himself to be a Prophet.[50] Nevertheless, such a baseless charge would alone suffice the accusers' intentions.

> They say, "He has made a claim to prophecy." If, in a broken state, I put forth an objection, it would be an opportunity for them to protest. But if I am silent, that would be an acknowledgment of my "heresy" and "unbelief." (*N* II, 358, §555)

ʿAyn al-Quḍāt writes this last of his letters in response to his student's reaction to the contents of *Exile's Complaint*, which the Shaykh somehow manages to show to him while in prison. The student is particularly disconcerted by the manner in which ʿAyn al-Quḍāt expresses a longing for his homeland in the treatise, which he presumably deems to be unfitting for so accomplished a spiritual master. In a modest voice, ʿAyn al-Quḍāt says that the longing expressed for his homeland is on account of his impatience, since patience is a virtue that he has not yet attained.

> O chevalier! If I am impatient, my claim to be patient would be a lie! If as a mortal man I have made any claim, I have claimed knowledge of patience, not the state of the men. (*N* II, 357, §554)

Another line of argument that ʿAyn al-Quḍāt takes up is to cite Q 5:75 alongside Q 19:23 with reference to Mary's virtue of truthfulness and her labor pangs, respectively. He uses these Quranic passages to demonstrate that sighing and the like are natural symptoms of distress, thereby implying that there is no spiritual deficiency on his part.

> O friend! Concerning Mary, it is said, *And his mother was truthful.*[51] Despite that, she was afflicted with blame: *"Would that I had died before this and was utterly forgotten!"*[52] You say, "What is this sighing for Hamadan?" If I love Hamadan, should I say that I do not love it? (*N* II, 361, §561)

In a sense, the words in this letter amount to a second "defense" against a different kind of accuser, this time the Shaykh's concerned and loving disciple. ʿAyn al-Quḍāt is ultimately comforted by the fact that he is not truly imprisoned. Quite the contrary. Despite his being shackled behind the walls of a Seljuq cell, he is already delivered, for

> prison is the prison of separation from the Beloved and deliverance is finding, namely finding the Beloved. (*N* II, 360, §557)

Divine Jealousy

Thus far the external dimensions of ʿAyn al-Quḍāt's imprisonment and execution have been recounted. Alongside the injustice of the charges and the level of political intrigue involved in bringing ʿAyn al-Quḍāt to his death was his own assessment of his predicament. As he tells us in *Exile's Complaint*, one of the outward causes for his death sentence had to do with the jealousy and envy (*ḥasad*) that many scholars had against him on account of his exceptional acumen, which resulted in his writing books at a young age that scholars could not even produce in their old age.[53] This was an indirect cause—when the real political reasons for ʿAyn al-Quḍāt's death were presented in the form of an accusation of heresy, the envious scholars to whom this accusation was brought then gave their tacit approval for his death. But the Shaykh gladly welcomes and even prays for death.

> Kāmil al-Dawla wa'l-Dīn[54] wrote to me. He said that in the city they[55] are saying, "ʿAyn al-Quḍāt is making godly

> claims," and that they are issuing a fatwa for my execution. O friend! If they want a fatwa from you, then you too give a fatwa! I give everyone this advice, namely that they write this verse on the fatwa: *Unto God belong the most beautiful names; so call Him by them, and leave those who deviate with regard to His names. Soon they shall be recompensed for that which they used to do.*[56] I myself am supplicating for this execution! Alas! It is still far away.[57] (*T* 251, §329)

ʿAyn al-Quḍāt is not troubled by his impending death because of his awareness of another cause for it that he identifies some four years before his actual execution.

> One of these days you will see how ʿAyn al-Quḍāt has found this success, offering his head in sacrifice in order to obtain headship! I indeed know how the matter will be.[58] (*T* 236, §306)

Such a sacrifice is of no concern to the Shaykh since death for him is life.

> You imagine that being executed on the path of God comes as a tribulation or is a tribulation? No, in our path execution is life! What do you say? Does one not love to give his life?! (*T* 235, §305)

ʿAyn al-Quḍāt makes rather cryptic allusions to what, from the divine perspective, was the true reason for his impending death. When we put the pieces of the puzzle together, his understanding for why he has to die has something to do with his disclosing the secret of lordship (P. *sirr-i rubūbiyyat*). This idea is informed by a famous early Sufi saying, sometimes attributed to Ḥallāj, to the effect that "Disclosing the secret of lordship is unbelief."[59]

> Alas! I dare not speak! Perhaps you have not seen the Law,[60] how it has become a watchman for those who speak about lordship. Whoever speaks about lordship in the era of the Law, his blood will be spilt! (*T* 230, §299)

Although fully aware of the need for silence, ʿAyn al-Quḍāt tells us that there are moments when he cannot contain himself and has to reveal the secret of lordship and all that it entails.

> Although on account of this discussion my blood will be spilt, I have no care and I shall speak, come what may! (*T* 266, §350).[61]

The secret of lordship, ʿAyn al-Quḍāt maintains, is guarded by nothing less than the divine jealousy (P. *ghayrat*).

> Alas! Look at how much tale-bearing and spying I have done, and how many divine mysteries I have placed out in the open, even though speaking about these mysteries is unbelief—"Disclosing the secret of lordship is unbelief"—and even though His jealousy overcomes all creatures, lifting them away! (*T* 269, §353)

In Sufi literature, God's *ghayrat* demands that His servants devote themselves to Him exclusively.[62] The Arabic word *ghayr* and the noun *ghayrat* indicate that the issue here has to do with others who stand between the lover and the Beloved. As Chittick puts it, "The function of God's jealousy is precisely to destroy the soul's relationship with anything other than the One."[63]

The secret of lordship is guarded by the divine jealousy in the sense that the latter does not allow others to come between the servant and the Lord. When discussing the highest rank of those on the spiritual path, ʿAyn al-Quḍāt hints at his position by citing a *ḥadīth qudsī* or sacred saying.[64] These people

> have reached the core of religion, have tasted the reality of certainty, and are in the protection of the divine jealousy: "My Friends are under My robe—none knows them but Me."[65] (T 42, §59)

What then is the "secret of lordship"? It has to do with the essential nothingness of the lover and the sole reality of the Beloved, before whom the lover is naught. In other words, the secret of lordship is the reality of God's oneness. This secret, when disclosed in human language, naturally entails dualistic language and the use of conceptual categories, thereby problematizing the illusory subject-object barriers and distinctions that govern ordinary, human frames of referencing.

One consequence of revealing the secret of lordship is the onset of all kinds of trials and tribulations. In the next passage, the judge of Hamadan cites the example of a certain drunken group of lovers. They met their fate, just as he will meet his.

> They began to speak in a drunken state: some of them were killed for it[66] and others were tried by God's jealousy, as will be the case with this helpless one. But I do not know when it will be. Right now, it is far. (*T* 205–206, §265)

Reworking a passage from Samʿānī's *Rawḥ al-arwāḥ* (*Repose of the Spirits*),[67] Maybudī explains the link between disclosing the secret of lordship and the divine jealousy with reference to the martyrdom of Ḥallāj.

> Shiblī[68] said, "On the night they killed Ḥusayn-i Manṣūr Ḥallāj, I whispered to the Real all night until dawn. Then I placed my head down in prostration and said, 'O Lord, He was a servant of Yours, a man of faith, a unity-voicer,[69] a firm believer, numbered among Your friends. What was this trial You brought down upon him? How did he come to be considered worthy for this tribulation?'
>
> Then I dreamt, and it was as if I was shown this call of exaltedness reaching my ears: 'He is one of Our servants. We informed him of one of Our mysteries and he disclosed it, so We sent down upon him what you saw. It is fine for a greengrocer to call out about his vegetables, but absurd for a jeweler to call out about a night-brightening pearl.' "[70]

ʿAyn al-Quḍāt also gives us a version of this story in *Paving the Path*.

> Alas! The day they hung that leader of lovers and foremost of recognizers Ḥusayn-i Manṣūr, Shiblī said, "I was whispering to God that night. I said, 'My God! For how long will You kill the lovers?' God said, 'Until I receive the compensation.'[71] I said, 'O Lord! What is Your compensa-

> tion?' He said, 'It is the lovers' encounter with Me and My beauty.' "[72] (*T* 235–236, §306)

We are now in a better position to cite two more texts, both of which are rather curious incidents reported by the Shaykh.

> Alas! For one month I was held in this holy Garden about which I speak, such that people imagined that I had died. With complete unwillingness, I was sent to a station in which I had been on another occasion. I committed a sin in this second station;[73] after some days, you will see that my punishment for this sin is that I will be killed. What are you saying? The one who impedes the lover from reaching the Beloved—watch the tribulation that comes to him! In this sense, pain has afflicted this helpless one. But I do not know whether or not I will ever find the remedy. (*T* 231–232, §301)

> This discussion is too high for just anyone to understand it, so some of the realized wayfarers have said that the path to God is infinite. No doubt, one must place the bag of servanthood in the dwellings of the desert of lordship seven hundred times each day! This statement is known to be strange. And the end of this report is known: I fear that ʿAyn al-Quḍāt will take a piece from the storehouses of the treasure of *and We taught him knowledge from Our Presence*[74] and will strike it against the hearts of some of his own friends! (*T* 300–301, §394)

The divine jealousy is what guards the closest confidants at the divine court in their realization of the essential oneness of reality. But when the secret of lordship is made known to others, it implies alterity and distinction on the conceptual level as much as it results in the disclosure of the secret between the lover and the Beloved to those who are unworthy of hearing it. The very robe that is the divine jealousy, which protects ʿAyn al-Quḍāt, is thus lifted when he reveals the secret of lordship. This thereby entails that it is now out there for others, who are unworthy, to know it. The robe then necessarily comes down; but this time it envelops the one who revealed the secret, suffocating him in the divine embrace.

Figure 4. The symbolic tomb of ʿAyn al-Quḍāt (Hamadan, Iran)

3

Heavenly Matters

Viewing his intellectual and spiritual perspectives as complementary, ʿAyn al-Quḍāt simultaneously sees God as the only true existent, all of reality as encompassed by levels of light, and the Prophet Muhammad as the purpose of creation.

هو

The Essence

Toshihiko Izutsu put it best when he described ʿAyn al-Quḍāt as "a mystic of profound spiritual experiences, and at the same time a thinker endowed with an unusually keen intellectual power of analysis."[1] We have already been given a window into the truth of the first part of Izutsu's statement. Now, we turn to the second part. The Shaykh certainly has a penetrating intelligence and is also extremely well versed in the rational methods of investigation that characterize the later Islamic intellectual tradition. As such, he addresses and develops many of the philosophical and theological problems bequeathed to him by his predecessors.[2]

As there is a significant degree of overlap between the Shaykh's spiritual life and his intellectual life, we will gradually come to see how all of the theoretical problems he tackles in his writings have important repercussions for and reverberations in his mystical theology.

In order to accomplish this task, we first turn to his treatment of God qua Absolute. In Islamic theological language, this is referred to as the Divine Essence (*dhāt*), which is completely beyond the grasp of people.

> How can one say something about the Essence or describe It? (*T* 269, §352)

In a technical Arabic discussion in *Paving the Path*, the Shaykh speaks of God's Essence as a substance (*jawhar*). More precisely, he says that It is an indivisible substance (*jawhar fard*), by which he means to say that God is absolutely simple and immaterial in every way.

> It is the Reality of reality, the One within whom there is no multiplicity, neither in potentiality nor in actuality—like a dot. Such is the Essence of the Maker, whom we call an indivisible substance. This dot cannot be divided and cannot be a receptacle for anything. It is free from multiplicity in existence, possibility, potentiality, and actuality. For It is One and is the Essence of the Maker. (*T* 337, §445)

ʿAyn al-Quḍāt adheres to a well-known saying that seems to originate with the early Sufi master Abū Saʿīd al-Kharrāz (d. ca. 286/899), "None knows God but God."[3] This is to say that God is so exalted, unique, and transcendent as to escape the grasp of any and all knowers. As the Source of what we typically refer to as existence, this supra-sensory Reality (*maʿnā*) is only known to people who have true insight (*baṣāʾir*) into the nature of things.

> For those who have insight that penetrates the veils of the unseen and the canopies of the spiritual realm, there is no doubt that there exists a supra-sensory Reality from which "existence" emerges in the most perfect of ways. (*Z* §33)

Only God can know Himself, while everyone other than God must settle with the manner in which He reveals Himself to them. For our part, we have been given the name "God" or "Allah" to speak of this nameless supra-sensory Reality who is otherwise utterly transcendent, unfathomable, and beyond our imagination.

> Outside of these veils, this supra-sensory Reality is what is called "Allah" in Arabic. By "those who have insight" I mean people who perceive the existence of this supra-sensory Reality without rational premises, as do the rationalists. This supra-sensory Reality is too exalted and holy for the gaze of anyone other than It to turn toward Its reality. Glory be to Him that anyone should even desire permission for this! For He is totally unapproachable by others in His Essence, but not by Himself. (Z §33)

Just as the sun cannot be seen by the minuscule vision of bats, so too can God's Essence not be known by our puny intellects. That we can even liken God to anything is on account of His generosity.

> His Essence and Self are what demand this unapproachability of others, just as the sun in its essence demands, by virtue of its sheer splendor, that it be unapproachable by the sight of bats: *And unto God belongs the loftiest similitude;*[4] "and among His signs is the sun."[5] But for His permission and the abundant generosity demanded by this permission, not a single person would have the audacity to liken Him to something. How could it be otherwise, since likening Him to things is impossible at any rate? *There is nothing like Him.*[6] (Z §34)

All likenesses ultimately fail to do justice to what God really is in Himself: sheer perfection beyond all perfection.

> The sun to which we likened God does not adequately address our aim, for, in its essence, the sun demands neither unapproachability by others nor anything else. This is because the sun's existence—along with all of its attributes—is derived from something other than it. . . . [He] is far above every perfection attained by the Prophets and the angels in His proximity, let alone the deficiencies imagined by those with weak insight—those to whom the Eternal has alluded as uttering and thinking *ugly thoughts about God; upon them is an ugly turn!*[7] (Z §34)

Rational Proof

For as inaccessible as God is in Himself, ʿAyn al-Quḍāt asserts that we can nevertheless know God on a level appropriate to our understanding and even advance rational arguments in order to prove His existence. He does the latter by proceeding with the most general and all-encompassing of things, namely existence or being, which can be got at through the human intellect (*ʿaql*) alone.

> The role of the intellect is to simply demonstrate God's existence by way of the existence of existents. (Z §47)

In Islamic philosophy, God is commonly referred to as the Necessary Existent (*wājib al-wujūd*). This means that God necessarily exists by virtue of Himself and is not dependent upon anything outside of Himself for His existence. All other existents (*mawjūdāt*) are fundamentally contingent in themselves and are only necessitated into existence through their belonging to a causal nexus of necessitated existents that is ultimately held together by God, the ultimate ground for the necessity of the existence of all other existents. ʿAyn al-Quḍāt pithily explains this point as follows.

> Indeed, in existence there is no existent with an essence that necessitates the reality of existence other than *the One, the Paramount*.[8] (Z §34)

The Necessary Existent in Itself does not have a beginning or an end. He is what the Shaykh calls *al-qadīm al-ḥaqīqī* or the "Real Eternal,"[9] and more commonly simply the Eternal (*al-qadīm*). His Beginningless knowledge is the "fountain of all existents"[10] as He Himself is the Source of existence.[11]

> Were the Necessary not eternal, He would not be necessary. Likewise, were He not the Source of existence, He would not be necessary. (Z §47)

Drawing on the concept and reality of existence that applies to God and everything other than God in varying ontological degrees, the

Shaykh argues that the very existence of the Eternal itself demands that all things proceeding from It be temporal and thus contingent kinds of existents.

> "Certain truth"[12] in proving the Eternal lies in demonstrating it by way of that existence which is the most general of things, for if there were not an Eternal in existence, there would, fundamentally, not be an existent in existence whatsoever. This is because existence divides into that which encompasses the originated and the Eternal, that is, into that whose existence has a beginning and that whose existence does not have a beginning. If there were no Eternal in existence, there would, fundamentally, not be that which is originated, since it is not in the nature of that which is originated for it to exist by virtue of itself. Indeed, that which is existent by virtue of itself is the Necessary Existent. And that which is necessary in itself cannot be conceived as having a beginning. (Z §31)

ʿAyn al-Quḍāt then puts forth an argument to prove the existence of the Eternal, referring to it as a demonstrative proof (*qiyās burhānī*) that proceeds from existence itself. The proof yields the following watertight insight: the existence of derivative things itself means that there exists a point of derivation that Itself is not derivative. After all, there cannot be "derived" things if they are not derived from a root source that itself is not derived in any way whatsoever.

> Thus, it can be said: [1] "If there were an existent in existence, it would necessarily entail that there be an Eternal in existence." This is a certain premise: it is inconceivable for anyone to doubt it. Then it can be said, [2] "Existence is clearly known." This is the second premise, which, like the first premise, is certain. Thereafter, [3] the existence of an Eternal existent necessarily follows from these two firm premises. Such is the demonstrative proof of the Eternal by way of existence. Be it succinct or extended, further exposition is inconceivable. (Z §31)

Withness

ʿAyn al-Quḍāt has a robust view of the relation between God and the world and the world and God. On the one hand, God is with everything in existence—a fact that is designated by what the Shaykh calls God's withness (*maʿiyya*). On the other hand, nothing is "with" Him in any way at all.[13] The entire contingent, causal order of existents is sustained at every moment by God's withness, without which the order would come to naught.

> God is existent, and there is nothing with Him, nor can it ever be conceived that something will be with Him. For nothing shares the rank of withness with His existence. Thus, nothing is with God, but He is with everything. Were it not for His withness with everything, no existent would remain in existence. (Z §116)[14]

In more technical terms, the Shaykh says that God, the Necessary Existent, is coextensive with everything in existence (*musāwiq al-wujūd*), but nothing is coextensive with His existence.

> There is no existent whose existence is coextensive with the existence of the Necessary, nor can it be conceived to be the case. Indeed, the Necessary is coextensive in existence with the existence of everything. And His coextensivity with what is not yet brought into existence is like His coextensivity with the first existent, with no distinction between them. (Z §141)

This position, the Shaykh insists, is not only the fruit of rational argumentation and intellectual know-how. It is best arrived at through a particular kind of vision that can only be obtained through the eye of recognition (P. *ʿayn-i maʿrifat*).

> When the recognizer looks with the eye of recognition, he perceives as correct our statement that the existence of the Necessary is coextensive in existence with every existent. But the intellect and conventional ways of knowing grow weary

> before they perceive this. Thus, the recognizer says, "God is with everything, all the while being prior to everything by way of an infinite priority." And he says, "There is not a thing in existence that is with God, nor is it posterior to Him. It is also inconceivable for there to be something in existence that has this attribute." (Z §141)

> Be wary of rejecting our statement that there is nothing with God, nor is there anything posterior to Him. For you will then be like a blind man who rejects colors and even disbelieves in their existence. Indeed, our statement is true. It is clearer and more manifest to the eye of recognition than primary concepts are to the eye of the intellect! (Z §142)

We will return to ʿAyn al-Quḍāt's detailed discussion of the recognizers and recognition in chapter 7. For our present purposes, it is important to keep in mind that his position on divine coextensiveness and its implications can be verified by the intellect, but only to a certain extent.

> The intellect may perceive the correct meaning of our statement that God is with everything and is prior to everything. But that notion is nothing like what is perceived by the eye of recognition. Our statement that there is nothing with God and nothing posterior to Him is, fundamentally, one of those things whose meaning it is absolutely inconceivable for the intellect to perceive. (Z §142)

Divine Names and Attributes

Beyond proving God's existence and explaining how God is with everything, can anything else be said about Him? One would be tempted to answer in the negative if it were not for the fact that God is not only metapersonal but also quite personal. After all, He reveals Himself in scripture, speaking about Himself in terms that its recipients can understand and to which they can respond. These terms appear to us as names (*asmāʾ*) and attributes (*ṣifāt*), both of which take center stage in much of Islamic God-talk.

> O dear friend! "The search for knowledge is an obligation upon every Muslim."[15] The men know with certainty that the most important thing and the most obligatory of obligations is the recognition of God and His attributes. (*N* II, 254, §382)

The Shaykh has a great deal to say about these key terms and explains why they are so important for the religious and spiritual life. We can relate to God's names and attributes, but the same cannot be said about the divine Essence, which we can never know. God's names and attributes are like the rays of the sun, and the sun is like the Essence. The names transmit the warmth that comes from the sun, but we dare not look directly at the sun itself.

> The rays of the sun can be seen since they are caressing, but their source cannot be seen since it is burning. (*T* 304, §399)

The divine names reveal different aspects of God, thus conveying His inexhaustible self-disclosures (*tajalliyyāt*) to their recipients.

> God has a thousand and one names, and in every name He discloses Himself in a thousand ways. Every kind of self-disclosure gives rise to a state in the wayfarer, and every state brings forth a subtlety and a different action in him. (*N* I, 74, §95)

Despite the fact that the names are many and their effects diffuse, they do not make God, given His pure simplicity (*basāṭa*) and unity (*waḥdāniyya*), in any way composite and multiple. In somewhat paradoxical terms, we can say that each divine name names God, but no divine name actually names God. The names are many, but the Named is one.

> A drop from the ocean can itself be called the "ocean." For if you say, "A drop is other than the ocean," that would be correct. And if you say, "A drop is from the ocean," that would also be correct. (*T* 336, §443)

> O friend! Water has several names. In Arabic it is called *mā'*, and in Persian *āb*. Something that is in ten languages

> has ten names. The names are many, but the essence and the named are one. (*T* 263, §346)

In Islamic theology God has seven primary names, each of which has a corresponding attribute. These attributes are life (*ḥayāt*), knowledge (*ʿilm*), desire (*irāda*), power (*quwwa*), hearing (*samʿ*), sight (*baṣar*), and speech (*kalām*). ʿAyn al-Quḍāt will at times add an eighth attribute, that of subsistence (*baqāʾ*), and in doing so he seems to be following a very early Ashʿarī position. The Shaykh states in no uncertain terms that each divine attribute conveys the other, meaning that each one sufficiently communicates what God is in His revealed totality. When we make distinctions between God's attributes it is on account of our tendency to see things through our own frames of reference.

> The meaning of God's knowledge is that everything comes into existence from Him. God's power also has this meaning, namely that something comes into existence from Him. There is thus no disparity between these two attributes, but people understand them by way of habit. (*N* I, 178, §273)

Be that as it may, we can speak of the divine names and attributes as distinct by virtue of their effects. In other words, God can be called "knowing" and be said to have the attribute of knowledge in light of the fact that there are things that He knows. Likewise, He can be called "Creator" and be said to have the attribute of creating in light of the fact that there are things that He creates. On this score, there is a real distinction between God's knowledge and His ability to create, and ʿAyn al-Quḍāt is perfectly aware of this. But we cannot say that the divine attributes are God's Essence. Doing so would spell a kind of unification (*ittiḥād*) between It and the divine attributes, thereby dissolving and nullifying the latter's ontological status. Having said that, the divine attributes cannot be wholly other than the Essence as this would compromise God's oneness, leading us into the murky waters of polytheism.

> Here, know a tremendous difficulty: the attributes of the Real are not His Essence Itself. If all of His attributes were His Essence Itself, this would entail unification. But the attributes are not other than His Essence, since otherness would entail divine multiplicity. Thus, one can

> speak of the attributes as subsisting in His Essence. (*T* 304, §399)

It is considerations such as these that lead the Shaykh to, in many contexts, uphold a well-known position concerning the relationship between God's attributes and His Essence: the divine attributes are not God, but they are not not God. They can be said to somehow subsist in His Essence (*qāʾima bi-dhātihi*) but in a way that does not make God, who is characterized by pure oneness (*waḥda*) and unicity (*aḥadiyya*), more than one.

> "The Creator subsists with subsistence, is one with oneness, and is existent with existence."[16] He is saying that the Subsisting is one thing, and subsistence another; the Existent is one thing, and existence another; the One is one thing, and oneness another. Since these meanings subsist in God's Self, one cannot speak of the disjunction of the attributes from the Essence. (*T* 304, §400)

> Whoever views the world as eternal is far from His unicity; and whoever calls His attributes temporally originated is unaware of His tremendousness.[17] (*N* I, 173, §264)

ʿAyn al-Quḍāt's understanding of the ontological status of the divine names and attributes is not so cut and dried.[18] Like Ibn ʿArabī and his followers,[19] the Shaykh upholds a view bequeathed by Avicenna (d. 428/1037) in which the divine names and attributes are seen as relations (*nisab*) and not as actual ontological entities.[20] The Shaykh also speaks of the divine attributes and the names to which they refer as being the results of the differing standpoints (*ʿibārāt*) that emerge by virtue of the relationships that necessarily obtain when the Necessary Existent turns Its face to the impoverished, contingent existents.

> If you reflect upon the relation of the Essence Itself, which is Necessary in Itself, you will discover that It is one without multiplicity in any way whatsoever. When the wayfarers look at this Essence with the eyes of their hearts, they discover It to be this way, with no distinction. However, on account of the multiplicity of the relations of

> this Essence to the other existents that derive existence from this Essence—not from themselves—the wayfarers have to depend upon the alternation of Its standpoints such that the realities of these relations can be conveyed, by way of these standpoints, for the weak-minded to understand. (*Z* §81)

The divine-human relationship demands, in other words, the presence of the differing effects of divine names and attributes. For when God listens to the prayer of one of His servants, we speak of Him as the "hearer." And when He forgives a servant, He is the "forgiver." These names and attributes are relations, and relations are real things. Ontologically speaking, however, they are not actual "things." This is akin to the example of a woman who is at once a daughter, parent, spouse, and educator. She is a child for her mother, a mother for her child, a wife for her husband, and a teacher for her student. The woman's names and attributes are the results of the various kinds of relationships that she assumes vis-à-vis different people. Although her names and attributes are many, they are not independent, ontological entities, nor do they compromise her unity and status as a woman. The woman remains a woman, while her various relationships in the world entail that she do and be different things for different people—and thus be named accordingly. ʿAyn al-Quḍāt describes this point as follows.

> His desire pertains to the existence of the objects of desire, His power to the existentiation of the objects of power, and His knowledge to the temporal origination of the objects of knowledge. . . . His hearing, seeing, power, desire, and knowledge are all perfections of His Essence. If you call the Essence "desire," It is all desire. If you call It "power," It is all power. If you call It "hearing," It is all hearing. . . . His entirety is power if you call the existents objects of power, desire if you call them objects of desire, and knowledge if you call them objects of knowledge. (*N* I, 144, §209)
>
> Thus, since this Essence is related to the effusion of the existents that emerge from It, and it is known that they are contingents and that it is undoubtedly the Necessary who brings the contingent into existence, It is called "power" from the standpoint of this relation between It and the existents,

and sometimes It is called "desire" from the standpoint of another relation. But the weak-minded think that there is a difference between power and the Powerful, and desire and the Desiring! This is the very limit of intellectual reflection. (Z §81)

Oneness of Existence

ʿAyn al-Quḍāt took his formal, logical proofs for the existence of God to their natural conclusion: if all existents in reality derive their existence from God, the only One who truly has existence, then the things in existence are quite literally nothing. This position is commonly associated with what, from the time of Ibn ʿArabī onward, would be called "the oneness of existence" (*waḥdat al-wujūd*).[21] As is well known, the doctrine that there is nothing in existence but God was clearly articulated by authors who preceded ʿAyn al-Quḍāt and can be traced to the Quran itself.[22]

In the eyes of the people of recognition, there is no self in existence other than He. (*N* I, 232–233, §383)

Oneness is a concomitant of the Essence of the true Necessary Existent. How can oneness not be Its concomitant when unicity, which is more particular than oneness, is a concomitant of It . . . ? (*Z* §81)

When you reach the Essence, all is unicity. Here, there is His existence and nothing else. Alongside His eternity, there is no eternity at all; and alongside His existence, there is no existence at all for any other.[23] (*N* I, 173, §264)

Alongside His existence, there is no existence apart from it. It is assuredly like this, namely that alongside His existence there is no existence apart from it such that it is an absolute unity. Since there is no doubt at all concerning absolute unity, it necessarily follows that existence is one, and that it belongs to Him. (*N* III, 397, §219)

> Your existence is not outside of two possibilities: either it subsists on its own or through the existence of other than itself. If it subsists on its own, then there is no distinction between your existence and God's existence because there is not more than one existence in existence that subsists on its own. . . . And whatever does not subsist on its own but subsists through something does not have existence. Thus it necessarily follows that there is not more than one existence in existence, and that one existence is God. (*N* III, 398, §221)

> From the perspective of reality everything in existence is perishing, and the only thing that subsists is the face of *the Living, the Self-Abiding*.[24] It is just like a perishing form in a mirror—only the form outside the mirror subsists insofar as general observation is concerned, satisfied as it is with sensory imagery. In the eyes of the recognizer the form outside the mirror is also perishing, just like the form inside the mirror, with no distinction between them. (Z §95)

> The truth is that God was existent and there was nothing with Him. And right now He is existent and there is nothing with Him. And He will be existent, and nothing will be with Him. His Beginninglessness is present with His Endlessness with no distinction between them. (Z §107)

The Shaykh makes it crystal clear that what we call the oneness of existence accounts for a certain insight into the nature of things that is only accorded to a special group of people. There are several different approaches that one may take with respect to the God-world relationship. The first group of people, who maintain that "there is nothing in existence but God,"[25] are distinct from the second group, who say that "there is nothing in existence but God and His acts (*afʿāl*)."[26] Then there is a third group who uphold the view that "there is nothing in existence but God, His acts, and His attributes."[27]

ʿAyn al-Quḍāt tells us that the view of the second group "is toward this world by way of the intellect."[28] By contrast, the view of the first group is fixed "on the next world,"[29] which is to say that those who see that there is nothing in existence but God do so by having been given a glimpse into the true nature of things, which can only be seen on the other side of death. In short, those who uphold the second view see the sun (God) and its rays (God's acts),[30] whereas the third group sees the sun (God), its rays (God's acts), and the sun's luminosity (God's attributes).[31] But only those in the first group behold the Sun and become blinded by Its dazzling brilliance, leaving them incapable of seeing anything but light.

Levels of Light

Having his vision occasionally returned to him, ʿAyn al-Quḍāt is able to see all of existence—perhaps like those in the second group—as a cascade of lights proceeding from the supernal Sun.

> Existents and created beings have been adorned and made eminent in levels of light. (*T* 122, §170)

One way we can frame the relationship between God and the world is to speak of God as light and the world as rays of that light. This perspective, informed by the Quran's famous Light Verse (24:35), was by ʿAyn al-Quḍāt's time standard fare in Islamic thought. Although the great founder of the school of Illumination Shihāb al-Dīn Suhrawardī would build an intricate metaphysical system around the doctrine of God as the "Light of lights" (*nūr al-anwār*), one of the earliest musings on the ontological levels of light can be found in their raw form in ʿAyn al-Quḍāt. The Shaykh's point of departure seems to be Ḥallāj's statement to the effect that God is the "Source of existents,"[32] which he takes to mean that "God and His light are the Source of lights (*maṣdar al-anwār*)."[33]

It can also be noted that this discussion on the levels of light is informed by ʿAyn al-Quḍāt's position concerning the relationality of the divine attributes: just as the divine attributes emerge as relations between the Necessary Existent and contingent existents but do not make the Necessary Existent more than one, likewise, the lesser lights emerge as relational rays that emerge from the one and only real light but do not make It more than one. Following Ghazālī, ʿAyn al-Quḍāt argues that in themselves these lights are metaphorical lights, whereas God is the only true light.

Every metaphorical light becomes a reality in real light. (*T* 324, §424)

Although bodies are existent at night, they are all tenebrous, and colors are not at all apparent. When day comes, everything is illumined, and colors are apparent—a light shines on each body, and every particle becomes mixed with a bit of light. . . . Now, these bodies that are existent at night are also existent during the day. There is no increase or deficiency at all except in the sun. . . . Likewise, existence in itself only belongs to the Eternal, and whatever is other than It can only be nonexistent in itself. If you posit something without the Eternal, from beginning to end it is fundamentally nothing but nonexistent, for when you think of it without the Eternal, it can only be enclosed by nonexistence. (*N* I, 132–133, §§190–191)

The theologians and ignorant scholars say that it is inappropriate to call God "light." Why? Because, light is an expression of what does not have subsistence for two temporal moments; and it is temporally originated. This statement is correct. But to say that God's light is this light—such a description is wrong. Among His names, one of them is "Light." This light is the illuminator of all lights. (*T* 255, §335)

Alas! How beautiful an explanation did the Proof of Islam Abū Ḥāmid Muḥammad al-Ghazālī offer! He gave a whiff of this light: "'Light' is an expression of that through which things are manifest."[34] That is, light is that without which things cannot be seen and through which darkness is manifest. If light has this meaning, then the ascription of real light pertains to God and applies to other lights metaphorically.[35] All existents in the cosmos were nonexistent. Then, through His light, power, and desire, they became existent. Since the existence of the heavens and the earth is from His power and desire, *God is the light of the heavens and the earth*[36] only pertains to Him. Can any of the sun's rays ever be seen in darkness? No, for the manifestation

> and exposure of the sun's rays are through the existence of sunrise. If there was no sunrise, the rays could not be seen and would appear as nonexistent. (*T* 255–256, §336)

ʿAyn al-Quḍāt also suggests that God is light (*nūr*) qua substance, but that qua manifestation, His light emits a lesser light (also, *nūr*). It is this ray that is akin to the accident of a substance and, as we will see in chapter 9, accounts for all of the metaphorical lights in the cosmic order.

> "Substance" is an expression for the Source of existence, whereas "accident" means to abide in a substance. I am not speaking about the substance and accident of the sensible world. I am speaking about the real substance and accident. If only you could understand! Alas! God is existent. He is therefore a substance. But substance is not without accident. Thus, God's existence is a substance, and light is an accident of that substance. (*T* 257, §339)

ʿAyn al-Quḍāt maintains that we can only integrate the various orders of light into our being by praying to the Source of all light Itself, as did the Prophet.

> Perhaps you have not read this supplication: "O Light of light!"[37] He is requesting an increase in light from light. He said, *"Complete our light for us."*[38] Do you know when this meaning is facilitated? When the robe of otherness is lifted—when the enterer becomes the entered, and *the ultimate end is unto thy Lord*[39] appears. (*T* 324, §424)

The Goal of Creation

Much of traditional Islamic piety is centered around the image and person of the Prophet Muhammad.[40] And it is indeed commonplace to find Sufi authors declare the Prophet to be the goal of creation.[41] As ʿAyn al-Quḍāt explains, everything in the cosmic order has come about because of his holy and sanctified presence.

> All existents were created on account of Muhammad. (*T* 180–181, §238)

As we will see in later chapters, the Shaykh's emphasis on the levels of light that make up the cosmos is directly related to his understanding of the cosmic function of the Prophet. At present, it is important to keep in mind that ʿAyn al-Quḍāt's thinking is informed by several key Islamic scriptural sources, namely Q 21:107, which calls the Prophet *a mercy unto the worlds*, and such *ḥadīth qudsī*s as, "Were it not for you, I would not have created the two worlds" and "I created the world for you, and I created you for Myself."[42] ʿAyn al-Quḍāt offers us a way to understand these texts by drawing on an image from falconry.

> What do you hear?! Muhammad is the divine falcon, and all existents are his birds and prey. (*T* 181, §238)

A falcon receives its nourishment from its prey; and, by implication, the sultan who sends that falcon out for the chase is directly nourished by it since he takes pleasure in watching the falcon hunt its prey. Thus the falcon pursues its prey, and the sultan in turn preys on the falcon and never lets him go.[43]

As God's chosen one (*al-Muṣṭafā*), the Prophet enjoys a special rank with Him. This begins with his very place amid the constellation of existent things in the cosmic order. For one thing, people travel to God. But Muhammad comes from God to them.

> All of the wayfarers went to God from themselves. But Muhammad came to the creatures from God.[44] (*T* 301, §395)

> This station[45] is the end of the perfection of the wayfarers. However, it pertains to someone who travels and ascends from here, and from here goes there; that is, he goes to Him from himself. But someone who comes from there to here does so from Him with himself. (*T* 343, §454)

The same applies to the other Prophets: Muhammad is unique among them, as the Shaykh demonstrates with respect to Abraham and Moses.

> Listen! You have never heard that Abraham was the possessor of tasting, Moses the possessor of pleasure, and Muhammad the possessor of sweetness? What do you know about what I am saying?! Nay! I have told you[46] that seeing honey is one thing and eating it is one thing. But being honey is quite another thing! (*T* 310, §408)

> As for the group that is the sought,[47] Muṣṭafā came as their leader and his community came, following him: *He loves them, and they love Him.*[48] Muhammad is the root of their existence and the others are followers. *He came*[49] was said about Moses; *He carried*[50]—"We brought him"—was said about Muṣṭafā. Having come is not like having been brought. The Prophets swore by the names and attributes of God. But God has sworn by the soul, head, hair, and face of Muṣṭafā: *By thy life;*[51] *By the morning brightness, and by the night when still.*[52] To Moses it was said, *"Look upon the mountain."*[53] To Muṣṭafā it was said, "We are looking at you—you too entirely look at Us." *Hast thou not considered thy Lord, how He spreads out the shade?*[54] (*T* 20, §31)

The great poet and ideological founder of Pakistan Muhammad Iqbal (d. 1357/1938) once wrote that it is possible to reject God but that it is impossible to reject the Prophet.[55] What he meant was simply that a person can lose sight of God, in all of His transcendence and abstractness, whereas the person of the Prophet perfectly embodies the divine ideal in an accessible human form. Of course, as ʿAyn al-Quḍāt reminds us, by coming to the Prophet we necessarily gain access to God.

> "O Muhammad! We taught you what you did not know: *He taught thee what thou knewest not; God's bounty toward thee is tremendous.*[56] O Muhammad! Take on Our character traits, and from the bounties and character traits that We have given to you, pour a mouthful on the helpless ones so that whoever sees you, has seen Us, and whoever obeys you, has obeyed Us." This is the meaning of *whosoever obeys the Messenger has obeyed God*[57] and *he teaches you what you knew not.*[58] (*T* 185, §242)

> Act in conformity with Muṣṭafā and ask God all day, "O God! Whiten my face with the light of Your noble face."[59] (*T* 264, §347)

> Listen! Have you not heard what that great one said? "What Muhammad is for people, God is for us; and what God is for people, Muhammad is for us." This is the station of *God has not placed two hearts in the breast of any man.*[60] Thus, what is present is absent, and what is absent is present. This is "The witness sees what the absent one does not see."[61] (*T* 327–328, §430)

Despite the fact that the Prophet is a mercy for all sentient beings, many will not recognize him. If a person fails to see him for who he is, the Shaykh contends, it is by virtue of this person's own inner ugliness and vile nature. The Prophet is like the warm sun—those upon whom the sun casts its warmth are either prepared to receive it or are unprepared to do so.

> Since the coming of Muhammad is a favor for the believers, what did the unbelievers get from it?[62] *Surely it is the same for them whether thou warnest them or warnest them not; they do not believe.*[63] What benefit did Abū Jahl and Abū Lahab[64] find from the verse, *and We sent thee not, save as a mercy unto the worlds*[65]? Have you not seen that the sun is a comfort for the entire world and that mercy is for all the world's inhabitants? But if the sun shines on a pit of garbage, repulsive scents will emerge and appear from it, and if it shines on a bed of roses, pleasant scents will emerge and come from it. These defects do not come from the sun. Rather, these defects and disparities come from the roots and contours of those things. (*T* 185–186, §243)

This point naturally brings us to a deeper problem: why is it that there are such disparities in the world to begin with, not only with respect to guidance and misguidance, but more generally with respect to good and evil, right and wrong, and perfection and imperfection? In the following chapter, we will see how the Shaykh approaches these and related questions in a number of creative ways.

Figure 5. The tomb of Avicenna (Hamadan, Iran)

4

Earthly Concerns

ʿAyn al-Quḍāt goes to great lengths to address the manner in which our perspectives and actions shape and color our understanding of the way things are, which often obscures how they actually are.

هو

Good and Evil

The Shaykh has a keen interest in the problem of good and evil, and his treatment of it filters into and informs his thinking on a variety of different issues. The long and the short of it is that he does not affirm the reality of evil. But this is a very complicated matter, inquiry into which is sure to lead most people down a rather perilous road.

> It is no surprise at all that God knows and that we do not know. What is surprising is that whatever He knows, we try to know or have the desire to know. By my life! I am not saying that perceiving this premise—namely that there cannot be evil—is easy. If it were easy, the secret of destiny would be unveiled to people in general. About this, Muṣṭafā said, "When destiny is mentioned, restrain yourselves!"[1] He did not say this because knowing this

> issue is not appropriate; rather, he said it because when a person delves into it, he will inevitably fall into error. And if he does not fall into error, then it is inevitable that he will necessarily utter far-fetched and vile words, thereby bringing about discord. (*N* II, 292–293, §441)

In his stance on the question of the existence of good and evil ʿAyn al-Quḍāt follows Avicenna's well-known and historically influential position.[2] God is sheer goodness and thus all that there is reflects the plenitude of divine goodness. This leaves no room for absolute evil, which is not to say that there is nothing bad in the cosmos. There are plenty of bad things, people, and events in our world. But they exist only in a relational manner (*nisbatī*), not in an absolute sense.

This is to say that our conventional usage of the word "evil" applies to situations and circumstances in which disparities certainly do exist. Without these disparities, which by definition entail relational evils, the world would not be the world, and things would not have their own natures. In illustrating this point, Avicenna gives us the classic example of fire: it is a source of warmth, but by virtue of its nature, it can also burn a pious person.[3] Taking up this line of argumentation, ʿAyn al-Quḍāt explains the relational nature of evil.

> On the whole, one must say that evil is nonexistent in itself. That is the truth, however far-fetched it is for human understanding. The Messenger's statement and the scholarly consensus must be interpreted—namely why they affirmed the existence of evil. This is just like when the father and mother of a child call cupping "evil" with reference to what is apparent and in relation to the child's perception, since he perceives nothing but pain. But the parents know the reality: cupping is not evil; rather, it is good! (*N* II, 294, §444)

ʿAyn al-Quḍāt's example of cupping would in our times perhaps be equivalent to a child's parents taking him to the doctor in order to get vaccinated. The needle will doubtlessly be painful and leave the child in a miserable state. The pain of the injection and the ensuing soreness are bad and "evil" in the child's eyes. But for the child's parents, the needle will protect him from a variety of harmful viruses.

The needle is bad in relation to the child, but objectively good for him and hence good in the eyes of his parents who have an eye on the child's overall well-being.

Despite their relational nature, it is perfectly normal to speak of evils in the cosmos, which necessarily do exist. What the Shaykh wants us to keep in mind is that all evils are nevertheless nonexistent (*maʿdūm*) in the face of God's absolute goodness and bounty.

> It is certainly known to the Prophets and Friends of God that nothing but the good comes into existence from God, and that all of His actions are good. However, it might be that not everyone will know that whatever exists is good and is not evil. The bad is relational, but it is nonexistent in itself. Thus, the name "evil" exists and is affirmed, although in reality it is nonexistent; it is merely affirmed in accordance with the understanding of people. But in relation to God's mercy, generosity, and bounty, the existence of the reality of evil is known to be impossible.[4] (*N* II, 294, §444)

Cosmic Well-Being

Since God is the Good and intends the good, all that comes about in the cosmic order is good. ʿAyn al-Quḍāt's thinking here is informed by his commitment to both Avicenna's understanding of the order of the good (*niẓām al-khayr*) and Ghazālī's best of all possible worlds thesis.[5] One of the implications of these positions is that everything is where it is supposed to be and cannot be otherwise. But this also includes the presence of evils, which naturally arise in the cosmic order and are necessary features of its overall well-being (*ṣalāḥ*).

> Whatever has come and will come into existence from God, all of it is of the utmost beauty and perfection. Yet this is in relation to the order of the cosmos, not in relation to the order of those particulars that are pleasant to you and to me. In general, it is known to people that fire, water, the sun, and the moon are necessary in relation to the order of the cosmos. But rain destroys the home of a poor man,

> fire burns a child, someone becomes sick because of the moon,[6] and particular harms occur to a person on account of the sun. (*N* I, 401, §667)

> If your well-being lies in being present in Hamadan, it would not be fitting for you to be in Ushnuh.[7] Do not be heedless of this: *And thy Lord creates what He will, and chooses; no choice have they.*[8] You must realize that whatever is, was, and will be in existence is nothing but well-being. This is the most perfect of perspectives, better than which one cannot be conceived whatsoever. (*N* I, 343, §573)

> The Godhood accords with the universal order, not in conformity with my caprice and yours: *Were the Real to follow their caprices, the heavens and the earth and those therein would have been corrupted.*[9] (*N* I, 401, §668)

"Caprices" in the preceding Quranic verse translates the Arabic plural *ahwāʾ* (s. *hawāʾ*), which literally means "winds." When a person has *hawāʾ*, he is possessed by whimsical desire and caprice. Like the wind, this desire is fleeting: it will pass away in due course only to be followed by another momentary desire. Since God acts in accordance with the way things are and not in accordance with what we want, He does not take into consideration our transient personal wishes and fleeting fancies. If one can look past his subjective wants and to the divine purpose in the cosmos, ʿAyn al-Quḍāt insists that he will be able to see it as entirely imbued with purpose, meaning, and perfection, leaving him no room to entertain the thought that things could have been better. After all, such a view, which is based on one's shortsighted caprice, would be tantamount to questioning the wisdom of the Wise who created the cosmos and who has its inhabitants' best interests in mind.

> Whatever is in existence, something better than it cannot be conceived. For He is *"the most just of judges,"*[10] *"the most merciful of the merciful,"*[11] the most knowing of the knowing, and the most powerful of the powerful. If something from Him came into existence but for which there could be something better, of all of these statements, one of them

> would be an error! O dear friend! It is a terrible deficiency for you not to know, and for you not to know that you do not know! (*N* I, 345, §576)

> If you do not believe, then listen to God: *Praise be to God, who created the heavens and the earth, and made darknesses and light.*[12] Alas! What perfection does blackness have without whiteness, and whiteness without blackness? No perfection at all! The divine wisdom required it to be this way. By virtue of His wisdom, the Wise knows it must be and should be this way. In this court, all are at work. If a mote of deficiency is found in His creation, it would entail a deficiency on the part of the Wise and of wisdom. (*T* 122, §170)

What, then, can be said about the fact that we witness various evils that plague the world and ourselves? Rather than negate their existence, ʿAyn al-Quḍāt first advises us to recognize from whence our awareness of these evils obtains.

> If you look at existence from the perspective of your puny intellect, many matters would appear to your eyes as bad, such as sickness, poverty, and the various tribulations by which people are tried. (*N* I, 401, §668)[13]

Casting our partial vision and understanding of the nature of things aside, we open ourselves up to seeing the beauty, goodness, and order inherent in the cosmos. This vision moves from theory to practice once we have cultivated what the Shaykh calls "Muhammadan eyes" (P. *dīda-yi Muḥammadī*).

> If you were to look at all of existence thousands and thousands of times, not even a mote of a deficiency would appear to your eyes. Have you not seen what Muṣṭafā, whose prophetic eyes were anointed with the collyrium of the light of the Godhood, said? "Look at the one *who created seven heavens one upon another; no disproportion dost thou see in the All-Merciful's creation. Cast thy sight again; dost thou see any flaw? Then cast thy sight twice again; thy sight will return to*

> *thee, humbled, wearied."*[14] But one must have prophetic eyes. No, rather, he must have Muhammadan eyes so that his gaze roams over all of existence and does not see a single deficiency in any place. (*N* I, 402, §670)

Against Dualism

In several of his *Letters* ʿAyn al-Quḍāt takes particular issue with the Zoroastrians and, following a Hadith, their counterpart in Islam the Qadariyya. The latter in this context are not simply a reference to the early Islamic theological group who defended human freedom over and against divine determination or *qadar*, but, specifically, the first Muslim school of rational theology, the Muʿtazila.[15]

With respect to the Zoroastrians, the Shaykh contends that they are ontological dualists since they believe in two orders of divine reality—one god who brings about good and another who brings about evil.[16] In Zoroastrian cosmology and theology, Yazdan is the good or positive principle, corresponding to the god of light, while Ahriman is the bad or negative principle, corresponding to the god of darkness.

> The Zoroastrians say, "God is two: One is Yazdan (who is light) and the other is Ahriman (who is darkness). Light commands obedient deeds and darkness ugly deeds. Light is the day's appointed time and darkness the night's place of return. Infidelity comes from one and faith from the other." (*T* 305, §401)

ʿAyn al-Quḍāt is at odds with the Zoroastrian stance on the existence of a principle of absolute evil because he does not believe in the existence of absolute evil. As we have seen, for our author the relational evils that are in the world necessarily emerge within the cosmic configuration that has been created by God, the absolute Good who only intends the good.

Be that as it may, how and why are the Muʿtazila equated with the Zoroastrians by ʿAyn al-Quḍāt? First let us turn our attention to the typical manner in which they are identified with one another in the Shaykh's writings.

> The Zoroastrians say that evil does not come into existence from God, which is unbelief because another god must then be affirmed. Such is the religion of the Zoroastrians who affirm Yazdan and Ahriman. And this is "The Qadariyya are the Zoroastrians of this community."[17] (*N* II, 281, §423)

> One group says that evil does not come into existence from God, and so they affirm light and darkness. In Islam, there is a group that has also perished in this regard. They are called the "Qadariyya." Muṣṭafā equated them with the Zoroastrians: "The Qadariyya are the Zoroastrians of this community." (*N* II, 269, §402)

Note that ʿAyn al-Quḍāt is careful not to ascribe ontological dualism to the Muʿtazila, who were radical monotheists. They were also not distinctively known for any kind of doctrine of light and darkness. What the Shaykh is getting at by citing the Hadith that equates the Zoroastrians and the Muʿtazila is that they are in fact different kinds of dualists. Whereas the Zoroastrians are ontological dualists, the Muʿtazila are moral dualists. This is because they uphold a doctrine that situates the source of good in God and the source of evil in man. Moreover, they emphasize human freedom at the expense of divine determination. Insofar as they teach that actions have their source outside of God and in man himself, the Muʿtazila therefore also qualify for ʿAyn al-Quḍāt's charge of dualism.

We will soon turn to the Shaykh's perspective on human agency and his attendant critique of the Muʿtazilī overemphasis upon human freedom. Before doing so, it is essential to account for the underlying cause of the respective dualisms of the Zoroastrians and the Muʿtazila, namely doctrinal alteration by those whom ʿAyn al-Quḍāt calls "bad transmitters."

Bad Transmitters

On the level of formal theology, ʿAyn al-Quḍāt adheres to the standard Islamic doctrine of the alteration (*taḥrīf*) of previous religions. As with so many other aspects of his thought, his thinking on this particular issue is intricate and quite original.[18] He maintains that religions other than Islam are true from one perspective, which is an insight he arrived at through tasting.

> If it were not that these meanings had become known to me by way of tasting, would the thought ever have occurred to me that fire-worship, idol-worship, sash-wearing,[19] and the Zoroastrian religion are, from one perspective, correct? (*N* II, 308, §465)[20]

Each religion has come from God and has been taught and transmitted by its original founders and early teachers, whom the Shaykh refers to as those wayfarers who have reached God (P. *rasīdagān*). A religion becomes altered and corrupted by virtue of the nonwayfarers and those who have not reached God (P. *nā rasīdagān*) within that religion who take control of it and fail to properly communicate the meanings of their respective tradition's sacred texts, doctrines, and rites. Over a prolonged period of time, this leads to the corruption of the original message of the religion in question.

> O chevalier! In wayfaring it has become certain to me that the principles of every religion are correct, but that over long periods of time the transmitters have altered these religions: "There are no flaws in reports apart from their transmitters."[21] (*N* I, 158, §234)

> From my perspective, every religion in the world is at root correct since the principles of the religions have been transmitted by wayfarers who have arrived. But when a person who has not at all traveled the path takes control of a religion, from there onward that religion will inescapably fall into error. (*N* II, 269, §402)

These nonwayfarers who corrupt religion come part and parcel with the spread and teaching of any religion, and this includes the various subcommunities that make up the religion of Islam.[22]

> In Islam, I see that the seventy some-odd sects are false.[23] Each of them has fallen into error with respect to the Quran

> and the Hadith, having failed to understand them—before understanding the Quran and the Hadith they took control of them with their corrupt imaginings. (*N* II, 269, §402)

ʿAyn al-Quḍāt most commonly refers to those who alter a religion's teachings as "bad transmitters" (P. *nāqilān-i bad* and *ruwāt-i bad*).[24]

> From my perspective, this religion[25] is altered. But I do not know whether this alteration occurred after the coming of Islam or before it. Verification shows that all religions are just like this—they have fallen into the hands of bad transmitters: "There are no flaws in reports apart from their transmitters." (*N* II, 269, §402)

It is not only alteration in religion that brings about error. A person's adherence to the rites and doctrines of his religion also entails an error. The reason for this will be made evident in chapter 10. For now, we will suffice with a statement from the Shaykh that undoubtedly also comes by way of tasting.

> Every religion is transmitted by wayfarers. In terms of alteration, that which is altered is an error and that which is not altered is a waystation. But if the wayfarer resides in a waystation, it is an error. Kufa is on the path until we reach the Kaaba. But Kufa is not the Kaaba! (*N* II, 307, §464)[26]

Compulsion and Freedom

Having caught a glimpse of ʿAyn al-Quḍāt's thought-world as it concerns the human understanding of and interaction with good and evil, the nature of the universal order, and religious diversity, we now turn to the pivot of all of these points of inquiry: the embodied and acting human subject. ʿAyn al-Quḍāt avers that man has the power of choice to chart his own course in the world.

> Since there is a locus of choice, different actions come into existence from man through the medium of choice. If he wants, he moves to the left; and if he wants, he moves to

> the right. If he wants, he rests; and if he wants, he moves.[27] (*T* 190, §247)

It would be incorrect to read this statement as tantamount to what is today known as "libertarianism" or absolute free will. As an independent actor, the Shaykh sees man's situation as being more akin to the game of chess: he can move about freely, but these actions are circumscribed by the rules of the game itself. Thus the Shaykh argues that man's choice (*ikhtiyār*) is the result of his being compelled (*muḍṭarr*) and subjugated (*musakhkhar*) by divine destiny, which is a position that goes back to Avicenna.[28] We can say, in other words, that man is compelled by God to act freely.

> O dear friend! Whatever is in the kingdom and the Dominion[29]—every single thing—is subjugated to do a specific task. But man is not subjugated to do a specific task. Rather, he is subjugated to freely choose.[30] (*T* 189, §247)

> When you do an action by means of something, you have equally done so through subjugation. Even though I have written this letter by means of a pen, I have done so without the participation of a pen. (*N* II, 268, §401)

> If I write and if I do not write—in both of these, I am subjugated and compelled. This is because, when I write, although I do so with choice, in writing with choice, I am compelled. And when I do not write, although I do not do so with choice, in not writing, I am compelled.[31] (*N* I, 338, §564)

In attempting to delimit absolute human freedom of action, ʿAyn al-Quḍāt is of course responding to the Muʿtazila, whom we have already encountered as moral dualists.[32] For ʿAyn al-Quḍāt, the Muʿtazila err precisely because they do not see the hand of divine destiny in the very freedom of human action itself, thereby positing human will alongside divine will.

> By means of his choice, man is compelled, overpowered, and subjugated. A group became the Qadariyya over this

> question. They said, "Free choice is not compelled—man is free to choose, not compelled to choose." They did not know this much, namely that whoever is compelled and subjugated is so by means of a specific attribute that is in him. Thus man himself is compelled by means of his choice. (*N* III, 338, §100)

> Since . . . each attribute necessitates another act and for each capacity there must be another condition, this also applies to man for he is subjugated by destiny.[33] (*N* III, 337, §99)

The "attribute" that ʿAyn al-Quḍāt speaks of is that of choice, which he likens elsewhere to fire: just as fire must burn because of its inherent attribute of burning, so too must man choose because of his inherent attribute of choice.[34]

The Shaykh also wishes to demonstrate how intricately connected human actions are in his causal world picture—a picture that is ultimately in the hands of the Divine Painter.[35] He does this by recourse to an example from the involved act of writing.

> Now, listen: knife, pen, inkpot, and ink—all four are subjugated by man, and each one is put to work by the other. The subjugation of each of these four is by means of an attribute that is in it, and which is not in the other three things. When man wants to make a pen, he does so with a knife, for in the knife there is an attribute by means of which the pen has the capacity to be cut. This attribute is neither in the inkpot, nor the ink, nor the pen. Likewise, there is an attribute in the pen by which it becomes a tool for writing when it is subjugated by man for this purpose. And there is an attribute in the inkpot by which it becomes a lodging-place and depository for the ink. (*N* III, 336, §95)

It would be quite incorrect to assume that the Shaykh has no more to say about the nature of human freedom and its relationship to divine destiny, or that he does not take his initial insights on constrained human freedom to an entirely new level. That he does, and we will later have occasion to see the practical implications of his theory of action. Let us here call attention to what may seem like a contradiction at worst and a paradox at best: if man has limited freedom of choice, why, then, does the Quran say that God creates human beings and their actions? For the Shaykh, this is as much a paradox as it is a riddle.

> All of these realities in this discussion are riddles: *"God created you and what you do."*[36] If it were not like this, this verse would not be true. *Is there a creator other than God who provides for you?*[37] (*N* II, 268, §401)

Guidance and Misguidance

One thing that this riddle indicates is that everything other than God is sheer metaphor and unreality, just as lights in our world pale before God's light. This has major implications for ʿAyn al-Quḍāt's defense of Satan or Iblis, which we will discuss in detail in chapter 9. Despite their objective reality, sin and misguidance for the judge of Hamadan are merely metaphors for the guidance and misguidance that ultimately go back to God, the only true Actor.

> O dear friend! If it were not that *He leads astray whomsoever He will and guides whomsoever He will,*[38] what would Iblis and Gabriel[39] do? Granted that Iblis misguides people, but who created Iblis with this attribute? . . . He also says, *We unleash the satans on the unbelievers, to incite them cunningly.*[40] (*N* II, 7, §9)

> O dear friend! Every act that you see ascribed to someone other than God is metaphor, not reality. God is the true doer. Where He says, *Say, "The angel of death will take you,"*[41] it is metaphor. The reality of it is that *God takes souls at the moment of their death.*[42] Muhammad's guidance is metaphor and, likewise, Iblis' misguidance is metaphor. The reality is that *He leads astray whomsoever He will and guides whomsoever He will.*[43] Granted that Iblis misguides people. But who created Iblis with this attribute? Perhaps this is why Moses

says, *"It is naught but Thy trial whereby Thou leadest astray whomsoever Thou wilt, and guidest whomsoever Thou wilt."*[44] Alas for the sin! It is all from Him! What sin is there for someone else?[45] (*T* 188–189, §246)

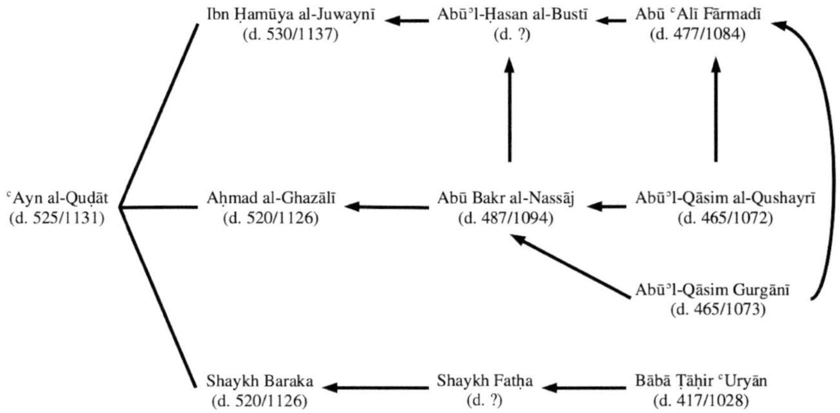

Figure 6. ʿAyn al-Quḍāt's spiritual network

5

Inside Out, Outside In

ʿAyn al-Quḍāt has the unique ability to at once practice, preserve, and penetrate the outward form of religion, thereby drawing attention to the inner reality and significance of the central rites of Islam, as well as some of its spiritual virtues and core eschatological teachings.

هو

Intention and Sincerity

Preceding any and every religious act in Islam one must have the intention (*niyya*) to perform the act in question. Islamic law does not distinguish between a person's good or bad intentions to perform any religious action. One may have the intention to pray at the masjid and carry out the prayer in accordance with this intention. Whether the person's intention to pray is motivated by a genuine desire to come closer to God or is motivated by other nonreligious factors, such as getting closer to his future employer praying next to him, does not enter into the concerns of Islamic law. Either a person has the intention to do something or does not. If there is no intention, the performance of a religious act is not legally valid.

On a spiritual level, there are varying reasons that inform a person's very intentionality, as in the example of the person praying in the masjid. The fundamental text cited in the Islamic tradition, and particularly emphasized by Sufis, are the words of the Prophet, "Deeds are by intentions. And every person shall have what he intends."[1] That is to say, every person will see the fruit of his intentions, possibly in this life, but certainly in the afterlife. After identifying human desire (*irāda*) with intention in the context of his explanation of this tradition,[2] the Shaykh elaborates on this teaching.

> If religious desire dominates over man, most of his deeds will be accepted. But if worldly desire dominates, most of his deeds will be rejected: *And We shall turn to whatever work they have done and make it scattered dust.*[3] When love for the world dominates a person's disposition, his intention for obedient deeds will inescapably be corrupt. (*N* I, 24, §25)

Sufi authors particularly identify a good and pure intention with the virtue of sincerity (*ikhlāṣ*). When a person has the best of intentions in performing any act of devotion, he is characterized as being sincere in that particular act. As his good intentions inform all of his actions, the extent of his sincerity widens correspondingly. A person who is entirely sincere in carrying out his religious obligations can direct the arrow of his sincerity toward different things.

One may, for example, be completely sincere and have the best intentions to be a good servant of God in order to obtain the rewards of Paradise that the Quran promises to the righteous. This kind of sincerity amounts to nothing less than sincerity for Paradise and its content, which ʿAyn al-Quḍāt specifically identifies as the sincerity typically found among the renunciants (*zuhhād*). But he is quick to point out that this type of sincerity stands worlds apart from another kind of sincerity, which sees even the desire for Paradise as an impediment upon the path toward self-realization. As the Shaykh explains, one must not be sincere for that which comes as a consequence of a godly life, but for God to be in one's life, both here and in the hereafter. This type of sincerity is reserved for the elect (*khawāṣṣ*), namely those who recognize God.

> When one's intention is pure of the contaminations of this world, that is called the "sincerity of the renunciants," the reward for which is Paradise: *Those who believe and perform*

> *righteous deeds, theirs shall be the Gardens of Paradise as a welcome.*[4] But when one's intention is pure of the contaminations of the next world, that is called the "sincerity of the recognizers," the reward for which is the encounter with God: *Whosoever hopes for the meeting with his Lord, let him perform righteous deeds and make no one a partner with his Lord in worship.*[5] (*N* I, 25–26, §27)

> The Paradise that the commoners have been promised is a prison for the elect, just as the world is a prison for believers.[6] Perhaps it is from this perspective that Yaḥyā Muʿādh-i Rāzī[7] said, "The Garden is a prison for the recognizers, just as the world is a prison for believers."[8] The elect are with God. What are you saying? God is in Paradise?! Yes, He is in Paradise, but in His own Paradise—that Paradise about which Shiblī said, "There is no one in the Garden other than God."[9] If you want, also listen to what Muṣṭafā says: "God has a Garden in which there are neither Houris, nor palaces, nor milk, nor honey."[10] Do you know what is in this Paradise? It is "what no eye has seen and no ear has heard, and what has never occurred to a mortal man."[11]
>
> To a person for whom this is Paradise, seeking the Paradise of the commoners is an error. This tribe is pulled to Paradise by chains of light and gentleness. But they do not go and do not accept it: "How strange are a people who are led to Paradise in chains but are unwilling to go!"[12] One's high aspiration must be like that of Āsiya, the wife of Pharaoh. In her supplication, she said, *"My Lord, build for me a house near unto Thee in the Garden."*[13] This *near unto Thee* is nothing but the Garden of the elect. (*T* 135–136, §187)

Assent

As a professional judge (*qāḍī*), ʿAyn al-Quḍāt was keenly aware of the formal limitations of legal scholars insofar as they are only legal scholars and uncommitted to the spiritual life. This is why he bluntly says that "the jurists are knowers of this world, not knowers of the religion."[14] That is, the jurists, qua their discipline, are only concerned with the realm of the body and deal with measurable and quantifiable realities, all of which have their place in the religious life but are not its be-all and end-all.

It is with this thought in mind that ʿAyn al-Quḍāt singles out Abū Ḥanīfa (d. 150/767) and al-Shāfiʿī (d. 204/820), the eponymous founders of the Ḥanafī and Shāfiʿī legal schools respectively. It was the destiny of both figures to play an extremely important role in developing the discipline of Islamic jurisprudence and legal theory. If they lived in an era when the exoteric religious sciences were firmly established, as was the case by ʿAyn al-Quḍāt's time, then these formidable leaders would have only concerned themselves with the inward dimension of religion.

> O dear friend! If Shāfiʿī and Abū Ḥanīfa—who are emulated by the community—were in these times, they would have found many benefits in the lordly sciences and traditions conveying spiritual statements, and would have entirely been devoted to these statements. They would have been occupied with nothing but the divine sciences, and would have spoken about nothing but them! (*T* 198–199, §257)

What then must one do in order to become a "knower of the religion" and someone who is concerned with the "lordly sciences"? The answer is rather straightforward: delve into the outward form of the Sharia and reach its inner core, its reality (*ḥaqīqa*). As ʿAyn al-Quḍāt explains, "When the meaning is seen, the form becomes a veil."[15]

From a spiritual perspective, the actions that make up Islam's five pillars of practice are all windows into a much deeper meaning behind their outward appearances. But one must not be misled into thinking that the Shaykh is somehow opposed to the rites and practices of Islam. For him, the Sharia in its most outward form is filled with beauty—if one cannot perceive this external beauty, then he will never be able to see the beauty of the realities contained within it.

> Alas! What am I, and what are you? This talk of reality itself cannot be contained, so how can it be contained in the world of the Sharia?! You have still not seen the beauty of the Sharia, so how will you see the beauty of reality? (*T* 242, §316)

The first of the five pillars of Islam is that of assent (*taṣdīq*).[16] This refers to the testimony upon the tongue of a deeply held conviction in one's heart concerning the oneness of God and the messengerhood of Muhammad, and is referred to as the Shahada or act of bearing witness. Its shortened form is, "[There is] no god but God; Muhammad is the Messenger of God." On its most basic level, the Shahada is the basis of the entire Sharia and of Muslim religious life.

> The least degree of this assent is when it incites man to observe the commandments and shun the prohibitions. When this foundation is obtained from assent, man's movements and stillnesses will accord with the Sharia. (*T* 70, §98)

The deeper one goes into the Shahada, the more he increases in righteous action, guidance, and certainty.

> When man becomes firm and rooted in the Sharia, the path to the selfhood of his self will be shown to him. "If you obey, you will be rightly guided"[17]—from obedient deeds, nothing but guidance comes out: *Those who strive in Us, We shall surely guide them in Our ways*.[18] When this guidance appears, the assent of the heart becomes certainty.
>
> The Commander of the Believers ʿAlī b. Abī Ṭālib gave news about this state like this: "Were the cover to be lifted, I would not increase in certainty." This assent is the cultivation of form for the people of religion upon the path of religion, and for the people of wayfaring upon the path of wayfaring. Assent is such an inciter that it effectuates wholesome works. When wholesome works are effectuated, the works themselves take man to certainty. (*T* 70–71, §98)

The certainty one can obtain through immersion in the Shahada may lead him to see and experience the states of the afterlife here and now—a theme that will resurface later on in the present chapter.

> When he reaches certainty, *on that Day the earth shall be changed into other than the earth*[19] will be disclosed to his eyes.

> He will taste the next world, and the states and knowledge of that world. (*T* 71, §98)

Purity and Prayer

ʿAyn al-Quḍāt attaches great importance to the daily prayer and is critical of those of his contemporaries who ceased to pray. At the same time, the Sharia does not hold a person who has lost his mind accountable to perform the obligatory rites of Islam. In this context, ʿAyn al-Quḍāt defends one Sufi in particular, Shaykh Muḥammad Maʿshūq-i Ṭūsī, who was a contemporary of the great Sufi master Abū Saʿīd b. Abī'l-Khayr (d. 440/1049).[20] As someone who had been pulled directly into the divine Presence (*majdhūb*) and had lost his senses, Shaykh Ṭūsī did not perform the daily prayers.[21]

But insofar as one is mentally sound and legally responsible for performing the daily prayers, pray they must. The Shaykh insists that one's level of penetration into the outward form of the daily prayers will always be commensurate to the awareness of his own situation as someone who stands before God, detached from the world and in the holiest of presences. This awareness should not only obtain during prayer. It must also accompany each of the conditions and acts that precede the prayer, beginning with the ritual ablution (*wuḍūʾ*).

> Perhaps you have not heard what Shiblī said: "Ablution is disconnection and prayer is union; he who does not disconnect does not unite."[22] If disconnection from what is other than God is not obtained in ablution, the union of "I have a moment with God"[23] will not be obtained in prayer. (*T* 79, §112)

In the *Letters*, ʿAyn al-Quḍāt outlines four levels of purity (P. *ṭahārat*). The beginning of purity is outward purity (P. *ṭahārat-i ẓāhir*), which consists in one's body and garments being free of filth. Then comes purity of the senses (*ḥawāss*), which entails such things as guarding the eyes from looking at what is forbidden by the Sharia, listening to gossip, and so on. Third is purity of mind (*dimāgh*), which the Shaykh tells us is to protect oneself from illusion and fancy, both being satanic in nature. Finally there is purity of the heart (P. *ṭahārat-i dil*), which is to guard the self from negative incoming thoughts (*khawāṭir*) and anything else that would impede one's progress along the spiritual path. Purity of the heart is best contrasted with outward purity, which in itself can never suffice as real purity.

> When the heart is impure, of what use is outward purity? . . . O friend! On the path to God, outward purity is an appearance and purity of the heart a pillar. When the pillar has cracks in it, of what use is the appearance? (*N* I, 111, §159)

When in a state of ritual purity, one faces the Kaaba, the required direction of prayer (*qibla*). At times, the Shaykh is thrown into a special state in which the entire order of space and time are folded up, leaving him in a realm that is timeless, placeless, and directionless.

> Alas! I do not know what I am saying! In this station, direction is lifted. Whatever thing the spirit faces that thing becomes its *qibla*. *Wheresoever you turn, there is the face of God*[24] is there. Since there is neither night nor day, how can one find the five times for prayer? This is also the meaning of "My Lord has neither night nor day."[25] (*T* 83, §119)

To mark the onset of the prayer, one performs the formula of consecration known as *takbīrat al-iḥrām*. This amounts to the statement *Allāhu akbar* ("God is the greatest") while one raises his hands past his ears, an act that symbolically gestures death to the world and even death to his own sense of self before the supreme Self.

> O dear friend! Have you ever gone to welcome *"Surely I am going unto my Lord"*[26]? Have you ever said, "God is the greatest!" such that you saw the existence of the kingdom and the Dominion as obliterated? In "God is the greatest!," have you ever seen affirmation after obliteration? (*T* 84, §121)

> When the prayer-performer says "God is the greatest!," *Nay, but We cast the real against the unreal, and it crushes it*[27] devours him. "I prayed" is itself thrown in the fire. What are you saying, he goes into the fire of *and it crushes it*?

> Nothing at all remains. . . . If nothing at all of the unreal remains, all that remains is God.[28] (*T* 82, §118)

The name for the ritual prayer, *ṣalāt*, derives from two words: the noun "joining" (*ṣila*) and the verb "I prayed" (*ṣalaytu*). The one in the act of prayer is joining himself to God, which amounts to the act of whispering to God (*munāja*), as stated by the Prophet.

> I know that the thought is occurring to you, "What is prayer?" The derivation of prayer is from "joining" and "I prayed." Do you know what "joining" is? The servant's whispering and speaking to God: "The prayer-performer is whispering to his Lord."[29] *Those who are mindful of their prayers;*[30] *Those who are constant in their prayers.*[31] (*T* 80, §114)

But it is not only the servant who prays and whispers. God, too, prays and whispers.

> O dear friend! God's prayer is that He whispers to the servant and speaks with him, and the servant's prayer is that he speaks with God. (*T* 81, §116)

From another perspective, God's "prayer" takes on no other object than Himself.[32] This was shown to the Prophet on the night of the Ascension (*miʿrāj*), just before he entered into the sanctuary of the Divine Presence Itself.

> That night when Muṣṭafā was taken on the Ascension, he reached a place where it was said to him, "Stop." Why was that said? "Because God is praying." Muṣṭafā asked, "And what is His prayer?" It was said, "His prayer is laudation for Himself. Glorified and holy is He, the Lord of the angels and the spirit."[33] (*T* 81, §116)

Fasting

ʿAyn al-Quḍāt draws on a number of Quranic verses and Hadiths to take us to the reality of fasting, which is what he calls the "fast of meaning" (P. *ṣawm-i maʿnawī*). This type of fast is quite distinct from the fast that Muslims must observe during the month of Ramadan and are encouraged to undertake at other times throughout the year. Whereas one must refrain from bodily pleasures and sustenance of every kind during the usual fast, the fast of meaning is quite different. In fact, it is the antipode of this kind of fasting, just as the inward is the antipode of the outward and meaning (*maʿnā*) the antipode of form (*ṣūra*). In the fast of meaning, "fasting" is characterized not by abstinence from food and drink but by partaking in food and drink. Needless to say, the Shaykh has in mind a very different kind of "food" and "drink" when it comes to the fast of meaning.

> In the Sharia, fasting is an expression of refraining from food and drink, namely the fast of the body. But in the world of reality, fasting is an expression of consuming food and drink. Which food? The food of "I spend the night with my Lord."[34] Which drink? The drink of *and unto Moses God spoke directly*.[35] This is called "the fast of meaning" and is the fast of the soul. It is God's fast: "The fast is Mine." Why? Because in this fast there is nothing but God. "And I recompense for it" also has this meaning. Since this fast is godly, the recompense for it is nothing but God. "I recompense for it,"[36] that is, "I am the recompense." (*T* 91, §129)

The divine name the "Self-Sufficient" (*al-ṣamad*) appears only once in the Quran, and it has posed some serious challenges to translators and modern interpreters.[37] One common view in the Quranic exegetical tradition is that *al-ṣamad*, when applied to God, refers to His freedom from any need, and, hence, His self-sufficiency. By the same token, the word can also mean "transcendent" in relation to God.[38] ʿAyn al-Quḍāt notes that, as a divine name, *al-ṣamad* denotes God's Essence, but it is in no way adequate to It.

> The "Self-Sufficient" has not completely explained the Howlessness[39] of the Essence! (*T* 269, §352)

It can be said that this divine name is characterized by a certain kind of oneness (P. *yakī*) and uniqueness (P. *yagānagī*).

> Read, *Say, "He, God, is One; God, the Self-Sufficient."*[40] The Self-Sufficient is oneness, and has the attribute of uniqueness. (*T* 268, §351)

But how is the divine name *al-ṣamad* as being qualified by oneness related to the notion that it signifies God as self-sufficient and transcendent? The Shaykh sees a connection here with the act of fasting, and in so doing he is following a teaching in the early Sufi tradition that goes back to the famous *Kitāb al-Lumaʿ fī'l-taṣawwuf* (*The Book of Gleams on Sufism*) of Abū Naṣr al-Sarrāj (d. 378/988).[41] The one who is fasting partakes in the divine attributes of God's self-sufficiency and transcendence, and hence His independence and uniqueness.

In other words, the act of fasting gives the servant a momentary experience that is entirely divine, since one who does not have food and drink in his body is empty of the world and all that it contains. Like God, the fasting person is free of need and in a state of oneness. Unlike God, he must break his fast, which explains why a perpetual fast is forbidden in the Sharia. Only God is perpetually self-sufficient, transcendent, unique, and one. God is the only one who perpetually fasts.

> At times, fast, and at times, break the fast. If all is fasting, it is forbidden, and if all is fast-breaking, it is one-coloredness. Perhaps it is from this perspective that Muṣṭafā said, "Whoever fasts endlessly does not have a fast."[42] The endless fast is itself oneness, for the Self-Sufficient is its attribute. This is the meaning of *"And He feeds and is not fed."*[43] God is the one who fasts eternally. (*T* 92, §130)

Pilgrimage and Alms Tax

In the same way that ʿAyn al-Quḍāt sees prayer and fasting as filled with inward meaning, so too is the case with the rites associated with the other major pillar of Muslim practice, the Hajj.

> In every action and movement en route to the Hajj there is a secret and a reality. But a person who does not see does not know! (*T* 95, §135)

Because the Sharia is imbued with outward and inward beauty, the same also applies to its fundamental symbols and sites of performance. Thus the Hajj's central symbol and point of focus, the Kaaba, is bathed in a luminous beauty that utterly transcends the reality of its physical appearance.

> The beauty of the Kaaba is not the walls and rocks that the pilgrims see. The beauty of the Kaaba is that light that will appear in a lovely form at the Resurrection, interceding for those who visited it. (*T* 94, §133)

Why do most people not see the Kaaba in its crystalline and transparent beauty? The Shaykh explains that this is because they only see the outward form of the Kaaba, which is made of clay (P. *gil*), just as they are. They thus can only see the Kaaba in their own image. But those who can journey into the Kaaba's interior, which corresponds to the heart (P. *dil*),[44] will see the Lord of the Kaaba.

> Whoever goes to the Kaaba of clay sees himself, and whoever goes to the Kaaba of the heart sees God. (*T* 95, §135)

The Shaykh also offers a unique reading of the last pillar of practice, the alms tax or *zakāt*. Adults who earn income and meet certain requirements for eligibility are required by the Sharia to pay the annual alms tax to those in need. And *zakāt* does not only pertain to one's income; it also pertains to the wealth that a person may have stored away, be it in the form of savings, gold, and the like. Now what can be said about the greatest treasure of all, namely God Himself? As God says in the famous Hadith of the Hidden Treasure, "I was a Hidden Treasure and I loved to be recognized. So I created the world in order to be recognized."[45]

For ʿAyn al-Quḍāt, this divine Treasure that is the source of all existence is Itself liable to *zakāt*. Just as people must distribute their wealth in the form of *zakāt*, so too must God distribute His "wealth" to the entire universe. This wealth is nothing other than mercy (P. *raḥmat*), which is distributed to God's servants—all of whom are in need of it—through His perfect representative, Muhammad.

> Watch out! Do you know what the alms tax of "I was a Hidden Treasure" is? That treasure is mercy: Your Lord

> *has prescribed mercy for Himself.*[46] To whom is the alms tax of this treasure given, and who will take it? Alas! *And We sent thee not, save as a mercy unto the worlds*[47] itself testifies to this statement. Muṣṭafā apportions that mercy to the elect of the community, and to the elect of the elect—*He it is who sends down tranquility into the hearts of the believers*[48]—and they apportion it to the generality of people—"The worst of men is he who eats alone."[49] Thus, whoever is in the Prophet's time[50] is not bereft of a share of this mercy in this world and the next world. (*T* 90–91, §128)

Praise and Gratitude

In a number of instances, ʿAyn al-Quḍāt dedicates his energies to an enigmatic Prophetic utterance, "If only the Lord of Muhammad had not created Muhammad!"[51] A number of Sufi authors have endeavored to explain its meaning,[52] and the Shaykh seems to be one of the earliest to have done so. Quite naturally, the Prophet's words do not imply any kind of imperfection on his part, being as they are a natural result of spiritual maturity along the path and a sign of effacement.[53] Among the meanings that our author sees in this statement is that it is a form of lament over the existence of the embodied human state that perforce does not allow one to fully praise God as He should be praised.

> The reality of Muṣṭafā's statement, "If only the Lord of Muhammad had not created Muhammad!," is this: "If only this body were not, so that I would sing the song of laudation—'I cannot enumerate Your laudation. You are as You have lauded Yourself'[54]—in the divine garden upon the rose of greatness." (*T* 199–200, §258)

The Prophet could only utter such a statement because he was in a state of annihilation and thus was speaking from the divine perspective, meaning he did not see a personal "he" but only a divine He.[55] This is why ʿAyn al-Quḍāt also includes the other Prophetic utterance in this context, "I cannot enumerate Your laudation. You are as You have lauded Yourself." That is, by one's not being "there," God can utter His own praise, which is the greatest kind of praise that can ever be enumerated or sufficiently encompassed by the human state.

This point is inextricably linked to the supreme virtue of gratitude (*shukr*), which the Shaykh discusses in a variety of contexts[56] and refers to as "the path to Paradise."[57] He gives us a window into precisely why gratitude has this special status when commenting upon Q 14:7, *If you are grateful, I shall surely increase you*. If one is grateful to God for the blessings of the afterlife, the increase that he will receive is God's acceptance even in this life, as was the case with Mary.

> When you are grateful for the blessings of the next world, He will take you and say, "You, be with Me; for you are worthy of Me!" *Thus her Lord accepted her in a beautiful way*.[58] (*N* II, 95, §133)

In the present life, the act of gratitude also has cosmic repercussions.

> From the gratitude of tongue and body, the heavens and the earth are filled with light. This is gratitude for the blessing of He created *for you whatsoever is in the heavens and whatsoever is on the earth, altogether*.[59] (*T* 246–247, §323)

In addition to gratitude of the tongue and body there is what ʿAyn al-Quḍāt calls gratitude of the spirit (P. *shukr-i rūḥ*). He alludes to it early in *Paving the Path*: "It is required and necessary for the wayfaring man to be grateful; but he cannot be grateful. Gratitude is done for him."[60] What the Shaykh is getting at is that this particular kind of gratitude is when a person realizes that he can never properly be grateful to God for His manifold blessings, a fact that is affirmed by Q 14:34, *And were you to count the blessings of God, you could not number them*. The poor slave consequently becomes utterly effaced before the divine Benefactor, leaving his spirit open to another form of gratitude altogether.

> When he sees himself as obliterated, in the midst of *Praise be to God unto whom belongs whatsoever is in the heavens and whatsoever is on the earth*[61] a call from the divine world will be given: "I Myself am your deputy—I will be grateful to Myself on your behalf, and will count My gratitude in place of your gratitude."[62] Perhaps you have not read that among His names, one is the Grateful and one the Praise/Praised.[63] That is, "He praises Himself through Himself."[64]

> The Grateful is the one who, as your deputy, is grateful on your behalf. Alas! Perhaps in this context that great one said, "I praised the Lord through the Lord."[65] But what do you know of the worth of this statement?! A person to whom "I recognized my Lord through my Lord"[66] appears knows the worth of this statement.[67] (*T* 246, §322)

Imaginalization

What allows the Shaykh to see the inner dimension of the outward form of religion is imagination (*khayāl*). Although imagination in a more general sense can be traced back to a number of earlier Islamic sources, it is commonly acknowledged that, as a conceptual category and a separate world, it came to the forefront largely due to the influence of Suhrawardī and then Ibn ʿArabī.[68] For his part, ʿAyn al-Quḍāt speaks extensively of imaginalization (*tamaththul*), a word that takes its cue from Q 19:17.[69] The function or process of imaginalization ties into many important aspects of the Shaykh's teachings. At its most basic level, it allows him to express the interplay between form and meaning and, consequently, to explain (as did his master Aḥmad Ghazālī before him[70]) the manner in which the spiritual realm interpenetrates the material realm.

> Most divine mysteries are known through imaginalization and are seen through it. Alas! *He imaginalized himself to her as a mortal man, well-proportioned*[71] is a complete answer. Gabriel showed himself to Mary from the spiritual world in the garb of a mortal man by way of imaginalization, and she saw him as a man in human form. (*T* 293, §385)

> Alas! What does anyone know about what state this imaginalization has?! In imaginalization, there are stations and states. One station of imaginalization is that whenever anyone sees a speck of that station and is in it, the station snatches him away from himself. When he is not in that station, he does not have a single moment of separation and sorrow. Reflection arises from this station. One of Muṣṭafā's stations was reflection, and another sorrow. ʿĀʾisha[72] said, "The Messenger of God was perpetually in reflection, always in sorrow."[73] (*T* 294, §386)

> One time, Muṣṭafā's Companions saw Gabriel in the form of a Bedouin. There was another time when Gabriel showed himself to Muṣṭafā in the form of Diḥya al-Kalbī.[74] If it was Gabriel, who is spiritual, how did he assume form so that he could be seen as a Bedouin in the garment of a mortal man? And if it was not Gabriel, who then was seen? Know that it was imaginalization, pure and good. (*T* 293–294, §385)

Through the lens of imaginalization, one can understand many seemingly anthropomorphic Hadiths and verses from the Quran, as well as the function of the divine names themselves. In fact, the reality of imaginalization comes from God Himself, the Form-Giver (*al-muṣawwir*) who perpetually discloses Himself to human beings in myriad forms.

> Alas! "I saw my Lord on the night of the Ascension in the most beautiful form."[75] This "most beautiful form" is imaginalization. If it is not imaginalization, then what is it? "God created Adam and his offspring in the form of the All-Merciful"[76] is also a kind of imaginalization. Alas! One of His names is *the Form-Giver*,[77] that is, He is the maker of forms.[78] But I am saying that Form-Giver means the displayer of forms. (*T* 296, §388)

> Do you even know in which bazaar these forms are on display and are sold? In the bazaar of the elect. Listen to Muṣṭafā, where he says, "There is a market in the Garden in which forms are sold."[79] This is "the most beautiful form." Look at what report Imam Abū Bakr Qaḥṭabī[80] gives about imaginalization: "I saw the Lord of exaltedness in the form of my mother." Do you know who this "mother" is? Know *the unlettered Prophet*[81] and read *and with Him is the Mother of the Book*.[82] (*T* 296–297, §388)

The Shaykh insists that whatever the imaginalized forms a person encounters, these forms have everything to do with his own spiritual and intellectual makeup, which is to say nothing of such things as his education, background, character, culture, and language. This mode of imaginalization corresponds to what is known in the later philosophical Sufi tradition as "connected imagination" (*al-khayāl al-muttaṣil*). We experience this mode of imagination most vividly in our dreams wherein the meanings of things take on forms and forms take on meanings. That is to say, the dream states that we encounter allow us to see attributes in embodied states, and to see embodied states in terms of their attributes.

Since dreams are re-presentations of the states of our souls and more generally our consciousness, the more sanctified and holy our souls, the more likely it is that we will encounter sanctified and holy imaginalized forms in our dreams. Since the dreaming subject is none other than the waking subject, like our dreams, we can and do encounter imaginalized re-presentations of the states of our souls in our waking states. It is this aspect of imaginalization with which the Shaykh is most concerned in his writings.

> One time, my master[83] said, "O Muḥammad![84] I have seen Muṣṭafā seven hundred times—I imagined that I was seeing him. Today, I have come to know that I have been seeing myself!" (*T* 298, §390)

> Wait until you reach that station where seventy thousand forms are displayed to you. You will see every form in the shape of your own form and will say, "Which one of these forms am I?" How is it possible for seventy thousand forms to come from one form? This is because seventy thousand attributes are inserted, mixed, and emplaced into every object of attribution and essence. Each specificity and attribute is imaginalized in a form and becomes an individual entity. When man sees all of these attributes, he imagines them to be himself. But they are not him. Rather, they are from him. (*T* 297, §389)

The later philosophical Sufi tradition also speaks of another order of imagination, what is called "disconnected imagination" (*al-khayāl al-munfaṣil*).[85] This mode of imagination proceeds from above the imagining subject and comes from a more primordial and archetypal world that is rather independent of the individual, connected imagination. The latter of course shapes the mode of reception of the imaginal forms that come from the realm of the disconnected imagination. This is a point that ʿAyn al-Quḍāt does not explicitly make, although it is clearly assumed in his writings. In some contexts, he gives us a window into his thinking on the question of the spiritual roots of the forms in our world, taking as his example the four elements or what are also known as the four "pillars." These pillars have a reality that simultaneously transcends and in-forms them.

> Wait until you reach reality from form. Then you will know that the root is reality, not form. What do you say, that your reality is like the reality of the realizers?[86] O dear friend! Wait until you reach that place where the reality of the elements, the natures, and the pillars are displayed to you in the same way as are the four pillars (water, earth, air, and fire) and the four formal natures (heat, coldness, dryness, and moisture), all of which have a relation to the world and upon which the world hinges. Then you will be taken to a place where the reality of these will appear to you, and you will become alive. You will obtain true life. (*T* 165–166, §221)

Elsewhere, the Shaykh says that the four elements have as their source the world of the spirit (P. *ʿālām-i rūḥ*), which has its own corresponding four "elements." In this context, ʿAyn al-Quḍāt attributes a statement to Avicenna: "The four elements are eternal."[87] Our author then draws the natural conclusion: just as the four elements of this world are that by which the world operates, the elements of the spiritual world are that by which the Garden (*janna*) operates. But, he complains, "people have a trivial understanding of how reality works, and remain very far from these meanings!"[88]

The key to understanding "the work of reality" is once again imaginalization. Imaginalization can give us a direct window into the next world, which is the principle and root of our present world and the arena of the eschatological events a person encounters after the death of his body.

> See how the discussion drags me from one place to another! But that is done. What I meant is what I said: the foundation of the existence of the next world is through imaginalization, and recognizing imaginalization is no trifling matter! (*T* 293, §385)

> You do not know this! Wait until you are shown the foundation of the world of imaginalization. Then you will know how and what the affair is. The foundation of the

> next world and the world of the Dominion is all through imaginalization. To become aware through imaginalization is no trifling matter! (*T* 287, §374)

Since the human soul is the locus of this "radical interiorization of Islamic eschatology,"[89] the positive and negative eschatological realities that a person will encounter before and after death are the imaginalized projections of the states of his own soul.

> So long as the wayfarer is outside of the veils of the earth and the heavens, the Resurrection will not happen for him, for the Resurrection is only within the veils, because God is within the veils: *and with Him lies knowledge of the Hour.*[90] (*Z* §181)

> A mystery is always a mystery as such, and what is out in the open is always out in the open as such. Both "change" only as the states of the wayfarers change. (*Z* §183)

> Everything that will happen on the Day of Resurrection is a mystery to human knowledge. It is inconceivable for anyone to encompass it while he remains in this world and is not free from the bonds of fantasy and the error of imagination. (*Z* §179)

> Seek the grave inside yourself! . . . The seekers' graves are their bodies.[91] (*T* 288, §375)

> The first thing from the next world that is known to the wayfarer is the states of the grave. The first imaginalization that he sees is in the grave. For example, the snakes, scorpions, dogs, and fire that have been promised to those deserving punishment appear to him in the grave through imaginalization. This is also inside of man, for it is from him. Therefore, it is constantly with him. Alas! What do you hear?! (*T* 288–289, §376)

> The questioning of Munkar and Nakīr[92] is also in the self. All of our veiled contemporaries have come with this problem:

how can two angels go to a thousand people in a single moment? [They therefore resolve that] one must simply have belief in this. But on this point Bū ʿAlī Sīnā[93] gave a world of clarification in just two sentences: "Munkar is one's ugly works, and Nakīr is one's wholesome works."[94] He said that Munkar is one's sins, and Nakīr is one's obedient deeds. Alas! How beautiful has it been said! That is, the soul is the mirror of blameworthy qualities, while the intellect and heart are the mirror of praiseworthy qualities.[95]

When a person looks, he sees his own attributes imaginalized. His existence is his punishment, yet he imagines that somebody else is punishing him. But the punishment is itself him, and is from him! If you want it from Muṣṭafā, then listen to when he explained the punishment of the grave: "They are merely your works brought back to you."[96] (*T* 289, §377)

In this resurrection, *secrets are laid bare*[97] is on display. *And what lies within breasts is made known*[98] removes the veil from the face of actions. . . . When your entirety is illumined, this is the address: *O tranquil soul! Return to thy Lord, content, contenting. Enter among My servants. Enter My Garden.*[99] (*T* 326, §427)

In this Garden, He will address them: "Do you want something from Me?" They will say, "O God! We want annihilation and selflessness from You." So He will have them taste the wine of union and proximity in their constitution. Wherever the wine goes, it will alchemically transform. This is *a wine most pure.*[100] (*T* 292, §383)

Death before Death

Another key theme that the Shaykh takes up in a number of different contexts is the well-known Sufi notion of dying to one's ego and attachment to the world before the physical death of the body. Although ʿAyn al-Quḍāt does not cite it in his writings, this teaching is entirely informed by the Prophetic injunction, "Die before you die."[101] A rather evocative Sufi saying that illustrates this perspective comes by way of Ḥātim al-Aṣamm (d. 237/851), a major spiritual disciple of the master from Khurasan Shaqīq al-Balkhī (d. 194/809).[102] Ḥātim noted that not a day passes by but that the devil addresses him, hoping to cause anxiety in him over the basic necessities of life: "What will you eat? What will you wear? Where will you live?" In response to his enemy's attempts to spiritually decenter him, Ḥātim, who was already dead to the world, would reply, "I will eat death. I will wear the funeral shroud. And I will live in the grave."[103]

ʿAyn al-Quḍāt calls the death of the ego the "death of meaning" (P. *mawt-i maʿnawī*) and "real death" (P. *marg-i ḥaqīqī*). These correspond to what in later Islamic texts is referred to as the "voluntary return" (*al-rujūʿ al-ikhtiyārī*). The death of the body, on the other hand, corresponds to what is known as the "compulsory return" (*al-rujūʿ al-iḍṭirārī*). Whereas every human being will necessarily experience biological death, it is only those who do the hard work of dying to the ego who will truly be resurrected, judged, and brought into the divine Presence even while still in the body.

> The first station for man is to obtain the death of meaning. When he obtains this death, "his resurrection has happened"[104] will be disclosed to him. (*T* 322, §421)

> "Whoever wants to see a dead man walking upon the earth, let him look at Ibn Abī Quḥāfa"[105] has explained this death. Anyone who does not have this death does not find life. I mean, what you know as "death" is not real death, which is annihilation. Do you know what I am saying? I am saying that when you are you and are with yourself, you are not you. But when you are not you, you are all yourself:
>
> Neither am I I, nor are You You, nor are You me.
> I am myself, You are Yourself, and You are me.
> Such am I with You, O Beauty of Khotan,[106]
> that I err when I am You, or You are me.
> (*T* 287–288, §374)

> O friend! You have seen the world of the kingdom and its wonders. Wait until you also see the world of the Dominion

> and its wonders! You have not yet seen the world of the Dominion, so what can you know of the Divine world? (*T* 307, §404)
>
> O friend! That world is all life in life, and this world is all death in death. As long as you do not pass death, you will not reach life: *And surely the abode of the next world is life indeed.*[107] In another place Jesus said, "The one who is not born twice shall not enter the Dominion of the heavens."[108] He said that the wayfarer must be born twice. One time he is born from his mother, where he sees himself and this evanescent world; and one time he is to be born from himself so that he can see the everlasting world and God.[109] (*T* 319–320, §418)
>
> Alas! What will you hear?! For us, death is this: one must be dead to all that is other than the Beloved until he finds life from the Beloved and becomes living through the Beloved. (*T* 288, §374)
>
> If you want something more complete, listen to how God gives news about a group: *They will say, "Our Lord, Thou hast caused us to die twice over, and given us life twice over."*[110] Know this second death as beyond the death of the body and recognize this second life as other than the life of the body! If you want to know something more complete about the life and death of meaning, listen to what Muṣṭafā said in a supplication: "O God! I live through You and die through You."[111] (*T* 320, §418)

The idea of dying to the self before bodily death is not just an abstract teaching or some kind of an aspirational ideal for ʿAyn al-Quḍāt. It is very real and attainable, and is the only worthwhile human pursuit. Attaining this goal is certainly difficult but not impossible, so long as one is willing to and actually does walk the spiritual path. This point naturally sets our sights on what the Shaykh has to say about the path, those traveling upon it, and the help that they will need along the way.

Figure 7. Page from a manuscript of ʿAyn al-Quḍāt, *Zubdat al-ḥaqāʾiq*

6

Wayfarers and Masters

ʿAyn al-Quḍāt places a great deal of emphasis on the science of Sufi psychology and the attendant need to walk the spiritual path under the guidance of a realized master.

هو

Habit-Worship

One of the most prominent themes in ʿAyn al-Quḍāt's writings is his critique of habit (P. *ʿādat*).[1] The word in Arabic derives from a verb that has to do with returning and doing something again and again. For the spiritual seeker, paying careful attention to the kinds of things she returns to, and thus her habits, is essential. For, at bare minimum, negative habits imply major spiritual flaws and impediments for the soul in this life and after death.

> From the beginning, no position is better for one than abandoning habit. (*T* 21, §33)

> Most people are controlled by the satans of habit and are afflicted by them. (*N* I, 82, §107)

> O dear friend! From the very beginning, the seekers of God have spoken of abandoning all habits. (*N* II, 252, §379)

> Know with which people you will be mustered: "Whoever loves a people shall be mustered with them."[2] If you are on the path of the lovers and a lover of the lovers, you will be mustered with them. If you are on the path of the wholesome and a lover of the truthful, you will be taken with them into the Garden. If you are on the path of this world and the people of habit, you will be mustered with them. (*N* I, 65–66, §83)

Religious actions that are done more out of a force of habit than anything else also fall short. Since they are not carried out with the fullness of one's intentions and presence of mind, performing such actions cannot lead to human perfection.

> Habit and zealousness are also inciters for prayer, fasting, and charity. However, they are not correct inciters. (*N* I, 69, §88)

> One unit of prayer that you do at the command of a heart-master[3] is better than a thousand units of prayer whose inciter is habit. (*N* I, 44, §50)

> Strive in this, namely that you should perform all of your actions in such a way that they are all accepted. One action like this is better than thousands and thousands of obedient deeds performed out of habit. (*N* II, 422, §666)

> If a person's deeds are unaccompanied by ostentation, associationism, and hypocrisy but are mixed with habit, he will never reach the perfection of Uways, Junayd,[4] and Shiblī. (*N* I, 54, §67)

The Shaykh normally frames the problem of habit as specifically being one of "habit-worship" (P. *ʿādat-parastī*).[5] A soul given over to serving its habits cannot be in a state of submission (*islām*), taking as it does other gods alongside God.

> The habit-worshippers are distant. (*N* II, 92, §129)

> The people of the world are content with habit-worship. Where are they from, and where is this discussion from? Read this again and reflect upon it a thousand times! (*N* II, 92, §128)

> So long as there is a mote of habit-worship in you, the reality of submission will not turn its face to you. (*N* II, 478, §747)

> How can you call a habit-worshipper a submitter? Submission is that you acquiesce to God and worship Him. (*T* 68, §94)

Another kind of habit-worship is "legalism" (P. *sharīʿat-warzī*). In and of itself, punctiliousness in matters of the Sharia is meritorious and necessary. But when one becomes too legalistic to the point that the practice of the Sharia becomes an end in itself instead of a means to the greater End, legalism is a major idol and impediment upon the homeward journey. What one needs is not legalism but "realism" (P. *ḥaqīqat-warzī*).

> The world of habit-worship is the Sharia, and legalism is habit-worship. So long as you do not perceive habit-worship and let go of it, you will not be in realism. These words are known in the Sharia of reality, not in the Sharia of habit! (*T* 320, §419)[6]

The Shaykh links habit-worship not only with legalism but also with idol-worship (P. *but-parastī*) itself.

> O dear friend! If you want the beauty of these mysteries to be disclosed to you, then let go of habit-worship, for habit-worship is idol-worship. Do you not see how the arrow of this group goes? *"We found our fathers upon a creed, and we surely follow in their footsteps."*[7] Whatever you have heard from people, forget it! "A vile guide for man is his conjecture."[8] Whatever you have heard, ignore it, for "The tale-bearer shall not enter the Garden."[9] Whatever appears, do not look at it! *And do not spy.*[10] Whatever is difficult for

> you, only ask with the tongue of the heart and be patient until you arrive: *Had they been patient until thou camest out unto them, it would have been better for them.*[11] Accept the advice of Khiḍr:[12] *"Question me not about anything until I make mention of it to thee."*[13] (*T* 12–13, §18)

> Do you know why we do not see the beauty of submission? Because we are idol-worshippers and have joined this group: *"These, our people, have taken gods apart from Him."*[14] We have taken the idol of the soul that commands to ugliness[15] as our object of worship. *So hast thou considered the one who takes his caprice as his god?*[16] also has this meaning. We will see the beauty of submission when we replace the bag of caprice as our object of worship with God as our object of worship. (*T* 68, §94)

> You have been content with false habit! The path of the men who smash the idols of habit to pieces is one thing, and the path of the effeminates, wimps,[17] and false claimants who take the idol of habit as their object of worship is quite another thing! (*N* I, 225, §370)

The habit-worshipper is an idolater because he puts his own habitual attachment to himself and his desires above God. In the final analysis, the habit-worshipper is nothing but a self-worshipper.

> When you worship your soul and caprice, you are not a servant of God. Listen to what Muṣṭafā said: "Caprice is the most hated god that is worshipped on the earth."[18] He said that the worst god that is worshipped on the earth is one's caprice and soul. In another context, he said, "Cursed be the servant of the dirham! Cursed be the servant of his wife and the dinar!"[19] (*T* 68, §94)

> As long as you are not free from self-worship, you cannot be a God-worshipper; as long as you are not a servant, you will not be free. . . . As long as you do not flee from self, you will never reach the Self. . . . As long as you are not poor, you will not be rich; as long as you are not annihilated, you will not be subsistent. (*T* 25–26, §38)

> How much do you hear? Come out of habit-worship! Even though you have been in school for seventy years, you have not become selfless for a single moment! (*T* 340–341, §452)

Body and Soul

In *Paving the Path*, the Shaykh gives us a general outline of his understanding of the levels of the human self, or what is generally referred to as "spiritual psychology." At a basic level, there is the body (*qālab*, lit. "bodily frame") and the soul (*nafs*). In addition to these, a person also has within himself a heart and a spirit. The body and soul are dark and dense entities, as they are closer to the earth, whereas the heart and spirit are luminous and subtle entities, as they are closer to the light of God.

> O dear friend! Man does not have one attribute. Rather, he has many. There are two inciters in every person: one is from the All-Merciful and the other from Satan. The body and soul are satanic, and the spirit and heart are from the All-Merciful. The first thing that entered the body was the soul. Had the heart preceded the soul, it would never have allowed the soul into the world. Relative to the heart, the body has density. The soul has the attribute of darkness, while the body is earthly and also has darkness. They have become intimate and familiar with one another. The soul's home is the left side of the body, and the heart's home is the breast. At every moment, the soul increases in caprice and misguidance. But every hour, the heart is adorned with the light of recognition: *What of one whose breast God has expanded for submission so that he follows a light from his Lord?*[20] (*T* 195, §252)

The dark, earthlike body is the most outward of all aspects of human selfhood. In and of itself, the body is nothing, although it takes on meaning and reality by virtue of being the particular locus of the soul.

> From the perspective of dusthood and human mortality, all bodies are one. But their realities are diverse. (*T* 252, §330)

Habit-worship pertains to both the domains of the body and the soul, but it is more exclusively a problem of the soul. This explains why the Prophet said, "Your greatest enemy is the soul between your two sides."[21] Technically speaking, there are levels of "soulhood" that are based on a taxonomy derived from the Quran. At its basest level, the soul is entirely egotistical, immersed in character traits that are blameworthy (*madhmūma*) and caught up in the pursuit and fulfillment of lusts and desires. Derived from Q 12:53, this aspect of the soul is referred to as the "soul that commands to ugliness" (*al-nafs al-ammāra bi'l-sūʾ*), or more simply the "commanding soul." It is the "greatest enemy" to which the Prophet was referring.[22] The more one is immersed in the pursuit of desires and the cultivation of blameworthy character—hence the soul's dark, downward, and egotistical tendencies—the more "bodily" will he be, which is how habit-worship exercises its influence upon the body.

The more a person's entirety is characterized by habit-worship, the more is he a self-worshipper and the stronger is his false sense of selfhood. This illusion is fueled by the egotistical attachment to the self and longing for the world and worldly things. Such a habit-worshipper, even if he be a sincere aspirant upon the spiritual path, will always find himself in existential danger.

> O friend! There is a station—until the wayfarer is in it, he is in danger. This is the meaning of "The sincere ones are in tremendous danger."[23] It can be called the station of caprice and desire. . . . As long as you do not bring the bag of selflessness and desirelessness from the world of caprice to the divine desert, you will not be delivered from fear. *As for one who fears standing before his Lord and forbids the soul from caprice.*[24] He is saying that whoever steps out of the world of caprice steps into Paradise. (*T* 233–234, §303)

Q 75:2 speaks of *the blaming soul* (*al-nafs al-lawwāma*), which is the soul that recognizes and seeks to address the problems caused by the soul that commands to ugliness.[25] The blaming soul takes a person to task for his immersion in acts of disobedience and moral ugliness. It amounts to a degree of human self-awareness and self-reproach, both of which are necessary and healthy attitudes toward recovery from one's fallen state. The only way a person can overcome the predicament of habit-worship is to bring down the walls of the ego through spiritual struggle (*mujāhada*) so that all that remains is selflessness and nothingness.

> O friend! You have never slayed your soul by opposing it. *"Slay your souls!"*[26] With what? "With the swords of struggle and opposition."[27] (*T* 219, §281)

> Perhaps you have not heard what Dhū'l-Nūn said: "If you can sacrifice your spirit, then come! But if not, then do not occupy yourself with the technicalities of the Sufis!"[28] If you are ready to sacrifice your spirit at the first step, then come along! But if you cannot, then of what use will the technicalities, metaphors, and formal expressions of the Sufis be to you? (*T* 14–15, §21)

With much combat against the ego and a life sanctified by prayer and the remembrance of God, the blaming soul can be transformed into one that Q 89:27 refers to as "tranquil" (*muṭmaʾinna*).[29] This is the soul at its finest and fullest, with a state of tranquility and repose that becomes second nature because of a person's having conquered his ego, internalized character traits that are praiseworthy (*maḥmūda*),[30] and brought the soul in line with his intelligence and, most importantly, the spirit.[31] The net effect is not only a whole and sound soul and sense of self, but also a whole and sound body and a closer connection to the heart.

The Heart

The seat of human consciousness is the heart (*qalb*; P. *dil*),[32] or what Henry Corbin poetically referred to as one of a person's "organs of mystic physiology."[33] The heart is the very stuff of the human self but also has a mysterious connection to God, which is why James Morris speaks of it as being an "invisible human-divine reality."[34] In its totally pure and unsullied state, the heart is the locus through which one may perceive spiritual realities. To gain complete access to the heart, ʿAyn al-Quḍāt says that one must first cultivate detachment from the self, the world, and worldliness, all of which stain the heart with the dross of darkness and duality.[35]

> So long as your heart is not cleansed of attachments—*Did We not expand for thee thy breast?*[36]—it will not be full of the knowledge, light, and recognition of *What of one whose breast God has expanded for submission so that he follows a light from his Lord?*[37] (*T* 65, §88)

> God does not have any condition for you but that you empty your heart. (*N* II, 92, §128)

The process of emptying and cleansing the heart is tantamount to the act of walking the spiritual path, which itself is a synonym for the inner journey and the search for one's lost heart.

> Whoever does not have a heart is not a human—*It is they who are heedless.*[38] Seeing that you are human and have reached maturity, praying, fasting, performing the Hajj, and paying the alms tax are obligatory upon you. But ahead all of these, the search for the heart is obligatory: *Have they not journeyed upon the earth that they might have hearts by which to understand?*[39] Why is the path not traveled so that a heart can be found? (*N* II, 370, §577)

> Search for the heart and grab hold of it! Do you know where the heart is? Search for it "between the two fingers of the All-Merciful."[40] Alas! If the beauty of the "two fingers of the All-Merciful" were to lift the veil of exaltedness, every heart would be cured. (*T* 146, §198)

As Q 22:46 states, *Surely it is not the eyes that go blind, but it is hearts within breasts that go blind.* This is to say that, when corrupted by vile character traits, sin, and the forgetfulness of God, the heart will be unable to be fully conscious and aware of Him. But when it is sufficiently cleansed, which is to say that when a person finds her heart, she will find God there. For only the heart is expansive enough to contain the divine Presence. In the following passage, ʿAyn al-Quḍāt explains this point by offering a commentary on the famous *ḥadīth qudsī*, "Neither the heavens nor the earth embrace Me, but the heart of My faithful servant does embrace Me."[41]

> What kind of knowledge do the heavens have of God that they can bear Him? And what kind of proximity does the earth have with God that it can be His abode? The heart of the believer is at once God's intimate, His lover, and the abode of His mysteries. (*T* 24, §36)

> Perhaps you have not heard what Muṣṭafā was asked: "Where is God?" He said, "In the hearts of His believing servants." This is "The heart of the believer is the house of God."[42] Search for the heart so that the pilgrimage is the pilgrimage of the heart. I know that you are saying, "Where is the heart?" The heart is here: "The heart of the believer is between the two fingers of the All-Merciful."[43] (*T* 92–93, §131)

> "The heart of the believer is the Throne of the All-Merciful."[44] Anyone who circumambulates the heart will find the goal, and anyone who errs and loses his way on the path of the heart will become so distant that he will never find himself. (*T* 24, §36)

Alongside being God's place of dwelling, the heart in Sufi literature is also described as the locus into which He looks.[45] This is why the Shaykh refers to it as the object of divine gaze (P. *manẓūr-i ilāhī*) and the looking-place of God (P. *naẓargāh-i khudā*).

> The heart knows what the heart is and who it is. The heart is the object of divine gaze and is itself worthy.[46] "God looks at neither your forms nor your actions, but He looks at your hearts."[47] O friend! The heart is God's looking-place. (*T* 146, §198)

Although God looks at every heart, only hearts that are purified and perfectly reflective can act as proper loci for His Self-contemplation. When God's eyes are fixed upon a person's purified heart, she can consult it and it can serve as her guide.

> When the moment comes, you will be brought into the world of *the All-Merciful taught the Quran*[48] and all of the

> divine mysteries in the circle of the *bāʾ* of the *basmala* or in the *mīm* of the *basmala*[49] will appear to you. Then *He taught by the Pen, taught man that which he knew not*[50] will be your teacher. All of this is imprinted in your heart. Your heart is the *Preserved Tablet.*[51] (*T* 155–156, §209)

> God's Pen itself tells the Tablet of your heart what is to be spoken[52] and your heart tells you what that is. This is all when you are the servant and aspirant of the heart. When the heart is the master and you are the aspirant, the heart is served and you are the servant. The heart is the commander and you are the commanded. When all of this worthiness appears in you, the heart will accept you and nurture you until your work reaches a place where the recompense and wage of your service will be given to you every day. (*T* 157, §211)

So reliable is the pure heart that one need only turn to it, and not to a mufti or legal expert, for knowledge of what one should "do."

> O dear friend! What do you hear? A whiff of the Hadith "The believer is a mirror of the believer"[53] is fitting here. Whoever does not know something and wants to know it has two ways. One way is for him to return to his heart, reflecting and contemplating until, by means of his own heart, he acquires it for himself. From this perspective, Muṣṭafā said, "Consult your heart, even if the muftis give you a fatwa."[54] He said, whatever happens, the locus and mufti must be a truthful heart.
>
> If the heart gives a fatwa, it is God's affair, so do it! If it does not give a fatwa, leave it! And learn avoidance, for "The angel has a suggestion and the devil has a suggestion."[55] Whatever fatwa the heart gives is godly, and whatever the heart repels is satanic. A portion of these two calls is in everyone, be they unbelievers or submitters.
>
> Our work in this is difficult, since our mufti is the commanding soul: *"Surely the soul commands to ugliness."*[56] Whoever has the heart as a mufti is godwary and felicitous,

> and whoever has the soul as a mufti is lost and wretched. (*T* 8–9, §12)

> The outward-seers say, "We have not heard these words from Shāfiʿī and Abū Ḥanīfa." Another one says, "ʿAlī says such-and-such," while another says, "Ibn ʿAbbās[57] says such-and-such." Alas! Do you not know this much, namely why Muṣṭafā said to Muʿādh-i Jabal,[58] "Pursue matters using your own opinion"[59]? He said, "Whatever is difficult for you, return its fatwa to your heart. . . . Accept it from the mufti of your own heart." I am speaking about the heart, not the commanding soul.
>
> When our mufti is the commanding soul and we set out in its tracks, our ensuing state will be worse. It is mandatory and an obligation for us to oppose our souls. Perhaps you have not heard what God told Prophet David in this statement: "O David! Come close to Me through enmity with your soul."[60] But what are we saying? The ignorant scholars will count you as among the ignorant! Knowledge is of two types—knowledge of the heart and knowledge of the tongue. They are content with knowledge of the tongue and have forgotten knowledge of the heart! (*T* 197–198, §256)

As a spiritual entity, the heart stands above the material body. And ʿAyn al-Quḍāt also tells us that between the heart and the body there is an intermediary entity called the "subtle human reality" (P. *laṭīfat-i ḥaqīqat-i insānī*). In Sufi psychology, this term can denote the soul as it has become more aligned with the heart and the spirit.[61] The soul is subtle because of its proximity to the heart, while it is dense because it is housed in the body. Given this intermediary station between spirituality and subtlety and light and darkness, the soul has some level of connectivity to both the body and the heart. It can therefore channel the heart's states to the body.

> Alas! From *did We not expand for thee thy breast?*[62] what have you understood? If the heart were merely placed in the body, it would not settle down in and be intimate with

> the body; and the body would be unable to bear the heart's states and would melt. Thus, this subtle human reality was placed as an intermediary and a barrier between the heart and the body. (*T* 143, §194)

> Alas! You have never known that the heart is a subtlety and is from the high world and that the body is dense and is from the low world. There was and is no congruity and affinity between them. But between the heart and the body an intermediary and a link is appointed—*God comes between a man and his heart*[63]—so that it is the interpreter of the heart and the body. That which is the heart's share, the heart will tell to that subtlety and that subtlety will then tell it to the body.[64] (*T* 142–143, §193)

Many who come into contact with holy people notice the presence of an unmistakable light on their faces, as well as a certain kind of suppleness and subtlety to their bodies.[65] For ʿAyn al-Quḍāt, such an experience is perfectly explainable: since the heart is the place wherein God looks, through the intermediary of the soul the heart can affect the body and transfer its light and color to it.[66] Participating in the heart's subtle and luminous nature, the body thereby also becomes a locus of the divine gaze and a source for the diffusion of grace (*baraka*) to the world.

> When the body takes on the color of the heart and becomes the same color as the heart, it too will be the object of God's gaze. (*T* 146, §198)

> When the Prophet would want his tongue to hear from the heart, he would say, "O Bilāl! Relieve us!"[67]—"Give me an hour with reality from the selfhood of myself." When he would want his heart to be the hearer of the tongue, he would say, "O Ḥumayra! Speak with me!"[68]—"O ʿĀʾisha, give me an hour with myself from reality and bring me to myself so that the world's inhabitants may benefit." He explained it this way: "I have been sent to perfect noble character traits."[69] (*T* 16, §24)

As we have seen in the previous chapter, the Shaykh identifies the luminous, inner reality of the Kaaba with the heart. When the light of the Kaaba fills one's heart, that light will, through the soul that stands between the heart and the body, display its effects upon the body itself. It is with this point in mind that ʿAyn al-Quḍāt explains a key story about the sanctified body of Abū Yazīd (Bā Yazīd) Basṭāmī and its relationship to the light of the Kaaba.

> Perhaps you have not heard this: Bā Yazīd Basṭāmī was coming and saw someone. He said, "Where are you going?" The person said, "To the house of God." Bā Yazīd said, "How many dirhams do you have?" He said, "I have seven dirhams." Basṭāmī said, "Give them to me and circle around me seven times, and you will have visited the Kaaba."[70] What do you hear?! The Kaaba of the light that comes from "The first thing that God created was my light"[71] was in the body of Bā Yazīd, so the man's visitation to the Kaaba was achieved. (*T* 94, §134)

The Spirit

Above the heart is the spirit (*rūḥ*; P. *jān*). If one has not found his heart, he will never be able to get to the spirit, the vision of which is a prerequisite for the vision of God.

> You still have not seen the heart, so how will you see the spirit? And since you have not seen the spirit, how will you see God? (*T* 155, §209)

What, then, is the spirit, and how can one see it? In and of itself, the spirit defies all classification and is guarded by nothing less than the divine jealousy.

> Do not imagine the spirit to be just another created thing. The spirit has a different exaltedness and subtlety. (*T* 151, §204)

> When the heart is obtained by you and you recover it, the spirit will show the beauty of exaltedness to you. Alas! If the Sharia had not fastened the shackle of reality's madness, I would have spoken about what the spirit is! But the divine jealously does not allow for it be spoken of. (*T* 148, §201)

The spirit belongs to each human being, which means it has a special relationship to the body.

> The spirit's control over the body is through subjugation, not nature and choice. "We enter compelled, subsist in bewilderment, and exit unwillingly"[72] is what has been transmitted from the Greek sage. (*N* II, 54, §70)

More important than the preceding point is that the spirit mysteriously resides both inside and outside the body, just as God is mysteriously inside and outside the world.

> Wait until you know what relation the spirit has with the body—whether the spirit is inside or outside it. Alas! The spirit is inside and outside the body and is inside and outside the world. The spirit is also neither inside nor outside the body, and is neither inside nor outside the world. Alas! Understand what has been spoken: the spirit is not connected to the body, but is not disconnected from it. God is not connected to the world but is not disconnected from it.[73] (*T* 157–158, §212)

Despite the spirit's connection in some sense to the body, the Shaykh insists that it does not belong to the realm of creation, much less this lowly world. To illustrate his point, he cites a statement that goes back to Abū Bakr Qaḥṭabī:[74] "The spirit does not enter under the lowliness of *'Be!'*"[75] On the face of it, what this means is that the spirit does not have a relation to the created order, which emerges as a result of the divine, existentiating command *"Be!"*

Abū Bakr al-Kalābādhī (d. 380/990) weighs in on Qaḥṭabī's statement in his Sufi primer entitled *al-Taʿarruf li-madhhab al-taṣawwuf* (*Introduction to the School of Sufism*). He says that spirit "is nothing but life-giving; and life and life-giving are attributes of the Life-Giver, just as creating and creation are attributes of the Creator."[76] Kalābādhī then provides the scriptural proof text cited by those who adhere to this understanding, namely Q 17:85: *Say, "The spirit is of the command of my Lord."* Kalābādhī then explains that this text is meant to illustrate one concrete point: since God's command is His Word, which is uncreated, the spirit, which belongs to God's command, is also uncreated.

It is difficult to discern Kalābādhī's own position on the ontological status of the spirit due to a certain textual problem in *Introduction to the School of Sufism*.[77] But when we come to the commentary upon Kalābādhī's text by Abū Ibrāhīm Mustamlī Bukhārī (d. 434/1043) in what is likely the first book on Sufism in the Persian language,[78] the spirit is described as being in no way eternal.[79] Be that as it may, ʿAyn al-Quḍāt is happy to say that the spirit is eternal, and this because it is inextricably linked to God's creative power and His uncreated command.

> When the beauty of the spirit is put on display, wherever the rays of this beauty reach, it gives worth to that thing and that thing finds worth. O dear friend! *Say, "The spirit is of the command of my Lord"*[80] is itself a complete explanation, but only for the people of recognition. This is because the spirit is of the command, and the command of God is desire and power. Listen to this verse: *His command when He desires a thing is only to say to it "Be!," and it is.*[81] (*T* 149–150, §202)

> The spirit is from the entirety of the command. Thus, the spirit is the command, not the commanded; it is the doer, not the done; it is the subjugating, not the subjugated. (*T* 150, §203)

Q 15:92 and 38:72 state that God's spirit relates to His existentiating breath—the source of all life itself—and thus animates the human body.

> The spirit was sent from the world of God to the body. This is, *I breathed into him of My spirit*.[82] Wait until *thus have We revealed unto thee a spirit of Our command*[83] appears to you. Then it will tell you the meaning of *they ask thee about the spirit. Say, "The spirit is of the command of my Lord."*[84] (*T* 148–149, §201)

> Alas! I do not know what you will understand! I am saying that when the love of *He loves them*[85] charges forth with desire, desire charges forth with the command: *His command when He desires a thing is only to say to it "Be!," and it is.*[86] What is this command? *Say, "The spirit is of the command of my Lord"*[87] testifies to what the command is and what it is for. The command alchemically transforms the dot of servanthood—what you call the "body." (*T* 156, §210)

When God says *"Be!"* or when He causes things to exist by virtue of His breath, what emerges from His command and breath falls under their purview. But the spirit is of God's command, and all creation results from God's in-breathing of His spirit. Whichever way we look at it, the spirit is ultimately uncreated and eternal.

> The spirit is not from the created world; it is from the world of the Creator and has the attribute of eternity and Beginninglessness. (*T* 150, §203)

ʿAyn al-Quḍāt adds a further nuance to his treatment of the spirit. The spirit of the Prophet—or what he likes to call the "spirit of Muṣṭafā" (P. *jān-i Muṣṭafā*) and the "spirit of Muhammad" (P. *jān-i Muḥammad*)—is the means by which ʿAyn al-Quḍāt himself imparts knowledge to his students. First, God's spirit communicates with the spirit most like it and closest to it, that of the spirit of Muhammad. The Prophet's spirit in turn relates the message from God to the heart of ʿAyn al-Quḍāt. The Shaykh then passes these teachings from his heart on to his disciples by way of spoken and written words.

> Whatever you read in and hear from the *Letters* and dictations of this helpless one, you have not heard from my tongue—you have heard it from my heart; you have heard it from the spirit of Muṣṭafā. And whatever you have heard from the spirit of Muṣṭafā, you have heard from God: *he does not speak out of caprice. It is naught but a revelation!*[88] Another explication: *Whosoever obeys the Messenger has obeyed God.*[89] *Surely those who pledge allegiance unto thee only pledge allegiance unto God. The hand of God is over their hands*[90] also has this meaning. *They ask thee about the spirit. Say, "The*

> *spirit is of the command of my Lord"*[91] is the source of all of this.[92] (*T* 17, §26)

One of the implications of this passage is that the spirit of the Prophet is the direct cause and even agent for the inrushes that come to ʿAyn al-Quḍāt's heart. This is why the Shaykh states that through the recital of certain litanies involving the aspirant's immersion into the words of the Shahada, he has received many spiritual openings (P. *futūḥī-yi rūhī*).[93] Then he cites one special supplication (*duʿāʾ*)[94] and extols its value: "This supplication is written in the heart of the Preserved Tablet. The reciter of this supplication is none other than Muhammad, and all others are little children!"[95] If, like ʿAyn al-Quḍāt, we can be with the Prophet, then we will become "men." The only way to make progress in this direction is to walk the royal path to the court of the King, as many have done before us.

Wayfaring and Seeking

ʿAyn al-Quḍāt places a premium on the human attainment of repose and felicity, which can only be attained by following the spiritual path (*ṭarīqa*; P. *rāh*). The one who takes this journey is called a *sālik* or wayfarer, and the task of wayfaring is referred to as *sulūk*.

> Be certain that you have no task other than to arrive at repose, as much as you can. (*N* I, 87, §117)

> Sincerity in seeking is itself the condition. (*T* 22, §33)

> Every perfection that man reaches entails a deficiency of his perfection in the face of Perfection. (*N* III, 397, §219)

> O chevalier! The science of inheritance is wayfaring, not the inheritance from mother and father. (*N* I, 225, §371)

> O friend! If you want to reach these realities, you must undertake wayfaring and give yourself entirely to it. (*N* I, 86, §117)

> There are many paths to the Real. But of all paths, this path is the most marvelous, the rarest, and the least dangerous. (*N* I, 274, §454)

> When the moment comes, it will show itself: *Soon shall I show you My signs; so seek not to hasten Me!*[96] And seek so that you may quickly find: *Perhaps God will bring something new to pass thereafter.*[97] When you go, you will arrive and see. But so long as you do not go, you will not arrive: *Have they not journeyed upon the earth and observed?*[98] *"Was not God's earth vast enough that you might have migrated therein?"*[99] refers to journeying and traveling. If you travel, you will see the wonders of the world in every waystation: *Whosoever emigrates in the way of God will find upon the earth many a refuge and abundance.*[100] In every waystation advice will be given to you, and advice you will take: *And remind, for surely the reminder benefits the believers.*[101] (*T* 13, §19)

> The believer at the end of the path is a bird who flies in the divine world. Without means and without a plan, his sustenance is brought to him. . . . What is this sustenance? The encounter with God: "There is no repose for the believer apart from the encounter with God."[102] (*T* 70, §97)

ʿAyn al-Quḍāt says that God will always show the way to the one earnestly in search of Him.[103] Seeking (*ṭalab*) and discipleship (P. *irādat*) are therefore necessary conditions for the spiritual life.

> O dear, great friend! The first thing for the seeker and the most important goal for the truthful aspirant is seeking and discipleship, namely seeking the Real and reality. He should constantly be on the path of seeking until seeking shows him the way. (*T* 19, §29)

Lest one surmise that the path to God is somehow "out there," the Shaykh reminds us that this is certainly not the case. The path to God is inside the self.

> O friend! The path must also be sought in the self. *"This indeed is My path made straight; so follow it."*[104] Ibn ʿAbbās

> said that the straight path is the road of the Sharia in the world. Anyone who is on the straight path of the Sharia is indeed on the straight path of reality, and anyone who missteps on the path loses his own reality and throws himself into error. The path is the inner reality of man. (*T* 289–290, §378)

> The path to God is neither on earth nor in the heavens. Moreover, it is neither in Paradise nor upon the Throne.[105] The path to God is in your inner reality. *And within yourselves*[106] refers to this. (*T* 286–287, §373)

To be more specific, the path to God is inside the heart, which is where God resides.

> The seekers of God search for Him inside themselves because He is in the heart, and the heart is in their inner reality. This is strange to you, but whatever is in the heavens and on the earth, God has created all of it in you. Whatever has been created in the Tablet, the Pen, and Paradise, its like has been created in your makeup and inner reality. And whatever is in the divine world, its reflection appears in your spirit. (*T* 287, §373)

> I said, "O King! How can I search for You?
> And how can I even describe Your honor?"
> He said, "Search for Me on neither the Throne nor in Paradise.
> But in your own heart, for in the heart is where I dwell." (*T* 24, §36)

> One day someone asked Muṣṭafā, "Where is God?" He said, "In the hearts of His servants"[107]—He must be sought in the hearts of His servants. This is the meaning of *He is with you wheresoever you are.*[108] (*T* 148, §201)

> O dear friend! The path to God is not from the right and left, from above and below, from far and near. The path to God is in the heart and is one step: "Leave yourself and come!"[109] (*T* 92, §131)

> Do you know what I am saying? I am saying that the seeker must not search for God in the Garden, this world, or in the next world—he should not seek in whatever he knows and sees. The very path of the seeker is inside of him. He must take the path in himself: *and within yourselves—do you not see?*[110] All existents are the heart-traveling seeker: there is no path to God better than the path of the heart. "The heart is the house of God"[111] also has this meaning. (*T* 23, §35)

The more one travels the path as an individual seeker (*ṭālib*), the more he comes to realize that he is, in fact, not the seeker but the one who is sought (*maṭlūb*). Herein lies the secret of wayfaring—it is not the desire of a person that takes him to God, for God's desire is prior to his desire. Insofar as the seeker is real, God is the seeker and the seeker is the sought; but insofar as the seeker is unreal, God is both the Seeker and the Sought.

> When seeking lifts the niqab of exaltedness from its lovely face and removes the burqa, the seeker's entirety will be ravaged in such a way—from the seeker this much will appear—that he will discern whether he is a seeker or not. The Sought will accept him. This is the state of "Whoever seeks and perseveres shall find."[112] (*T* 19, §29)
>
> O dear friend! From the perspective of form, seekers are in two groups: the seekers and the sought. The seeker is the one who searches for reality until he finds it. The sought is the one for whom reality searches until it finds intimacy with him. (*T* 19, §30)
>
> When you reach the Sought, searching is also a veil on the path. (*T* 24, §36)
>
> Concerning a group of the Prophet's community, it has been explained: "He who draws near to Me a hand's span, I draw near to him an arm's span. He who draws near to Me an arm's span, I draw near to him two arm spans. And he who comes to Me walking, I come to him running."[113] If there is one step from the seeker, there are two pulls

> from the Sought. However, in reality, the seeker himself is the Sought. If He is not sought,[114] He does not "seek"; and if awareness of Him is not cultivated, He will not be "aware." (*T* 20, §31)

Renunciation

One of the guiles of the path, and something that hardens the substance of the soul, is the idea that one has some kind of agency whereby he is doing the wayfaring, the spiritual struggle, and so forth. Such an attitude can quickly lead to pride and self-admiration on the one hand, and a false sense of the nature of reality on the other. After all, as ʿAyn al-Quḍāt insists, there is nothing in existence but God. Wayfarers thus must give up any and all pretense, including their own sense of self-worth and accomplishment. They are nothing and have nothing. A logical corollary of this position is that, if there is no world to give up and indeed nothing in actuality to renounce, then there is fundamentally no value to be placed on such things as renunciation (*zuhd*). For those who have attained spiritual realization (P. *muḥaqqiqān*), the true renunciant is the one who is not, for only God is.

> For the realizers, "renunciation" and "renunciant" are nothing. This is because the world in itself does not have worth such that the one who abandons it becomes a "renunciant."[115] (*T* 311, §409)

> In relation to the life of the next world, the life of this world appears as a speck. *The day they see it, it will be as if they had tarried but an evening or the morning thereof*[116] itself explains this. Listen to what Muṣṭafā says: "This world with respect to the next world is nothing but the likeness of one of you when he dips his finger in the ocean—let him consider what it is that the finger returns with."[117] Abandoning this paltry thing is obligatory. But this abandoning is not renunciation. (*T* 312, §410)

> I mean, this world and the next world do not belong to the renunciant that he should abandon it. They belong to God! How can the renunciant abandon something that does

> not belong to him? Thus, renunciation has no meaning at all. (*T* 312, §410)

> Wait until the next world is also forsaken so that all there is is *the truth of certainty*.[118] *The truth of certainty* is a tremendous affair and a high rank! (*T* 72, §99)

> That which belongs to God cannot be abandoned. Whatever is the expectation and goal of the wayfarer is his object of worship, and abandoning an object of worship is inconceivable. Thus, there is never a renunciant or renunciation. (*T* 312–313, §410)

The Ripened Master

Among all of the remarkable people whom ʿAyn al-Quḍāt had the opportunity to meet, he tells us of a certain "little girl in Baghdad who gives news of peoples' incoming thoughts, which is not at all possible for others."[119] Although only seventeen or eighteen years old,[120] she had a great deal of knowledge without formal learning[121] and could even perceive colors despite being physically blind.[122] But ʿAyn al-Quḍāt insists that these impressive feats are not enough for traveling the path.

The girl from Baghdad was given to much travel. This, the Shaykh notes, was a major cause for the dissipation of her spiritual potential, although she was completely oblivious to the problem.[123] But what she lacked most was a ripened master (P. *pīr-i pukhta*) who could show her how to travel inwardly.[124] "Ripened master" is a key expression in the Shaykh's writings, although he only uses it four times.[125] It refers to a mature and experienced Sufi guide, namely someone who has successfully traveled the path and is consequently able to help other wayfarers along in their homeward journeys.

> The first counsel that the master gives to the aspirant is, "Do not tell anyone about your apparitions!" (*T* 32, §46)

> The mark of the master of the traveled path is that all of the aspirant's actions and statements, from beginning to end, are known to him. (*T* 30, §44)

> Who is "the one firmly rooted in knowledge?"[126] Read: *Nay, it is but clear signs in the breasts of those who have been given knowledge.*[127] Where shall this breast be sought? *What of one whose breast God has expanded for submission so that he follows a light from his Lord? Woe to those whose hearts are hardened!*[128] Where shall this light be found? *Surely in that is a reminder for whosoever has a heart.*[129] This is all lost to one who has lost his way, but it is all clear to a guide. It is for this reason that Muṣṭafā said, "There is a kind of hidden knowledge that is not known to knowers, except for knowers of God. Thus, when they speak of it, none denies it except those who are heedless of God."[130] (*T* 5, §6)

> One must seek and search for the reality and meaning of the master, not his body and form. For in witnessing the master, the aspirant will find one hundred thousand benefits. (*T* 31–32, §45)

> If you want, also listen to Muṣṭafā, where he says, "Seek bounty from the merciful ones of my community, living under their shelter."[131] This is permission for the master to come with as much of himself as he wants in nurturing the aspirant. This nurturing keeps the aspirant occupied with worship and inquiring into the states of the master. (*T* 332–333, §439)

> If the master orders the aspirant to do an act in opposition to his religion, he should do it. For if, in trying to conform to the master of the way he does not oppose his own religion, he would still be an aspirant of his own religion, not an aspirant of the master! (*N* I, 270, §448)

A ripened master is very much like a doctor who treats his patients, administering medicine to them in accordance with their illnesses and in conformity with their natures.[132] Without the help of a spiritual doctor the girl from Baghdad is nothing but an ill patient, despite the façade of being in perfectly good and even extraordinary health. In other words, by not having a master to aid her, she was a spiritual novice, regardless of her impressive knowledge and clairvoyant abilities.[133]

> Those who have put the treatment and the doctor aside, it would be better for them to sink in their illness! For, *Had God known of any good in them, He would have made them to hear.*[134] Thus, since a discerning doctor upon the path of wayfaring is necessary—according to the consensus of the masters—it is obligatory to have one. From this perspective it is said, "He who has no master has no religion."[135] (*T* 10–11, §15)

> When there is a master, all is easy. But when there is not, there is danger. "There is no religion for one who has no master" is the statement of the masters. (*N* I, 74, §96)

> When you devote fifty years of your life to serving the master with your head held high, one day you will fall under his gaze and attain every good fortune. Do you know what you are hearing? "He who does not taste, does not recognize." (*N* II, 368, §573)

> Now, the illness of religion and Islam is receptive to one color. "Islam is built upon five"[136] itself has given the specific prescriptions—there are five prescriptions that are the treatment and medicine for all believers. But the inner work and the way of the heart do not have restriction and measure. It follows that for every situation there must be a master: a discerning doctor who can treat the aspirant and prescribe a different remedy for every different ailment. (*T* 10, §15)

As ʿAyn al-Quḍāt notes, the presence of a spiritual guide in one's life is a divine gift.[137] By following the master and listening to his instruction, the aspirant can be confident that he is using this gift properly. After all, what better way would there be for one to use a gift given to him other than to do so in the way that its bestower intended that it be used? As a gift from God, the master's desire is thus an embodiment of God's desire, which means that the master's command is tantamount to God's command.

> The command of the master is the command of God. (*T* 35, §49)

> Every act that the master commands the aspirant to do is a divine robe of honor that he has given to him. Wherever the aspirant will be, he will be under the protection of that robe of honor.[138] (*N* III, 434, §274)

> If the master tells the aspirant to do a certain invocation, or to go on a certain pilgrimage, or to give something in charity, or to fast, all of these will protect the aspirant. . . . This is because it is not the command of the master. It is the command of God: *Whosoever obeys the Messenger has obeyed God;*[139] *Surely those who pledge allegiance unto thee only pledge allegiance unto God.*[140] (*N* III, 434, §274)

> When you fear the master, you fear God: *Whosoever obeys the Messenger has obeyed God.*[141] "The knowers are the heirs of the Prophets."[142] When you neglect the master's command, you neglect God's command: *Surely those who call thee from behind the apartments, most of them understand not.*[143] (*N* I, 47, §54)

In reality, devotion and service to the master spell devotion and service to God.

> As long as you do not become a master-worshipper, you will not be a God-worshipper. Do you imagine that it was not from this perspective that Muṣṭafā said,[144] "A man is abundant with his brother"? This is the master's nurturing. As for the aspirant, he has been bound to a precondition: "A man follows the religion of his intimate friend"[145]—that is, a man should follow the religion of his brother and master. O friend! There is a station that is called "intimate friendship." In that station, there is no servanthood—all is intimate friendship. (*T* 333, §439)

Despite the fact that service to the master is the condition sine qua non of the spiritual life, our author is careful not to attribute superhuman status to him and maintains that no master is infallible (*maʿṣūm*).[146] Thus, one should not search for this attribute in him.[147] It is much better for the aspirant to look past his spiritual master's outward form and into his inner reality, which can only be seen with the eye of the heart (P. *chashm-i dil*).

> In witnessing the master, the aspirant will find one hundred thousand benefits! (*T* 32–33, §45)

Without a guide one will surely err, losing his way even when he thinks that he is walking in the right direction.

> What will help the one seeking to purify his inner self is for him to wholeheartedly keep the company of people who know by way of tasting, spending time with them and serving them. By "people who know by way of tasting" I mean those who purify their inner selves from vile character traits to such an extent that, from God's generosity, such knowledge pours down on them that is impossible to attain by acts of devotion alone. (*Z* §132)

> The seeker's greatest felicity lies in entirely devoting his spirit and heart to serving one of the people who have arrived, who is annihilated in God and in witnessing Him. (*Z* §133)

> Be wary of being deluded by your knowledge, thus busying yourself with wayfaring but without a leader to guide you and being misguided in ways that you do not even know. (*Z* §137)

> [O]ne of the errors that overcomes the learned when they entertain the idea of wayfaring is that they think that they can do without someone who recognizes the dangers of the path, and who can guide them every step of the way. How rare it is for one of the rationalist theologians and philosophers to be free from this self-admiration, which produces pride in not wanting to follow the recognizers! (*Z* §137)

Just as it is an obligation upon an aspirant to follow a master, so too is there an obligation upon the master to direct those students who come to him. This is because the master's function is to be God's vicegerent (*khalīfa*) on earth, representing Him and guiding others to Him.

> It is also obligatory for the master to accept this vicegerency, as instructing aspirants is an obligation upon the path. (*T* 11, §15)

The greatest difference between a master and an aspirant is that the former is dead to himself and lives in God, the supreme Self. An aspirant, on the other hand, is still not dead to himself. Paradoxically, this means that the student seeks to relinquish himself, whereas the master, having already done so, can only aid the student in his quest for self-transcendence by helping him as a "self." In other words, so selfless is the master that he can only properly guide his students when he operates within the normal confines of human embodiment and selfhood.

> Perhaps you have not heard what that great one said: "All of the aspirants desire the station of the masters, but all of the masters wish for the station of the aspirants."[148] This is because the masters have come out of themselves. How will anyone who is with himself find good fortune and joy? Perhaps it is from this perspective that that great one said, "All of those in the world desire to be taken away from themselves for one moment, but I desire to be given back to myself for one moment." The aspirants are with themselves. But the one who is with himself has no share in uniqueness and selflessness. (*T* 242, §315)

Those who live in the divine Presence need not consult a master any longer. Free of the dross of duality, their hearts are pure and pristine—they need only consult their hearts to know the will of God and thus fully live and act in the present moment.

> O friend! Hearts are divided into two types. One faces the Pen of God and is written upon—*God has inscribed faith in their hearts*.[149] The right hand of God is the scribe. Thus, whatever one does not know, when he returns to his own heart, he comes to know by this means. (*T* 9, §13)

Those who are not at this stage are of the second type.

> The second type is still unripe, and a raw heart does not face the Pen of God. When there is someone whose heart is a mirror and a Tablet for the Pen of God, the one with an unripe heart can ask him, and then he will know. From this perspective, he will know what it is to see God in the mirror of the master's spirit. (*T* 9, §13)

> If a person does not have this worthiness and readiness, namely that he know by means of his own heart, he should seek and ask the heart of another person who has found this worthiness—*Ask the people of the Reminder if you know not*[150] so that someone else's heart is your mirror. (*T* 9, §12)

A spiritual master is someone who is called by God to position the mirror of his heart outward so that others whose hearts are imperfect may look into it and see God in it. But it is not only the aspirant who sees through the heart. In order for the master to make himself available to the aspirant, he has to both be in himself and see his own self, which can only happen when he sees himself in the impure heart and soul of the aspirant.

> Do you not know what discipleship is? It is to see God in the mirror of the master's spirit. (*N* I, 269, §446)

> The master is the mirror of the aspirant, for in him the aspirant sees God. The aspirant is the mirror of the master, for in him the master sees himself. Abū Bakr[151] never said, "No god but God" without "Muhammad is the Messenger of God" because he saw what *whosoever obeys the Messenger has obeyed God*[152] is. (*N* I, 269, §446)

> The master sees himself in the mirror of the aspirant's soul, and the aspirant sees God in the soul of the master. (*T* 9, §13)

> The master is a mirror for the aspirant, for he can see God in the master, and the aspirant is a mirror for the master, for he can see himself in the soul of the aspirant. (*T* 30, §44)

It is not only aspirants and masters who see themselves in the hearts and souls of others. The Shaykh tells us that God also sees Himself in them. To be sure, we can only catch a glimpse of ʿAyn al-Quḍāt's vision in this regard with reference to his complex Sufi epistemology, to which we now turn.

Figure 8. ʿAyn al-Quḍāt Square (Hamadan, Iran)

7

Knowledge Transcendent

ʿAyn al-Quḍāt sees the cosmos as a play of mirrors, each of which reflects an aspect of the Divine to a special kind of knower while also serving as a locus for the Self-perception of the All-Knowing.

هو

Brothers and Mirrors

In the previous chapter we encountered the well-known Hadith, "The believer is a mirror of the believer."[1] This tradition is typically invoked in contexts of spiritual pedagogy. When, for example, two believers spend time together, each will reflect some of the attributes (be they positive or negative) that the other has in himself. When a person sees his attributes through the mirror of a fellow believer, he is able to understand himself better, thank God for his positive attributes, and change his negative ones.

Those like ʿAyn al-Quḍāt never fail to point out that "believer" (*muʾmin*) is also a divine name. That is to say, God the Believer reflects to those who believe in Him their own attributes, and they, likewise, reflect His attributes back to Him. This is why Basṭāmī exclaimed, "O my Lord! You are a mirror for me and I am a mirror for You!,"[2] and why Aḥmad Ghazālī sang, "O God! The mirror of Your lovely face is this heart."[3]

> Alas! "The believer is a mirror of the believer." That is, He sees Himself in us. "The believer is the brother of the believer." That is, we see ourselves in His light. O friend! He is a believer in our servanthood and we are believers in His lordship. Thus, we are both believers. (*T* 274, §359)

> Alas! What do you hear? *Peace, the Believer, the Protector*[4] are God's names. Since He is the Believer, and Muṣṭafā is a believer, and the wayfarer is a believer—all are mirrors for one another. "The believer is a mirror of the believer" has explained all of this. (*T* 271, §355)

The Shaykh goes on to tell us that when a believer sees a believer in his mirror, and vice versa, the bonds of brotherhood are formed. They now become one in fraternity, seeing each other not in the mirror of belief but in the "mirror of brotherhoods" (P. *āyina-yi ikhwāniyyat*).

> First, brotherhoods are put in order and unification obtains. Then, one properly sees "The believer is the brother of the believer" in the mirror of brotherhoods. (*T* 271–272, §355)

The majority of authorities in the tradition maintain that the status of being the Prophet's Companion (*ṣaḥābī*) is limited to those individuals who met him and believed in him when he was alive on earth. ʿAyn al-Quḍāt tells us that the greatest of his Companions—like Abū Bakr and ʿUmar—also enjoyed the special status of brotherhood with the Prophet because of their intense love for him. As one would imagine, for the Shaykh this companionship and brotherhood are not limited to those who encountered the Prophet during his lifetime. One can become the Prophet's Companion by loving his Companions and conforming to their character traits on the one hand, and by loving the great Friends of God who came after them on the other.[5]

That the Prophet himself had spiritual Brothers is evidenced by one of his statements, which the Shaykh cites often.[6] In it, the Prophet exclaims, "O how I long to meet my Brothers!"[7] Longing that is divine in nature is, as ʿAyn al-Quḍāt states, "on account of presence and vision, not absence and deprivation."[8] It can thus be said that one is already with the Prophet and is his Brother if he truly loves him, which is one of the meanings of the well-known Prophetic saying, "A man is with the one he loves."[9]

This kind of realized love is tantamount to a state of true submission (*islām*) to God. When one is in such as state, he becomes an "Arab" in accordance with another Prophetic saying, "Whoever submits is Arab, and the believer's heart is Arab."[10] For ʿAyn al-Quḍāt, such an "Arab" is given the supreme gift of becoming the Prophet's Brother.[11] One characteristic of the Prophet's Brother, who is synonymous with the Friend of God, is that he can easily peer through the veil of causal phenomena, seeing everything in existence for what it really is. This takes us to the Sufi science of reading the signs (*āyāt*) of God in the cosmos and within the human self.

Commenting on the Quran's unique semiotics, Sachiko Murata notes that it is fundamentally concerned with the fact "that we must perceive things not so much for what they are in themselves but for what they tell us of something beyond themselves."[12] The Friend of God has perfected this operation and beholds all things as indicators that point to God. A couplet that Sufis love to quote in this context is that of the famous Abbasid poet Abū'l-ʿAtāhiya (d. 211/826):

> In everything there is a sign
> indicating that He is one.[13]

ʿAyn al-Quḍāt of course accepts this perspective and also introduces the symbology of mirrors in this context as something like its natural complement: we can say that all things point to God, and we can also say that they mirror divine reality. What we behold are signs, traces, and reflections of the divine order itself. This is why the Shaykh is of the view that every aspect of the cosmos can serve as a mirror for the vision (*muʿāyana*) of God. He explains the logic of this position in the context of his commentary upon Abū Bakr's famous statement, "I do not look at anything except that I see God in it."[14]

> Each thing is a mirror for the vision of Him—one finds benefit and recognition in each thing. (*T* 56, §75)

Despite the fact that everything in the cosmos is a mirror that reflects rays from the divine Sun, there is only one mirror that can display It in all of Its manifest glory. Beholding this mirror, we can see God in as unmediated a manner as possible.

> Looking at the sun of *God is the light of the heavens and the earth*[15] without the mirror of Muhammad's beauty will burn the eyes. But by means of this mirror, the beauty of the sun can be observed continuously. (*T* 103, §145)

Knowers and Recognizers

In order to behold the mirror of the Prophet's spirit one cannot simply be a knower (*ʿālim*). He must rise above his conventional epistemic faculties and become a recognizer (*ʿārif*). An early Sufi saying tells us that "The recognizer is above what he says, but the knower is below what he says."[16] This in many ways nicely summarizes ʿAyn al-Quḍāt's perspective on the chasm between the knowledge of the realized Sufi and the knowledge that is gained through the usual means of learning. It also explains why, after giving a standard theological explanation that proves the existence of God, the Shaykh notes, "This is correct, but it is not the path of the Prophets and the Friends."[17]

Such is the case because the recognizer is taught directly by God, whereas the commonplace knower, even if he is a "knower" of God, relies upon his own intellectual efforts to acquire the objects of his knowledge. From this perspective, the self-absorbed philosophers and theologians who rationally exert themselves are closer to ignorance than to real knowledge, which is recognition (P. *maʿrifat*) conferred from up above.

> What you know is not recognition of God. So have etiquette! (*N* I, 92, §126)

> You say, "Can I perceive recognition of God through intellectual proof?" O chevalier! Of what use is the intellect for the one who does not recognize Him? And nobody recognizes Him. (*N* I, 92, §126)

> O friend! A group among the philosophers and rational theologians call themselves "recognizers." *That is the extent of their knowledge.*[18] They imagine that, from the path of

> nonsense, a person will arrive at recognition. No, never! O friend! What business do I have with this? (*N* I, 113, §163)

> How can the worshippers of caprice talk like the men on the path of God? The one who still fears God's creation and does not fear God is, in the eyes of the people of the path, an unbeliever who has not even arrived at the station of associators! How is he worthy enough to speak like one of the people of recognition? O chevalier! In the grasp of the recognizer, the seven heavens and the earth are paltry. If he should say, "I am the Real!,"[19] excuse him! (*N* I, 113, §163)

In contrast to those who are below what they say, those who are destined for recognition are above what they say because their statements cannot encompass the palpable directness of their mode of knowing.

> The supra-sensory realities that I have discussed in these chapters are witnessed by way of tasting in a manner not less than the intellect's witnessing primary concepts; it is just that it is only possible to convey these supra-sensory realities by means of these words. The truth—*in which there is no doubt*[20]—is that "Whoever recognizes God becomes speechless."[21] That is, he has no way to convey to people's minds the meaning he has understood by way of tasting. (Z §122)

> All knowledge in relation to *the truth of certainty*[22] is just like the imagination of an imagining man in relation to the imagined intellect, or the forms that are seen through the medium of a mirror and the like. (*T* 72, §99)

> Apart from this world we have another world.
> Apart from Hell and Paradise, there is another place.
> The free ones live through another spirit—
> for that pure gem there is another mine.
> Worthlessness and scoundrelhood are love's capital—
> for Quran-reciter and renunciant there is another world.
> But, we are told, this is yet another sign.
> For apart from this tongue, there is another tongue.[23] (*T* 4, §5)

Another way ʿAyn al-Quḍāt explains the difference between recognition and regular knowledge is to draw on natural imagery. Those who are not taught directly by God and receive knowledge from themselves and others have knowledge that is sterile and fruitless, much like dry land. But those who are taught directly by God have deep and vast knowledge, much like an expansive ocean. Having lost themselves in the ocean of knowledge, they realize that they do not know anything and have nothing to hold on to.

> What can one draw from the ocean? So long as you do not become an inhabitant of the ocean, whatever you find will have a measure and a limit. How does the navigator limit and describe the ocean, and how does he draw from it? He pours back whatever he draws because he has a station in the ocean. But what news does land have of the ocean? *Corruption has appeared on land and in the ocean.*[24] Whatever is learned from people is land and land-like, and whatever is learned from God—*The All-Merciful taught the Quran*[25]—is ocean and ocean-like. And the ocean has no end: *And they encompass nothing of His knowledge.*[26] (*T* 8, §11)

> Alas! Knowledge does not have an end, and we will not reach an end. Of course, we want to embrace Him, but we will not reach Him. We have neither knowledge nor ignorance, neither seeking nor abandonment, neither accomplishment nor non-accomplishment; we are neither drunk nor aware, neither with ourselves nor with Him. What tribulation is more difficult than this?! (*T* 353, §468)

A major difference between the recognizer and the knower is that the latter witnesses the order of time and existence on a purely outward and superficial level while the recognizer perceives them as they really are. Her exalted vision allows her to see that all created things continually wink in and out of existence in accordance with the principle of *tajdīd al-khalq* or the "perpetual renewal of creation," which is signaled by Q 50:15.[27]

Since it is only God who exists and is the only one who is truly living, everything other than God is sustained at every moment by His creative power. The conventional knower, beholding as she does only the outward nature of things, habitually associates existential continuity with the created order when it is not actually present or real. The recognizer on the other hand peers through this illusion and sees how God's creative act perpetually sustains all things that, in themselves, cannot endure for a single moment. She finds herself no longer implicated in the cosmic flow and experience of the usual order of time, space, and creation.

> Every existent perpetually exists and is made perpetually continuous through *the Living, the Self-Abiding*.[28] In every moment, another existence similar to the one preceding it is renewed for it. The recognizers clearly witness this, whereas it is impossible for the knower to perceive it. So reflect continuously on what I have said. . . . Perhaps the reality of these matters will be disclosed to you! (Z §121)

It can even be stated that the recognizer witnesses the perpetual nature of creation in accordance with the degree to which she is perpetually in the remembrance of God. The Shaykh refers to this state of constant invocation, which is the most important thing a disciple can learn from a spiritual master, as "heart-work" (P. *ʿamal-i dil*).

> Nobody but a knower of God has hidden knowledge. I do not know if you have ever known who the knower of God is: "Seek knowledge, even to China."[29] You must go to China and beyond; then you will find "The knowers of my community are like the Israelite Prophets."[30] Upon which path must one go? The path of work. I am not speaking of body-work. I am speaking of the path of heart-work. It is well known that the Prophet has said, "Whoever acts in accordance with what he knows, God will bequeath to him knowledge of what he does not know."[31] (*T* 5–6, §7)

The Scale of the Intellect

The Shaykh also sheds light on the gaping gulf between the knower and the recognizer when he discusses the nature, power, and limits of the human intellect (*ʿaql*). On the one hand, the intellect is an essential, God-given scale (*mīzān; qisṭās*) by which truth can be measured against falsehood and right can be discerned from wrong.

> O friend! Do you know what the scale is? It is the scale of the intellect: "Take yourselves to account before you are taken to account."[32] Alas! Read, *We have indeed sent Our Messengers with clear proofs, and We sent down with them the Book and the scale.*[33] This scale is the intellect by which the weight of all beliefs, statements, and acts are measured.[34] This *straight scale*[35] is in one's inner reality. (*T* 290, §379)

Be that as it may, the scale of the intellect is limited in the kinds of things that its pans can measure. With respect to the realities of all things (*ḥaqāʾiq jamīʿ al-ashyāʾ*), a rationalist theologian, a philosopher, or anyone else who wants to know them with the scale of the intellect will always fall short. The Shaykh explains why this is so.

> The rationalist theologian who desires such knowledge is like a man who sees a scale in which gold is being weighed and desires that a mountain, for example, be weighed against it. But that is impossible. However, it does not mean that the scale is untrue in what it can weigh and measure. (*Z* §186)

The deeper, more profound, and weightier the reality, the less amenable is it to the scale of the intellect. This is particularly true of the three pillars of faith (*īmān*)—the realities of God, prophecy (*nubuwwa*), and eschatology (*maʿād*).

> The intellect is a valid scale, and its measurements are certain and real with no unreality in it; and it is a just scale: it is inconceivable that it can ever be unjust. Having said that, when an intelligent person desires to weigh everything against the intellect, even the matters of the next world, the reality of prophecy, and the realities of the Beginningless divine attributes, that is a desire for the impossible. (*Z* §187)

> [E]ach existent has absolutely no relation to the embrace of Beginningless knowledge, so how is it fitting for the intellect to desire to perceive it? (*Z* §58)

> God is above the intellect and encompasses it, so how is it conceivable that the intellect should encompass Him and His attributes when the part can never encompass the whole? The intellect is one of the tiny specks of existence effectuated by God. (Z §58)

It can be asked how the intellect, being entirely immaterial, can fail to grasp the realities of faith, which themselves are also immaterial. What the Shaykh has in mind is not that the intellect cannot know them; indeed it can, but only at a level that itself is not adequate to what these realities are. To truly understand God, prophecy, and eschatology requires a more transcendent epistemological platform, or what ʿAyn al-Quḍāt calls the "stage beyond the intellect."

Beyond the Intellect

ʿAyn al-Quḍāt adapts the phrase "the stage beyond the intellect" (*al-ṭawr warāʾ al-ʿaql*) from Ghazālī.[36] He also calls it "something else beyond knowledge and the intellect" (*shayʾ ākhar warāʾ al-ʿilm wa'l-ʿaql*), "what is beyond knowledge and the intellect" (*mā warāʾ al-ʿilm wa'l-ʿaql*), "the stage after the intellect" (*al-ṭawr baʿd al-ʿaql*), and simply "beyond the intellect" (P. *warā-yi ʿaql*). In relation to the intellect, the stage beyond the intellect is as the soul is to the body.[37] Perceiving the stage beyond the intellect thus presents many mysteries to our ratiocinative faculties, similar to how the sight's objects of perception present mysteries to the sense of smell and primary concepts are utterly unknowable to the bodily senses.[38] Needless to say, in this world, the stage beyond the intellect can only be accessed by a bona fide recognizer.[39] From this perspective, all other knowledge is simply child's play.

> When something of this stage is in your soul, your thirst would simply not be satisfied even if all of the intelligibles were to pour down upon you all at once. As a hungry person will not be satisfied by water and a thirsty person will not be satisfied by bread, so too will the apprehension of intelligibles not satisfy the quest of the recognizer singled out by that stage beyond the intellect. (Z §54)

The Shaykh also explains that an intense light will appear inside of a person when the stage beyond the intellect is encountered.[40] This special stage thereby entails certainty in the aforementioned objects of faith, and is accompanied by further illumination and expansiveness of soul.

> When your heart has expanded for faith in the unseen, God will cause a light to pour into your inner self, the likes of which you have not witnessed before. This is one of the traces of that stage that appears after the stage of the intellect. So intensify your search, for that alone is what you need in order to find! (Z §176)

When its lights dawn upon the human soul, the desire to weigh eschatological realities against the scale of the intellect will slowly vanish.

> With the illumination of the light of the stage beyond the intellect, this desire will diminish, bit by bit, just as the light of the planets diminishes at the crack of dawn, bit by bit. (Z §188)

The intellect is a sure criterion for many objects of knowledge and the act of knowing brings with it a delight and joy that is itself immaterial. But a person cannot repose in God's beauty by virtue of the intellect alone, much less be propelled to pursue and taste the Object of his quest.

> The intellect delights in perceiving the existence of the Real. However, this is not a delight in the perception of His perfection. Rather, it is delight insofar as He is an object of knowledge, as is the case with other objects of knowledge, such as mathematics, medicine, and the like. (Z §65)

> One of the special attributes of the stage after the intellect is that when one perceives the existence of the Real there necessarily follows a tremendous longing for Him that cannot be conceived through expressions or a thorough search. (Z §65)

> Love is one of the things specific to the stage beyond the intellect. For those who have witnessed the states of love, there is no doubt that the intellect is far from perceiving these states. To the understanding of the person restricted by his intellect and who has not had an intimate taste of love, there is no way for the lover to convey the meaning of that love with which he is so intimate. That can only happen when such a person stands in the same position as the lover who tastes love. (*Z* §71)

Since the Object of knowledge is God, who is infinite, knowledge of God is infinite. The Shaykh therefore tells us that there is not just one stage, but many stages (*aṭwār*) beyond the intellect.

> [T]here are in fact many stages beyond the intellect—and none knows their number but God. (*Z* §60)

On one level, everyone will access at least the first stage beyond the intellect after death since it will correspond to an awareness of the reality of the afterlife—which is beyond the intellect—by virtue of existential, posthumous participation in it.

> [T]here are many stages, and every single person will inevitably reach the stage beyond the intellect, even if it is after death. (*Z* §184)

But unlike those who will access the first stage of the intellect after death, the recognizers can reach the higher stages beyond the intellect even while embodied in the present life.

> [I]t is impossible for everyone to reach the stages that are only possible for a few. Rather, it is true and necessary that, without shedding the body he is clothed in, a person can reach many stages beyond the intellect (which are beyond this world); but it is inconceivable that others can reach most of these stages, be it in this world or in the next. This is the truth that the recognizers witness by means of their insight, just as the intellect beholds the fact that ten is greater than one. (*Z* §184)

As we saw in the introduction, ʿAyn al-Quḍāt's position on the stage beyond the intellect was cited by his detractors as one of the reasons for his "heresy." They read it to mean that the Friends of God are superior to God's Prophets and Messengers. Before delving into the Shaykh's own presentation of the issue, it is important to know how he understands the Friends of God to be similar to the Prophets. As he affirms in his *Letters*, the Friends of God can witness the states of the afterlife even before dying, just as the Prophets can. The distinction has to do with the difference in the degree of intensity of this kind of witnessing, with the Prophets beholding these realities in a way that is more intense, vivid, and real than what the Friends of God witness.[41]

The Friends can even perform some of the miracles that the Prophets can perform, such as bringing the dead back to life, as was the case with ʿAyn al-Quḍāt. The great difference between the miracles done by the Prophets and those performed by the Friends of God is that the former take place out of some necessity linked with their prophetic function, whereas the latter occur only fortuitously.[42] As discussed in chapter 1, the Friends have charismatic gifts whereas the Prophets have miracles proper. The Shaykh is careful to point out that these observations do not mean that the Friends of God have a rank similar to or higher than that of the Prophets: "From these meanings that have been discussed, do not in any way understand by them that the Prophets are lower than the Friends in degree."[43] Prophets are one thing, and Friends of God are something else.

> The thought might occur to you that perhaps the friendship of the Friends is higher and better than prophecy. O dear friend! In this presence, the degree of messengerhood is one thing, and the distinction of proximity and friendship is quite another thing! (*T* 45, §62)[44]

The difference in degree between the Prophets and the Friends of God also ties into their difference in degree with respect to the stages beyond the intellect: the lower stages are accessible to the Friends of God, whereas the higher stages are only reserved for God's Prophets and Messengers. The Shaykh typically describes prophecy as being a stage that is beyond the general stage beyond the intellect, and more specifically as being beyond the stage of friendship (*walāya*), which itself is a stage beyond the intellect.

> The intellect of a person who has not been blessed with even a little experience of this stage will not accept its existence as true merely by way of premises. Faith in prophecy is almost impossible for him since prophecy is an expression of a stage beyond that stage. . . . And whoever does not believe in this is far away, essentially not accepting prophecy as true. (*Z* §67)

> What then do you think of those who disbelieve in the stage of friendship with God, which appears beyond the intellect, and beyond which the stage of prophecy appears? (*Z* §67)

Whatever stage beyond the intellect a person may attain, one thing is certain: the knowledge in question is no longer of a discursive kind. In other words, it is not a way of knowing that can be characterized by the standard subject/object dichotomy. This implies that ultimately knowledge, knower, and known are one, and that perception, perceiver, and perceived are one.

Self-Recognition

As noted in the introduction, the fourth chapter of *Paving the Path* is on self-recognition. In fact, ʿAyn al-Quḍāt says that the entire chapter is specifically dedicated to explaining the well-known Sufi saying, "He who recognizes himself recognizes his Lord."[45] The Shaykh explains the importance of the pursuit of self-recognition, noting that those who do not have it and thus do not recognize God are estranged (P. *bīgānī*) from their true selves.

> One must recognize himself so that he may recognize his Lord. They do not have self-recognition, so how can they have recognition of God?! They are estranged. (*T* 178, §236)

We have seen earlier how Dhū'l-Nūn famously said that he came to recognize God not through himself, but through God Himself. That is, since the self stands in the way of true knowledge of God, a person can never attain it through himself. He quite literally must seek it through God, the only real Self. The Shaykh explains this point as follows.

> But you are with yourself. When you find something, it is like finding yourself. The seekers and lovers of God seek Him through Him. So they find Him through Him. The veiled ones seek Him through themselves. So they see themselves, and have lost God. What do you hear? Do not consider this a trifling statement! If you want, listen to how Muṣṭafā explains and shows it: "The believer takes his religion from God and the hypocrite sets up his own opinion and takes his religion from it."[46] He said that the believer takes his religion from God, but the hypocrite takes it from his caprice. This is, *Hast thou considered the one who takes his caprice as his god?*[47] (*T* 319, §417)

We are also told that "through God" specifically means through God's light. Since light is synonymous with existence, it is the ground through which one can come to see his own self.

> The compass of His light consumes the entirety of our existence. This is the meaning of *Sight grasps Him not, but He grasps sight.*[48] Thus, in this station, man knows how to see his existence in the mirror of self-sufficient light. (*T* 273, §357)

> Alas! You heard *and whensoever We will, We shall entirely change their likenesses.*[49] What does it mean? Spend an hour with me so that you can know what *entirely change* means! It is God's light that enters man's makeup. (*T* 62–63, §85)

> How fine alchemical transformation is! Where is it from, and where is it going? *He follows a light from his Lord.*[50] It is light with light. (*T* 63, §85)

> When He wants us to see ourselves in His light—*Or have they not contemplated the dominion of the heavens and the earth?*[51]—His light assails our spirits: *"Surely kings, when they enter a town, corrupt it."*[52] (*T* 273, §357)

> This is the meaning of "My heart saw my Lord"[53]—we see ourselves in His light. (*T* 273, §357)

A good deal of ʿAyn al-Quḍāt's attention in outlining the steps to self-recognition is devoted to explaining how someone who is self-recognizing (P. *khwud-shinās*) will inevitably also become Muhammad-recognizing (P. *Muḥammad-shinās*), which itself will pave the way for recognizing God qua manifestation.

> When man reaches this station—namely that he becomes drunk from the wine of recognition—when he reaches the perfection of drunkenness and the end of his own finality, the spirit of Muhammad—*A Messenger has indeed come to you from yourselves*[54]—is displayed to him. "Blessed be the one who sees me and believes in me."[55] The robe of his passing days is prepared: he will find a wealth beyond which there is no other wealth. Whoever obtains recognition of his own self obtains recognition of the spirit of Muhammad. And whoever obtains recognition of the spirit of Muhammad has placed the foot of aspiration in recognizing the Essence of God. This is also the meaning of "He who sees me has seen the Real."[56] Whoever is not self-recognizing is not Muhammad-recognizing. What then is the state of the recognizer of God? (*T* 56–57, §77)

> There are three types of recognition of God. One is recognition of the Essence, the other recognition of God's attributes, and the other recognition of His actions and rulings. O dear friend! Recognition of God's actions and His rulings is obtained from self-recognition: *and within yourselves—do you not see?;*[57] *We shall show them Our signs upon the horizons and within themselves.*[58]
>
> The more perfect the self-recognition, the more perfect the recognition of God's actions. Then recognition of God's attributes is obtained, for recognition of the spirit of Muhammad is obtained: *A Messenger has indeed come to you from yourselves.*[59] As for recognizing God's Essence, who would have the gall? The Prophet himself said, "Reflect on God's blessings,[60] but do not reflect on God's Essence."[61] Apart from symbolic expressions, it is forbidden to try to explain recognition of God. (*T* 60, §81)

> "Glory to the one who has not given people a way to recognize Him except through the incapacity to recognize Him."[62] Anyone who has not been given a path to recognize His Howless Essence, nay, anyone who searches for the path of recognition of His Essence, a mirror is prepared for the spirit of his own reality, and he looks in that mirror—he recognizes the spirit of Muhammad. Thus, the mirror is prepared for the spirit of Muhammad. The mark of this mirror has come: "I saw my Lord on the night of the Ascension in the most beautiful form."[63] In this mirror, *Faces that Day shall be radiant, gazing upon their Lord*[64] is found, and a cry is given in the world: *They did not measure God with His true measure;*[65] that is, they did not recognize God with His true recognition. This station is high and rare. Here, nobody reaches, and nobody knows. (*T* 58–59, §79)

There is a most intimate connection between the knower and the known precisely because, as the Presocratic doctrine tells us, "Only like can know like." In self-recognition, the knowing subject no longer posits an "other" or "object" outside of himself to know. The more he recognizes his true self, the more he recognizes its contents, which are God's divine attributes buried deep within his soul. Likewise, the more he sees his true self in this life, the more of God will he see in the next life.

> O dear friend! Prepare for self-recognition, for recognition in this world is the seed for the encounter with God in the next world! What do you hear? I am saying that whoever has recognition today will see God tomorrow. (*T* 59, §80)

The Shaykh further notes that self-recognition also brings with it the gift of seeing God in this life. A self-recognizer does not simply perceive God, but comes to perceive through Him and becomes the objects of perception (*mudrakāt*) and perception itself. He then comes to know the meaning of Abū Bakr's profound statements, "Glory to the one who has not given people a way to recognize Him except through the incapacity to recognize Him" and "The incapacity to perceive perception is perception."[66]

> O chevalier! So long as a person is in sense perception, his perception can only be a finite attribute. When he reaches intellectual perception, the individual parts of his objects of perception will become infinite. But when he reaches recognition, he will be the objects of perception: the individual parts will be boundless, and in his perception the infinity of the intellectual world will become finite. (*N* I, 213–214, §344)

> So too is it the case when, on another occasion, the recognizer steps into the other world where the individual parts of this new world are like the infinity of his objects of perception in the previous world. I have passed through these worlds, but in this world of yours I do not entirely know how to speak and am unable to do so, in order for you to know. (*N* I, 214, §344)

> When rays of the sun shine forth, despite the stars' expanse, their properties do not remain. Here, the wayfarer tosses away his own will and eyes forever, until all is seen. (*T* 63, §85)

> Alas! Recognition of the Lord gives to man such self-recognition that in that recognition he recognizes neither the recognizer nor the recognized. Perhaps it is from this perspective that Abū Bakr Ṣiddīq said, "The incapacity to perceive perception is perception." That is, recognition and perception consume the entirety of the recognizer so that he cannot perceive whether or not he is the perceiver. (*T* 58, §78)

There remains for the true self-recognizer neither perceiver nor perception, but only the perceived, and neither recognizer nor recognition, but only the recognized.

> Here, nothing at all remains of the recognizer, and recognition has also been obliterated—all is the recognized. *Truly affairs are journeying unto God*[67] also says this. In this station

> *He loves them, and they love Him*[68] shows oneness, and this dot displays itself to the desert of the Invincibility.[69] Thus, what could Ḥusayn have said other than "I am the Real!," and what could Bā Yazīd have said other than "Glory be to Me!"?[70] Here, the wayfarer is nothing—there is only the creator of the wayfarer. Beyond this station, what station is there? (*T* 62, §84)

Self-Perception

As we have seen, self-recognition implies self-seeing. Yet ʿAyn al-Quḍāt would like to remind us that this is only one side of the equation. From the perspective of God, His Self-perception and Self-seeing are so intimately bound up that whether we recognize the true nature of the self or not, as the only real Self, God knows and sees nothing but Himself, both in ourselves and in Himself. Since God is all that there is, there is no perceiver in existence but the Perceiver who is the ground for all perception and is Himself the Perceived. Only God can see God.

> His perception is through Himself. (*N* III, 398, §221)

> O dear friend! He Himself knows Himself, and He Himself recognizes Himself. . . . The intellect does not reach here. If you have something beyond the intellect, you will know what I am saying. (*T* 283, §367)

> Nothing in existence can perceive God but God. From His perspective, no existence but His existence has existence. Thus, whatever perceives God's unity is itself He, for He is the one who perceives. (*N* III, 397, §219)

> Just as God can only recognize God, so too can God only see God. *"Show me!"*[71] had the color of jealousy. *"Thou shalt not see Me."*[72] He said, "O Moses! With your exertion and striving, you will not see Me; with your selfhood alone, you cannot see Me. You can only see Me through Me." From this station, Dhū'l-Nūn Miṣrī explained it this way:

> "I saw my Lord through my Lord. Had it not been for my Lord, I would not have been able to see my Lord."[73] Here, the words of Abū'l-Ḥusayn Nūrī[74] appear to us: "No one other than my Lord has seen my Lord." He said, "Nobody sees Him, for He Himself sees Himself." (*T* 305–306, §402)

> O friend! What have you understood from this tradition where Muṣṭafā says, "Reflect on God's blessings, but do not reflect on God's Essence"? Here, the world of the Sharia is thrown into turmoil! . . . The Essence of the Real can only be seen by the Real since He takes man away from himself. This is *Sight grasps Him not*,[75] for He takes the wayfarer away from himself. And this is *but He grasps sight*,[76] for all is God. (*T* 303–304, §399)

Recall from the introduction that ʿAyn al-Quḍāt also spends a good deal of time in his *Letters* answering his less esoterically inclined students' theological and philosophical questions. Given his exalted view of the nature and goal of knowledge and his disdain for intellectual hair-splitting, such a fact may come as a surprise. But it should not, as it is in line with the Shaykh's function as a teacher and spiritual guide. He takes all of his students on their own terms, responding to them as their training and preparation demand. But when it comes to explaining the mysteries of the book of existence, the Quran, the Shaykh makes exceptions for nobody.

Figure 9. Aḥmad Ghazālī imparting spiritual instruction to a student, possibly ʿAyn al-Quḍāt

8

Quranic Origins

ʿAyn al-Quḍāt's understanding of the Quran is informed by a unique vision concerning not only what the Word of God is, but how one should live a life of meaningful engagement with and transformative immersion in it.

هو

Paradise Found

ʿAyn al-Quḍāt is not fixated on such questions as the Quran's various linguistic senses and the contexts in which it was revealed, even though he was thoroughly conversant in all of the Quranic sciences. For ʿAyn al-Quḍāt, the Quran as the Word of God penetrates the planes of time and space and transcends the physical Arabic text in which it is written. What, then, is the Quran, and how can it be known? The logical place to look for ʿAyn al-Quḍāt's answers to these and related questions would be his incomplete Quran commentary.[1] Unfortunately, this book has not survived. But fortunately, in his writings that have come down to us, the Shaykh has a great deal to say about the nature of the Quran and how one may come to understand it.[2] From one perspective, he tells us that the Quran is tantamount to Paradise itself.

Paradise is the Quran, but you are unaware! (*N* I, 22, §24)

> The Quran is the Paradise of the Real. What do you hear? Do you imagine that you know what the Quran is? (*N* I, 22, §24)

Equating the Quran with Paradise is entirely sensible, since the Quran has always been present, communicating itself to those fortunate enough to be its intimates.

> The Quran is an everlasting address to its own friends. (*T* 169, §225)

From another perspective, ʿAyn al-Quḍāt likens the Quran to a rope, in keeping with a well-known Prophetic saying that describes the Quran as a rope extending from heaven to earth.[3] This rope allows the one who grasps it to be pulled into the very presence of God and back to Paradise.

> Alas! The Quran is a rope that pulls the seeker until he reaches the Sought. (*T* 168, §224)

As that which leads people back to God, the Quran in theory supplies all of the provisions that people need for their homeward journey. With this in mind, ʿAyn al-Quḍāt says that if we combine the first letter of the Quran, namely the Arabic letter *bāʾ* (1:1) with the final letter of the Quran, namely the Arabic letter *sīn* (114:6), we get the Persian word *bas*, which means "enough." What is between the first letter of the Quran and its last letter—the entire Quran—is therefore enough for the one seeking God.[4]

Vastness and Worthiness

Being all that a believer needs, the Quran explains everything and contains everything.

> Whatever is, was, and will be, all of it is in the Quran: *nor is there anything moist or dry, but that it is in a clear Book.*[5] (*T* 169, §225)

> The Quran is the catalogue of Beginningless knowledge, and Beginningless knowledge is the fountain of existence. (*N* I, 166, §251)

> I have written a thousand times that you do not know the Quran and are still asleep! (*N* I, 43, §49)

> All is in the Quran, but you are still asleep! (*N* I, 25, §27)

> O dear friend! What have you understood from this verse, where God says, *Had We made this Quran descend upon a mountain, thou wouldst have seen it humbled, rent asunder by the fear of God?*[6] And Muṣṭafā said, "The Quran is richness, with no poverty after it and no richness apart from it."[7] (*T* 168, §224)

> All is explained in the Quran, but what do people know of the Quran?! (*N* I, 333, §558)

> By my life! All is explained in the splendorous Quran—*nor is there anything moist or dry, but that it is in a clear Book.*[8] But where have you seen the Quran? (*N* I, 349, §582)

In the last text cited ʿAyn al-Quḍāt asks where one "sees" the Quran. This is an important concept that we will have the opportunity to address momentarily. At this stage it is sufficient to keep in mind that wherever the Quran is to be seen in order to learn its mysteries, ʿAyn al-Quḍāt undoubtedly has access to that unique vantage point.

> The Quran is so vast that whatever I want, I find it in there. O chevalier! The Quran is tremendous: *We have indeed given thee the seven oft-repeated, and the tremendous Quran.*[9] (*N* I, 43, §49)

In order to gain direct access to the vast treasuries of the Quran, ʿAyn al-Quḍāt introduces a rather straightforward program of action. First, one must faithfully seek God[10] and cultivate faith, for one will never be able to understand the Quran without faith: "You do not have faith, so what will you do with the Quran?!"[11] Second, one must confront habit-worship, a theme that we encountered in chapter 6.

> The splendorous Quran has every indicator of His Existence, but people have not put habit aside! Without doubt, the veil of habit has them blind. (*N* I, 5, §7)

> If you want to see the beauty of the Quran, let go of habit-worship; and whatever you have heard, forget it! "A vile guide for man is his conjecture."[12] (*N* II 102, §145)

Habit-worship is tantamount to idol-worship and is thus completely antithetical to the Quranic notion of God's oneness. Attachment to one's deeply ingrained habits, be they psychological or physical and pertaining to some desired gain in this world or the next world, causes one's inner ugliness to dominate, thereby forcing the Quran's beauty to recede to the background.

But to "let go" of habit-worship does not in itself guarantee that one will be able to perpetually see the Quran's beauty. Only the beauty of the Quran itself can cause a person to leave habit-worship altogether—what ʿAyn al-Quḍāt refers to as a person's "coming out" of habit-worship. When habit-worship is fully overcome, one is then characterized as being among "those worthy of the Quran" (P. *ahl-i Qurʾān*).

> O dear friend! When you see the beauty of the Quran, you will come out of habit-worship such that you will become worthy of the Quran: "Those worthy of the Quran are worthy of God, and are His chosen ones."[13] These worthies are those who have reached the reality of God's Word itself. *Do they not contemplate the Quran?*[14] comes from them because the Quran has accepted them. This is the meaning of *they are more worthy of it and deserving of it.*[15] (*T* 176–177, §234)

Following a long-standing tradition in Islam, ʿAyn al-Quḍāt conceives of the Quran as a bride. The bride's beautiful face is not seen by most people and is in effect veiled thousands of times over.

> O dear friend! When the Quran lifts the niqab of exaltedness from its face and removes the burqa of majesty, it will cure all of those ill because of their distance from the encounter with God—everyone will be delivered from their pain. Listen to what Muṣṭafā says: "The Quran is the medicine."[16] (*T* 168, §224)

> The Quran is in thousands and thousands of veils![17] But you are not privy and still have no way to get inside them! (*N* I, 349, §582)

> For the Quran to lift the niqab of exaltedness from its face and show itself to one who is privy is no trifling matter! (*N* I, 351, §584)

> In another place the Prophet said, "The Quran was sent down in seven readings, each of which is clear and sufficient."[18] When the bride of the Quran's beauty shows herself to those worthy of the Quran, they see traces in seven forms, each with complete transparency. It is perhaps from this perspective that he said, "Those worthy of the Quran are worthy of God, and are His chosen ones." (*T* 3, §4)

But who are those that are "privy" to such an honor? It is not those who are worthy of the Quran since, as we have seen, becoming worthy of the Quran is itself predicated upon the Quran displaying its beauty to a person, causing him thereby to completely relinquish habit-worship and then become worthy of the Quran. Those who are privy are those who are virtually worthy of the Quran. They have this status because they have hearts worthy of beholding the Quran's beauty.

> Beware! Do not think that the Quran will ever accept just any stranger and speak to him. The Quran gives a wink of its beauty to a heart that is worthy. *Surely in that is a reminder for whosoever has a heart*[19] testifies to this. (*T* 177, §234)

The next question would be how this worthiness of heart comes about. ʿAyn al-Quḍāt's answers are inextricably related to his teachings concerning the right and wrong way to read and interact with the Quran.

Knowing and Hearing

One topic that ʿAyn al-Quḍāt constantly addresses in his writings is that of the correct understanding of the Quran. He is rather unapologetic about the criteria that he takes for granted. His convictions can be summed up in the following remarks.

> Look at Muṣṭafā, when he will complain about you and the likes of you: *"O my Lord! Surely my people have taken this Quran for foolishness."*[20] Do you imagine that you are not one of these people? In truth, you are, but you do not know! (*N* II, 76–77, §105)

> It may be that a person reads the Quran so many times but knows nothing of the Quran! (*N* I, 242, §400)

> Do you imagine that you know the Quran? By God, you do not know! (*N* I, 91, §124)

The Shaykh's criteria for a sound understanding of the Quran have little to do with mastery of Arabic and the science of Quranic interpretation (*tafsīr*). With respect to *tafsīr*, he argues that one cannot accept the meanings of verses based on the reports and explanations of traditional authorities, even if the authority be the great Ibn ʿAbbās. This is because there is a world of difference between assenting to the realized understanding of someone else and knowing why it is that they have such a conviction.[21]

> Knowing is one thing, and memorizing the statements of others is quite another thing! (*N* II, 47–48, §63)

For ʿAyn al-Quḍāt, what is worse than following the opinions of someone else in matters of Quranic interpretation is one's own superficial understanding of the text of the Quran. In the context of a letter to one of his disciples, ʿAyn al-Quḍāt drives home the point that dedication to an outward understanding of the Quran is a sign of ignorance and ultimately indicates a failure to understand the intent of religion and revealed scripture.

> Whoever is committed to the outward is a complete moron; and if he is content with the outward, he is lifeless, suspended at the lowest point of humanness, and totally unaware of the reality of the revealed religions of the Prophets. (*N* I, 351, §584)

ʿAyn al-Quḍāt's disdain for the standard approaches to Quranic interpretation does not stop here. It is well known that the analysis of the Arabic language, with respect to its lexicography, grammar, style, and rhetorical forms, is the hallmark and foundation of the science of Quranic interpretation. Despite being a first-rate scholar of the Arabic language, ʿAyn al-Quḍāt sees mastery of Arabic as rather unessential to understanding the Quran.[22] Rather than being proficient in Arabic, one's heart must become "Arab."[23]

> Wait until you become Arab, until you know the tongue of Muhammad: "Whoever submits is Arab, and the believer's heart is Arab." (*T* 184, §242)

Not knowing the Quran is tantamount to being unable to hear it. Two cases in point are the early enemies of Islam Abū Jahl and Abū Lahab. They were among the most eloquent users of the Arabic language and certainly "heard" the Quran; yet they did not accept the Quran as the Word of God and thus did not follow the Prophet.[24]

In ʿAyn al-Quḍāt's writings it is Abū Jahl in particular who is the prototypical unbeliever tone-deaf to the divine Word.

> *Dead, not living;*[25] *Surely thou dost not make the dead hear;*[26] *Only those who hear will respond. As for the dead, God will resurrect them.*[27] A dead man who does not hear cannot answer. *Respond to God and the Messenger when he calls you.*[28] The purpose of this is because you say, "I know the Quran." If this is Quran-knowing, then Abū Jahl also knew the Quran! God says, *They are debarred from hearing.*[29] (*N* I, 42, §47)

Despite his extensive knowledge of Arabic, what Abū Jahl lacked was self-recognition.[30] As was seen in the previous chapter, it is particularly a lack of self-recognition that leads to one's being estranged from the truth, which is why ʿAyn al-Quḍāt singles Abū Jahl out with this unenviable designation.[31]

What is required, in other words, is much more than just formal training and know-how. For starters, one must be intellectually and even existentially prepared.

> Alas! "Speak to people in accordance with their intelligence"[32] is perfect advice. . . . This is because whatever a person hears that is not commensurate to his station and in accordance with his understanding, he will be unable to perceive and handle. O dear friend! You imagine that the glorious Quran is addressed to one group, or a hundred tribes, or one hundred thousand tribes? Rather, every verse and every letter is addressed to a certain person, but is intended for another person—rather, another world. . . . What is said to Zayd is not what is said to ʿAmr; and what Khālid sees, Bakr, for example, does not see.[33] (*T* 6, §8)

One must also be mature in the spiritual sense, just as a baby must be mature before it can eat complex foods.

> O dear friend! Do you imagine that Abū Jahl heard *Praise be to God, Lord of the worlds*,[34] or that he was intended? From the Quran he heard, *Say, "O unbelievers!,"*[35] and that was his share. But *Praise be to God* was Muhammad's share, and so Muhammad heard. If you do not believe, then listen to what ʿUmar said: "Muṣṭafā used to utter words to Abū Bakr that I heard and knew. There were times when I heard but did not know, and there were moments when I did not hear and did not know." What are you saying? The Prophet was withholding from ʿUmar? No, never! The Prophet was not withholding from him. However, a nursing baby is kept away from roasted lamb and sweetmeat since his stomach cannot handle them—until he matures. At that time, food and drink will not harm him.[36] (*T* 7, §9)

As should be clear by this point, Abū Jahl is for ʿAyn al-Quḍāt an archetype of a certain kind of person who claims to know the Quran based on his knowledge of Arabic alone, even if, unlike Abū Jahl, such a person does accept the Quran as the Word of God. This is why there are some who believe in the Quran and recite it, but to their own detriment. As the famous saying attributed to Mālik b. Anas (d. 179/796) goes, and which ʿAyn al-Quḍāt cites a number of times in his writings,[37] "Many a reciter of the Quran is there whom the Quran curses."[38]

Although "cursed" through the Quran for different reasons, what Abū Jahl and this kind of believer share in common is their surface-level perception of what the Quran is.

> What you hear and read—that is not the Quran! If it were, why did Abū Jahl not hear? And why is it said, *Surely thou dost not make the dead hear*?[39] I mean, he heard the outward. (*N* II, 76, §105)

Sufis typically juxtapose the superficial and outward (*ẓāhir*) understanding of the Quran with a more esoteric or inward (*bāṭin*) understanding.[40] The Shaykh is no different in this regard.

> I take it that anyone can perceive the outward interpretation; but who knows and sees the inward interpretations? (*T* 3, §4)

Penetrating the ocean of the Quran, one becomes immersed in a whole new world of meaning and understanding. This knowledge is not necessarily for everyone, especially those only given to the outward sense of scripture.

> ʿAbd Allāh b. ʿAbbās said, "If I were to interpret the verse, *Surely your Lord is God, who created the heavens and the earth in six days, then mounted the Throne,*[41] you would stone me."[42] Abū Hurayra[43] said, "If I explain the verse, *God it is who created the seven heavens, and from the earth the like thereof. The command descends among them,*[44] you would declare me an unbeliever."[45] (*T* 7, §10)

In the following passage a synonym for the inward sense of the Quran is employed, namely kernel (*maghz*). This is to say that the Quran has a shell (P. *pust*) and it has a kernel. The shell is the surface of the Quran, the outward aspect of it, whereas the kernel is what the shell is for, and is in fact its reality.

> Alas! People are content with the outward of the Quran—all they see of it is the shell! Wait until the Quran's kernel is eaten: "The Quran is God's banquet on earth."[46] Look at how Muṣṭafā will complain about these people: *And the Messenger will say, "O my Lord! Surely my people have taken this Quran for foolishness."*[47] (*T* 177–178, §235)

ʿAyn al-Quḍāt returns to the outward/inward nature of the Quran many times in his writings. In some contexts, he also frames his inquiry using the form/meaning dichotomy, which was commonplace in Sufi texts from the sixth/twelfth century onward. In order to move beyond the Quran's form and access its meaning, one must "ingest" the kernel of the Quran and not simply behold its outer shell. The key here is reflection.

> If you want to find Him, then read the Quran with reflection, for "God has disclosed Himself to His servants in the Quran."[48] Read it so that you know what work you have to do—*until it becomes clear to them that He is the Real.*[49] (*N* I, 84, §112)

The kind of reflection ʿAyn al-Quḍāt is calling for is not discursive reasoning. Like Ghazālī, the sage of Hamadan is of the view that discursive reasoning will not take one to the meaning of scripture. What is needed is a certain degree of inner purity. In another one of his *Letters*, ʿAyn al-Quḍāt poses several rhetorical questions to a student, emphasizing the importance of purity as a precondition for truly reading and hearing the Quran.

> Do you imagine that you have ever read or known a single letter of the Quran? Not at all! *None touch it, save those made pure;*[50] *The idolaters are surely unclean;*[51] "God is goodly,

> and He only accepts the goodly"[52]; *good women are for good men;*[53] *"Well done! Now enter it, abiding."*[54] (*N* I, 21–22, §24)

What exactly is it that is supposed to be pure? This takes us back to the notion of a worthy heart, which is a synonym for a heart that is in its pristine and pure state. Such a heart is filled with light and knowledge, which are synonymous with the Quran.

> Keep your hearing and sight pure from what is inappropriate until you hear the Beginningless Word and see the Beginningless beauty. Keep your tongue pure from disobedience until you can read the Quran. Keep your heart pure from inward disobedience until you understand the meaning of the eternal Word. (*N* I, 149, §217)

When the heart is cleansed of its worldly attachments, it will then be ready to read, understand, and reflect upon the Quran. In the following passage, which is a fine example of what can be called ʿAyn al-Quḍāt's Quranic Persian prose, he states his point in very lucid terms.

> Alas! The lock of humanness is upon hearts, and the bond of heedlessness around thoughts. This is the meaning of *Do they not contemplate the Quran, or do their hearts have locks upon them?*[55] When the openings of victory and God's help come forth—*When God's help and victory comes*[56]—they will remove this lock from the heart. *We shall show them Our signs upon the horizons and within themselves*[57] will be manifest, and the sprouts of *And God made you grow forth from the earth like plants*[58] will be harvested. The wayfarer will come out of himself. He will see the Dominion and the kingdom, and the King of the kingdom will reign: *Thus did We show Abraham the dominion of the heavens and the earth.*[59] He will come out of himself. (*T* 11–12, §16)

What ʿAyn al-Quḍāt means by the lock upon the heart being opened fundamentally entails what the Sufis call unveiling (*kashf*). When he speaks of reading the Quran, he is therefore not concerned with the act of reading, just as he is not concerned with the act of thinking when he speaks of reflecting upon the Quran. The active role of the individual entails combat with the self and overcoming his base nature. The passive aspect is when God causes the individual to be overcome by the divine audition. This is made possible by virtue of hearing and listening to the divine Word.

Sufis have always placed critical importance upon listening to scripture, which is emphasized by such verses as Q 7:204, *And when the Quran is recited, hearken unto it, and listen, that haply you may receive mercy*. After all, as ʿAyn al-Quḍāt tells us, "From the mystery of revelation to speech there are many levels and degrees."[60] The practice of immersed listening to the recited Quran consequently engenders increasingly deeper modes of contemplation among listeners, thus resulting in ever new and more profound understandings upon every aural encounter with the Quran.[61]

ʿAyn al-Quḍāt's emphasis on hearing the Quran is no different in this regard. For him, as was the case with many of the Sufis who preceded him, the ability to hear the Quran correctly in this world is itself a reflection of a higher, primordial prefiguring when all human souls stood before God in a timeless "time" and testified to His oneness and lordship. This is known in Islamic texts as the Day of the Covenant, and is signaled by Q 7:172, *"Am I not your Lord?"*[62]

> O dear friend! Recall that Day when the beauty of *"Am I not your Lord?"*[63] was displayed to you and you were hearing the audition of *And if any of the idolaters seek asylum with thee, grant him asylum until he hears the Word of God.*[64] There was no spirit that did not see Him, and there was no ear but that it heard the audition of the Quran from Him. (*T* 106, §150)

Among the people whom ʿAyn al-Quḍāt cites as being worthy of the Quran was Shaykh Baraka.[65] He only knew the Fātiḥa and a few other short Quranic chapters—in other words, he had enough formal knowledge of the Quran that one would need in order to perform the five daily prayers. Shaykh Baraka's student, by contrast, had a very extensive knowledge of the Quran and had the entire Quran committed to memory. Despite this fact, ʿAyn al-Quḍāt insists that Shaykh Baraka knew the Quran much better than he did. Whatever of the Quran ʿAyn al-Quḍāt did know was due to his service to this master.[66]

In keeping with two well-known Prophetic sayings,[67] ʿAyn al-Quḍāt would say that Shaykh Baraka had died to himself, and thus his resurrection had already taken place. Having already reached the next world, he could hear the Quranic address in its primordial audition.

> Alas! The lowest station for a man who is aware of the Quran is that he reaches the next world, for the one who does not reach the next world has not heard the Quran. "Whoever dies, his resurrection has happened" applies to him, since the resurrection stirs up in himself. (*T* 177, §234)

The hearing to which ʿAyn al-Quḍāt is alluding is called "inner hearing" (P. *samʿ-i bāṭinī*). People who have this attribute stand in stark contrast to those who are estranged from the divine Word and simply hear it as the clashing of words and sounds.

> The one who does not have hearing, what does he hear? (*N* I, 390, §652)

> Those estranged from the Quran have no share from it but letters and words—they hear the outward because they do not have inner hearing. (*T* 169, §225)

The Imprint of Letters

In a letter to one of his students, the Shaykh says that one may arrive at a world wherein "the chapters of the Quran are one letter, but without the imprint (*naqsh*) of letters."[68] Although the Shaykh does not develop this point elsewhere in his writings, one way to understand it involves the letter *bāʾ* of the *basmala* formula, "In the Name of God, the All-Merciful, the Ever-Merciful."

Meditations on the *bāʾ* of the *basmala* abound in Sufi literature. This is primarily because it acts as a preposition that is attached to the word "God" (Allah). Thus, it is not only the first letter of the entire Quran but the linguistic and ontological link for the emergence of God's self-revelation in scripture. Many Sufi authors have stated that the *bāʾ* contains all of the mysteries of the Quran and in fact enshrines the entire Quran itself. To this effect, in *Paving the Path* ʿAyn al-Quḍāt cites a report wherein Ibn ʿAbbās finds himself mesmerized by ʿAlī's profound knowledge of the vastness of the *bāʾ* of the *basmala*.

> ʿAbd Allāh b. ʿAbbās said, "One night, I was with ʿAlī b. Abī Ṭālib. He commented upon the *bāʾ* of the *basmala* until morning, and I saw myself as if I were a pitcher next to a tremendous ocean." (*T* 7, §11)[69]

If various forms of Sufi literature bear witness to extensive discussions upon the *bāʾ* of the *basmala*, just as if not more attention is devoted to meditating upon the significance of the dot that is beneath the *bāʾ* itself (ب). If the *bāʾ* takes in the entire Quran, then the dot (*nuqṭa*) under the *bāʾ* contains the dotless *bāʾ*, and, hence, all that it contains.

> Alas! On the wayfarer's path there is a station that, when he arrives there, he knows that all of the Quran is in the dot of the *bāʾ* of the *basmala*. (*T* 172, §228)

Beyond conferring upon a person the ability to see all of the Quran in this one dot, this station allows him to see "all existents"[70] in it as well. This explains why ʿAyn al-Quḍāt also states that this single dot has the power to obliterate the entire cosmic order.

> O chevalier! The Quran has been sent to creation in as many as a thousand veils.[71] Were the majesty of the dot of the *baʾ* of the *basmala* to come upon the Throne or the heavens and the earth, they would immediately be crushed and melted. *Had We made this Quran descend upon a mountain, thou wouldst have seen it humbled, rent asunder by the fear of God*[72] also has this meaning.[73] Hail to the one who explained all of this, saying, "Each letter in the Preserved Tablet is greater than Mount Qaf."[74] Do you know what this Tablet is? It is the Preserved Tablet of the heart. (*T* 173, §229)

Taken together, the *bāʾ* of the *basmala* and the dot contained under it may be that to which ʿAyn al-Quḍāt is referring when he speaks of the chapters of the Quran as being "one letter." That is, the *bāʾ* is this one letter, and since the letter *bāʾ* itself has its origin in the dot beneath it, the dot accounts for that nonformal aspect of this letter, which is tantamount to speaking of the dot as being "without the imprint of letters."

Letters and Dots

A natural corollary to ʿAyn al-Quḍāt's approach to the Quran and his immersion in its words and letters is to be found in his theory of its mysterious detached letters (*al-ḥurūf al-muqaṭṭaʿa*) that appear at the beginning of twenty-nine Quranic chapters. There is a great deal of speculation in the Islamic tradition as to the meanings of these letters, with opinions ranging from their ultimate unknowability to their being gateways that open up to higher realities.[75]

Whereas people only understand the Quran from what ʿAyn al-Quḍāt calls "the path of habit,"[76] he makes it clear that his vision of the detached letters, like his other teachings, is based on tasting.[77] Among the things he has tasted with respect to the detached letters is that "all of the mysteries in the vast plain of existence are placed in the letters,"[78] and that "there is no end to the mysteries of these letters."[79]

These mysteries are not to be read of in books or even extracted from the pages of the Quran through an analytical engagement with it. The reality of the detached letters is made known to ʿAyn al-Quḍāt through the same means by which he has been able to unlock the mysteries of the Quran in general: the purification of the heart, which allows one to hear the meanings contained in the Quran from God Himself. This is why ʿAyn al-Quḍāt indirectly links knowledge of the detached letters with what the Sufis refer to as the science of the heart.

> In God's Word, the detached letters are what gladden the hearts of His lovers. (*N* II, 98, §136)

In one passage, the Shaykh even identifies his faith in the detached letters with faith in the Quran.

> Were I not to find these detached letters in the Quran, I would not have any faith in the Quran! *Surely in that is a reminder for whosoever has a heart.*[80] (*N* I, 126, §181)

Incidentally, we find a reference to this declaration of ʿAyn al-Quḍāt in the Sufi Quran commentary of Ismāʿīl Ḥaqqī Burūsawī, the *Rūḥ al-bayān* (*The Spirit of Clarity*).[81] He first paraphrases the Shaykh's words: "Were there not a place for the detached letters in the Quran, I would not have faith in it," and then curiously notes that many scholars in ʿAyn al-Quḍāt's day declared him an unbeliever on account of this statement.[82] Then comes Burūsawī's defense: "But the matter is rather easy for the people of understanding. What he meant was [that he would not have faith in the Quran had he not] had cognizance of the unmanifest, supra-sensory realities of the detached letters," which can only serve to deepen the faith of a person solely concerned with knowing spiritual realities.

How, then, can one have such "cognizance" of the inner nature of the detached letters? As far as ʿAyn al-Quḍāt is concerned, the answer is rather straightforward. Such an understanding springs from a heart that has become worthy of receiving the meanings of the divine Word. But the heart can only be in such a state when one relinquishes individual agency or the habit of insisting on his selfish and individualistic quest for knowing. As with the other topics that he addresses in his writings, there can be no talk of ʿAyn al-Quḍāt and "his" understanding of the detached letters.

> These detached letters are a veil over the beauty of the beginning of recognition. Since this is the beginning of recognition, what would you say about its end? Has anyone's expression ever reached it? Take heed! (*N* II, 246, §371)

> How could I ever be so bold as to write an explanation of the detached letters, such as *Ṭāʾ, Hāʾ*;[83] *Yāʾ, Sīn*;[84] *Ḥāʾ, Mīm*;[85] and *Alif, Mīm, Ṣād*?[86] (*N* II, 308, §465)

ʿAyn al-Quḍāt's not having agency in being able to explain the detached letters contrasts with the boldness of the detached letters themselves. In a beautiful myth that recounts the Quran's terrestrial origins, the Shaykh states that every chapter, verse, word, and letter of the Quran shied away from containing the reality of divine love. But the detached letters were happy to take on the task.

> O chevalier! Do you not want to know why these letters are in the Quran? When the talk of love got to the summit of time and space—*Surely We offered the Trust unto the heavens and the earth and the mountains*;[87] *unto God belongs the loftiest*

> *similitude*[88]—it addressed the chapters, verses, words, and letters. All of them took a step back, for they knew that *"if the ocean were ink for the Words of my Lord, the ocean would be exhausted before the Words of my Lord were exhausted."*[89] What room was there for chapters, or verses, or words? But those meaningless letters took a step forward. (*N* I, 334, §559)

When an exposition of the detached letters overpowers ʿAyn al-Quḍāt, there is much to say. In the first instance, he tells us that these letters appear as conjoined (*mujmal*).[90] Why? So that those who are strangers to the Quran are debarred from understanding the mysteries to which they refer.

> O dear friend! To the lovers, He wants to give news of the mysteries of the kingdom and the Dominion in the garb of letters so that the strangers are not aware. (*T* 175, §232)[91]

This "garb of letters" does not only pertain to the detached letters. The entire Quran is itself enshrouded in this garb, whose function remains the same—to communicate something to the believers in and lovers of the divine Word that cannot be conveyed to those who reject the message.

> The Quran was sent to this world in the garb of letters. Thousands of spirit-stealing winks were placed in each letter. Then this call was given: *And remind, for surely the reminder benefits the believers.*[92] He said, "You lay down the snare of messengerhood and the invitation. Our snare will know those who are Our prey, and will have no desire at all for those estranged from Us." *Surely it is the same for the unbelievers whether thou warnest them or warnest them not; they do not believe.*[93] (*T* 168–169, §224)

Despite the fact that all of the Quran's letters are inaccessible to those estranged from it, the detached letters better serve the function as primary gateways into that vast expanse that is the Beginningless Word. This is because they indicate an originary form of the Quran and are the keys to unlocking its true meanings.

> Do you imagine that you have known the Quran? In the eyes of the men, the beginning of Quran-knowing is that

you know *Kāf, Hā', Yā', ʿAyn, Ṣād;*[94] *Alif, Lām, Mīm;*[95] *Ṭā', Hā';*[96] and *Yā', Sīn.*[97] Since you do not know its beginning, how will you know what its end is? By the majesty and worth of the Beginningless and the Endless, this section that I have written is tasting!

Whatever is known before knowledge of these letters is ignorance—but you are unaware! What are you saying? So long as you do not know the letters, how will you know the Word? Since the teacher is God—*He taught by the Pen;*[98] *The All-Merciful taught the Quran;*[99] *He taught thee what thou knewest not;*[100] "My Lord taught me etiquette"[101]—the first letters that were written upon the Tablet were *Yā', Sīn;*[102] *Ṭā', Sīn, Mīm.*[103] If you do not know it in this way, you are the same as the unbelievers in understanding; and unbelievers have no business in understanding the Quran! (*N* I, 42, §47)

Alas! Perhaps you have not heard this report from Muṣṭafā:[104] "Everything has a heart, and the heart of the Quran is *Yā', Sīn.*"[105] These are all traces of the secret that the Unique has with Aḥmad[106] which, apart from the lovers, nobody understands. (*T* 175, §232)

The end of the Quran is when you know the station of Moses: *unto Moses God spoke directly.*[107] In the beginning, you know the detached letters; but between the beginning and the end there are infinite degrees! (*N* I, 42, §47)

O chevalier! Do you know what these detached letters are? The infinite, Beginningless Word from beauty without neglect. In the eyes of people in general, these letters are meaningless. *"If the ocean were ink for the Words of my Lord, the ocean would be exhausted before the Words of my Lord were exhausted, even if We brought the like thereof to replenish it."*[108]

Do you say that some ink can write all of the Quran? Then what is this? *And if all the trees on earth were pens, and if the ocean and seven more added to it [were ink], the Words of God would not be exhausted.*[109] Thus, all that is known is from this, but you have known nothing! O friend! That

> which cannot be written by the oceans is wrapped up in the exaltedness of these letters. (*N* I, 126, §182)

For ʿAyn al-Quḍāt, the detached letters are not confined to the twenty-nine Quranic chapters in which they are found. Those who only see the Quran's detached letters in this conventional way are, as he says, still neophytes.[110] This is because they are on the plane of forms and written expressions. For those who are spiritually accomplished, the entire Quran consists of detached letters since the Quran descended from the world of mystery (P. *ʿālam-i sirr*), which is the plane of meaning above and beyond forms, writing, and speech.

> O dear friend! In this world about which I speak, all the connected letters are disconnected. (*T* 175, §233)

> O dear friend! For the men, the Quran's guidance is in the detached letters speaking to them and displaying their beauty to them. (*T* 177, §234)

In other words, in the world of mystery, insofar as we can speak of an articulated Quran, the entire Quran subsists as so many individual, detached letters. In our world, these letters form together, giving us clusters of words and sentences and effectively the entire written Quranic text. During the downward descent of the detached letters, some of them did not descend fully—they therefore stand apart from the letter combinations that make up most of the Quran.

But how can one see the entire Quran as consisting of detached letters? This can only happen when one becomes proficient in the alphabet of love (P. *abjad-i ʿishq*). When this happens, things change entirely, for the one skilled in this alphabet is now able to behold the Quran's beauty in its full plenitude.

> O dear friend! You still have not reached that place where the alphabet of love is written for you. The trace of this alphabet's writing is when the connected letters become disconnected. This is *We have joined the Word for them*.[111] Then, the trace of all of this is *We have separated the signs*.[112] On the path, all of this is called "writing the alphabet of love upon the Tablet of the wayfarer's heart."[113]

> Wait until the beauty of these verses appears to you—*God has inscribed faith in their hearts*[114]—to the point that all of the Quran, along with its meanings, becomes easy for you: *We have indeed made the Quran easy to remember; but is there anyone to remember?*[115] (*T* 176, §233)

A person's learning the alphabet of love for ʿAyn al-Quḍāt is tantamount to his coming out of himself, a theme that we have encountered several times already. This is to say that the more one is able to penetrate the Quran by virtue of penetrating his own soul through the science of wayfaring, the more will he come to see the attached letters of the Quran as in fact detached.

To illustrate his unique perspective on the detached letters the Shaykh draws on the words in Q 5:54, *He loves them* (يحبهم / *yuḥibbuhum*), which has always been a favorite among Sufis in their discussions on love.[116] The more one spiritually matures through wayfaring and the higher the ascent of his soul, the more will he begin to see يحبهم / *yuḥibbuhum* as actually comprised of detached letters (ي ح ب ه م / *Yāʾ*, *Ḥāʾ*, *Bāʾ*, *Hāʾ*, *Mīm*). That is, the beauty hidden behind the veil of the word cluster will be seen in its primordial form, that of detached letters.

> When one becomes more ripe, the connected letters will become disconnected. This is what people read: *yuḥibbuhum* [*He loves them*[117]]. And they imagine that it is connected! When from behind the veil one comes out of himself, beauty will present itself to his eyes in the disconnected letters, and he will say all of it like this: *Yāʾ*, *Ḥāʾ*, *Bāʾ*, *Hāʾ*, *Mīm*. But who has the capacity to listen?! (*N* II 98, §137)

The Shaykh does not stop there. He tells us that if one ascends the rungs of human perfection, he will eventually come to see even the detached letters that make up the entire Quran in a more primitive state, that of a dot (P. *nuqṭat*). In the following passage, which is in parts identical to the passage we have just seen, he lays down his position.

> When people read *yuḥibbuhum wa-yuḥibbūnahu* [*He loves them, and they love Him*[118]], they imagine it to be connected. When one comes out of the veil and beauty itself is presented to his eyes in the disconnected letters, the verse will be like this, if he is a beginner: *Yāʾ*, *Ḥāʾ*, *Bāʾ*, *Hāʾ*, *Mīm*.[119] When

> he reaches another plane, all of the letters will become a dot. (*T* 175–176, §233)

One might be tempted to view ʿAyn al-Quḍāt's reference to the "imprint without letters" as an allusion to the detached letters and their resulting in this primordial dot. On this reading, the detached letters all devolve on a single detached letter and, like the dot under the *bāʾ* of the *basmala* that accounts for the nonformal aspect of the letter *bāʾ*,[120] the dot functions as the nonformal source of this single letter (amounting to the "imprint without letters").

Such a reading is possible, even though ʿAyn al-Quḍāt also states that the detached letters do not simply devolve on just one dot, but on dots (*nuqaṭ*).

> If the wayfarer's affair reaches a more perfect portion, the letters will all become dots—his sustenance would be from the dots under the *yāʾ* and the *bāʾ* in *yuḥibbuhum* [*He loves them*[121]], nothing else. The letters would not remain. (*N* II, 99, §138)

It is important to keep in mind that, in the two texts just cited, the Shaykh is not presenting us with two contradictory pictures of what it looks like when the wayfarer emerges from himself and goes beyond the detached letters. Rather, he is providing us with a key insight into the two modes in which the wayfarer will encounter the originary form of the detached letters, oscillating as he inevitably will between the states of contraction (*qabḍ* = a dot) and expansion (*basṭ* = dots).

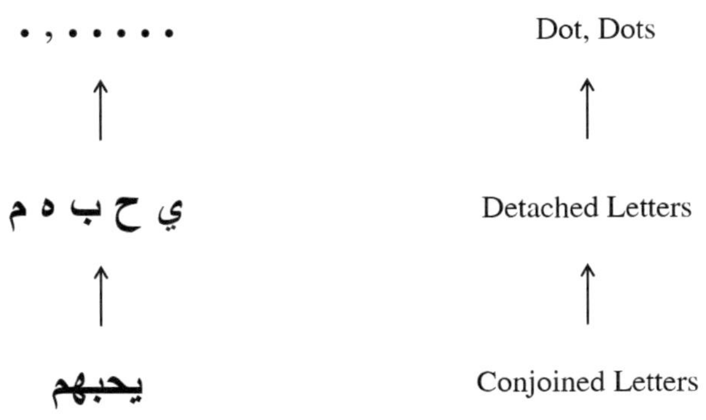

Figure 10. From conjoined letters to a dot/dots

Dots, Nothingness, Subsistence

It is not only the detached letters that amount to dots. The wayfarer himself must become nothing but a dot. He will then come to know God, see Him in everything, and hear His hidden praise uttered by all sentient beings.

> O chevalier! The wayfarer reaches a place where he hears the glorification of the particles of existence.[122] (*N* I, 390, §653)

> What do you know? How can you say "God" about God? As long as you are not a dot, you have not said "God." (*T* 36, §50)

> When the ground of annihilation and the body is changed into the ground of subsistence and the heart, man will be taken to a place wherein he will see the splendorous Throne in a speck, and in every speck he will see the splendorous Throne. (*T* 55, §75)

> Alas! The man at the end of the path sees the seven heavens and the seven earths in every speck. (*T* 55, §75)

As for the dots that are the source of the detached letters, ʿAyn al-Quḍāt maintains that there is something even more originary and primordial than them. Tearing the veils of separation and transcending the multiple levels of illusory existence, the primordial dots themselves will be pulverized into nothingness.

> When man is given another way from inside a certain veil, the dots are also obliterated. (*N* II, 99, §139)

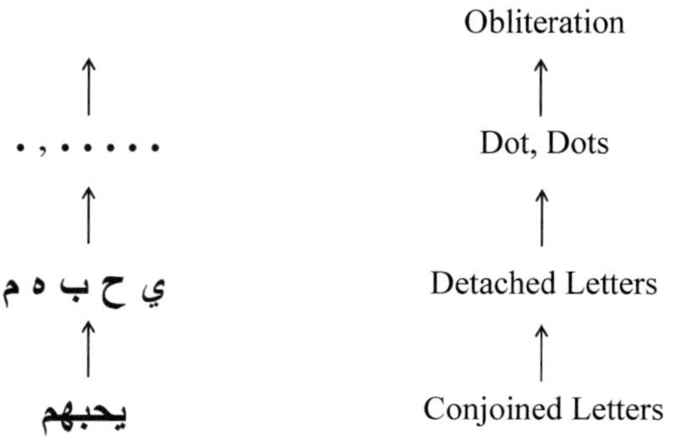

Figure 11. From conjoined letters to obliteration

As for the wayfarer who has become a dot, if he continues to ascend, he will reach the world of certainty (P. *ʿālam-i yaqīn*). The world of certainty is synonymous with a more intense level of a person coming out of himself—what the Sufis refer to as "annihilation" (*fanāʾ*) and "obliteration" (*maḥw*). Neither dots nor the individual remain, for everything is reduced to its ontological root, which is nonexistence.

> Alas! In the world of certainty the wayfarer sees his self as obliterated and sees the Obliterator as God—*God obliterates what He will, and establishes.*[123] (*T* 53, §72)

This is precisely when the wayfarer comes to understand the Quran, since its luminous rays have completely consumed the dark shadows that necessarily obtain from the once dichotomous world of reciter/recited and reader/written. Here, we can only speak of that which is recited and that which is written. This stage of obliteration in which there remains nothing beyond the dots takes us to the allness of the Quran, where there is only primordial hearing and primordial writing.

> When the reader arrives at the Book—*and with Him is the Mother of the Book*[124]—he has arrived at the Quran's meanings. The beauty of the Quran's radiance obliterates his self in such a way that neither Quran, nor reciter, nor Book remain. Rather, all is the recited, and all is the written. (*T* 3–4, §4)

ʿAyn al-Quḍāt further states that the soul's being obliterated only accounts for the first phase of the realized wayfarer's engagement with the Quran. Those like him who have died to their egos and have been resurrected in the divine audition can even see past the black ink of the Quran and right into the primordial parchment (*muṣḥaf*) upon which it is written.

> The people of the world read the Quran on the black part of the parchment, but I read it on the white part! *We have divided their livelihood among them;*[125] *And God has favored some of you above others in provision.*[126] (*N* II 99, §139)

White Parchment

↑

Dot, Dots

↑

Letters

↑

Black Words

Figure 12. From black words to white parchment

Elsewhere, the Shaykh tells us that the whiteness he has in mind is light.[127] This light can only be witnessed when one leaves the darkness of his own illusory existence. We are thus led to that key dimension of ʿAyn al-Quḍāt's Quranic vision that can be called his doctrine of affirmation (*ithbāt*) or subsistence (*baqāʾ*) in the Quran.

> Alas! We see in the Quran nothing but black letters and white paper! When you are in existence, you can see nothing but blackness and whiteness. But when you come out of existence, the Word of God will obliterate your own existence. Then, from obliteration, you will be taken to affirmation. When you reach affirmation, you will not see another blackness—all you will see is whiteness, and will recite, *and with Him is the Mother of the Book.*[128] (*N* II, 99, §139)

Qua embodied individual, the realized soul returns after having been obliterated by the divine Word to read the Quran not as a wholly other reader, but as someone who himself is mysteriously absent from and still somehow inscribed in the very pages that he recites. Here, there are no dark shadows and no forms; there is only light and formlessness. Put differently, all blackness is vanquished, and only whiteness is witnessed.

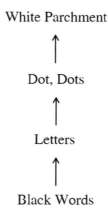

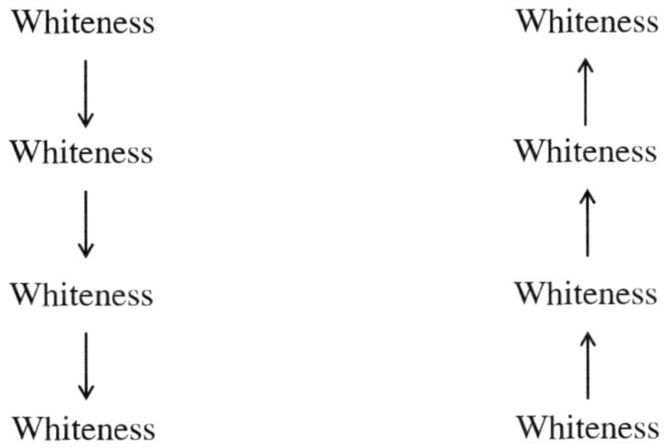

Figure 13. From whiteness to whiteness

As stated in the introduction, ʿAyn al-Quḍāt's highly original theory of the detached letters was taken up by Mullā Ṣadrā in his Quranic writings and may have been influential upon Najm al-Dīn Kubrā's synesthetic theory. At the same time, it does share some interesting similarities with the treatment of the detached letters by the great Andalusian Sufi and Quran commentator Ibn Barrajān (d. 535/1141). Ibn Barrajān also sees the detached letters as representing a more primordial, celestial aspect of the Quran, and thus as taking in the entirety of the written Quranic text. Yet one major point of difference between them is that ʿAyn al-Quḍāt sees the detached letters as ultimately originating in a nondifferentiated dot or nondifferentiated dots, while Ibn Barrajān assigns no function to dots in his treatment of the detached letters.[129]

ʿAyn al-Quḍāt's perspective on the detached letters can be seen as being formed partly in conversation with earlier discussions in Islamic theology and Quranic exegesis having to do with the nature of the Quran's descent.[130] It may likewise have an eye on the art of Arabic calligraphy wherein letters are made out of initial dots, and which Sufis see as representing the emergence of immanence from transcendence, or multiplicity from unity.[131] Be that as it may, if we were to ask the Shaykh himself, he would surely say that his vision of the Quran's detached letters comes from his having died to his ego and been resurrected in the eternal, living Word of God.

Figure 14. The tomb of Bābā Ṭāhir (Hamadan, Iran)

9

Muhammad and Iblis

The horizon of ʿAyn al-Quḍāt's consciousness is dominated by the complementary realities of light and darkness, and their respective personifications in the forms of Muhammad and Iblis.

هو

Periphery to Center

We have already seen some ways in which ʿAyn al-Quḍāt discusses the Shahada, "No god but God; Muhammad is the Messenger of God" (لا إله إلا الله محمد رسول الله). His understanding of the first part of the Shahada, "No god but God" (لا إله إلا الله), is in part indebted to the teachings of two major Sufi figures in his spiritual network, Abū'l-Ḥasan Bustī (fl. fifth/eleventh century)[1] and Aḥmad Ghazālī.[2] Yet the Shaykh also approaches the Shahada from many different angles. At its most basic level, the path of "No god but God" leads one to true belief.

> "No god but God" is another statement. "No god but God" is another being. By God's exaltedness, if the beauty of "No god but God" were to shine a speck onto the kingdom and the Dominion, all would come to nothing by virtue of the majesty of the worth of the everlasting! Wait until you travel to "No god but God." Then you will see "No god but God" propped up before your eyes and you will become "No god

> but God." *It is they who truly are believers*[3]—at that moment, you will become a believer. (*T* 77, §108)

From another perspective, the Shaykh envisions a circle. Its outer rings represent the "No" of negation (*nafy*), namely "No god," and are what hold the soul back from reaching the circle's inner dimension, which is represented by the affirmation (*ithbāt*) "but God."

> "No" is the circle of negation. The first step must be taken in this circle. But one must not stop and stay there, for if the wayfarer stops and stays in this station, the sash of unbelief and associationism will appear. (*T* 74, §102)

> What news does the wayfarer have from "but God"?![4] You will find that every one of the hundred thousand wayfarers seeking "but God" places his foot in the circle of the "No" of negation, desiring the pearl of "but God." (*T* 74, §102)

> Alas! Do you know what danger the circle of "No" has? In the circle of "No," the world is captive. One hundred thousand souls are made soulless and have become soulless. In this path, the soul can reach "but God." But the soul whose traversing the path is not given to "but God" will not have perfection. When "one of the pulls"[5] comes out, man finds salvation and deliverance at its hands: *Our host will surely be victorious*.[6] (*T* 75, §104)

Arrival at the affirmation of "but God" is only possible by first transcending the negation of "No." In its full expression, this negation of divine reality is represented by "No god." That is to say, in order to arrive at God's unity and oneness, a person must negate all false gods. The ground will then be cleared for the soul to receive nothing "but God" (see figure 15, right).

> Give ear and listen to what taste these words have for the masters of insight, and how it is that they speak. O dear friend! I do not know what of "No god but God" you taste. Strive in that so that you leave behind "No god" and reach the reality of "but God." When you reach "but God," you

will find safety and will become safe: " 'No god but God' is My fortress. Whoever enters My fortress is safe from My punishment."[7] (*T* 73, §101)

Returning to the image of a circle, the Shaykh also conceives of "No god" (لا إله) as representing the arena in which the wayfarer journeys to God. He envisions it as the first ring of the circle, which is characterized by ignorance, the state of unrealized servanthood, and darkness. The second ring represents "but God" (إلا الله) and marks the end of the wayfarer's journey to God. It is characterized by knowledge, the state of realized servanthood, and light.[8] Traveling from the periphery to the Center, and going from the dark world of "No god" to the light-filled world of "but God," the wayfarer emerges from the various layers of darkness into the light. This then opens him up to the inside of the circle, its empty Center wherein resides the luminous reality of God (see figure 15, left).

> Alas! For my part, I do not know what has been said! "No god" is the world of servanthood and the primordial disposition, and "but God" is the world of divinity, friendship, and exaltedness. Alas! The going forth of the wayfarers is in the circle of "no God"—"God created people in darkness." When they reach the circle of "but God," they will step into the circle of "God"—"Then He sprinkled some of His light upon them."[9] (*T* 74, §102)

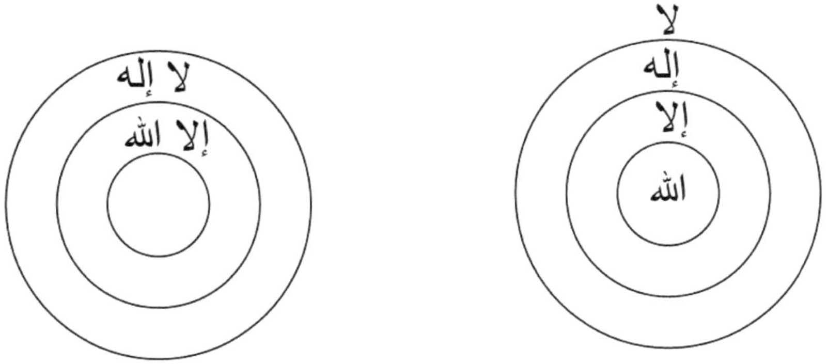

Figure 15. From "No god" to "God"

What we have not yet encountered is the method the Shaykh outlines in order to traverse these various circles and arrive at the Center. He assures us that doing so is a rather easy task.

> O dear friend! When the attraction of God's beauty arrives, coming out of these circles is easy. O dear friend! Knowing, hearing, and speaking about these pages is not the business of every person. Beware! Do not imagine that some of these words have been read or heard! They have been read, but from the Tablet of the heart—*God has inscribed faith in their hearts.*[10] They have been heard, but from the school of *Had God known of any good in them, He would have made them to hear.*[11] Here, "Whoever says 'No god but God' enters the Garden"[12] becomes known to you. (*T* 78, §109)

Note how ʿAyn al-Quḍāt speaks of the "attraction of God's beauty" as the condition that will liberate the wayfarer from the labyrinth of circles. In front of the negation of "No god" and the affirmation of "but God" stand many veils, but particularly the luminous veil of the second part of the Shahada, "Muhammad is the Messenger of God" (محمد رسول الله).

> Now, where are you? For the people, "No god but God" is in thousands and thousands of veils; so there is nothing for them but the veil of "Muhammad is the Messenger of God." (*N* I, 280, §466)

For the beginner, the light of the veil of "Muhammad is the Messenger of God" allows for greater access to "No god but God" which appears "dark" to him at first sight because he starts his journey from the darkness of "No god." With the help of "Muhammad is the Messenger of God," the wayfarer can then come to behold the light of "but God."

> Alas! The sincere wayfarer is taken to a place where the light of "Muhammad is the Messenger of God" is presented to him. In this light, the wayfarer knows what "but God" is. He achieves "recognizes himself" in the light of Muhammad, so "recognizes his Lord" becomes his hard cash. (*T* 76, §106)

When the wayfarer reaches the Center of the circle, he finds nothing there but God. From the standpoint of the Center, proceeding from "Muhammad is the Messenger of God" to the reality of God is like going from darkness to light, just as from the standpoint of "Muhammad is the Messenger of God" "No god but God" is covered in darkness.

> Here, the words of that great one[13] appeared to him[14] when the aspirant asked him some questions: "Who is your master?" He said, "God." "Who are you?" He said, "God." "Where are you from?" He said, "God." Perhaps it is from this perspective that, when that great one was asked, "Where do you come from?," he replied, "He." "Where are you going?" He said, "He." "What do you want?" He said, "He."
>
> What news do you have from this world?! The distance from this station to where the light of Muṣṭafā is is as much as the distance from black to white or movement to rest! All of the travelers have reached someone through whom abides the world of the kingdom and the Dominion. Some have known him as the light of Aḥmad, and some as self-sufficient beauty. (*T* 348, §461)

But anyone who has not yet reached the end of the path or the middle of the Circle can only see "but God" through the luminous light of "Muhammad is the Messenger of God." In such a state, he is characterized by associationism (*shirk*) since he requires a partner in the form of the second part of the Shahada to access the first part of the Shahada.

> Alas! Do you know what this associationism is? In the veil of the light of "Muhammad is the Messenger of God," the light of God is seen. That is, in the mirror of the spirit of "Muhammad is the Messenger of God," God is seen—"I saw my Lord on the night of the Ascension in the most beautiful form."[15] (*T* 76, §107)
>
> What do you know of "Muhammad is the Messenger of God"? If it appears with "No god but God" and you see

> it as a partner, it is called "associationism": *if thou dost associate, thy work will surely come to naught*[16] is known. (*N* I, 279, §465)

This form of associationism is not to be understood as polytheism or in any other negative terms. It simply is the situation of the one seeking God, who naturally must come to the Formless through forms.

> I have told the beginners that the beauty of "No god but God" can only be seen in the veil of "Muhammad is the Messenger of God." (*N* I, 280, §466)

> The first station is that the light of "No god but God" is seen in the veil of the light of "Muhammad is the Messenger of God," like the moon in the midst of the sun. (*T* 77, §108)

But the wayfarer must mature and transcend associationism altogether.

> The perfection of discipleship is that one sees the light of "No god but God" better in the veil of "Muhammad is the Messenger of God." One cannot see without a veil because his eyes are still raw—until they ripen. (*N* I, 280, §466)

> Alas! If the sincere wayfarer does not see the light of "Muhammad is the Messenger of God" as linked and connected to the light of "No god but God," it is associationism: *if thou dost associate, thy work will surely come to naught.*[17] He must pass by associationism. Here, it becomes known to you why Muṣṭafā used to say, "I seek refuge in You from associationism and doubt."[18] (*T* 76, §106)

The Center is the realm of light, unity, and oneness. The wayfarer can only access it by coming from the periphery, which is the realm of darkness, multiplicity, and associationism. The closer he moves to "No god but God" and eventually the Center of God, the more will he see "Muhammad is the Messenger of God" as deeply connected and linked to "No god but God" and not distinct from it. He is then ready to relinquish his state as associator and become a submitter (*muslim*).

> For the beginner, he can only see God in the veil of Muhammad. But when he is at the end, the light of Muhammad is removed from their midst: "*Surely I have turned my face toward the one who* [. . .]"[19] becomes the hard cash of the moment. "*We worship none but Him, sincere*"[20] becomes the *qibla* of his sincerity because he sees the light of "Muhammad is the Messenger of God" as naughted and subjugated under the light of God. (*T* 76–77, §107)

> When his eyes ripen, "Muhammad is the Messenger of God" will not disappear? No, never! This is a wrong opinion! However, its subjugation under the severity of "No god but God" will become apparent. It is like this for the one at the end. (*N* I, 280, §466)

> If you see "Muhammad is the Messenger of God" subjugated under the severity of "No god but God," you can be called a submitter. Man's perfection is in this: the light of "Muhammad is the Messenger of God" is seen in the light of "No god but God" just as the light cast over a planet is better seen in the light of the sun. Or rather, it is like moonlight, which is better seen in the light of the sun. (*N* I, 279, §465)

> The second station is that the light of Muhammad is seen in the light of God, like the light cast over planets in the midst of moonlight. Alas! Can you hear or say the letters of "No god but God"? Bā Yazīd repented from it when he said, "The repentance of people is from their sins. But my repentance is from saying 'No god but God.' "[21] Alas! Do you know why he repented from "No god but God"? In this context, Muṣṭafā said, "The best of what I and the Prophets before me have said is 'No god but God.' "[22] What are you saying? For the Prophets and Friends of God, was "No god but God" a statement from the tongue, or from the heart? (*T* 77, §108)

Muhammadan Light

When the Shaykh speaks of "Muhammad is the Messenger of God" as being a veil of light over "No god but God," he takes for granted the Sufi doctrine of the Muhammadan reality (*al-ḥaqīqa al-Muḥammadiyya*) and its complementary notion, that of the Muhammadan light (*nūr Muḥammadī*).[23] Although a number of figures before ʿAyn al-Quḍāt wrote on the Muhammadan light, he is the first author in the tradition to emphasize its uncreated nature.[24] In the following passage he refers to the light of the Prophet as an attribute of God and links it to God's name the "Self-Sufficient." As such, the Prophet's light is God's "most special attribute" (P. *ṣifat-i akhaṣṣ*).

> Alas! Perhaps you have never read that God has an attribute called the "most special attribute," and which is hidden from all people. Perhaps this most special attribute that is hidden from all is the light of Muhammad? Do you know what I am saying? (*T* 268, §351)

> O friend! Since His Essence is one, what are these eight multiple attributes? Wait until you see this one attribute—you will then have reached these eight attributes. This one attribute has such a specificity and perfection that eight specificities have been placed in it. (*T* 268, §352)

Since the Quran manifests the divine attribute of speech (*kalām*) and God's attributes can never be created, a traditional Islamic teaching concerning the nature of the Quran is that it is the uncreated Word of God (*kalām Allāh ghayr makhlūq*). The Quran also identifies itself with light, and it connects Muhammad's light to it. This allows ʿAyn al-Quḍāt to draw the natural conclusion: like the Quran, Muhammad's light is also uncreated.

> Perhaps you have not read or heard this verse in the Quran: *There has come unto you, from God, a light and a clear Book.*[25] It calls Muhammad "light" and it calls the Quran, which is the Word of God, "light": *and those who follow the light that has been sent down with him.*[26] In the Quran you see black letters on white parchment. But parchment, ink, and lines

> are not light! What, then, is "The Quran is the uncreated Word of God"? (*T* 2, §2)

The reason "Muhammad is the Messenger of God" is a veil of light thus becomes clear: it is the realm of the Prophet, who is nothing but divine light.

> Alas, O friend! All of the Prophets are light, but Muhammad is more light than all of them. (*T* 323, §422)

> Alas! Continue on until you see the Tuba[27] tree; then you will know what *the lote tree of the boundary*[28] is, as well as what kind of tree *the olive*[29] is. It is "I spend the night with my Lord." The root of all of these is one. It has many names. Sometimes it is called "tree," sometimes "Mount Sinai," sometimes "olive." Read *By the fig and the olive*.[30] Listen to the Word from a tree: "he was called from the tree,"[31] "*O Moses!*"[32] A tree *issuing from Mount Sinai*[33] will take you right to the secret of the olive. Do you know what Mount Ṭūr is? It is this mountain: "*but look upon the mountain*."[34] Ibn ʿAbbās said, "That is, look at the light of Muhammad." He called the light of Muhammad a "mountain" since both mine and land are all from his light. *Qāf. By the glorious Quran*[35] testifies to this mountain.
>
> Have you heard *kindled from a blessed olive tree*?[36] This olive is "not eastern or western"[37] because, in the divine world, light is called east and fire is called west. What do you hear, that it is neither luminous nor fiery? Rather, it is upon luminosity, *even if no fire had touched it—Light upon light*.[38] You still have not seen the tanning of fire, so when will you see the beauty of light? Who has seen the light so that you can also see? And who has tasted the olive so that you can also taste? Wait until *God guides unto His light whomsoever He will*[39] alchemically transforms you. Then you will know what I am saying.[40] (*T* 263–264, §347)

> Since Muṣṭafā is light, what is this verse? "*Our Lord, complete our light for us*."[41] If you do not believe this verse, what is this supplication? "O God! Give me a light in my face, a

> light in my body, a light in my heart, a light in my limbs, and a light in my bones."[42] The more light there is, the more light must one request. *"Our Lord, complete our light for us."* Here, God's light is being requested, not a light other than His. (*T* 323, §423)

A natural corollary to the Shaykh's explication of the Muhammadan light is his concern to disassociate him from any trace of humanness. The Prophet's physical body is not a human body at all. Rather, it is light embodied, and is the origin of all cosmic diversity.

> When Muṣṭafā was brought out of nonexistence—"The first thing that God created was my light"—his light became the origin and source of all diversities and kinds. (*T* 266, §349)

> States are disparate—you cannot understand every state. And to understand all states as one is a mistake. In one state, Muhammad was called a man. This state was in one world, but in that world, there is nobody other than Muhammad and God. Since God wanted to give him eminence in this world, He called him an orphan: *Did He not find thee an orphan and shelter thee?*[43] (*T* 301–302, §395)

> Alas! Whoever calls the pure spirit of Muṣṭafā "mortal" is an unbeliever! Listen to what God says: *They say, "Will a mortal man guide us?" So they disbelieved.*[44] In another place, He says, *"Shall we follow a single mortal man from among us? Then we would surely be astray and mad!"*[45] This is a spirit that is purified of human mortal nature and is cleansed of this world. *"I am only a mortal man like you"*[46] refers to a body that is not of this world. (*T* 164–165, §220)

Why is the Prophet's body "not of this world"? It is because it is entirely characterized by God's light.

> Alas! When the body is with reality and takes on the color of reality, that is an indication of the body's disappearance from the world. When the sun of reality is with nonexistence, the light of the body disappears. (*T* 249, §327)

> Alas! Muṣṭafā is with that which is light. O friend! He is a light, for he is *upon light*.[47] I know that you are saying, "So what is the use of this discussion?" It is this: "He who sees me has seen the Real."[48] This is the meaning of "God created Adam in the form of the All-Merciful."[49] (*T* 323, §423)

Transparent objects are shadowless, as are opaque bodies that stand directly under the sun. So too is it the case with the Prophet's body which is luminously transparent and stationed beneath the divine Sun.

> Alas! I dare not speak, for the worlds will be thrown into turmoil! Look at what Sahl b. ʿAbd Allāh[50] said: "In the cloak of a mortal man, Muṣṭafā appeared with a body to people through similarity and imaginalization." If he did not, his heart was nevertheless light. So what relation does light have with the body? *There has come unto you, from God, a light and a clear Book*.[51] Thus, if he was not light and was a body, then *thou seest them looking upon thee, but they see not*[52] would not have an explanation for itself. But if he had a body just as you and I do, why did he not have a shadow, just as we have? "He used to walk, but he had no shadow."[53] (*T* 248, §326)

Although the Prophet's body does not cast a shadow, the Shaykh says that his reality is itself a shadow of the Sun of existence.

> O friend! Do you know why he did not have a shadow? Have you ever seen a shadow for the sun? A shadow does not have form, but it does have reality. When the sun of exaltedness rises from the world of nonexistence, its shadow is cast over the world of existence as *a luminous lamp*.[54] (*T* 248, §326)

ʿAyn al-Quḍāt also indicates that knowledge of and absorption in the light of Muhammad is an end in itself for wayfarers on the spiritual path. This would correspond to what is known in Sufi literature as "annihilation in the Messenger" (*fanāʾ fī'l-rasūl*), which is a stage that follows annihilation in God (*fanāʾ fī'llāh*).[55]

> Alas! Give ear to this statement: the end and conjunction of all of the wayfarers is with the light of Muṣṭafā;[56] but I do not know with whom Muṣṭafā's end and conjunction will be! "He who sees me has seen the Real" has explained this statement. (*T* 303, §398)

> When the wayfarer achieves recognition of the light of Muhammad and the allegiance of *Surely those who pledge allegiance unto thee only pledge allegiance unto God*[57] is bound, his work in this world and the next world is complete: *This day I have perfected for you your religion*.[58] (*T* 57, §77)

The Black Light of Iblis

It is well known that ʿAyn al-Quḍāt's emphasis on the positive role of Satan or Iblis is inspired by earlier figures. However, there are many features of his Satanology that are entirely unique to him. This pertains not only to his defense of Iblis as a fallen lover of God but also to his theological and philosophical views, understanding of faith and unbelief, theory of aesthetics, and cosmogonic doctrine.[59] In order to come away with a sense of the multidimensionality of the figure of Iblis in the Shaykh's worldview, we will turn to each of these topics, beginning with the latter.

Black light (P. *nūr-i siyāh*) in Persian Sufi literature is typically a reference to God's Essence, which is so intensely luminous that it is blinding.[60] When ʿAyn al-Quḍāt speaks of black light, however, he most often does so with reference to Iblis.[61] In the following passage, he recounts how, at an earlier point in his spiritual journey, his master Aḥmad Ghazālī pointed him to the reality of this black light.

> "O Muḥammad! You still have not reached the middle of servanthood, and the way has not been given to you to the veil of that black light who is the chamberlain of *'I shall certainly cause them to err, altogether.'*"[62] (*T* 49, §67)

Having arrived at the "middle of servanthood," the sage of Hamadan begins to get a glimpse into what this black light is.

> When the wayfarer arrives at the second birth, the veils of the Dominion that remain between him and God will be lifted, one by one. The last veil is a black light. (*N* I, 91, §124)

As we have seen, the person of the Prophet is shadowless; but in relation to the divine light, his luminous reality is its shadow. Likewise, in relation to the Prophet's light, the world is his shadow.

> Muhammad's shadow was cast over the world when the root of the sun set. What are you saying? The shadow will remain?! It will never remain: *that Day We shall roll up the sky like the rolling of scrolls used for writing.*[63] (*T* 249, §326)

The shadow that is cast by the Prophet's light corresponds to the world because it is the realm of the black light of Iblis, the ambit of misguidance and deviation. Along the circle of the Shahada, the blackness of Iblis' shadow derives from the darkness of "No god," while its luminosity derives from the affirmation of "but God," which is the realm of the light of Muhammad.

> You know that Muhammad is the shadow of the Real. Have you ever known what the shadow of Muhammad's sun is? Alas! Perhaps you have not seen the black light outside of the dot of "No" in order to know what Muhammad's shadow is. (*T* 248, §326)

The black light of "No god" is symbolized as a guard who blocks the way to "but God."

> O chevalier! If *unto Moses God spoke directly*[64] is perfection, then Iblis is of this perfection. Do you know who Iblis is? He is the officer of the empire from whose blow the one hundred and twenty-four thousand Prophets have been afflicted: *And no Messenger or Prophet did We send before thee, but that when he had a longing, Satan would cast into his longing.*[65] (*N* I, 96, §133)

> Alas! Do you know who the king of Abyssinia is? He is the chamberlain of "but God." But you call him "Iblis."[66] (*T* 30, §43)

> He comes forward and blocks the way for them until these helpless ones remain in the world of "No," worshipping their caprice and becoming self-worshippers. (*T* 74, §103)

> When they get to the end of the desert of what is other than God, the guard of the presence of "but God" arrests them, confused and bewildered. (*T* 74, §102)

Personified as Satan, the black light of "No god" has the sole function of deluding, misguiding, and confusing all of those who dare set foot in the direction of "but God."

> Do you know what that black light is? *He was among the unbelievers*[67] was his robe of honor, and the sword of *"By Thy exaltedness, I shall certainly cause them to err"*[68] was unsheathed. Without choice, he was cast as a meddler into the darknesses of *the darknesses of land and ocean.*[69] The guardian of exaltedness came, serving as the doorkeeper of the presence of "I seek refuge in God from Satan the accursed." (*T* 119, §168)

The guard's specific task is to block the way in order to set apart those who sincerely aspire to be with the King from those who only claim to do so.

> Do you know what "He who resembles a people is one of them"[70] is? This is also the meaning of *Say, "If you love God, follow me, and God will love you."*[71] As long as the doorkeeper of this Presence was not given access, this station could not be found. Who is this doorkeeper? *"By Thy exaltedness, I shall certainly cause them to err, altogether."*[72] If the king did not have a doorkeeper, all would have been the same in proximity to the Sultan—there would be no disparities at all, and the wimps would also place their feet upon the

> path. This doorkeeper is the discerner of claimants—who is sincere, and who is a mere claimant? (*T* 342–343, §454)

In the following discussion, Iblis is featured by his other name in the Islamic tradition, ʿAzāzīl,[73] which derives from the Hebrew Azazel mentioned in Leviticus 16:8–10.

> Do you know what this sun is? It is the light of Muhammad that comes forth from the East of Beginninglessness. Do you know what moon this is? It is the black light of ʿAzāzīl[74] that emerges from the West of Endlessness. (*T* 126, §175)

Between the opposite poles of the East of Beginninglessness and the West of Endlessness is the key to understanding the situation of existence.

> In the Dominion, I went inside the veils of the unseen and it was announced: "O one with insight, take a lesson[75] from opposites!" (*N* I, 253, §421)

Although Muhammad and Iblis are opposites, later in this chapter we will see that they are not mutually exclusive entities as much as they are complementary realities. Iblis' darkness is, in fact, not darkness but overshadowed light.

> In relation to the divine light, he is called "darkness." If not for this relationship, he is light. (*T* 118–119, §166)

Commenting on two statements by al-Ḥasan al-Baṣrī, "The light of Iblis is from the fire of exaltedness . . ."[76] and "If Iblis' light appeared to people, he would be worshipped as a god,"[77] the Shaykh makes the following observation.

> What are you saying?! They would worship him as a god? They will not worship him! You are wrong! But listen to this verse: *Hast thou considered the one who takes his caprice as his god?*[78] Since the light of Iblis is from the light of exaltedness, it indeed can be like this. (*T* 211, §270)

Despite their varying forms, the lights of Muhammad and Iblis necessarily derive from God's light and themselves are the luminous roots of the cosmic order.

> The upshot of this discussion is that God is a substance and light an accident. Substance was never without accident and will not be. I have spoken about these heavens and the earth through symbols, namely that two of His lights are the roots of the heavens and the earth—their reality is these two lights. One is the light of Muhammad, and one the light of Iblis. (*T* 258, §340)

Face, Mole, Tresses

ʿAyn al-Quḍāt frames the foregoing discussions in more concrete terms when he speaks of God as symbolizing a beautiful, round face (P. *rūy*) and cheek (*khadd*). Every beautiful face needs a mole (P. *khāl*), and the face in general would not be alluring if there were no long locks of hair or tresses (*jaʿd*) to conceal it.

> Alas for anyone who sees the lovely face with such a cheek, mole, tress, and eyebrow and does not say "I am the Real," like Ḥusayn![79] Wait until Bā Yazīd Basṭāmī sets you up in the midst of this meaning and makes you aware of the reality of this affair! (*T* 119, §168)

> O dear friend! Do you know which lovely face this is? What is the tress of the lovely face? In which station are the cheek and mole? There are stations and meanings for the traveler that, when they are displayed to him in the world of form and bodiliness and he is intimate with their image and takes them as a reminder, he can only speak of them in the garment of letters and through such expressions as "lovely face," "cheek," "mole," and "tresses." (*T* 29, §41)

As will become clear in the following chapter, the Shaykh's vision of beauty takes him beyond all forms and to Beauty Itself. It is from this perspective that he declares the Beloved's face and its distinctive features as aids along the path of perceiving Beauty.

> O dear friend! What do you know about what the cheek, mole, and tresses of the Beloved do with the lover? As long as you do not arrive, you do not know. (*T* 117, §164)

> O chevalier! That which I know, you will never know! The mole and face of the Beloved are for the perfection of beauty. Wait until you see Beauty itself! (*N* III, 279, §4)

Yet the symbolic significance of the Beloved's face and its mole and tresses cannot be understated. Apart from pointing the way to Beauty, these images concretely convey the complex structure of the relationship between God, Muhammad, and Iblis. For starters, the mole represents Muhammad,[80] and the tresses Iblis.

> How can strangers know what the black mole on the face of the Beloved is?[81] (*N* I, 415, §695)

> People have heard Iblis' name. But what they do not know is that he is shown so many kindness that nobody else will ever see. Alas! Why? Because he is linked to the cheek and the mole. (*T* 121, §169)

We can quite naturally also say that the mole symbolizes the light of the Prophet and the tresses the black light of Iblis.

> What do you say? Does the lovely face have beauty without tresses? The lovely face would never assume form without cheek, mole, and tresses. Thus, when the traveler reaches this station, he will have two states and two lights will come forth[82]—one expressed as a mole and one as tresses. One is the light of Muṣṭafā, and the other the light of Iblis. The wayfarer's work will forever be with these two stations. (*T* 30, §43)

Muhammad and Iblis are light but they figure as "dark" images in order to point up their contrast to the white and luminous face of God. In its turn, God's face is a symbol for "No god but God," which means that the mole and from one perspective the cheek (upon which the mole rests) is a symbol for "Muhammad is the Messenger of God."

The face of "No god but God" is not complete without the mole of "Muhammad is the Messenger of God." The Shaykh refers to this mole as the "mole of perfection" (P. *khāl-i kamālī*) since it is a distinctive mark and trace that allows the otherwise elusive face of "No god but God" to be seen.

> Do not consider the cheek and mole of the Beloved to be other than the face of the light of "Muhammad is the Messenger of God"—"The first thing that God created was my light." By virtue of the beauty of the light of the One, the light of Ahmad became a cheek and a mole. If you do not believe, say, "No god but God, Muhammad is the Messenger of God."
>
> Alas! If the heart is not lost between the cheek and the mole of this lovely face, it will say, "What secrets do this cheek and mole of the Beloved have with the lover?" Having lurked in the midst of the cheek and mole and fled, how will such a heart that has gone astray be found? (*T* 117, §164)

> Alas! What do you hear? The black mole is the token of "Muhammad is the Messenger of God," which has become a seal and an adornment upon the face of "No god but God." The cheek of the lovely face is never without the mole of perfection. The beautiful cheek of "No god but God" would never be perfect without the mole of "Muhammad is the Messenger of God," and would be inconceivable. The spirits of one hundred thousand lovers are lost in the mole of this lovely face! (*T* 29, §42)

The mole completes the face, yet both require hair for their completion.

> What are you saying? Do cheek and mole ever have perfection without tresses, eyebrow, and hair? No, by God, they do not! Do you not see that in the prayer it is mandatory to say, "I seek refuge in God from Satan the accursed"?[83] Because of this meaning, disdain, conceit, and boldness are reviled, as Iblis himself is the leader of the proud and the self-seers. *"Thou hast created me from fire, while Thou hast created him from clay"*[84] also refers to this disdain. (*T* 121, §169)

Although ʿAyn al-Quḍāt does not explicitly relate the tresses to the function of the "No god" of "No god but God," such a reading is certainly implied as it allows for a perfect parallel between the Shaykh's treatment of these symbols of beauty with the circle of the Shahada. That is, one can only arrive at the round, blinding, and luminous face of "but God" through the mole of "Muhammad is the Messenger of God," which serves as its index. And covering the face of "but God" are the dark tresses of "No god," which is the domain of Iblis.

True to his function as guard of "but God," the tresses of the black light of Iblis reveal something of its beautiful and luminous face insofar as Iblis' reality is light. But insofar as Iblis is "black" and thus distant from God, the tresses ultimately conceal the face of "but God" and serve as a barrier between God and His beloveds. And just as a lover should not mistake his beloved's beautiful locks of hair for her face, so too should the one seeking the divine face not halt at its tresses. As much as the mole of "Muhammad is the Messenger of God" takes one to the face of "but God," the tresses of the black light of Iblis, as "No god," will block the way to it. Passing through the veil of tresses, one then is led to the mole and eventually to the face itself.

> Between man and the encounter with God one veil remains—when this veil is passed, there is nothing other than the beauty of the encounter with God. (*T* 29, §42)

Faith and Unbelief

Seen as black light or the tresses of "No god," Iblis for ʿAyn al-Quḍāt is not an altogether negative cosmic force. In more ways than one, Iblis' seemingly less desirable role and function is no less important than that of Muhammad. This point takes us to the third dimension of ʿAyn al-Quḍāt's Satanology which deals specifically with the complex dynamics of the Muhammad-Iblis nexus as it pertains to guidance and faith and misguidance and unbelief.

For the Shaykh, the created order is a manifestation of God's names and attributes which are summed up in two antithetical but complementary functions: gentleness and severity. The former corresponds to God's names and attributes of beauty (*jamāl*) and the latter to those of majesty (*jalāl*). God's names and attributes of gentleness and beauty in turn correspond to Muhammad and His names and attributes of severity and majesty to Iblis.

> O dear friend! When, from the Essence of oneness, the dot of God's greatness placed its foot in the Beginningless and Endless circle, it descended on nothing until the desert of the attributes had spread out in the world of the Essence. And this desert is nothing but the beauty of *And We sent thee not, save as a mercy unto the worlds*,[85] and the majesty of *"And surely My curse shall be upon thee until the Day of Judgment."*[86] (*T* 73, §101)

> Have you ever known that God has two names? One is *the All-Merciful, the Ever-Merciful*,[87] and the other *the Compeller, the Proud*.[88] He brought Iblis into existence from the attribute of compellingness and Muhammad into existence from the attribute of mercifulness. Thus, the attribute of mercy is Muhammad's nourishment and the attribute of severity and wrath Iblis' nourishment. (*T* 227, §294)

Any and all guidance and mercy in the cosmos goes back to Muhammad. But not every receptacle is able to receive it. This is akin to the light of the sun—whatever comes into contact with it is colored by what it is, in substance.

> The sun makes the washer's garment white and his face black. These two effects differ, but their effectuator is one. This is because the same thing that made the washer's face black is what made his garment white. Now, if by virtue of these two differing effects the sun were given two names and it were said that "the sun blackens and whitens," fools would imagine that the causer of whiteness is other than the causer of blackness. But that is an error. (*N* I, 180, §279)

When the sun of the Prophet's guidance is brought to different people, they will likewise receive it in accordance with what they are. Abū Jahl, for instance, could not accept guidance. Thus, the Prophet's mercy for him simply brought about what was already inside of himself, which was nothing but wretchedness (P. *shaqāwat*).[89] In the following passage, ʿAyn al-Quḍāt juxtaposes the Prophet's light with the nature of Abū Jahl and, a fortiori, the black light of Iblis.

> Muṣṭafā is the means of mercy to the inhabitants of the world, but with respect to Abū Jahl, he is the means for the appearance of the perfection of wretchedness from Abū Jahl's substance. You have never heard what the black light of Iblis and Abū Jahl say to the light of Ahmad, from head to toe? Listen to these lines!
>
> O sweet-lipped one, such pure poison you are for me.
> You are a mercy for others, but a punishment for me.
> You twist my hands, and have nothing for me.
> You are a sun for the world, but darkness for me.
> (*T* 187–188, §245)

Framed differently, the Shaykh tells us that Muhammad symbolizes faith and Iblis unbelief. As respective manifestations of God's names and attributes of beauty and majesty, they each fulfill their corresponding tasks of guidance and misguidance.

> In our religion, unbelief and faith are one color. (*N* II, 206, 303)

> I do not know what you understand from "unbelief." Unbeliefs are many because the wayfarer's waystations are many. Unbelief and faith are conditions and requisites for the traveler at every moment. (*T* 49, §68)

> "If God wanted to forgive His servants, He would not have created Iblis."[90] If He wanted all of His servants to be brought near, He would not have placed Iblis as an intermediary and a veil between Himself and them. (*T* 217, §277)

> Iblis is also one of His acts. (*N* II, 232, §349)

> Peoples' guidance is consigned to Aḥmad and their misguidance to Iblis. (*T* 189, §247)

Do you know who Iblis is? He is an inviter on His path. But he invites away from Him and Muṣṭafā invites with Him. (*N* I, 304, §509)

O dear friend! Water is the means for a fish's life and nourishment, but it is the means for the death of others. Here, what *the Word of thy Lord is fulfilled in truth and justice*[91] is becomes known to you. Here, you come to know why the sun of God's light—the substance of Muṣṭafā—is the means of illumination and light, and why the substance of Iblis is the means of misguidance, endarkening, and darkness: faith arises from the light of Muhammad and unbelief and humiliation arise from the "light" of Iblis.

Listen to this meaning from Muṣṭafā, who says, "I have been sent as a caller, but guidance does not come from me in any way; Iblis was created as a misguider, but misguidance does not come from him in any way."[92] Alas! What can be done? *None alters His Words.*[93] In another place, He says, *and you will never find alteration in the custom of God*[94]—it also has this meaning. "Whoever God guides, none shall lead him astray; and whoever He leads astray, no guide has he."[95] Alas! What have you understood from these verses? *Yāʾ, Sīn. By the wise Quran*[96]—perhaps the explanation of this has not been given to you. (*T* 186, §244)

If you do not believe, listen to the Quran: *Thus did We show Abraham the dominion of the heavens and the earth.*[97] What did he see in this dominion? Give ear: *when the night grew dark upon him, he saw a star. He said, "This is my Lord!"*[98] When he saw the star of his own spirit, he said, *"This is my Lord!"* Why did Abraham say this? Because of what Kaʿb the "Rabbi"[99] said: "In the Torah, we have read that 'the spirits of the believers are from the light of God's beauty and the spirits of the unbelievers are from the light of God's majesty.' " Thus, whoever sees the beauty of his own spirit has seen the beauty of the Beloved, but it is not the beauty of the Beloved.

> If a believer sees his own spirit, he has seen the beauty of the Friend. But if an unbeliever sees his own spirit, he has seen the majesty of the Friend. This is why He says, *When he saw the moon rising, he said, "This is my Lord!"*[100] When in that station Abraham saw the moon—which is the light of Iblis, he said, *"This is my Lord!,"* for it is from the light of God's majesty. Then he left that. *When he saw the sun rising*—when he saw the sun of the light of Ahmad, for in that world, the spirit of Ahmad is a sun—he said, *"This is my Lord!"*[101] (*T* 212–213, §272)

It will be recalled that for ʿAyn al-Quḍāt everything in the cosmos is precisely where it is supposed to be and cannot be otherwise. He also says that it is best to view things in relation to their opposites, otherwise we will not be able to understand their precise reality. Only through the relations of opposites can we situate everything in existence intelligently and meaningfully. One cannot know subsistence without annihilation, white without black, day without night, and so on.

We can even relate the Shaykh's argument in favor of the existence of evil as only being a relational reality to the "evil" function of Iblis.[102] Iblis' task is to lead people to the bad and the negative, but this can only be meaningful in relation to the light of the Prophet's guidance and his leading them to the good and the positive. This is to say that, through Muhammad and Iblis' respective functions of guidance and misguidance, the cosmic economy of faith and unbelief is brought into perfect equilibrium and harmony. There cannot be guidance without misguidance, light without darkness, belief without unbelief, truth without falsehood, and Muhammad without Iblis.

> Anyone who suffers and is half-slain in the world of Iblis is cured in the world of Muhammad; for unbelief is the stamp of annihilation and faith the stamp of subsistence. As long as there is no annihilation, subsistence will not be found. In this path, the more the annihilation, the more perfect the subsistence. (*T* 233, §302)

> O dear friend! This is wisdom: whatever is, was, and will be must not and cannot be otherwise. Whiteness could never

be without blackness. Heaven cannot be without earth. Substance is inconceivable without accident. Muhammad could never be without Iblis. Obedience without disobedience and unbelief without faith cannot be conceived. Likewise is it with every opposite. This is, "Things are distinguished through their opposites."[103] Muhammad's faith cannot be without Iblis' unbelief.

If it is possible for *He is God, the Creator, the Maker, the Form-Giver*[104] to not be, then it is possible for Muhammad and the faith of Muhammad to not be. If it could be conceived that *the Compeller, the Proud*[105] and *the Paramount*[106] not be, then it could be conceived that Iblis and his unbelief not be. It is therefore clear that Muhammad's felicity cannot be without Iblis' wretchedness, and Abū Bakr and ʿUmar cannot be without Abū Jahl and Abū Lahab. This is, "There is no Prophet but that he has a counterpart in his community."[107] There is never a Friend of God but that a sinner is inseparable from him. There is never a Prophet without a heedless person, nor a truthful person without a sinner. (*T* 186–187, §245)

Two Commands

The implications of the three aspects of the Shaykh's Satanology we have so far encountered are brought to life when it comes to the fourth, which specifically focuses on the actual person and tragic image of Iblis.

According to the standard reading of the Quranic account of Iblis, he was one of the Jinn commanded by God to prostrate to Adam along with all of the other angels.[108] The angels obeyed, but Iblis refused, citing his superiority over Adam on account of Adam's being made of clay and his being made of fire. Iblis was consequently banished from Paradise for disobeying God and became hated and despised by Him. Iblis then became God and mankind's sworn enemy and promised to misguide as many of God's followers as he could until the Day of Judgment.

In premodern Islam, a number of Sufis have weighed in on the meaning of the Iblis narrative,[109] with some figures, beginning with Ḥallāj and then later Aḥmad Ghazālī, coming to his defense.[110] Here we find Iblis as a tragic, fallen lover of God who was banished from Paradise on account of his refusal to bow down to other than Him. Iblis only "disobeyed" God because the other option given to him amounted to going against his Beloved, which he could not do. He is therefore a monotheist at all costs. As Aḥmad Ghazālī puts it, "Whoever does not learn God's unity from Satan is an unbeliever."[111]

Building on the defense of Iblis in Ḥallāj, Aḥmad Ghazālī, and others, ʿAyn al-Quḍāt offers the single most sustained and robust case in favor of the person of Iblis in all of Islamic literature. Although some details in the Shaykh's account follow that of his predecessors, he ultimately presents us with a number of novel interpretive twists and turns, and even relates the story of Iblis to his theory of human freedom.[112]

On a theoretical level, and in keeping with the Shaykh's understanding of the necessity of guidance and misguidance and the general function of opposites in the cosmic order, Iblis is simply a necessary piece to the puzzle of existence and the means by which humans may attain perfection.[113] On a practical level, what people are to do with the figure of Iblis is to take a lesson, just as they are to take a lesson from the person of Muhammad.

Let us first consider the exalted status that Iblis enjoyed as a confidant of God, before his banishment from Paradise.

> Iblis was nurtured by God's generosity, was proximate to the Presence, and was the teacher of the angels.[114] His hut faced the base of God's Throne without intermediary, "and God spoke words to him."[115] He was one of the elect who stood with Him. (*N* I, 314, §524)

Given his special rank with God, it is no wonder that Iblis would refuse to bow before another. Indeed, his refusal to bow down to anyone other than God effectively communicates the positive spiritual attitude of jealousy (P. *ghayrat*) vis-à-vis God.[116] As a jealous lover who was exclusively devoted to his Beloved, Iblis put forth a perfect reason for why he could not bow down to Adam: he was made of fire, which is all consuming, and Adam of clay, which is lesser than fire. Human beings should likewise be characterized by the fire of jealousy for their Beloved, refusing to bow to anyone other than Him and willing to burn to ashes anything that stands in their way.

> If you want to recognize perfect jealousy, then go and also obtain *"Thou hast created me from fire, while Thou hast created him from clay"*[117] so that you know what jealousy is. (*T* 316, §414)

Yet it can be asked why, if Iblis was such a jealous lover, he decided to go against his Beloved's wishes. Is it not a more perfect form of love to simply do what one's beloved asks of him? ʿAyn al-Quḍāt's answer is quite unapologetic, taking us to the heart of the matter. Iblis did not, in reality, go against God's wishes. Rather, his refusal to bow down to Adam was in fulfillment of God's true intention—that Iblis should not bow down to Adam.

> In the open, God said to him, *"Prostrate unto Adam!"*[118] But in secret, He said to him, "O Iblis! Say, *'Shall I prostrate unto one whom Thou hast created of clay?'"*[119] (*T* 227, §293)

> God said to Iblis—just as Gabriel and Michael[120] heard it—*"Prostrate unto Adam!"*[121] But in the unseen of the unseen, He said, "Do not prostrate unto anyone other than Me." (*N* II, 412, §650)

> In the open, he said, *"Prostrate!"* Acting in accordance with what he was ordered to do in secret, this poor wretch said, "I shall not prostrate unto one whom You have created of clay!"[122] So He said, "Surely My curse shall be upon thee."[123] Iblis replied, "Since this robe of honor is from You, who cares whether it comes with curses or mercy?" On the path to God, among those to come first and those to come last, Iblis saw nothing but children. (*N* II, 187, §280)

It is important here to grasp the sense of God's "command" (*amr*) to Iblis. Authors in the Islamic tradition speak of two distinct divine commands. There is the "prescriptive command" (*al-amr al-taklīfī*) and the "engendering command" (*al-amr al-takwīnī*). The prescriptive command corresponds to the dos and don'ts of the Sharia, that is, those things that God has told people to do but which they have the choice to obey or disobey. The engendering command, however, is altogether different since human choice or volition does not factor into the equation.[124]

As Q 36:82 states, *His command when He desires a thing is only to say to it "Be!," and it is*. That which results from the divine command *"Be!"* is the engendering command in action. In the following passages, it is made clear that God's command to Iblis to bow down to Adam took the form of a prescriptive command; but, in actuality, it was overridden by the engendering command, which the Shaykh rightly refers to as God's desire.

> One must be an aspirant who has the attribute of Iblis so that something comes from him. In the command to him the motive was one thing, but in the Beloved's desire for him the motive was quite another thing! Knowing the command of the Beloved is one thing, but knowing the desire of the Beloved is quite another thing![125] O chevalier! The command is outside, and the desire inside.
>
> If, for example, a father says to his child, "Do not praise me too much so that you embarrass me," and that child increases in honoring his father, the child would not be opposing him. By my life, he would be opposing his father's command, but he would not be opposing his desire. If Sultan Maḥmūd were to tell Ayāz, "Go serve someone else," and Ayāz were to go, he will have erred.[126] A person who would obey the command in such a situation is raw. (*N* I, 75, §98)

> O friend! Perhaps you have not seen someone who, knowing the desire of his friend and beloved, opposes his command in conformity with his desire. What do you hear? Iblis knew God's desire, namely that He did not want Iblis to prostrate when He said, *"Prostrate unto Adam!"*[127] It was a test—who, by His command, would prostrate to someone else? All prostrated, except the teacher of the angels—it was inescapably like this. The teacher must be more ripe than the student! (*N* I, 96, §132)

As already discussed, for ʿAyn al-Quḍāt humans are compelled and subjugated to act by nature. Iblis is likewise compelled into action; but unlike human beings who are subjugated by God to act in accordance with their inborn attribute of free choice, Iblis is compelled to act in accordance with his inborn attribute, that of misguidance.[128] Iblis is therefore chosen and compelled by the hands of destiny to be what he already was, is, and will be.

> He threw him into the ocean with his hands tied behind his back.
> Then He said, "Watch out! Don't get wet!"[129] (*N* II, 412, §650)

> O dear friend! Iblis knows what this is. God said, *he was among the unbelievers*.[130] It was necessary. What was he to do, not lose hope in God's mercy? O chevalier! Having seen the face of the perfection of majesty and observed the selfhood of his self, without doubt, he lost hope. It is in this state that he said,

> You set my heart on fire and throw oil on my spirit.
> Then You say, "Hide our secret!" (*N* II, 418, §660)

An Ideal Lover

As should be clear by now, the Shaykh's retelling of the story of Iblis serves as a concrete example of his doctrine of imaginalization. It can also be argued that the figure of Iblis ties into a wide range of ʿAyn al-Quḍāt's other teachings beyond his theodicy and theory of human action. Iblis can, for example, be related to the exoteric dimension of religion and hence habit-worship. As symbolizing darkness, he can also be identified with the black letters upon which the Quran is written, while the light of the Prophet would then be identified with the primordial white parchment.

But in the constellation of ʿAyn al-Quḍāt's spiritual and intellectual universe, Iblis shines best when seen as an ideal lover of God who smiles at, and even takes joy in, his terrible fate.

> How fine has Ḥusayn Manṣūr-i Ḥallāj spoken in the *Book of Ṭawāsīn*:[131] "Chivalry is not fitting for anyone except Iblis and Aḥmad."[132] (*N* II, 187, §281)

> "Chevalier" and "arrived man" pertain to Aḥmad and Iblis. The others are nothing but children on the path! (*T* 223, §288)

With respect to Iblis in particular, his example of chivalry has many lessons to teach us sophisticated human beings.

> O chevalier! That place where Iblis is, you do not have a way to it. (*N* I, 97, §133)

> If someone in existence knew how to listen to the story of Iblis, especially its mysteries, his story would be extremely dear to him. (*N* II, 416, §657)

> Doing God's work is not foolishness! *And We do not send it down, save in a known measure.*[133] In every action there must be a command. First, there must be a command in the Beginningless inscription, then in the mark of Muṣṭafā, and then in the trace of Iblis.[134] (*N* III, 378, §182)

> There is only one of my friends who can listen to some of his story. So who would dare tell it, and who can hear it?! For how are people in general going to understand the story of someone whose foot-dust the elect of the elect have not even caught wind of?
>
> I take it you have heard that he was the teacher of the angels. For so many thousands of years his hut was at the base of the Throne. You imagine this was a trifling matter? Such was Iblis, whose beginning was like this. Now he has reached a state where "he is the toy of the children in Your alley." Read this letter a thousand times and memorize it! (*N* II, 417, §658)

Iblis' chivalry is on full display when he chooses the love for God over all else, even if it means being abandoned by God and cursed by Him. So exalted is Iblis' status that, in the tradition of Sufi masters in ʿAyn al-Quḍāt's spiritual network, he had earned the titles "Master of masters" (P. *khwāja-yi khwājagān*) and "Leader of the abandoned ones" (P. *sarwar-i mahjūrān*).

> That unique one in existence, that leader of the abandoned, that secret of destiny, that mole upon the face of Endless beauty,[135] that object of the empire's jealousy—Shaykh

> Abū'l-Qāsim Gurgānī[136] used to call him the "Master of masters." (*N* II, 416, §657)

> If after this poverty[137] shows itself to you, your face will become black—just like the abandoned ones—and you will be cut away from the court of the Beginningless. Then you will know what kind of person Iblis is, for it has been as much as a thousand years that he has been abandoned. (*N* II, 160, §237)

> I heard from Khwāja Aḥmad Ghazālī that Shaykh Abū'l-Qāsim Gurgānī would never say "Iblis." Rather, when he would say his name, he would say, "That Master of masters!" and "That Leader of the abandoned ones!" When I recounted this to Baraka,[138] he said, "'Leader of the abandoned ones' is better than 'Master of masters.'" (*N* I, 97, §134)

Despite the fact that Iblis is banished from the divine Presence, God nevertheless has his eternal solicitude in view. Consequently, Iblis is not thrown into the world without his share of sustenance (*rizq*) and nourishment (*ghadhā*). These come in the form of the curses (P. *laʿnat*) that are hurled upon Iblis by both God and humans—all of these of course being appropriate to the function of "misguidance" that the divine desire seeks of Iblis and by virtue of which guidance and the path to God become more distinct and clear. Being the share allotted to him from his Beloved, Iblis rejoices in the sustenance that comes to him, even if others consider it to be blame and condemnation.

> One of the stations of the perfection of love is that if a person hears the name-calling of the Beloved, it is more delightful to him than receiving gentleness from others. (*T* 221–222, §284)

> That chevalier Iblis said, "If others flee from Your assault, I will take it on my neck!" (*T* 224, §289)

> "Do as You wish: I am content with whatever You do. If others flee from Your curse, for me it is a crown on my head and an embroidered robe."[139] (*N* II, 187, §281)

> The beauty of God's beloveds was never displayed to Him until Iblis was cursed. Until a bad eye was cast, one could not arrive at perfection itself![140] (*N* I, 415, §695)

> In terms of the reality of the situation, Iblis took the path of proximity in distance. (*N* I, 315, §525)

Indeed, by being cursed, Iblis receives the nourishment he needs to continue his task of misguiding and leading others into error.

> He has taken misguidance as his profession and curses have become his nourishment: *"By Thy exaltedness, I shall certainly cause them to err, altogether."*[141] (*T* 30, §43)

> Of all the errors that occur along the wayfarer's path, one is that he sends prayers[142] upon Iblis. This is an error because his gift is in the love of being cursed, which is more beloved to him. (*N* I, 97, §134)

If there is any doubt, ʿAyn al-Quḍāt assures us that in the afterlife Iblis will enter into God's all-encompassing forgiveness and mercy, when the scope of guidance and misguidance come to an end.

> As for Iblis' outcome, there is "so ask forgiveness"[143] and "their recompense is forgiveness."[144] Such people are not called sinners. Rather, they are called "workers": *How excellent is the wage of the workers!*[145] Since sins will be wiped away and nothing but forgiveness will remain, how will Iblis be harmed by any sins? (*N* II, 69, §94)

If this recounting of the story of Iblis can do nothing but awaken in wayfarers a sense of the aspiration and love that they must have upon the spiritual path, ʿAyn al-Quḍāt will consider his job done.

> What fine aspiration! He said, "I am prepared for endless pain, so give me the everlasting mercilessness that is my due!" (*N* II, 187, §281)

> He had chosen separation from the Beloved over prostration to someone else. How wonderful is the perfection of

> love! *The gaze swerved not, nor did it transgress.*[146] (*N* I, 96, §132)

In the final analysis, the story of Iblis can act as a complete mirror for anyone aspiring to live a life in conformity with the Beloved.[147] ʿAyn al-Quḍāt also leaves open the possibility that a true aspirant can even surpass Iblis, as was the case with Shaykh Fatḥa.[148] Be that as it may, Iblis' story is our story.[149] Just as pleasure and pain and praise and blame are equal in the eyes of Iblis, so too should they be for us, even as we struggle to climb the mountain of self-transcendence atop of which all dualities vanish into thin air. Such was the perspective of Iblis, for whom God's gentleness and severity were one and the same.

> Alas! You have not heard what that great one said? "He who does not delight in the striking of the Beloved is not truthful in his claim of love."[150] Whoever does not suffer from the cruelty of the Beloved does not know the worth of His loyalty; whoever has not tasted separation from the Beloved will not find the delight of union with Him; whoever does not know the name-calling of the Beloved as gentleness is far from the Beloved. (*T* 244–245, §318)

> If a carpet is black, and if it is white—both of these are one. Whoever sees them as distinct, with respect to love, he is still raw. From the hand of the Friend, what honey is there and what poison? What sugar and what colocynth? What gentleness and what severity? The person who is a lover of gentleness or a lover of severity is a self-lover, not a lover of the Beloved. Alas! When the sultan gives a robe and special crown to someone, that is enough—nothing remains in the reckoning of lovers. Alas! They said to Iblis, "Why do you not throw off the black carpet of *My curse*[151] from your shoulder?" He said:
>
> I will never sell the carpet—never!
> For if I sell it, my shoulder will be bare.[152]
> (*T* 224, §289)

> What are you saying? If your beloved gives you a black carpet[153] as a keepsake, would it be acceptable to you if she

> were to take it back, compensating you with mixed fabrics? Certainly not! The lovers know the value of the Beloved's keepsake. It is worldly love to say that the mixed fabrics are better than the black carpet. For the lovers, His curse and mercy are the same. This is perfection in love, beyond which there is no perfection. (*N* I, 97–98, §135)

That leader of the abandoned ones Iblis is a perfect lover precisely because he relinquishes his self in favor of God's Self. He thereby comes to love all things not through his own eyes, but through the eyes of his Beloved, and not as he loves them, but as his Beloved loves them.

All of this love-talk naturally takes us to the Shaykh's multifaceted vision of love, beauty, and the manner in which they interpenetrate one another. At this point it would be correct form to state that we will now turn to love. But as ʿAyn al-Quḍāt would have it, it is in fact more correct to say that love will now turn to us.

Figure 16. Mount Alvand (Hamadan, Iran)

10

Love Transcendent

For ʿAyn al-Quḍāt the purpose of human life is the pursuit and attainment of love, which is synonymous with God who is at once the Subject and Object of both love and beauty.

هو

Love as Guide

ʿAyn al-Quḍāt maintains that love (P. *dūstī, maḥabbat; ʿishq*) and God are one, and that all human beings are objects of divine love. Since God is the Lover and human beings His beloveds, there is a standard subject-object relationship here: God, as the Lover, loves His creatures, who are His beloveds. As ʿAyn al-Quḍāt insists, human beings are also lovers and God is their Beloved. This leads him to an exposition of the subtle dynamics that are involved in what can be called the "circle of love," where the subject of love is simultaneously its object.

To come to this all-encompassing standpoint we must take small steps. In the first instance, the Shaykh tells us that love is an obligation (P. *farīḍat*) upon wayfarers because reaching God is obligatory for them.

> O dear friend! Reaching God is obligatory. And, inescapably, whatever it is through which one reaches God itself becomes obligatory for seekers. Love causes the servant

> to reach God. Thus, for this reason, love is an obligation upon the path.
>
> O dear friend! One must have the attribute of Majnun, who, by simply hearing the name of Layla, could throw away his spirit! For the unattached one, why would he care for the love of Layla? What is an obligation upon the path of Majnun is not an obligation for the one who is not a lover of Layla. (*T* 97, §138)

By speaking of love as an obligation upon the path, ʿAyn al-Quḍāt has in mind the spiritual path and the more general path of life. This is to say that, no matter who the person may be, his life must be characterized by love—if not for God, then at minimum, for what He has created.

> Alas! Love is an obligation upon the path for everyone. Alas! If you do not have love for the Creator, well, then be ready to love creation so that the worth of these words is obtained by you. (*T* 96, §137)

Love for even ephemeral things is nothing to sneeze at. After all, ʿAyn al-Quḍāt tells us that "all existents are God's act and handiwork."[1] Love for lesser things can therefore lead to God, who is love itself.

> O dear friend! There is a fine point here: there is no detraction and deficiency in loving something in order to perfect one's love. . . . If Majnun loves the dog on Layla's lane, that is not love for the dog. It is love for Layla! (*T* 139, §190)

For the wayfarer who is actively walking upon the spiritual path, this teaching is even more significant. He is conscientious of the fact that all things in existence point to God and that he must cultivate love for them. But some things are more beloved to God than others. The wayfarer's love is thus concentrated on the most beloved of God's creation, Muhammad, then his own master, then his own self, and then the means by which he and others subsist.

> Whoever loves God, he will inescapably love His Messenger Muhammad, his master, and his own life. For the sake of

> performing obedient deeds, he loves bread and water as they are the means for his subsistence. He loves women so that his offspring subsists and loves gold and silver so that, through them, he can have access to obtaining water and bread. (*T* 140, §191)

Despite the fact that one must cultivate all kinds of loves in the hope of attaining love itself, the surest way to reach love is to let it guide one through the labyrinth of life.

> Be a student! Love itself suffices as your teacher. (*N* II, 128, §188)

> I say that, for the beginner, the guide to recognition of God is love. Whoever does not have love as a master is not a traveler upon the path. Through the Beloved, the lover can reach love, and by virtue of love, he can see the Beloved. (*T* 284, §368)

> The first collyrium with which the seeking wayfarer must be anointed is love. Our master said, "There is no master more penetrating than love"[2]—there is no master more perfect for the wayfarer than love. One time, I asked the master, "What is the guide to God?" He said, "Its guide is God Himself." (*T* 283, §368)

> Enter with love, until you see wonders! God loves a servant until His love reaches a point where He says to him, "Do as you please, for I have forgiven you."[3] (*N* I, 64, §80)

> Love is the conqueror, and I am the conquered. How can I ever compete with love?! (*T* 96, §136)

> Alas! What can be said about love? What indication of it is worthy and what explanation can be given? When entering love, a person should surrender and not be with himself. He should abandon himself and prefer love over himself. (*T* 96–97, §137)

Love and Loverhood

In *Paving the Path* the Shaykh says that "love is a veil between the lover and the Beloved."[4] This statement is of course not a definition of love per se, because love is a synonym for the Essence of God which is indefinable. Rather, ʿAyn al-Quḍāt is hinting at the subtle nature of the veil of love that conceals the lover from, and also reveals him to, the Beloved (and vice versa).

> Will you ever know what the sustenance and share of the Beloved is from and what the lover finds his share from, and what makes the lover live? An explanation of love can only be done through symbols and likenesses so that love can be spoken about. If not, what can be said of love and what should be spoken? (*T* 125, §174)

> The beginner-lover, for whom the world is a veil, is still unripe. When the love of Beginninglessness is brought, it is hidden between the spirit and the heart. Since love is veiled in this world, the world cannot obtain its secret—love itself has the world entranced and confounded! And love knows what is done to the world as it is always in sorrow and grief. (*T* 108, §153)

> O, alas! You can never understand what has been spoken! God's love is the substance of the spirit and our love is an accident for the substance of His existence. Our love is an accident for Him and His love is the substance of our spirits. If, for example, a substance without accident is conceivable, then a lover without a beloved and without love is possible. But this is never possible and conceivable! In this state, love, lover, and beloved abide through one another; between them, otherness should not be sought. (*T* 113, §160)

Despite the transparent obscurity of love, one thing is for certain as far as ʿAyn al-Quḍāt is concerned: the "confidants of divine intimacy," those who have taken on God's attributes but whose "reality is tied to human mortality,"[5] stand in stark contrast to those whom he calls "wimps" (P. *nā mardān*). These wimps are the antipodes of the chevaliers Muhammad and Iblis. As such, wimps have nothing to do with love and love has nothing to do with them.

> Love is forbidden to wimps. (*N* I, 22, §24)

> The confidants of love themselves know what state love is. But wimps and effeminates only get blame from love, and blame is nothing. (*T* 110, §157)

As we saw in chapter 6, a wimp is a habit-worshipper. He is also a self-lover (P. *ʿāshiq-i khwudī*), and a self-lover has the attribute of "faintheartedness" (P. *bad-dilī*). This alone disqualifies him from engaging in the demanding and difficult business of love.

> O friend! You are a self-lover, but trading cannot be done with faintheartedness! (*N* I, 123, §178)

The self-lover is ultimately someone who loves something—to which he assigns ultimate worth—over and above the Beloved, be it his own desires, sense of self, the world, Paradise, and so forth.

> A thousand people are seekers of the seal, but there is not a single seeker after the pearl and the gem! (*T* 111, §158)

> O chevalier! If there is neither desire for God nor desire for Paradise inside yourself—if indeed you belong to a people who *love the ephemeral and forsake the next world*[6]—then your recompense is this: *And a barrier is set between them and that which they desire, as was done with the likes of them before. Surely they were in confounding doubt.*[7] But if you would be *and who are certain of the next world*[8] and would not be *they were in [confounding] doubt*, and if you would let go of *until it becomes clear to them that He is the Real,*[9] then you would be held back by neither this world nor the next. Now, look inside yourself: does love for this world dominate, or love

> for Paradise, or love for God? *"On this day, your soul suffices as a reckoner against you."*[10] (*N* I, 65, §83)
>
> The veil of heedlessness and distance is placed before those estranged from themselves and unworthy of love until they fall far away: *"You were indeed in heedlessness of this."*[11] In another place, God complains of this group: *They know an outward aspect of the life of this world, but of the next world they are heedless.*[12] Love is a specific task and everyone has it. But nobody has business with the Beloved! This heedlessness is a sign of misfortune. (*T* 107, §151)
>
> Alas! *Between them and that which they desire*[13] is complete Hell for the people of insight. *"They are called from a place far off."*[14] This distance from the Presence of exaltedness is Hell, but nobody knows! Today, the veiled ones know what punishment through fire in this world is. But wait until they reach the world of certainty! (*T* 291, §382)
>
> "Follow the religion of old women."[15] How extremely well has he spoken! That is, O incapable one who cannot bear love! Choose foolishness, for "Most of the people in the Garden are foolish. . . ."[16] Whoever seeks Paradise is called "foolish." The worldly person is a seeker of Paradise, but there is not a single seeker of love! (*T* 111, §158)

In contrast to those who foolishly seek Paradise are the Friends of God. For them, the very sight of their Beloved is Paradise itself.

> When His Friends see Him, they are in Paradise. But when they are without Him, they consider themselves to be in Hell. (*T* 291, §381)

In order to reach the Beloved as the Friends have, and hence to be in Paradise like them, what one must do is first make himself worthy of love, and hence worthy to receive God.

> Whoever is not worthy of love is not worthy of God. Love can speak to the lover, and the lover knows the worth of

> love. The one unconcerned with love only thinks it to be a fable. He deprives himself from the name "love" and the claim to love. (*T* 111, §157)

To become worthy of love, one must first cultivate the right kind of spiritual attitude. This necessarily spells single-minded devotion to love, as well as the cultivation of purity of heart.

> O dear friend! Give ear to *He loves them, and they love Him.*[17] When *they love Him* is put in place, it can entirely face *He loves them* and arrive at it. *They love Him* can say *He loves them* because *He loves them* embraces all of *they love Him*. The sun can be for the entire earth since its surface is vast. But so long as the house of your heart does not entirely face the sun, not a single ray of the sun can be its share.
>
> "And among His signs is the sun"[18] itself testifies that *He loves them* has such an attribute of vastness that it can be for every person. But as long as *they love Him* is not entirely given to *He loves them*, it will not find its rays in their entirety. In the cloister of *they love Him*, *He loves them* says what love is, and who the Beloved is. (*T* 128, §177)

> The reality of seeking obtains when the gaze of the seeker is entirely turned toward the sought. It is then that seeking and finding are twins. The reality of this search can be expressed by the attraction of iron to a magnet: if the iron is unalloyed, the magnet will attract it, with nothing to impede the iron's attraction to the magnet. But if the iron is mixed with some gold, silver, or the like, this will compromise its attraction. Likewise, when the iron is uncontaminated, its fully actualized attraction to the magnet will ensue. It is then that finding—namely the iron reaching the magnet—will necessarily occur. (*Z* §72)

In the preceding passage the Shaykh equates finding the Beloved with reaching the Beloved. More commonly, as in the *Letters*, he relates the finding in question to a concept we have already encountered, that of self-recognition. If a person finds himself and therefore recognizes himself, he comes to love the Object of his quest—the Beloved—who is his innermost self. The Beloved resides deep within his heart, which is why he only has to search within himself to realize love.

> Apart from its trappings without reality, do not imagine that you and your likes have known love! Love is only achieved by the one who obtains recognition. (*N* II, 153, §224)
>
> The seeker's task is to search in himself for nothing but love. The lover's existence is from love. How can he live without love? Recognize life from love and find death without love!
>
> My two days of life in this world
> would be a shame were I to live alone.
> Dying before You is the moment I live,
> and living without You is the moment I die.
> (*T* 98, §139)

Trial and Tribulation

If a person wishes to take the path of love, he has one guarantee: the journey will be filled with all kinds of obstacles and pitfalls, and will be one of pain and suffering.

> First I was given my idol of pure wine without dregs.
> By this ruse was my heart taken.
> Then I was turned over to the snare of separation—
> the same kind of trade with idiots and fools!
> (*T* 106, §150)
>
> [W]hen the moment of "People are asleep; when they die, they awaken"[19] comes about and everyone is made aware of their own reality, then they will know that there is nothing but idols, and that only madness, heedlessness, and distance have appeared. (*T* 108, §152)

The Shaykh explains that the veils of distance and separation are necessary in order for lovers to perfect their love so that they can eventually see God unveiled before their very eyes.

> Alas! Do you know why all of these curtains and veils are placed upon the path? So that, day by day, the lover's eyes ripen until he is able to bear the burden of encountering God without a veil. (*T* 104, §148)

ʿAyn al-Quḍāt says that suffering (P. *miḥnat*) is inscribed into the very nature of love (P. *maḥabbat*) through a primordial transposition of letters. When *maḥabbat* (محبت) was written on the Preserved Tablet, its *bāʾ* or "b" transmuted into the *nūn* or "n" of *miḥnat* (محنت).

> Alas! The first letter that appeared on the Preserved Tablet was *maḥabbat*. Then, the dot of the *bāʾ* turned into the dot of the *nūn*—that is, *maḥabbat* became *miḥnat*. (*T* 245, §320)

In other words, loverhood and suffering are inseparable insofar as the lover sees himself as distinct from God.

> In this path, there is no tribulation more difficult than your own existence, and there is no poison deadlier than the false wishes of the aspirants. (*T* 50, §68)
>
> The believer must suffer from tribulation so much that he becomes tribulation itself and tribulation becomes his very self. Then, he will be unaware of tribulation. Alas! This is the meaning of *"Surely kings, when they enter a town, corrupt it."*[20] (*T* 244, §318)

What the lover must do is be patient with his false sense of independent existence and with his Beloved, taking on the divine name the Patient (*al-ṣabūr*).[21] Eventually, that tribulation (*balā*) with which he was so patient will become the very means by which he arrives at God.

> Alas! You imagine that tribulation is given to just anyone? What do you know of tribulation? Wait until you reach a

> place where you sell your spirit for God's tribulation! Perhaps it is from this perspective that Shiblī said, "O God! Everyone seeks You for gentleness and comfort, but I seek You for tribulation." Wait until "one of the pulls of the Real" alchemically transforms you. At that time you will know what tribulation is! (*T* 243, §318)

Every tribulation the aspirant experiences on the path is actually a caress of gentleness (*luṭf*) from the Beloved, even though these caresses may come in the guise of severity (*qahr*). The severity is necessary because the aspirant is still raw (P. *khām*) in his love. This is tantamount to saying that he is insincere and unfaithful toward his Beloved, directing as he does his love and aspiration at other things. Through the intense fire of tribulation, the substance of his soul can slowly ripen.

> The sign of love is sincerity. You never know what I am saying! In love, harshness and faithfulness are necessary until the lover becomes cooked by the gentleness and severity of the Beloved. If not, he will be raw, and nothing will come from him. (*T* 221, §283)

> Alas! What business does the ball have that the Sultan should strike it with the polo stick of gentleness or the polo stick of severity? What business does the ball have with desire? This is also *And We carry them over land and ocean.*[22] Do you know what this land and ocean are? *And whosoever is wary of God, He will appoint a way out for him*[23] is the mirror of these two, that is, He will take him out of human mortality and send him to lordship. The *land* is servanthood and the *ocean* lordship. *And We provided them with good things*[24] gives them nourishment—*He will provide for him whence he reckons not.*[25] "I spend the night with my Lord; *'He feeds me and gives me drink'*"[26] testifies to this station. When the ball reaches this station, it is struck by Him—the Sultan strikes the ball with the polo stick of love in the field of divinity. (*T* 179–180, §237)

> Alas! When you turn toward these words and trade with them, you will reach a place where it must be said that

> the Friends of God are nourished by His gentleness and severity. They become drunk from the wine of union[27] a thousand times every day, but at the end of each day they are laid low under the foot of separation from Him. The lover is still an aspirant, and in this world the aspirant is placed atop the tree of separation. (*T* 222, §285)

> O dear friend! Do you know what the beauty of Layla says to the entranced love of Majnun?[28] It says, "O Majnun! If I give a wink, even if there are a hundred thousand people with the attribute of Majnun who all come forward, they will be slain by my wink." Give ear to what Majnun says: "Do not worry! If your wink will annihilate Majnun, union and your generosity will give him subsistence." (*T* 110, §156)

As the aspirant ripens and matures along the path of love, he may come under the illusion that he is a "lover." This claim (*daʿwā*) of love will itself be accompanied by its fair share of trials and tribulations. The Shaykh likens such a claimant to a nightingale (P. *bulbul*) who presents itself as a lover of the rose (P. *gul*). The rose has thorns that ensure that only the nightingale who is a true lover would dare fly toward it, knowing full well that all claims of love will be tested by the rose's piercing thorns. In short, if the aspirant talks the talk, he better prepare to walk the walk.

> You have not seen that the nightingale is a lover of the rose? When the nightingale gets close to the rose, it cannot bear it—it lunges itself into the rose. But the thorns under the rose have a station: they cause the rose to kill the nightingale. . . . If the rose were without the thorns' torment, every nightingale would have made the claim of being a lover. But with the existence of the thorns, not a single one out of a hundred thousand nightingales makes the claim of love for the rose. (*T* 341–342, §453)

Madness and Burning

In another context, ʿAyn al-Quḍāt likens the nightingale to a crazed lover of God. Like the nightingale who weeps and wails to be with the rose, the spiritual madman (P. *diwāna; majnūn*) sighs and laments for his Beloved.

> You have not seen that man driven mad by love, who is like a nightingale that sings on account of separation from the rose, letting out sounds and laments? When the nightingale sees the rose, out of yearning it laments as much as a thousand times. (*T* 207, §266)

At times, the Shaykh also identifies love with the sun from the perfection of whose illumination (*ishrāq*) the lover receives "neither power nor portion."[29] This is because the totalizing luminosity of the sun leaves no room for otherness, rendering the lover's intellect, whose operation is separative by nature, to nothing.

> When the sun of love appears, the star of the intellect is obliterated. (*N* II, 219, §327)

If the intellect stands no chance before love, words and actions will fare a lot worse.

> Here, what can "do" and "do not do" do? The rulings for lovers are one thing, and the rulings for intellectuals are quite another thing! (*N* II, 219, §328)

> Here, the fatwa of the muftis does not work. If speech had a chance with love, the task would be easy. But where God's command does not work, what can a fatwa do? (*N* II, 219, §327)

To truly be a lover one must give up everything: actions, words, intelligence, and egotistical self-love. When love takes over, it leaves the lover in a state of stupor, derangement, and madness (P. *sawdāʾī*), for "neither madman nor lover remain; only madness and love subsist."[30]

> However much I try to pass love by, love leaves me entranced and perplexed! (*T* 96, §136)

> The madness of love is of better worth than the cleverness of the world! . . . Whoever is not a lover is a self-seer and is wicked. (*T* 98, §140)

> Madness has made me so selfless and entranced that I do not know what I am saying! (*T* 237, §307)

> The lover is choiceless. Whatever the lover does comes into existence without his desire and issues forth without his choice.[31] (*T* 238, §308)

> To be a lover is to be selfless and pathless. (*T* 98, §140)

> Be in the tavern[32] for one month to see what the tavern and the tavern-dwellers do with you! O metaphorical drunkard! Become a tavern-dweller![33] Come so that we can go along for one moment! (*T* 341, §452)

> Alas! O friend, give ear! Have you ever seen that the madmen are placed in bonds? A group of the wayfarers are madmen over reality. With the light of prophecy, the lawgiver knew that the madmen would have to be placed in bonds. So the Sharia was made as their bond. Perhaps you have not heard what that great one said to his disciple: "Be a madman with God and sober with Muṣṭafā." (*T* 204, §263)

Annemarie Schimmel put it best when she described ʿAyn al-Quḍāt as someone who was "consumed by burning divine passion."[34] As such, not everyone will understand this love-stricken madman whose words "are not the taste of just anyone."[35] What one needs of course is the Shaykh's taste, which is "the taste of love."[36] This taste is of the ashes that result from the fire of love entirely consuming the lover.

> Wait until you reach a station where a fire will be given to you—the liver of your reality will be burnt from the heat of that fire. (*T* 240, §313)

> Love is a fire—wherever it is, nothing else can settle down there; wherever it reaches, it burns and turns into its own color. (*T* 97, §137)

> Do you know what the fire of the lovers' Hell is? You do not know! The fire of the lovers' Hell is love for God. Perhaps you have not heard what that great one said: "Love is God's greatest punishment."[37] Perhaps it is from this perspective that Shiblī said, "Love is a fire in the heart—it burns away everything other than the Beloved."[38] (*T* 238, §309)

When embarking upon the path of love, the lover's concern should solely be with love itself: "His goal is love and his life is from love; without love, he is dead."[39] Such a person is a "lover of the moment"[40] whose reaching the Beloved is contingent upon his becoming naughted.

> The least sign of this illumination is that you will come to naught, as it is only possible for a lover to reach his beloved after his having come to naught. So do not in any way suppose that your existence can come in the way of reaching God! Any explanation of this is inconceivable, for it passes beyond the limits of knowledge and the intellect. (*Z* §191)

The lover is neither happy to have arrived at love, nor is he sad to depart from it since "all of his self is given to love"[41] and he subsists in it alone, without a thought given over to "his" "self."

> When you become subsistent, you will be told what to do and what must be done: *Those who strive in Us, We shall surely guide them in Our ways.*[42] You will be placed in the crucible of love and at every moment it will be said to you, *Strive in God as He should be striven in*[43] until the fire causes you to be burnt. When you are burnt, you will become light—*Light upon light. God guides unto His light whomsoever He will.*[44] On its own, your light is unreal, but His light is real and reality. His light assails and your light vanishes and becomes unreal. Thus, you will entirely become His light: *Thus does God set forth the real and the unreal.*[45] *Nay, but We cast the real against the unreal, and it crushes it.*[46] (*T* 14, §20)

ʿAyn al-Quḍāt also relates the divine-human love relationship to the standard Persian Sufi imagery of the moth (P. *parwāna*) and candle (*shamʿ*). The moth, which represents the lover, of necessity lunges itself headfirst and without care into the candle, which represents the divine presence. All that the moth wants and sees is the fire of the candle. When it throws itself into the candle's fire, there is neither moth nor mothhood, for all is fire.

> When the moth becomes the fire, what portion can the fire take from the fire and what share can it find? But when the moth is distant from the fire, how will it take its share, and how will it settle with otherness? (*T* 283, §367)

> Without the fire, the moth is restless, but in the fire it does not have existence. So long as the moth flutters around the fire of love, it sees the entire world as fire. And when it reaches the fire, it throws itself in its midst. The moth does not know how to differentiate between the fire and other than the fire. Why? Because love itself is all fire. (*T* 99, §141)

> Love has a power that, when it permeates the Beloved, the Beloved draws in and consumes the entirety of the lover. The fire of love gives power to the moth and the moth flies toward the fire since it imagines the fire to be its lover. . . . The moth throws itself in the midst of the fire by virtue of its desire, and the fire of the candle, which is the moth's beloved, burns on until all of the candle is fire—neither love nor moth remain. (*T* 100, §141)

> If you want me to give an example of this, listen! The moth, who is a lover of the fire, has no share of it at all so long as it is indeed distant from the fire's light. When it throws itself into the fire, it becomes selfless and nothing of mothhood remains—all is fire. (*T* 242, §316)

Likewise, all that the lover can see is the form of his Beloved. This is because "the Beloved's beauty burns the vision of the lover until he takes on its color"[47] and is thus no more, for all is love.

The Religion of Love

In chapter 4 we saw how ʿAyn al-Quḍāt discusses a famous Hadith that speaks of Islam being divided into seventy-two or seventy-three sects.[48] The word for "sects" here is the Arabic term *madhhab*, which can also denote a legal school or more broadly a school of thought. In a still broader sense, the word can also mean "religion." This is how the term is figured in the following passages wherein ʿAyn al-Quḍāt interprets the seventy some-odd *madhhab*s as not subcommunities within Islam but as so many different religious communities. Their underlying meaning, our author tells us, "is displayed to a person who has gone beyond the seventy some-odd differing religions"[49] and who sees all things as rooted in God, the "Source of existents."[50]

> The first condition on the path of the seeker is that all of the well-known seventy-three religions be one and appear as one in his eyes. If he sees them as separate or makes them separate, he is a separator, not a seeker. (*T* 21, §33)

> O friend! If you were to also see what the Christians see in Jesus, you would become a Christian. And if you were to also see what the Jews see in Moses, you would become a Jew! Indeed, if you were to also see what the idol-worshippers see in idol-worship, you would become an idol-worshipper! The seventy-two religions are all waystations on the path to God. Perhaps you have not heard this story: one day Shaykh Abū Saʿīd Abū'l-Khayr came across a Zoroastrian and said, "Is there anything in your religion today that is not reported in our religion today?" (*T* 285, §370)

> *The Christians say that the Messiah is the son of God*[51] gives a trace of this about Jesus.[52] "Part of a man's felicity is in resembling his father" is the path of the wayfarers. *"Be lordly people"*[53] also shows the increase in their degree. (*T* 323, §423)

The true seeker has his eyes on unity and oneness and will never concern himself with divisions and factions which cause him to veer off course and into the direction of multiplicity, disunity, and dispersion.

> Alas! The partisans of the seventy-two religions dispute with one another, are opposed to everyone else because of their creed, and kill one another. But if all of them would come together and listen to the words of this helpless one, it would be conceivable to them that everyone follows one religion and one creed. Error and declaring God's similarity have cast people far from reality. *And most of them follow naught but conjecture. Surely conjecture does not avail against the truth in the least.*[54] (*T* 339, §449)

For the Shaykh, religious difference is inscribed into the nature of things and is necessary. This pertains to the branches of religion (*furūʿ al-dīn*) but not its roots (*uṣūl al-dīn*).[55] Like the waystations on a road, the branches are many; and like the road itself, the root is one.

> The wayfarer will necessarily have to go beyond all of these religions. O friend! Religions are waystations on the path to God. And wherever the wayfarer is, every day he will inevitably be in a waystation. (*N* II, 307, §463)

> The names are many, but the essence and the named is one. You are called "Ẓahīr al-Dīn," and "master," "scholar," and "mufti." If your reality would be changed for every name, you would be twenty Ẓahīr al-Dīns! Your names are not one—they are diverse. But the named is one. This is the meaning of *"Unto you is your religion, and unto me is my religion."*[56] Alas! Perhaps you have not heard what Muṣṭafā said: "Every striver is correct."[57] The striver thinks that his striving is correct, and every creed relies upon striving. (*T* 339, §449)

> Aḥmad granted a speck of love to the unity-voicers—they are the believers. Iblis granted a speck of love to the Zoroastrians—they are the unbelievers and idol-worshippers.[58] You have not heard what that great one said? "The roads are many, but the path is one." He said, "The roads on the waystations of lordship are many, but the path is one." (*T* 284, §369)

> O dear friend! Declaring God's similarity is a part of the path and belongs to the path. You should know that every person's religion is a waystation on the path to God, but residing in a waystation is an error. For a person coming from Khurasan, Hamadan and Baghdad are waystations en route to Makka. But it would not be fitting for him to reside in them, for a waystation can never be a place to reside in! If a person were to make a residence out of a waystation, the path would be cut off for him. (*N* II, 262, §395)

The "path" that ʿAyn al-Quḍāt has in mind is the religion of love, which is true *islām* or submission. This can only be truly known to those who, like the Shaykh, have lost themselves in their Beloved, beholding their Beloved wherever they may turn. When it comes to the perspective of the lovers of God, love is the only true religion.

> They follow the religion and creed of God, not the religion and creed of Shāfiʿī, Abū Ḥanīfa, and others. They follow the religion of love and the religion of God. When they see God, the encounter with God is their religion. When they see Muhammad, the encounter with Muhammad is their faith. When they see Iblis, for them, seeing this station is unbelief. (*T* 115–116, §163)

> O dear friend! Since the substance of the root—"God is the Source of existents"—is actualized through God's desire and love, nothing but its alchemical transformation appears: *He it is who created you; among you are unbelievers and among you are believers.*[59] The diversity in the colors of existents is no trifling matter! And one of God's signs is the diversity in the creation of people: "And among His signs is the diversity in your languages and colors."[60] (*T* 181–182, §239)

> Religion itself is *islām* and *islām* itself is religion. But it goes into disparate dwellings. Apart from that, the root is one. (*T* 66, §91)

> O friend! The religion and creed of the lovers is love—their love is the beauty of the Beloved.[61] (*T* 286, §372)

> Love for God is the religion and creed of the lover.[62] (*T* 292, §384)
>
> When one reaches the quest's end, there is no religion other than the religion of the Sought. Ḥusayn-i Manṣūr was asked, "What religion do you follow?" He said, "I follow the religion of my Lord."[63] (*T* 22, §33)
>
> For the great ones of the path, their master is God Himself. Thus, they follow God's religion and are sincere, not insincere. Insincerity is halting, and sincerity is advancing. (*T* 22, §33)
>
> If a religion takes a person to God, that religion is *islām*.[64] But if it does not give any awareness to the seeker, in the eyes of God, that religion is worse than unbelief. In the eyes of the travelers, *islām* is what takes a person to God and unbelief is what prevents and curtails the seeker, holding him back from the Sought. The seeker's work is with the Founder of the religion, not the religion.
>
> Let me start a fire, setting aflame this religion and creed!
> I put love for You in place of religion.
> How long shall I contain this hidden love in my wounded heart?
> The goal of the path is neither religion nor creed, but You. (*T* 22–23, §34)

Levels of Unbelief

As a complement to the Shaykh's exalted view of the religion of love is his detailed exposition of what can be called the levels of unbelief (*kufr*). Some have noted his indebtedness to Ḥallāj's treatment of real unbelief (*al-kufr al-ḥaqīqī*) in this regard, and there seem to be no good grounds to deny this connection.[65] ʿAyn al-Quḍāt also credits Avicenna with making an important distinction between metaphorical Islam (*al-islām al-majāzī*) and real unbelief. In the following passage, which has been interpreted variously,[66] he recounts a curious encounter between Avicenna (Abū ʿAlī Sīnā) and Abū Saʿīd b. Abī'l-Khayr.

> O friend! Perhaps you have not read what is recorded in the *Treatise on the Feast of the Sacrifice* concerning what Abū Saʿīd Abū'l-Khayr wrote to Abū ʿAlī Sīnā: "Point me to a guide." In the treatise, the master Abū ʿAlī replied: "The guide is to enter real unbelief and exit metaphorical Islam. You should only devote yourself to being one of three types of people: [1] a Muslim and an unbeliever; if you are beyond that, then [2] neither a believer nor an unbeliever; if you are below these, then [3] an associating Muslim. But if you are ignorant of these, then you should know that you are worthless and an utter waste of space."[67]
>
> In *The Lamps*, Shaykh Abū Saʿīd wrote, "These words took me to where a life of a hundred thousand years of worship could not take me."[68] But I say that Shaykh Abū Saʿīd has still not tasted these words! If he had tasted them just as Abū ʿAlī and the others who are wounded strangers had, he too would have been wounded and stoned by people. May a hundred thousand lives of that claimant be sacrificed for Abū ʿAlī on account of how he has torn away the curtain and shown the pathless path! (*T* 349–350, §463)

In ʿAyn al-Quḍāt's own terms, what is normally understood to be *kufr* or unbelief, namely the rejection of faith, is but the first stage of his unique four levels of unbelief. He calls the first stage of unbelief "outward unbelief" (P. *kufr-i ẓāhir*), which is metaphorical Islam plain and simple. It is the realm of the Sharia and is solely concerned with the conventional unbeliever or *kāfir*.

> Now, listen. The first unbelief that is outward is known to the generality of people: when one refuses or denies a trace and a single mark of the Sharia, he is an unbeliever. This is outward unbelief. (*T* 209, §269)

The most characteristic feature of outward unbelief is that it implies a strong duality between God and the servant. The second kind of unbelief, on the other hand, is different in nature. Corresponding to metaphorical Islam but with less intensity on the side of metaphor, it is called "unbelief of the soul" (P. *kufr-i nafs*) and is identified with habit-worship and caprice-worship (P. *hawā-parastī*).

> The second unbelief is attached to the soul, for the soul is an idol—"the soul is the greatest idol"[69]—and the idol is taken as a god. This is, *Hast thou considered the one who takes his caprice as his god?*[70] Perhaps it is from this perspective that Abraham said, *"And keep me and my children from worshipping idols."*[71] This unbelief is attached to the soul since it is the god of the caprice-worshippers. (*T* 209, §269)

Unlike outward unbelief, unbelief of the soul is typified by a reduced stress on duality between God and servant. This is because this level of unbelief is not the purview of the body but of the soul, which is a more inward dimension of human personhood than the body and is hence closer to the divine reality.

Furthermore, unbelief of the soul is the realm of Iblis and his function as misguider, whereas the third type of unbelief, "Muhammadan unbelief" (P. *kufr-i Muḥammadī*), is the realm of Muhammad and his function as guide. The Shaykh also refers to Muhammadan unbelief, which is tantamount to a residual form of metaphorical Islam, as "unbelief of the heart" (P. *kufr-i qalb*). That is to say that its purview is the heart and is thus typified by a much more subtle form of duality than that of unbelief of the soul.

> There is outward unbelief, unbelief of the soul, and unbelief of the heart. Unbelief of the soul has a relation to Iblis and unbelief of the heart has a relation to Muhammad. (*T* 209, §268)

If the first level of unbelief is for the conventional unbeliever and the second for the habit-worshipper, ʿAyn al-Quḍāt tells us that the third level of unbelief pertains exclusively to the "Muslim unbeliever" (P. *musalmān-kāfir*).

> Have you ever seen a Muslim unbeliever? On account of the beauty of "Muhammad is the Messenger of God" all

> of the believers became unbelievers, but nobody is aware. As long as you do not find these unbelievers, you will not arrive at faith in idol-worship. But when you arrive at the height of faith and see idol-worship in the court of "No god but God, Muhammad is the Messenger of God," an imprint will be made and your faith will be perfected at that moment. In this state, the perfection of the religion and the creed will appear.[72] (*T* 118, §165)

> Alas! Idol-worship, fire-worship, unbelief, and the sash of unbelief—all are in this station. From this perspective, Abū Saʿīd Abū'l-Khayr said, "Whoever sees the Prophet's beauty will instantly become an unbeliever." Why would he become an unbeliever? Because *there subsists the face of thy Lord, possessor of majesty and bounty*.[73] His entirety is pulled away in such a way that he prostrates immediately. What are you saying?! Prostrating to Muhammad is not unbelief! For the wayfarer, this station is "Muhammadan unbelief." Alas! From this perspective, Muṣṭafā said, "He who sees me has seen the Real."[74] He said, "Whoever sees me has seen God." The more one is in this station, the more the unbelief and associationism. (*T* 211–212, §271)

Note how the Shaykh identifies idol-worship with unbelief, fire-worship (a Zoroastrian practice), and so on. What he is getting at will become clearer when we turn to his aesthetic theory toward the end of this chapter. At present, it is important to observe that, just as ʿAyn al-Quḍāt has a complicated understanding of unbelief, so too does this apply to his understanding of idol-worship and associating partners with God (*shirk*). He insists that most people who believe in God are implicated into *shirk*. Why? Because the Quran says so.

> O dear friend! Give ear to this verse: *And most of them believe not in God, save that they are associators*.[75] He is saying that most believers are associators. O, how strange! (*T* 204, §263)

For the followers of Muhammad, who stand on the third level of unbelief and are thus "Muhammadan unbelievers," associating another with God is a natural feature of their faith. The association in question results from the subtle level of dualism that remains, where there is still God and the believer. Insofar as this is the case, the believer is an associator or *mushrik* which for ʿAyn al-Quḍāt is a positive designation. In fact, such a believer receives the title of being God's "associate" (P. *ham-sharīk*) and "partner" (P. *ham-maqām*).

> It becomes known to the wayfarer that *O you who believe! Believe in God and His Messenger*[76] is saying that, apart from this faith, there must be another faith. So, what is the opposite of this discussion? It is that, beyond this unbelief, there is another unbelief. This is, *And whosoever believes in God, He guides his heart.*[77] As long as man is still with his heart, he is a believer without guidance. But when he is selfless, guidance appears. *He leads astray whomsoever He will and guides whomsoever He will*[78] appears. When guidance is obtained in this way, he reaches a station where he becomes God's associate and partner. He becomes an associator. *If thou dost associate, thy work will surely come to naught*[79] itself says it like this so that the affair reaches a place where all becomes this: *And most of them believe not in God, save that they are associators.*[80] (*T* 324–325, §425)

When one passes the third stage of unbelief he enters upon the fourth and last stage, that of "real unbelief" (P. *kufr-i ḥaqīqī*) and what the Shaykh also calls "divine unbelief" (P. *kufr-i ilāhī*).

> Alas! O dear friend, give ear to divine unbelief! Look until you see the first unbelief. Then, travel until you acquire faith. Give your spirit until you see the second and third unbeliefs. Give up your spirit until, in doing so, you find the fourth unbelief. Then you will become a believer. At that time, *and most of them believe not in God, save that they are associators*[81] will say what faith is, and *I have turned my face*[82] will display itself to you. (*T* 214–215, §275)

> O dear friend! Give ear to what that great one said about these two stations: "Faith and unbelief are two stations beyond the Throne and two veils between God and the servant." This is because a man must be neither unbeliever

> nor Muslim. Whoever is still with unbelief and faith is still in these two veils. But the wayfarer at the end of the path is in nothing but the veil of God's greatness and His Essence. (*T* 122–123, §171)

> When the wayfarer also passes this,[83] he will see the God of these two stations and will become embarrassed and ashamed. Unity and faith will begin and the wayfarer will entirely say this: *"Surely I have turned my face toward the one who created the heavens and the earth."*[84] (*T* 211–212, §271)

ʿAyn al-Quḍāt even identifies real unbelief with "real faith" (*īmān-i ḥaqīqī*), which he also calls the "faith of Aḥmad" (P. *īmān-i Aḥmadī*).

> As long as you do not go beyond this unbelief, you will not become a believer who has the faith of Aḥmad. (*T* 341, §452)

> The unbelief of reality has a relation to God. After these, all is faith. Alas! What boldness I have to speak these words that cannot be contained in this world or that world! But I shall speak, come what may! (*T* 209, §268)

When the Shaykh ventures to speak about real unbelief/real faith, he must necessarily resort to rather unconventional theological language, pointing up as best as words can do the paradox of belief/unbelief that emerges the higher a person, qua embodied individual, ascends the scale of nonduality. On a number of occasions ʿAyn al-Quḍāt draws on the image of sash-wearing (P. *zunnār dāshtan*) and the sash (P. *zunnār*),[85] which was worn by non-Muslims in medieval Islamic societies in order for them to be distinguishable from Muslims. The sash thus commonly came to be known in Persianate contexts as the "sash of unbelief" (P. *zunnār-i kufr*). For our author, the sash is a distinctive feature of real unbelief and its wearers are of course the real unbelievers who are God's true servants, completely realized in divine oneness.

> Alas! People do not know what they want from unbelief and the sash!
>
> There is a meaning in wine that is not in grapes.[86]

> For them, unbelief and the sash are for the path to God and are specific to the work of their path. It is said that destruction is better than living without Him.
>
>> It is better to be slain in Your lane than to be distant from Your face. (*T* 206–207, §265)
>
> Alas! Wait until you reach this station! Then you will know what sash-wearing, idol-worship, and fire-worship are! (*T* 208, §267)
>
> O chevalier! Do you know what this is? Sash-wearing is the path of the men—as long as one is not established in His servanthood, the belt of servanthood will not be fastened around his waist. Until you are in servanthood, you are not free. When you become free from others, you can then be His servant. (*N* I 156, §230)

As far as the Shaykh is concerned, he himself is an apostate who has left his "religion."

> I would be an apostate if I would dare say what this station is! But it must be that you now know that I am an apostate! Do you know what I am saying? If you do not believe, listen to Muṣṭafā when he said, "Whoever changes his religion, slay him."[87] This is addressed to the doorkeepers of exaltedness, for *Whosoever seeks a religion other than submission, it shall not be accepted of him, and in the next world he shall be among the losers.*[88] (*T* 327, §428)

This religion that ʿAyn al-Quḍāt has left pales in the face of real unbelief. For the latter corresponds to the kernel of religion and the former to its husk.[89] As one peels away each layer of unbelief he finally reaches the kernel, which is where God is. Real unbelief is therefore the highest stage of faith because it entails the utter nothingness of the servant and the dissolving of all duality. Just as a conventional unbeliever negates what is there, namely God, the real unbeliever negates what is "there," namely himself.

This level of unbelief is exclusively the realm of God, the Believer; its purview with respect to the servant is neither body, nor soul, nor heart, but simply nothingness. The type of unbeliever in question is he whom ʿAyn al-Quḍāt calls the "poor one" (*faqīr*), that is, the servant who realizes the true nature of his ontological indigence.

> Your selfhood should live in Selfhood until you become all He. Then, poverty will appear, as poverty will be perfected: "When poverty is perfected, he is God."[90] That is, your entirety will be He. Unbelief will be and will not be. What are you saying?! This is "Poverty is almost unbelief."[91] Unity and oneness are here. Perhaps it is from this perspective that Ḥallāj said:
>
> > I have disbelieved in the religion of God, and unbelief
> > is obligatory for me,
> > though it is despised by the Muslims.[92]
>
> Look at this great one, the kind of excuse that he offers! O, would that I were in that unbelief that was his religion! (*T* 215, §275)
>
> Alas! In this station, one must also excuse Ḥusayn-i Manṣūr when he said, "There is no difference between me and my Lord except for two attributes: the attribute of essentiality and the attribute of subsistence. Our subsistence is through Him and our essences are from Him."[93] (*T* 129, §180)
>
> The poor one is the one who is in need neither of himself nor his Creator. This is because need is still a weakness and a deficiency, but the poor one has reached perfection: "When poverty is perfected, he is God." (*T* 130, §181)
>
> When an entranced one says that a drop in the ocean is to be called the ocean itself, it is just like when that chevalier said, "I am the Real!" He too should be excused—he was a real unbeliever. (*T* 340, §451)

A famous poem by Abū'l-Ḥasan Bustī, versions of which both Aḥmad Ghazālī and ʿAyn al-Quḍāt like to cite,[94] aptly illustrates how the wayfarer transcends all duality and conditionality. Moving past the realm above the obliterated primordial dots (see chapter 8), he also goes beyond the black light[95] and returns to his state of originary nothingness:

> I saw the makeup of the universe and the root of the world,
> and passed beyond defect and disgrace with ease.
> The black light beyond the dotless—
> that too I passed; neither this nor that remained.[96]

The self thus gone forth actualizes the saying, "When poverty is perfected, he is God." Free from this world and the next world, all that can be said is that there is only God and that the self never was/is.

> He receives neither news from the Beginningless nor a trace from the Endless. Alas! Being neither worldly nor otherworldly are both known to him because he is neither worldly nor otherworldly. All is God. (*T* 265, §347)

The highest reaches of poverty correspond to the actualization of what we would call "Sufism" (*taṣawwuf*). Since Sufism is the realization of poverty, the Sufi is none other than God.

> This renunciation is when man reaches a station called "Sufism," about which Shaykh Bā Yazīd gave an indication: "God purifies the Sufis from their attributes and makes them pure—so they are called 'Sufis.' "[97] The station of Sufism is first renunciation and turning away from all existents. Then God purifies the Sufi from all blameworthy and human attributes, so he becomes a true renunciant and Sufi. At that time, poverty appears: "When poverty is perfected, he is God."
>
> Perhaps it was in this context that that great one was asked about who and what a Sufi is. He replied, "He is God."[98] This is, "When poverty is perfected, he is God." "Poverty is my pride"[99] is the craft of this Sufi and renunciant. Alas! Who would dare say this? Give ear: one time Bā Yazīd was asked, "Who is the renunciant?" He said, "He is the poor one; the poor one is the Sufi, and the Sufi is God." You are an apostate if you do not spend your entire life trying to understand these words! (*T* 313–314, §412)

Level of Unbelief	Status	Sphere	Type of Unbeliever	Feature
Real unbelief (*kufr-i ḥaqīqī*)	Real faith (*īmān-i ḥaqīqī*)	God	Poor one (*faqīr*)	Nonduality
Unbelief of the heart (*kufr-i qalb*)	Metaphorical Islam (residual)	Muhammad	Muslim unbeliever (*musalmān-kāfir*)	Subtle duality
Unbelief of the soul (*kufr-i nafs*)	Metaphorical Islam (reduced)	Iblis	Habit-worshipper (*ʿādat-parast*)	Reduced duality
Outward unbelief (*kufr-i ẓāhir*)	Metaphorical Islam (*islām-i majāzī*)	Sharia	Unbeliever (*kāfir*)	Strong duality

Figure 17. Levels of unbelief

Self-Love

The link between ʿAyn al-Quḍāt's levels of unbelief and his expansive understanding of love is made most clear when considered in light of his doctrine of God's Self-love. We saw earlier that for ʿAyn al-Quḍāt, the spiritual master is the mirror through whom the aspirant on the path sees God and the aspirant is the mirror through whom the master sees his perfected self. A related dimension to this complex notion of mutual witnessing is the idea of the Muhammadan mirror, which, it will be recalled from chapter 7, represents the perfect locus through which God can display His names and attributes. This allows for wayfarers, to the extent of their abilities, to see God in as unmediated a manner as possible. At the same time, ʿAyn al-Quḍāt also wants to demonstrate how God's servants in general can act as mirrors in which He sees Himself. In the following passage, he cites his spiritual guide Aḥmad Ghazālī, who reports an intimate conversation between his own master[100] and God.

> "'My Lord, what is the wisdom in my being created?' The answer came: 'The wisdom in your being created is that I should see Myself in the mirror of your spirit and My

> love in your heart.'" He said, "The wisdom is that I see My own beauty in the mirror of your spirit and cast love for Myself into your heart." (*T* 272, §356)

If the Muhammadan spirit is the perfect locus for God's self-disclosure, all the other creatures are imperfect loci for His Self-disclosure, but nonetheless loci for the divine gaze. A key teaching here is the Hadith of the Hidden Treasure: "I was a Hidden Treasure and I loved to be recognized. So I created the world in order to be recognized." Since God recognizes Himself qua subjectivity, He also seeks to recognize Himself qua objectivity. Hence, He looks inside us in order to see His Self.

> O friend! When He wants to see Himself, He looks in the mirror of our spirits and sees Himself as Howless. (*T* 272, §356)

> The thought may occur to you, "Why did God effectuate existence? Is it because of a motive on His part?"—which is impossible!—or, "Did He effectuate existence for a different motive"?—which is also impossible, except by way of pure nature, though God cannot be described in that way. This question has bewildered many scholars and is the very thought that occurred to the prophet David, since he said, "O Lord! Why did you create the universe?" God replied, "I was a Hidden Treasure and I loved to be recognized." That to which God alluded in saying "I loved to be recognized" is what demands the effusion of existence from Him. Yet, only the recognizers can conceivably comprehend this meaning.[101] (*Z* §46)

> Servanthood is a mole raised up on the beautiful face of lordship. Here, you will know why that great one said, "There is no difference between me and Him except that I have come forth in servanthood."[102] The beauty of the face of lordship without the mole of servanthood does not have the attribute of perfection, and the mole of servanthood without the beauty of the face of lordship does not have existence! *I did not create jinn and mankind, save to worship*

> *Me*[103] testifies to both sides—lordship and humanness. "I was a Hidden Treasure and I loved to be recognized" explains the connection between servanthood and lordship. (*T* 275, §360)

One aspect of God's "all-possibility" is that of self-negation, which implies limitation, "descent," and localization. God delimits Himself in the perfect mirror in order to see Himself qua the totality of His manifestation. Likewise, He delimits Himself in imperfect mirrors in order to behold Himself qua the particularities of His manifestation. Another way to conceive of this is to say that the realm of manifestation is a display of the artisanry of the Artisan (*al-ṣāniʿ*), who naturally loves His artisanry and hence Himself.[104]

God's love is also linked to His love for that most perfect of mirrors, Muhammad. From one perspective, this love is a result of a certain "sin" (*dhanb*) that is attributable to Muhammad according to Q 40:55, 47:18, and 48:2. These verses have presented a number of difficulties to various theologians and legal scholars in the Islamic tradition particularly because the Prophet is seen in Islamic belief as having been divinely protected from sin (*maʿṣūm*).[105] For his part, the Shaykh does not try to explain the sin away.

> O, alas! Iblis' sin was his love for God! Do you know what Muṣṭafā's sin was? God's love for him. That is, Iblis' falling in love with God was Iblis' sin and God's falling in love with the Prophet was the Prophet's sin. *That God may forgive thee thy sins that went before, and those that are to come*[106] is a trace of this discussion. (*T* 229, §297)

> The entirety of this sin has been placed upon the spirit of Muṣṭafā. (*T* 229, §297)

For the Shaykh, God's falling in love with the Prophet is tantamount to God's love for Himself.

> Alas! God's love for Muṣṭafā is also Self-love. (*T* 218, §279)

> Alas! In love there is a station of which neither lover nor Beloved are aware. Of that station, nothing but Love is

> aware. This is, "Your love for something makes you blind and deaf."[107] What are you saying? Is it love for the lover or the Beloved? No, no! It is for the Beloved! So where is divine love from? It is self-evident that it is from a hallowed spirit. But where is the love of a hallowed spirit from? It is from the divine light. (*T* 279–280, §375)

> God is only a lover of Himself.[108] Thus, I say that love for Muṣṭafā is also God's love for Himself. Alas! Hear these words and listen to them with the ear of your spirit: God loves Muṣṭafā. He looked upon him out of all of the engendered things and treasuries and concealed him from the world's inhabitants. Perhaps you have not heard what that great one said: "The entire world has known God, yet they have not recognized Him. But they have not known Muhammad and have not recognized him." Alas! Perhaps "He who recognizes himself recognizes his Lord" has a relation to this statement. (*T* 220–221, §282)

> Alas! O listener of these words! By the spirit of Muṣṭafā, people have imagined that God's beneficence and love of creation is for them. It is not for them! Rather, it is for Himself. When a lover gives a gift to a beloved and is gentle to her, that gentleness he shows is not for her as much as it is out of love for himself. Alas! From these words you imagine that God's love for Muṣṭafā is for Muṣṭafā. But this love for him is for Himself! (*T* 217, §278)

In the final analysis, all that there is is Self-love upon the plain of terrestrial and cosmic forms.

> Perhaps you have not heard what that great one said: "God has fallen in love with Himself so much that He has no care for anybody and He does not turn toward anybody." And people imagine that He is their lover! If you want, listen to Shaykh Shiblī who was whispering to God one time and said, "O God! For whom were You?" He replied, "Nobody." "For whom are You?" He replied, "Nobody." "For whom will You be?" He replied, "Nobody."[109] (*T* 217, §278)

In the I of the Beholder

If God contemplates Himself in the various forms in the cosmos, then it is only fitting that we contemplate Him in these forms as well. To be sure, the great lover from Hamadan tells us that the human perception of God's beauty is the counterpart of His Self-vision that takes place through the mirror of the human spirit.[110] This insight allows ʿAyn al-Quḍāt to return to his preoccupation with the lovely face when he ventures into explaining the inextricable relationship between the witness and the object of his witnessing. After all, one of the perfect avenues to experience the divine presence is in a lovely face. What is required of the lover is to increase in the perfection of his love. The more of a lover he becomes, the more beautiful will the Beloved be.[111]

> The more perfect one's love, the more beautiful does the Beloved appear to him. (*T* 284, §368)

> O dear friend! Were the lover to see the beauty of the Beloved and drown in perceiving His beauty, the lover would not know what would happen! (*N* II, 28, §40)

Closely tied to the Shaykh's aesthetic theory is his tripartite understanding of love. There is "minor love" (P. *ʿishq-i ṣaghīr*), "major love" (P. *ʿishq-i kabīr*), and "in-between love" (P. *ʿishq-i miyāna*).

> O dear friend! I do not know if I am speaking about love for the Creator or love for creation! Love is of three kinds, but each love has different stages. There is minor love, major love, and in-between love. Minor love is our love for God and major love is God's love for His servants. (*T* 101, §143)

Unlike minor love and major love, in-between love is harder to get at.

> In-between love? Alas! I dare not speak of it since we have such a trivial understanding! But God willing, a trace of it shall be uttered by way of symbols. (*T* 102, §143)

The greatest distinction between in-between love and major love (which ʿAyn al-Quḍāt also calls *nihāyat-i ʿishq* or the "end of love") is that in in-between love the beholder of love and the Beloved are implicated in a disjunctive, subject/object dichotomy; but in major love, these barriers of duality disappear altogether.

> O dear friend! Do you know who our witness is and how we have come to the witness? Give ear to the explanation of major love and in-between love, and the witness and the witnessed. The explication of these two witnesses has appeared. In in-between love, a distinction can be found between the witness and the witnessed. As for the end of love, it is when a distinction cannot be made between them. (*T* 115, §162)

Whereas symbols and expressions can help in conveying the nature of in-between love, when it comes to major love, nothing will suffice.

> What do you know about what has been said? Alas for the love of God that is "major love"—no trace of it can be given at all in which the seer still subsists. (*T* 123, §172)

If we love God, that is "minor love." If God loves us, that is "major love." But if we witness God and He beholds Himself in forms, that is in-between love. The way to witness God is through a lovely face, denoted by the Arabic term *shāhid,* which also means a "witness." More specifically, one gazes at a beautiful form as a way of contemplating the eternal witness, a practice that in Persian Sufism came to be known as "devotion to the lovely face" (P. *shāhid-bāzī*).[112]

> What do you hear?! Alas! Has a lovely face not ever been shown to you, at which time your liver was torn to pieces by the love and jealousy of that lovely face? (*T* 295, §387)

> May my spirit be sacrificed for anyone who is a worshipper of the metaphorically lovely face, for a worshipper of the real lovely face is rare! But do not think that I am speaking about self-love, which is appetite. Rather, I am speaking about heart-love; and this heart-love is rare. (*T* 297, §389)

> That which is metaphorical, you refer to as a "lovely face." Whoever is a lover of God, his religion is the beauty of the

> encounter with God, and He is his lovely face. In reality, he is an unbeliever—the unbelief that, relative to others, is "faith." (*T* 286, §372)

> Alas! What report can be given of the station of witnessing, and who can give a report? You still do not know this much: a lovely face is for the Beloved. In this metaphorically lovely face—namely a beautiful face—a share of devotion to the lovely face of reality is placed in the heart. (*T* 297, §389)

> Alas for this station! The lovely-face devotees know how life with the lovely face is, and how death is without it. The witness and the witnessed explain to the real lovely-face devotees what life and death are. (*T* 320, §419)

> Since I said that the lovely-face devotees know this life and death—death being separation and life being encountering and yearning—what can be said about union? Alas! "There is no report like seeing."[113] Those unconcerned with love and devotion to the lovely face, what do they know? If you want to know more clearly, for us, death is unbelief and life is submission and unity. (*T* 321, §420)

From at least the time of Aḥmad Ghazālī onward, *shāhid-bāzī* had become standard fare in Persian Sufi circles. So widely accepted a phenomena was it that even the great Shams-i Tabrīzī, who is often very critical of individual Sufis and certain Sufi practices, had no qualms with it from the standpoint of the Sharia.[114] Shams would undoubtedly have been in full agreement with ʿAyn al-Quḍāt about one thing in particular: *shāhid-bāzī* is a divinely instituted practice and the greatest of the lovely-face devotees was none other than Muhammad.

> As long as the master of the tavern does not give an order, nobody would have the gall to try to look at the brides of the tavern of *Say, "The spirit is of the command of my Lord."*[115] The candle and the lovely face would not be placed in the tavern of unbelief. (*T* 341, §452)

> The head of the lovely-face devotees is Muṣṭafā. He gave a trace of unbelief and submission in this way: "O God! I live through You and die through You."[116] (*T* 321, §420)

> O friend! Also give ear to this report, which makes the elect of the community aware. He said, "Beware of glancing at beardless youths, for they have a color like the color of God."[117] In another place he said, "I saw my Lord on the night of the Ascension in the form of a beardless youth with curly hair."[118] (*T* 294, §385)

While we witness God through the mirror of earthly forms, God the supreme Witness also witnesses Himself through them.

> In this station, so long as you are not absent, you will not be present, and so long as you are not present, you will not be absent. (*T* 327, §429)

> If you think carefully, at times we are His witness and at times He is our witness. In one state, He is the witness and we are the witnessed, and in another state we are the witness and He is the witnessed. At the hands of this witness, the world has tossed away its spirit and has become spiritless. No one has ever found the remedy, and no one will ever find it! (*T* 295–296, §387)

> O friend! The witness in this station is one, and the witnessed is without number. It can be said to you in this way: do you not know that in oneness, numbers are themselves one? This station was given over to Ḥusayn-i Manṣūr, who said, "The parts of numbers are one in oneness."[119] (*T* 295, §387)

> In reality, the witness and the witnessed are one, but through expressions and allusions they appear as numerous. (*T* 295, §387)

At the level of major love, God, the only witness and the only witnessed, witnesses Himself in the mirror of nothingness, rendering all those who dare look in that direction deranged and mad.

> Alas! Those burnt by love are crazed! Being crazed has a relation to madness, and madness on the path has a relation to unbelief. Wait until you see our lovely face! Then you will know why one must be a madman! Have you ever seen someone driven mad by an idol? Listen to these lines:
>
> In the religion of the Sharia, unbelief is disgraced,
> for love-madness is crazed.
> Anyone who sees the unbelief of love,
> his lovely-faced idol becomes one. (*T* 204–205, §263)

In in-between love there is still a difference between the witness and the witnessed on the level of forms. This is why ʿAyn al-Quḍāt says that *shāhid-bāzī* is tantamount to unbelief, namely the third level of unbelief. The Shaykh calls the unbeliever engrossed in *shāhid-bāzī* a "metaphorical incarnationist" (P. *ḥulūlī-yi majāzī*). This is because the subject/object dichotomy in the act of witnessing still obtains. Standing in the station of the third level of unbelief, such a person also has the attribute of Muhammadan unbelief and is an associator.

At the end of the path, when all barriers are broken down and the metaphorical incarnationist reaches the fourth level of unbelief, he becomes an "incarnationist of meaning" (P. *ḥulūlī-yi maʿnawī*). This is the station of idol-worship and true unbelief, which is characterized by the faith of Aḥmad. At this time, belief and faith are fully realized—no one other than God has belief and faith in Himself.

> After all, you have heard that whoever sits with an unbeliever becomes an unbeliever. If you have not at all been influenced by my companionship, apart from the fact that you are not an incarnationist of meaning, at least be a metaphorical incarnationist! What are you saying?! Those who consider me to be without religion . . . just excuse them: *Say, "God!," then leave them.*[120] (*T* 328, §431)

> If it is possible that, from the hearing, sight, life, knowledge, and power of the Real some existents and beings can come about, then it is possible that, from God's hearing, sight, and power a secluded traveler of this kind can

> come about. . . . Here, incarnationism appears—it is the secret of "Take on the character traits of God."[121] (*T* 300, §394)

> Alas for the way of the women of this age, the ignorant scholars, and immature children who consider this path to be a type of incarnationism. May my spirit be sacrificed for the dust beneath the feet of this kind of "incarnationism"! (*T* 83, §119)

> When the lover at the end of the path becomes love and when the love of the witness and the witnessed become one, the witness is the witnessed and the witnessed the witness. You consider this to be a form of incarnationism, but this is not incarnationism. It is the perfection of unification and oneness! According to the religion of the realizers, there is no religion other than this. (*T* 115, §162)

> Alas! Here, incarnationism will appear. O friend! If you want endless felicity to be facilitated for you, for one moment keep the company of an incarnationist—namely a Sufi—so that you know what incarnation is. Perhaps it is from this perspective that that master said, "The Sufi is God." ʿAbd Allāh Anṣārī says that the scholar delights in knowledge and the renunciant delights in renunciation.[122] But what shall I say about the Sufi, for the Sufi is He? Since the Sufi is He, "he" is not an incarnationist. Whatever pertains to God, it also pertains to the unity-voicer's "incarnationism." In this station, whatever you hear from him, you have heard from God. (*T* 299–300, §393)

We have so far seen how the Shaykh moves between reality (*ḥaqīqa*) and metaphor (*majāz*) in communicating his profound vision of love and beauty. What allows for his conception of reality to be framed in these metaphorical and formal terms is nothing other than imaginalization.

> If love did not have the ruse of imaginalization, all of the travelers on the path would become unbelievers because,

> in most moments, they would see everything in one form and in one state. In seeing the moment like that, it would be one of blame. But when one sees increase in beauty and an added form at every instant or every day, love becomes greater and the desire to see the object of one's yearning greater. At every instant *He loves them*[123] is imaginalized for *they love Him*,[124] and *they love Him* is, likewise, imaginalized. Thus, in this station, the lover sees the Beloved at every instant in another form of beauty, and himself in a more perfect and more complete form of love.
>
> Every day I am in another state with Your love,
> and with Your comeliness another bond of beauty.
> In the sign of comeliness You have another beauty,
> in the sign of love I have another perfection.
> (*T* 124–125, §173)
>
> Alas! What do you know about what this station does for someone? I would be an unbeliever if whatever has been given to me is not for the sake of this station! Wait until a speck from this station is shown to you by way of the imaginalization of a formal station. Then you will know what this helpless one is in! Do you know what station this is? It is "devotion to the lovely face." (*T* 295, §387)
>
> No expression and trace other than *there is nothing like Him*[125] can be given to that which displays a better and more comely beauty at every moment and has the world of imaginalization at work. There is no other expression and explanation: "I cannot enumerate Your laudation. You are as You have lauded Yourself." If the Prophet sought the pardon of perceptionlessness and limitlessness, how can others give an explication? (*T* 123–124, §172)

God's beauty, which is indescribable, can only be experienced through the myriad forms in which it is revealed.[126] Imaginalization enables the experience of beauty through its function as that which allows for the carryover of meaning from nonduality to overt and subtle forms of duality, which is where the experiencing subject resides.

Reality (*ḥaqīqa*) = Nonduality			Metaphor (*majāz*) = Subtle duality	
God's Self-love in the mirror of nothingness	Major love (*ʿishq-i kabīr*)	IMAGINALIZATION	God's Self-love and human love for God through forms	In-between love (*ʿishq-i miyāna*)
God's Self-love in annihilated forms	Devotion to the lovely face of reality (*shāhid-bāzī-yi ḥaqīqa*)		Devotion to the lovely face (*shāhid-bāzī*)	Devotion to the metaphorically lovely face (*shāhid-i majāzī*)
God qua incarnation (*ḥulūl*)	Incarnationist of meaning (*ḥulūlī-yi maʿnawī*)		Seeing God in forms	Metaphorical incarnationist (*ḥulūlī-yi majāzī*)
God's Self-worship and Self-contemplation	Idol-worship (*but-parastī*)		Worshipping and contemplating God in forms	Associationism (*shirk*); for the associating Muslim *mushrik-muslim*)
Real unbelief (*kufr-i ḥaqīqī*); tantamount to faith (*īmān*)	Faith of Aḥmad (*īmān-i Aḥmad*)		Unbelief of the heart (*kufr-i qalb*); tantamount to unbelief (*kufr*)	Muhammadan unbelief (*kufr-i Muḥammadī*); for the Muslim unbeliever (*musalmān-kāfir*)

Figure 18. Imaginalizations of reality into metaphor

ʿAyn al-Quḍāt also says that another way the ineffable reality of divine love and beauty can be accessed is for the lover to search for them within the imaginalized forms of his own self. Having realized divine beauty and love in this way, the lover is, in the end, delivered from all forms, including the form of himself.

> Here, explanation is deficient and understanding shrunken. Here, man escapes himself. Alas! Listen to these lines:
>
> A traceless beauty love for You is,
> the root of its existence perfection is.
> At every moment imaginalized it is.
> Alas for this love! What a state it is! (*T* 124, §172)

Figure 19. Page from a manuscript of ʿAyn al-Quḍāt, *Nāma-hā*

Notes

Introduction: A Sage in Exile

1. For the determination of his first name, see chapter 5, n. 84 and the corresponding text in that chapter.

2. Other birth dates are given in the primary and secondary sources, but 490/1097 is the correct date. See Landolt, "ʿAyn al-Quḍāt." The medieval biographical materials on ʿAyn al-Quḍāt's life and death have been excavated in Papan-Matin, *Beyond Death*, 12–16 and 28–37, and Safi, *Politics of Knowledge*, 159–161 and 191ff. Assessments of Papan-Matin's study can be found in Radtke, "Review of Papan-Matin," and Rustom, "Review of Papan-Matin."

3. See Papan-Matin, *Beyond Death*, 12–13.

4. See chapter 1, s.v. "Charismatic Gifts."

5. ʿAyn al-Quḍāt mentions a certain "*farzand Aḥmad*" three times in his writings (i.e., *N* I, 363, §605; *N* II, 151, §221; *N* II, 438, §676), and always with the supplicatory formula "God preserve him," which he does not use with reference to anyone else. The contexts in which these references occur lean more in favor of Aḥmad being ʿAyn al-Quḍāt's biological child. Cf. Dabashi, *Truth and Narrative*, 75–76. For some critiques of this book, see Adhkāʾī, "Ḥaqīqat yā riwāyat?"; Meisami, "Review of Dabashi"; Safi, *Politics of Knowledge*, 167–172.

6. See Aminrazavi, *Wine of Wisdom*, 22–23 and 349, n. 14.

7. See the brief arguments given in Aminrazavi, *Wine of Wisdom*, 349, n. 14, and Landolt, "ʿAyn al-Quḍāt."

8. See his Persian anthology of ʿAyn al-Quḍāt's writings: *Khāṣṣiyyat-i āyinagī*, 21. See also page 22, where Mayel Heravi puts forward a theory for why some of ʿAyn al-Quḍāt's "enemies" would have wanted to create an association between himself and Khayyām.

9. See *Z* §§7–8, where he mentions a work that he wrote at the age of twenty-one on the demonstrative proof of prophecy.

10. For an Arabic edition and English translation of this work, see ʿAyn al-Quḍāt, *Essence of Reality*.

11. For the passage, see chapter 1, s.v. "Discovery."

12. *N* II, 459, §715. For Shaykh Baraka, see Pourjavady, *ʿAyn al-Quḍāt wa-ustādān-i ū*, 95–133, and Shams, "Baraka (Barakat) Hamadānī."

13. See, for example, his statements in *N* I, 46, §52, and *N* II, 113, §163.

14. Cf. *N* II, 302, §458. For the dating of his death, see Pourjavady, *Bābā Ṭāhir*, 9 (English introduction). Pourjavady's earlier dating can be found in *ʿAyn al-Quḍāt wa-ustādān-i ū*, 105.

15. Landolt, "ʿAyn al-Quḍāt." For more on Shaykh Ḥamūya, see *N* II, 51–52, §67, and Jāmī, *Nafaḥāt*, 414.

16. Jāmī, *Nafaḥāt*, 416–417, and Pourjavady, *Bābā Ṭāhir*, 41.

17. Cf. Pourjavady, *Bābā Ṭāhir*, 42 and 46–47.

18. *N* III, 395, §215.

19. See *N* II, 439, §690.

20. See *N* III, 403, §227 for the former, and *N* I, 433, §724, and *N* II, 35, §227 for the latter.

21. See *N* I, 433, §724. A helpful inquiry into the life, writings, and mythical portrayal of this great saint can be found in Pourjavady, *Bābā Ṭāhir*. For Bābā Ṭāhir's tomb, see figure 14.

22. See *N* I, 258, §428, and Pourjavady, *Bābā Ṭāhir*, 51.

23. Cf. *N* I, 27, §29, and Pourjavady's interpretation of this passage in *Bābā Ṭāhir*, 47–48.

24. Pourjavady, *ʿAyn al-Quḍāt wa-ustādān-i ū*, 104. Farmanish, *Aḥwāl wa-āthār-i ʿAyn al-Quḍāt*, x, gives a possible date of 515/1121, but with little substantial evidence.

25. For a study of Aḥmad Ghazālī's life, practice, and teachings, see Lumbard, *Aḥmad al-Ghazālī*.

26. For the passage, see chapter 1, s.v. "Discovery." For a detailed study of Aḥmad Ghazālī's influence upon ʿAyn al-Quḍāt, see Khātamīpūr, "Az Khurāsān tā Hamadān."

27. The text is entitled *Risāla-yi ʿAyniyya* (*Treatise Dedicated to ʿAyn al-Quḍāt*), which Jāmī held in very high regard (see *Nafaḥāt*, 414). A discussion of this treatise and its printed editions can be found in Lumbard, *Aḥmad al-Ghazālī*, 6–7 and 194, n. 5

28. See Aḥmad Ghazālī, *Mukātabāt*.

29. *N* III, 407, §236.

30. *N* III, 407, §236.

31. Kāmil al-Dawla is the recipient of thirteen different letters from his master. For more on him, see Safi, *Politics of Knowledge*, 190–191.

32. The wording in the passage is somewhat vague. It can mean that he was claiming to be God, or that he was making godlike claims. For the text in translation, see chapter 2, s.v. "Divine Jealousy."

33. *N* II, 358, §555. The text is translated in chapter 2, s.v. "Two Defenses."

34. The classic study of Ḥallāj's life, teachings, martyrdom, and legacy is Massignon, *Passion of al-Hallāj*. An analysis of how ʿAyn al-Quḍāt fits into the Ḥallājian mold can be found in Ernst, *Words of Ecstasy*, 73–84. Cf. Khawālidiyya, *Ṣarʿā al-taṣawwuf*, 135–172.

35. See chapter 1, s.v. "Charismatic Gifts."

36. See the texts in chapter 1, s.v. "Charismatic Gifts." See also the relevant text in chapter 1, s.v. "Muhammadan Encounters."

37. See the observations in Safi, *Politics of Knowledge*, 197–200.

38. Cf. the discussions in Griffel, *Formation of Post-Classical Philosophy*, 128; Lange, "Death of Dargazini"; Safi, *Politics of Knowledge*, 165.

39. For whom, see Lajevardi, "Bāyazīd Basṭāmī."

40. A fine English translation of this work is available: *A Sufi Martyr*.

41. *Sh* 9–10.

42. Cf. *N* II, 358, §555. As stated in n. 33, this text is translated in chapter 2.

43. *Sh* 10–11 and 27.

44. We will have occasion to see ʿAyn al-Quḍāt's arguments in action throughout the course of this book.

45. *Sh* 39–41.

46. See the astute observations in Safi, *Politics of Knowledge*, 198.

47. Cf. Griffel, *Formation of Post-Classical Philosophy*, 131–138 and 157–158, and Maghsoudlou, "La pensée de 'Ayn al-Quḍāt al-Hamadānī," 357.

48. Safi, *Politics of Knowledge*, 198–199.

49. For a helpful discussion of the Seljuq sultans' religiosity, see Tor, "'Sovereign and Pious,'" 39–62.

50. *N* II, 150–151, §§220–221.

51. See, for example, *N* I, 48, §58; *N* I, 87, §118; *N* I, 106, §149; *N* I, 114, §165; *N* II, 211, §314. In *N* II, 169, §§253–254, Matthew 6:3–4 is reworked into Arabic in the context of making the point (which also features in a famous Hadith) that one's giving with his right hand should be so discrete that it is not even "known" to his left hand. For more on ʿAyn al-Quḍāt's teachings on charity, see chapter 2, s.v. "Advice and Admonition."

52. ʿAyn al-Quḍāt was not unique among the *ʿulamāʾ* of his time in castigating the Seljuqs for their corrupt financial practices. Given the questionable nature of the Seljuqs' sources of income, some scholars were reticent or outright refused to work at the Niẓāmiyya colleges funded by them. Ghazālī, for one, made a famous vow not to take money from the rulers of his day. For a discussion of Ghazālī's complicated relationship with the Seljuqs both before and after his turn to the Sufi path, see Griffel, *Al-Ghazālī's Philosophical Theology*, 40ff.

53. For whom, see Shoarian-Sattari, "Abū al-Qāsim al-Dargazīnī."

54. See Safi, *Politics of Knowledge*, 191ff., which offers a critical reading of the historiographical sources that deal with ʿAyn al-Quḍāt's death and its relationship to ʿAzīz al-Dīn and Dargazīnī.

55. Safi, *Politics of Knowledge*, 194. See also Ernst, *Words of Ecstasy*, 114.

56. Lange, *Justice, Punishment and the Medieval Muslim Imagination*, 94.

57. See Lange, *Justice, Punishment and the Medieval Muslim Imagination*, 65–66.

58. An analysis of this letter can be found in Papan-Matin, *Beyond Death*, 48ff. See also chapter 2, s.v. "Two Defenses."

59. Landolt, "ʿAyn al-Quḍāt." For the administration of punishment under the Seljuqs, see Lange, *Justice, Punishment and the Medieval Muslim Imagination*, 61–98.

60. Landolt, "ʿAyn al-Quḍāt."

61. Landolt, "ʿAyn al-Quḍāt."

62. See figures 3 and 4.

63. See the list of his works in *Sh* 39–41.

64. See bibliography, s.v. "Works Misattributed to ʿAyn al-Quḍāt," and the helpful discussion in Papan-Matin, *Beyond Death*, 25–27. To Papan-Matin's listing we can also add a short treatise in Persian, the *Rāz-nāma* (*The Treatise of Mystery*), which was recently ascribed to ʿAyn al-Quḍāt based on a misreading of the details in a certain manuscript. See Tanındı, "Preliminary List of Manuscripts Stamped with Bayezid II's Seal," 993 (entry no. 61.1). As the opening pages of the manuscript in question (i.e., Ayasofya 4824) tell us, the author of the treatise is a certain Shams al-Dīn ʿAyn al-Quḍāt Hamadānī, also known simply as Shams al-Dīn Hamadānī. At any rate, the language, style, and content of this treatise preclude the possibility that our ʿAyn al-Quḍāt is its author.

65. An outline of some its foundational principles can be found in Lewisohn, "Sufism's Religion of Love," 152–173. For a comprehensive overview of Sufi love literature before the time of Aḥmad Ghazālī, see Lumbard, *Aḥmad al-Ghazālī*, 116–149.

66. See Landolt, "ʿAyn al-Quḍāt," and Papan-Matin, *Beyond Death*, 25–27.

67. Ritter, "Philologika VII," 94.

68. Mayel Heravi, for example, notes that it is attributed to a certain ʿAbd al-Malik Warakānī (d. 573/1178), but not without this attribution being contested. See Mayel Heravi, "Muqaddima," xiv and the corresponding note (n. 10).

69. Pourjavady, *Zabān-i ḥāl*, 176, n. 23.

70. See Shādruymanish, "*Lawāʾiḥ* az kīst?" Parts of *Flashes* have been studied in Lawrence, "The *Lawa'ih* of Qazi Hamid Ud-Din *Naguri*."

71. The best example of which is the extended discussion on the divisions of existents (*aqsām al-wujūd*) in *T* 337–339, §§444–448.

72. For which, see *N* I, 469, §481, and *N* II, 169, §253.

73. The sources for nearly one fifth of the poems that appear in ʿAyn al-Quḍāt's works are identified in Farmanish, *Aḥwāl wa-āthār-i ʿAyn al-Quḍāt,* 290–340.

74. One hundred and twenty of which are in *Paving the Path* and 355 in the *Letters*. For ʿAyn al-Quḍāt's citations of Persian verses that were likely taken directly from the writings of Aḥmad Ghazālī, see Khātamīpūr, "Az Khurāsān tā Hamadān," 95–98.

75. In addition to this work, 149 Arabic poems are cited in the *Letters,* fifty in *Exile's Complaint,* fourteen in the *Essence,* and six in *Paving the Path.* The sources for most of the Arabic verses in *Exile's Complaint* and the *Essence* have been traced in the translations of these works (see *A Sufi Martyr* and *Essence of Reality* respectively). For ʿAyn al-Quḍāt's use of Arabic poetry in the *Letters,* see the inquiry in Wāʿiẓ, "Abyāt-i ʿarabī-yi *Nāma-hā.*"

76. *N* II, 50, §49.

77. For their relationship, see de Bruijn, *Of Piety and Poetry,* 69–70. An insightful review of this book can be found in Chittick, "Review of de Bruijn."

78. Lewisohn, "In Quest of Annihilation," 298.

79. See Papan-Matin, *Beyond Death,* 22, as well as the last text in chapter 1, s.v. "Muhammadan Encounters." A thematic overview of *Paving the Path* can be found in Ariankhoo and Rustom, "ʿAyn al-Quḍāt's *Tamhīdāt.*"

80. Meier, "Stambuler Handschriften," 3.

81. See the observations in Pūrnāmdāryān and Ḥafīẓī, "Nigāhī ba-taṣḥīḥ-i *Tamhīdāt.*" Ḥafīẓī is currently preparing a new critical edition of the *Tamhīdāt.*

82. *T* 18, §27.

83. *T* 56, §72.

84. See his justification for this practice in "Muqaddima-yi muṣaḥḥiḥ," 27–28.

85. I have consulted nine manuscripts of *Paving the Path* (see bibliography, s.v. "Works by ʿAyn al-Quḍāt [Editions, Manuscripts, Translations]"), five of which were among those used by ʿUsayrān in his edition. In six of these nine manuscripts, the book is not divided into chapters; in the other three, where the chapter divisions are present, none of them are given a title. For the various manuscripts of *Paving the Path,* see Pūrnāmdāryān and Ḥafīẓī, "Nigāhī ba-taṣḥīḥ-i *Tamhīdāt,*" and ʿUsayrān, "Muqaddima-yi muṣaḥḥiḥ," 17–27.

86. See *T* 6, §8.

87. But he does mention the book by name in the *Letters.* See the passage in chapter 9, s.v. "Faith and Unbelief."

88. See chapter 9 and Rustom, "Devil's Advocate."

89. *T* 15–16, §23.

90. See, for example, the observations in Mayel Heravi, *Khāṣṣiyyat-i āyinagī,* 42.

91. I have indicated the most important parallels in the notes to the following chapters.

92. See *N* III, 441–444.

93. *N* I, 16, §17; N, II 482, §754; *N* II, 482, §755 respectively. For similar statements throughout the *Letters*, see *N* I, 23, §24; *N* II, 26, §37; *N* II, 377, §588; *N* III, 317, §67; *N* III, 425, §263; *N* III, 428, §265. Cf. *N* I, 480, §800; *N* III, 290, §18; *N* III, 325, §77.

94. *N* III, 290, §18. Cf. *N* I, 480, §800, and *N* III, 325, §77.

95. *N* I, 273, §453. Cf. *N* I, 115, §166.

96. *N* I, 149, §218.

97. *N* I, 381, §635.

98. *N* I, 1–87, §§1–118.

99. *N* I, 88–237, §§119–392.

100. See chapter 4, s.v. "Bad Transmitters."

101. See chapter 4, s.v. "Cosmic Well-Being."

102. We will have occasion to examine his unique doctrine of the Quran and how to existentially engage with it in chapter 8.

103. See, for example, *N* I, 383; *N* II, 157; *N* III, 340, §§106–107; *N* III, 351, §§127–128. Cf. *T* 85–88, §§123–125.

104. See Ghazālī, *Mukātabāt*, 1–3. Aḥmad Ghazālī's reply is on pp. 4–10.

105. See *W* 1–2 = *N* III, 401–402, §§224–226.

106. For Aḥmad Ghazālī's answer to one of his questions, see chapter 1, n. 32.

107. *RJ* 1–6 = *N* II, 483–488, §§756–766.

108. *RJ* 1 = *N* II, 483, §757. See also his mention of this work in *Sh* 40 and *Z* §2.

109. For this figure, see Safi, *Politics of Knowledge*, 190.

110. See Adhkāʾī, "Hamadān vi."

111. For whom, see Safi, *Politics of Knowledge*, 190.

112. *RJ* 1–5 = *N* II, 483, §§758–763.

113. *RJ* 4–5 = *N* II, 486–487, §§763–764.

114. *RJ* 5–6 = *N* II, 487–488, §§765–766. For some of these passages in translation, see Safi, *Politics of Knowledge*, 175–176.

115. For overviews of the philosophical Sufi tradition, see Faruque, "Sufi Metaphysical Literature"; Nasr, "Mystical Philosophy in Islam"; Rustom, "Philosophical Sufism." Detailed treatments can be found in Ali, *Philosophical Sufism*, and Dagli, *Ibn al-ʿArabī and Islamic Intellectual Culture*.

116. *Z* §8.

117. See *N* II, 459, §715, and *Z* §3.

118. See also the discussion of this work's content in Rustom, "Introduction."

119. Q 102:5.

120. *N* I, 73, §93.

121. See the texts in chapter 7, s.v. "Knowers and Recognizers."

122. *Sh* 26–30 and 39–41.

123. For a detailed study of her image in the Sufi tradition, see Cornell, *Rabi'a from Narrative to Myth.*

124. *Sh* 25. For inquiries into the role played by Sufi women in Muslim society, see Dakake, "'Guest of the Inmost Heart'," and Geoffroy, *Allah au féminin*, chapters 7–9. See also Salamah-Qudsi, *Sufism and Early Islamic Piety*, chapters 2–3, and the measured evaluation of this book in Farrell, "Review of Salamah-Qudsi."

125. *Sh* 40.

126. *NU* 243.1.

127. See Behmardi, "*Wajdiyyāt* of 'Ayn al-Quḍāt al-Hamadānī," 44–45.

128. Cf. *Sh* 40–41, where some verses from *Lovers' Excursion* are cited with approval.

129. Shīrāzī, *Ṭarāʾiq*, 2:568.

130. Although the latter does cite a poem that is also to be found in *N* II, 174, §261. See Samʿānī, *Repose of the Spirits*, 243. But this poem likely goes back to a common source that both ʿAyn al-Quḍāt and Samʿānī were drawing upon, much like the case that is discussed in the next paragraph.

131. See Papan-Matin, *Beyond Death*, 166–173. There is a sound English translation of this work: *Path of God's Bondsmen.*

132. For a diagram of this spiritual network, see figure 6.

133. A discussion of this poem can be found in chapter 10, s.v. "Levels of Unbelief."

134. For some possible leads, see chapter 8, s.v. "Letters and Dots"; Abuali, "Words Clothed in Light"; Corbin, *Man of Light*, chapter 4.

135. See Chittick, *Me and Rumi*, 81.

136. Nasafī, *Kashf al-ḥaqāʾiq*, 164–165.

137. Nasafī, *al-Insān al-kāmil*, 403.

138. That is, *sulṭān al-ʿāshqīn*. See Homerin, *Passion Before Me*, ix.

139. See Jāmī, *Nafaḥāt*, 414–416. Some relevant parts of this entry are translated in Safi, *Politics of Knowledge*, 252, n. 64.

140. See Rustom, *Triumph of Mercy*, 30–31.

141. Meier, "Stambuler Handschriften," 5. See also the listing of manuscripts of Turkish translations of *Paving the Path* in ʿUsayrān, "Muqaddima-yi muṣaḥḥiḥ," 27–28.

142. See chapter 8, s.v. "Letters and Dots."

143. This holds particularly true with respect to Shabistarī's famous Persian metaphysical poem the *Gulshan-i rāz* (*The Rosegarden of Mystery*).

For more on Shabistarī's life and thought, as well as the many connections between ʿAyn al-Quḍāt and Shabistarī, see Lewisohn's groundbreaking study, *Beyond Faith and Infidelity*.

144. Safi, *Politics of Knowledge*, 253, n. 66. ʿAyn al-Quḍāt's *Letters* may also have been read with the *Mathnawī* itself. See the hypothesis advanced in Safi, *Politics of Knowledge*, 253, n. 66.

145. See Safi, *Politics of Knowledge*, 252, n. 63.

146. See Pourjavady, "Introduction."

147. Shushtarī, *Majālis al-muʾminīn*, 4:515. For this period of Ṭūsī's life, see Meisami, *Naṣīr al-Dīn Ṭūsī*, 15–19.

148. I am grateful to William Chittick for alerting me to this reference from his forthcoming translation of Farghānī's major work of philosophical Sufism the *Muntahā'l-madārik* (*The Final End of the Perceptual Tools*).

149. See Jāmī, *Precious Pearl*, 37, 44, and 94. In his glosses, Jāmī also draws on ʿAyn al-Quḍāt's *Letters*. See *Precious Pearl*, 104.

150. Ibn ʿArabī, *Sharḥ Khalʿ al-naʿlayn*, 229.

151. See Aladdin, "Aspects of Mystical Hermeneutics," 405.

152. See Arif, "Defending Sufi Metaphysics in British India," and Malik, "Faḍl-i Ḥaqq Khayrābādī."

153. See Papan-Matin, "'Ayn al-Qudat al-Hamadhani."

154. See Safi, "Sufi Path of Love in Iran and India," 252–256; Safi, *Politics of Knowledge*, 169; Schimmel, *Mystical Dimensions of Islam*, 348.

155. See Maneri, *Mine of Meaning*, passim.

156. For some discussion on him in English, see Papan-Matin, *Beyond Death*, 174ff.; Papan-Matin, "Gisudaraz"; Safi, "Sufi Path of Love in Iran and India," 256–257.

157. Papan-Matin, *Beyond Death*, 187–189.

158. With this point in mind, see also nn. 73–75.

159. See the discussion in Pūrnāmdāryān and Ḥafīẓī, "Nigāhī ba-taṣḥīḥ-i *Tamhīdāt*," 127–128.

160. For a discussion of the various studies dedicated to ʿAyn al-Quḍāt over the past several decades, see Fishārakī and Mūsawī, "Kitāb-shināsī-yi ʿAyn al-Quḍāt Hamadānī dar Īrān," and Rustom, "ʿAyn al-Quḍāt between Divine Jealousy and Political Intrigue," 47–49. See also the listing in the present book's bibliography, s.v. "Works on ʿAyn al-Quḍāt Cited or Consulted."

Chapter 1. Autobiography

1. Discussions on Ghazālī's influence upon ʿAyn al-Quḍāt can be found in Griffel, *Al-Ghazālī's Philosophical Theology*, 81–87, and Maghsoudlou, "La pensée de 'Ayn al-Quḍāt al-Hamadānī," passim. For ʿAyn al-Quḍāt's posi-

tive assessment and criticisms of Ghazālī, see Maghsoudlou, "Étude," 31–33; Pourjavady, *ʿAyn al-Quḍāt wa-ustādān-i ū*, 135–179; Safi, *Politics of Knowledge*, 172–175. For the latter, see also *N* II, 318, §482, and *N* II, 380, §593. For the former, see the relevant text in this chapter, s.v. "Visions" (last passage) and the text in chapter 3, s.v. "Levels of Light."

2. Q 3:103. Cf. the climactic section in Ghazālī, *Munqidh*, 103.

3. For the full version of this saying, see Chittick, *Divine Love*, 294. It goes back to Shiblī (for whom, see chapter 2, n. 68).

4. *Z* §14.

5. In this book I render *azal* as either "Beginningless" or "the Beginningless," setting aside "Beginninglessness" for the adjective *azalī*; and I render *abad* as "Endless" or "the Endless," leaving "Endlessness" for the adjective *abadī*. In doing so, I am following Chittick, *Divine Love*, passim. For a discussion of these terms in ʿAyn al-Quḍāt, see Izutsu, "Creation and the Timeless Order of Things," 137–138.

6. I translate *huwiyya* as "Identity," although the term is normally rendered "Ipseity." Etymologically, "ipseity" refers to the self and selfhood of any "person," and, by extension, their individuality and "identity" as specific persons and entities.

7. Ibn al-Muʿtazz, *Dīwān*, 247.

8. *N* II, 344, §528. Cf. *N* II, 111, §160.

9. *N* I, 164, §248. Cf. *N* I, 163, §244.

10. *N* II, 111, §160.

11. See, for example, *N* II, 344, §528, as well as the insightful points in Boylston, "Writing the Kaleidoscope of Reality," 246.

12. An extensive inquiry into this trope in Sufism and Persian literature can be found in Pourjavady, *Zabān-i ḥāl* (for a brief discussion of ʿAyn al-Quḍāt in this regard, see part 1, pp. 173–177).

13. *T* 196, §254. A related teaching is the juxtaposition of the *lisān al-ḥāl* to the *lisān al-maqāl* ("the tongue of speech"), for which there is a famous Arabic proverb cited by ʿAyn al-Quḍāt once in his writings (*N* I, 402, §669): "The tongue of the state is more articulate and truthful than the tongue of speech."

14. *N* I, 215–216, §348. For a detailed discussion of tasting in Sufism, see Hirtenstein, "*Dhawq*."

15. See Ormsby, "Taste of Truth."

16. The letter in question is *Letter* 94, which is one of several wherein ʿAyn al-Quḍāt advances his theory of the alteration of other religions. See chapter 4, s.v. "Bad Transmitters."

17. See Chittick, *Me and Rumi*, 164. Of course, ʿUmar is the well-known second Caliph of Islam who died in 23/644. In Tirmidhī, Manāqib 18, no. 4046, the tradition is worded as follows: "God has placed the truth upon the tongue of ʿUmar, and in his heart."

18. For a study of this phenomenon in Sufi literature, see Renard, *Friends of God*.

19. This statement and the parenthetical remark below clearly indicate that ʿAyn al-Quḍāt was dictating this event to a disciple; as noted in the introduction, *Paving the Path* embodies ʿAyn al-Quḍāt's teachings by way of his oral instruction and formal writing.

20. That is, a *muqaddam*. Such a person is an advanced Sufi who has been designated by his master to fulfill his charge with respect to leading the formal Sufi gathering (*majlis al-dhikr*) and the spiritual direction of the master's disciples (and, in many cases, the initiation of new disciples), all the while remaining under the master's authority.

21. That is, Abū Saʿīd Tirmidhī, who was also a legal scholar.

22. This passage is to be found, with some adjustments, in *N* I, 374–375 (for a contextualization of it, see Radtke, "Review of Papan-Matin," 197).

23. ʿUsayrān's text has an added phrase here that obscures the point of the sentence: "there was a moment that" (*wa-waqt būdī kah*). I follow the much more sensible reading of this passage, for example, in MS Ayasofya 1839, fol. 110v, which does not include this wording.

24. Q 4:157. For an in-depth inquiry into the various historical interpretations and doctrinal positions to have emerged from sustained engagement with this verse, see Lawson, *Crucifixion and the Qur'an*.

25. Q 4:158.

26. For ʿAyn al-Quḍāt's use and understanding of the concept of Sufi chivalry (*futuwwa*; P. *jawānmardī*), see Rustom, "ʿAyn al-Quḍāt on Chivalry." See also chapter 9, s.v. "An Ideal Lover." Broader treatments of *jawānmardī* can be found in Nasr, "Spiritual Chivalry"; Ridgeon, *Morals and Mysticism in Persian Sufism*; Zargar, *Polished Mirror*, chapter 8.

27. The "men" (P. *mardān*) is a synonym for the Friends of God.

28. Q 2:189.

29. For the significance of the pronoun He (*huwa*) in Sufism (which serves as an epigraph in each of the present book's chapters), see Chittick, *Me and Rumi*, 378, s.v. "He." In part of an important supplication transmitted by ʿAyn al-Quḍāt (see chapter 6), *huwa* features prominently: "O He, O He, O He. O other than whom there is no He. O one whom none knows what He is other than He. O one whom none knows where He is other than He!" (*T* 38, §52).

30. An expression used variously in Arabic literature and derived from an event in the life of the Prophet Muhammad who visited Ṭāʾif and called its inhabitants to Islam; in rejection of his invitation, they had their lowest members of society curse him and attack him. See Lings, *Muhammad*, 98.

31. The "Supreme Name" indicates the greatest name of God, "Allah," the methodical repetition of which in Sufism is the highest form of *dhikr* or invocation. The "Trust" is referred to in Q 33:72; in Sufism, it is commonly identified with the primordial Covenant between God and human beings

mentioned in Q 7:172 (we will return to both of these verses in chapter 8).

32. After relating this vision, ʿAyn al-Quḍāt goes on to ask the recipient of this letter, his master Aḥmad Ghazālī, if it is correct or not, and what the meaning of it is. In his response (Ghazālī, *Mukātabāt*, 8), Shaykh Aḥmad tells him that it is a sound vision and then elaborates on how the secret of destiny, the Trust, and the Supreme Name relate to the "secret of love."

33. This combination of detached letters is also to be found at the beginning of Q 40–46, which are collectively referred to as the *ḥawāmīm*. For ʿAyn al-Quḍāt's unique understanding of the detached letters, see chapter 8.

34. "*Ḥā*ʾ, *Mīm*, ʿAyn, Sīn, Qāf" is a sacred Sufi formula, the best-known usage of which is to be found in the *Ḥizb al-baḥr* (*Litany of the Ocean*) of Shaykh Abū'l-Ḥasan al-Shādhilī (d. 656/1258).

35. ʿAyn al-Quḍāt also gives this interpretation in *T* 65, §88 (cf. *N* III, 331, §§87–88, and *N* III, 333, §90). In his reply to ʿAyn al-Quḍāt (Ghazālī, *Mukātabāt*, 9), Shaykh Aḥmad confirms his student's interpretation of "*Ḥā*ʾ, *Mīm*, ʿAyn, Sīn, Qāf" as true, and then identifies another "secret" behind this holy utterance.

36. For early Sufi explanations of the significance of the Arabic letter *alif*, see Rustom, "Forms of Gnosis," 340–341.

37. Q 3:7.

38. Cf. *N* II, 51, §67.

39. Cf. Corbin, *Man of Light*, 153–154, n. 93.

40. In premodern times, Hamadan was a thriving center for Jewish religion and culture. See Sarshar, "Hamadān viii."

41. Q 7:157.

42. With respect to Moses' luminosity, the Rabbi seems to be alluding to Exodus 34:29.

Chapter 2. Counsel and Confession

1. "Aspirant" translates *murīd*, which in Sufism denotes the person on the spiritual path in search of God.

2. For whom, see chapter 1, n. 27.

3. Q 33:41.

4. Q 2:152.

5. See *N* I, 114, §165.

6. Q 2:3 (this wording is also in Q 8:3).

7. Abū Dāwūd, Adab, 66, no. 4943.

8. Bukhārī, Jihād, 128, no. 3025.

9. Ṭabarānī, *Awsaṭ*, 1:146.

10. For ʿAyn al-Quḍāt's treatment of habit, see chapter 5, s.v. "Habit-Worship."

11. A similar saying is attributed to ʿAlī. See *Nahj al-balāgha,* 4:20.
12. Q 3:173.
13. Q 4:100.
14. Q 3:196.
15. Q 4:77.
16. Q 39:10 (cf. 4:97).
17. Q 4:100.
18. A recent discussion of the life and teachings of Dhū'l-Nūn can be found in Ebrahim, "Dhū al-Nūn al-Miṣrī."
19. Translated in Rustom, "Sufi Teachings of Dhu'l-Nun," 76.
20. We will have occasion to return to these two terms in chapters 4 and 6 respectively.
21. For these spiritual ailments and the method to cure them, see Ghazālī, *Condemnation of Pride and Self-Admiration.*
22. Cf. *N* II, 342, §525.
23. Q 4:143.
24. Q 59:13.
25. Q 47:12.
26. Q 2:21.
27. Q 11:6.
28. Cf. Q 32:80 and 77:20.
29. This passage has a number of similarities with the advice given in *N* II, 339, §519 (translated in Safi, *Politics of Knowledge,* 183), including the identification of Sultan Maḥmūd II (mentioned there by name) with a "filthy fluid."
30. Cf. Q 75:37, 76:2, and 86:6.
31. Q 29:17.
32. Q 7:194.
33. Q 13:16.
34. For the recognizers, see chapter 7.
35. Q 12:106.
36. Tirmidhī, Muqaddima, 39, no. 229.
37. One parasang or *farsakh* corresponds to approximately six kilometers. See Hinz, *Maße und Gewichte,* 62.
38. Bazzār, *Baḥr,* 1:175.
39. Bukhārī, Īmān, 16, no. 24.
40. Cf. *N* I, 90, §122.
41. Q 29:6.
42. See ʿAyn al-Quḍāt's account of his service to Aḥmad Ghazālī in chapter 1, s.v. "Discovery."
43. Cf. Griffel, *Al-Ghazālī's Philosophical Theology,* 85.
44. Q 50:22.

45. In Sarrāj, *Lumaʿ*, 70, this famous statement is attributed to the early Sufi figure ʿĀmir b. ʿAbd Qays (d. ca. 60/680).

46. Cf. *N* II, 414, §653.

47. See Gruendler, "Longing for Home."

48. Sakhāwī, *Maqāṣid*, 565. Cf. the interpretation of this saying offered by Shams-i Tabrīzī in Chittick, *Me and Rumi*, 265.

49. See introduction, n. 58.

50. See *N* II, 358, §555.

51. Q 5:75.

52. Q 19:23.

53. *Sh* 26–27. See also the observations in Schimmel, *Mystical Dimensions of Islam*, 296. Cf. Kīmīyāʾī, *Ḥasad*.

54. For this close companion of ʿAyn al-Quḍāt, see introduction, n. 31.

55. That is, the legal scholars in the city who were against ʿAyn al-Quḍāt.

56. Q 7:180.

57. For the context of this passage, see introduction, s.v. "Execution."

58. Cf. Ḥallāj's cryptic prediction, different readings of which can be found in Massignon, *Passion of al-Hallāj*, 3:51–52, and Sells, *Early Islamic Mysticism*, 277, no. 25.

59. ʿAyn al-Quḍāt cites this saying, without attributing it to Ḥallāj, a couple of times: *N* II, 197, §291, and *T* 269, §353. We will momentarily have occasion to cite the latter text. For a typical usage of this Sufi maxim, see Ghazālī, *Niche of Lights*, 2.

60. That is, the Sharia. For ʿAyn al-Quḍāt's understanding of the Law, see chapter 5.

61. The context of this statement involves a discussion concerning the true nature of the Prophet—is he the fruit of the tree of divinity or the tree itself?

62. For *ghayrat* and translations from some key Persian Sufi texts that discuss this concept, see Chittick, *Divine Love*, 396–416. See also Ghazālī, *Sawāniḥ*, 51.

63. Chittick, *Divine Love*, 396. See also the helpful discussion in Chittick, *SPL*, 304ff.

64. That is, a saying of God reported by the Prophet but which is not a part of the Quran. See Graham, *Divine Word and Prophetic Word*.

65. See Baqlī, *ʿAbhar*, 59, §125.

66. For the symbolism of drunkenness, see chapter 10, s.v. "Levels of Unbelief."

67. Samʿānī, *Repose of the Spirits*, 332.

68. An influential early Sufi and close companion of Ḥallāj who died in 334/936. For more on his life and teachings, see Avery, *Shiblī*.

69. That is, a *muwaḥḥid* or someone who declares God's unity.

70. Cited, with slight modifications, from Maybudī, *Unveiling of the Mysteries*, 345. A study of Maybudī's Sufi *tafsīr* can be found in Keeler, *Ṣūfī Hermeneutics*.

71. For compensation or bloodwit (*diya*) in Islamic law, see the commentary upon Q 2:178 in *SQ*, 76–77.

72. Cf. the texts in Chittick, *Divine Love*, 370–371 and 379.

73. Cf. the potentially pertinent points made in *N* II, 357, §554.

74. Q 18:65.

Chapter 3. Heavenly Matters

1. Izutsu, "Mysticism and the Linguistic Problem of Equivocation," 153.

2. For thorough treatments of ʿAyn al-Quḍat's indebtedness to his predecessors in the intellectual sciences (*al-ʿulūm al-ʿaqliyya*), see Maghsoudlou, "La pensée de ʿAyn al-Quḍāt al-Hamadānī," and Maghsoudlou, "Popularization of Philosophy in the Sufi Milieu."

3. See Chittick, *SPK*, 62. For more on Kharrāz, see Karamustafa, *Sufism*, 7–11.

4. Q 16:60.

5. An allusion to Q 41:37.

6. Q 42:11.

7. Q 48:6.

8. Q 12:39 (this wording is also in Q 13:16, 14:48, 38:65, 39:4, and 40:16).

9. *T* 338, §448.

10. *Z* §50 (see also *Z* §76). Cf. *N* I, 166, §251, which we will encounter in translation in chapter 8, s.v. "Vastness and Worthiness."

11. From the introduction it will be recalled that ʿAyn al-Quḍāt's accusers had identified the position that God is the Source of existence as one of his "heretical" views—heretical in their eyes presumably because it could be seen as a nod in the direction of the Ismaili doctrine of God as being "beyond existence." In actuality, the phrase *maṣdar al-wujūd* can be found in the writings of Ghazālī. See Ghazālī, *Maqāṣid*, 74, §§8–9. As we will see in this chapter, ʿAyn al-Quḍāt attributes an almost identical phrase to Ḥallāj.

12. An allusion to Q 69:51.

13. On this subject, see the penetrating remarks in Izutsu, "Creation and the Timeless Order of Things," 136–138, and Izutsu, "Mysticism and the Linguistic Problem of Equivocation," 166–170.

14. For ʿAyn al-Quḍāt's critique of Avicenna's understanding of God as the "Causer of causes" (*musabbib al-asbāb*), see the discussion in Izutsu, "Mysticism and the Linguistic Problem of Equivocation," 167–168.

15. For a version of this Hadith, see the text in chapter 2, s.v. "Sandal-Service."

16. ʿAyn al-Quḍāt ascribes these words to the major Ashʿarī theologian Abū Bakr al-Baqillānī (d. 403/1013). But as noted by Maghsoudlou, "La pensée de 'Ayn al-Quḍāt al-Hamadānī," 33, n. 83, the statement is contrary to al-Baqillānī's theory of divine attributes.

17. Cf. *N* II, 260–261, §393.

18. An interpretation of ʿAyn al-Quḍāt's position on the divine names and attributes can be found in Maghsoudlou, "La pensée de 'Ayn al-Quḍāt al-Hamadānī," 139–158.

19. For a detailed treatment of Ibn ʿArabī's understanding of the divine names, see Chittick, *SPK*, chapters 1–3.

20. An exposition of which can be found in Adamson, "From the Necessary Existent to God." For an introduction to Avicenna's life and thought, see McGinnis, *Avicenna*.

21. For some interesting remarks concerning the similarities between ʿAyn al-Quḍāt and Ibn ʿArabī vis-à-vis the oneness of existence, see Izutsu, "Creation and the Timeless Order of Things," 124–125.

22. Penetrating studies of *waḥdat al-wujūd* can be found in Chittick, *In Search of the Lost Heart*, 71–88, and Izutsu, *The Concept and Reality of Existence*, 33–55.

23. Cf. *N* II, 260–261, §393.

24. Q 2:255. The sentence in general is alluding to Q 55:26–27: *All that is upon it is perishing. And there subsists the face of thy Lord, possessor of majesty and bounty.*

25. *N* I, 133, §191.

26. *N* I, 134, §192.

27. *N* I, 138, §200. For a discussion of these three groups, see Boylston, "Writing the Kaleidoscope of Reality," 192–203.

28. *N* I, 134, §192.

29. *N* I, 134, §192.

30. *N* I, 134–135, §§193–194.

31. *N* I, 138, §200.

32. *T* 257, §338. See also *T* 181, §239; *T* 305, §401; *Z* §38; *Z* §124.

33. *T* 257, §338.

34. Cf. Ghazālī, *Niche of Lights*, 19.

35. Cf. Ghazālī, *Niche of Lights*, 20.

36. Q 24:35.

37. Dīnawarī, *Mujālasa*, 2:287–288.

38. Q 66:8.

39. Q 53:42.

40. For this phenomenon across different Islamic cultures, see Addas, *La Maison muhammadienne*; Gril, Reichmuth, and Sarmis, eds., *The Presence of the Prophet in Early Modern and Contemporary Islam, Vol. 1*; Ogunnaike, *Poetry*

in Praise of Prophetic Perfection; Meier, *Nachgelassene Schriften, Vol. 1*; Schimmel, *And Muhammad Is His Messenger*.

41. See the relevant texts presented in Chittick, *Divine Love*, 35–40.

42. ʿAyn al-Quḍāt cites this Quranic verse and these two traditions, which are not in the standard sources, in *T* 180, §238. For a version of the first of them, see Forouzanfar, *Aḥadīth-i Mathnawī*, no. 546.

43. *T* 181, §238.

44. See also the related discussion in *T* 266, §349.

45. The station being alluded to is that of love; see chapter 10.

46. Cf. *T* 235, §305, which is translated in chapter 1, s.v. "Tasting."

47. That is, they are sought after by God.

48. Q 5:54.

49. Q 7:143.

50. Q 17:1.

51. Q 15:72.

52. Q 93:1–2.

53. Q 7:143.

54. Q 25:45.

55. See Schimmel, *And Muhammad Is His Messenger*, 239.

56. Q 4:113.

57. Q 4:80.

58. Q 2:151.

59. Ghazālī, *Iḥyāʾ*, 1:493.

60. Q 33:4.

61. Aḥmad, no. 638.

62. My translation of this clause follows the corresponding correction to ʿUsayrān's reading in Pūrnāmdāryān and Ḥafīẓī, "Nigāhī ba-taṣḥīḥ-i *Tamhīdāt*," 128–129.

63. Q 2:6.

64. Abū Jahl and Abū Lahab (the Prophet's paternal uncle) were two of the Prophet's fiercest opponents. See the index s.vv. "Abū Jahl" and "Abū Lahab" in *SQ*.

65. Q 21:107.

Chapter 4. Earthly Concerns

1. Ḥaddād, *Takhrīj*, 1:112–113.

2. See Maghsoudlou, "La pensée de ʿAyn al-Quḍāt al-Hamadānī," 285–289, and Rustom, "Devil's Advocate," 76–77.

3. See Avicenna, *Metaphysics of The Healing*, 344–345 (IX.6, §16).

4. See also *N* II, 272–276, §§409–416.

5. See, respectively, Avicenna, *Metaphysics of The Healing*, 339 (IX.6, §1), and Ormsby, *Theodicy in Islamic Thought*.

6. A reference to traditional medical astrology where the moon's various movements have a direct effect upon a person's health. See Frawley, *Real Astrology*, 144.

7. According to *LN*, Ushnuh is a village near Isfahan. Cf. Minorsky, "Ushnū."

8. Q 28:68.

9. Q 23:71.

10. Q 11:45 and 95:8.

11. Q 7:151; 12:64 and 92; 21:83.

12. Q 6:1.

13. See also the related points in *N* II, 272–276, §§409–416, and *N* II, 292–293, §44.

14. Q 67:3–4.

15. For the historical background and polemic launched against the Qadariyya, who both were and were not identified with the Muʿtazila in early Islamic history, see Judd, "Were the Umayyad-Era Qadarites Kāfirs?"

16. *N* II, 309, §467. See also *N* II, 281, §422; *N* II, 309–311, §§468–469; *T* 305, §401.

17. Abū Dāwūd, Sunna, 17, no. 4693.

18. The most comprehensive treatment of this problem in ʿAyn al-Quḍāt is Boylston, "Islam from the Inside Out," 172–200.

19. For the symbolism of sash-wearing, see chapter 10, s.v. "Levels of Unbelief."

20. See also *N* I, 155, §229.

21. A saying that comes from a poem by al-Sharīf al-Raḍī (d. 406/1015). See Ibn Ḥamdūn, *Tadhkira*, 3:189. Cf. this passage from the *Letters* with the summary in *N* II, 281, §423.

22. See ʿAyn al-Quḍāt's case examples in *N* II, 299–300, §453; *N* II, 304, §459; *N* II, 411–412, §472. See also his statement in *N* I, 157–158, §233, and the helpful analysis and translated texts in Boylston, "Islam from the Inside Out," 194–198.

23. This is an allusion to a well-known Hadith that predicts the Muslim community will be divided into seventy-two or seventy-three sects, only one of which will be saved. For the two versions of the Hadith, see the commentary on Q 6:65 in *SQ*, 363 (seventy-two sects), and Ibn Māja, Fitan, 17, no. 4126 (seventy-three sects).

24. See, for example, *N* II, 281, §423 (*nāqilān-i bad*), and *N* II, 331, §504 (*ruwāt-i bad*).

25. That is, Zoroastrianism.

26. See also *N* I, 17, §18.

27. This passage also appears in slightly different form in *N* I, 337, §563. Cf. *N* III, 335–336, §94.

28. See Rustom, "Devil's Advocate," 80–83.

29. "Kingdom" translates *mulk* and "Dominion" *malakūt*. They refer to the corporeal and spiritual worlds respectively. See Murata, *Tao of Islam*, 118.

30. This text also appears in *N* I, 337, §563 with the difference that the latter ends with an added qualification: "But on the face of it, man is not subjugated to do a specific task."

31. ʿAyn al-Quḍāt's likely source in this passage is Ghazālī. See Maghsoudlou, "La pensée de 'Ayn al-Quḍāt al-Hamadānī," 276.

32. For an analysis of ʿAyn al-Quḍāt's response to the Muʿtazila on this issue, see Rustom, "Devil's Advocate," 80–81.

33. Cf. Maghsoudlou, "La pensée de 'Ayn al-Quḍāt al-Hamadānī," 271 and 277, n. 600.

34. *N* I, 337, §563. See also *T* 190, §247.

35. For a fine exposition of a wide variety of approaches to the relationship between causation and human freedom in Islamic thought, see Koca, *Islam, Causality, and Freedom*.

36. Q 37:96.

37. Q 35:3.

38. Q 16:93 (this wording is also in Q 35:8; cf. 13:27, 14:4, and 74:31).

39. Gabriel is the angel of revelation in Islam. He also appeared to Mary and the Prophet in human form (see chapter 5, s.v. "Imaginalization") and plays an important role in Islamic philosophy and cosmology. See Murata, "Angels," 327–330, and Rustom, "Storytelling as Philosophical Pedagogy."

40. Q 19:83.

41. Q 32:11.

42. Q 39:42.

43. Q 16:93.

44. Q 7:155.

45. *N* II, 6–7, §9 is almost identical to this passage.

Chapter 5. Inside Out, Outside In

1. Bukhārī, Badʾ al-waḥy, 1, no. 1.

2. See also *N* I, 69–70, §88.

3. Q 25:23.

4. Q 18:107.

5. Q 18:110.

6. An allusion to the well-known Hadith, "The world is a prison for the believer and a garden for the unbeliever" (Muslim, Zuhd, 1, no. 7606).

7. A major Sufi teacher who died in 258/872. See Iṣfahānī, *Ḥilya*, 10:51–70.

8. Cf. Kubrā, *Ta'wīlāt*, 3:363.

9. This statement by Shiblī, also cited in *T* 234, §303, is one of his "ecstatic utterances" (*shaṭaḥāt*). For more on this phenomenon as it pertains to Shiblī in particular, see Lory, "La transgression des normes du discours religieux." A study of Sufi ecstatic utterances can be found in Ernst, *Words of Ecstasy*; for ʿAyn al-Quḍāt's *shaṭaḥāt*, see Ernst, *Words of Ecstasy*, 72–84 and 110–115, and Mudarrisī and ʿArab, "Shaṭḥiyyāt-i ʿAyn al-Quḍāt Hamadānī."

10. See Āmulī, *Tafsīr*, 5:196, n. 117, and 6:96.

11. Bukhārī, Badʾ al-khalq, 8, no. 3280.

12. Abū Dāwūd, Jihād, 124, no. 2679.

13. Q 66:11.

14. *N* III, 364, §150.

15. *T* 34, §48.

16. For an insightful discussion on assent as it pertains to the notion of faith in general, see Chittick, *In Search of the Lost Heart*, 7–9.

17. Cf. Q 24:54.

18. Q 29:69.

19. Q 14:48.

20. A study of his life and image can be found in Meier, *Abu Saʿīd-i Abū l-Ḫayr*.

21. For Maʿshūq-i Ṭūsī's image in Persian Sufi literature and ʿAyn al-Quḍāt's treatment of him, see Pourjavady, *ʿAyn al-Quḍāt wa-ustādān-i ū*, 84–94. See also the related discussion in *N* III, 353, §132.

22. Cf. Shiblī's statement in Iṣfahānī, *Ḥilya*, 10:378.

23. For the full version and another usage of this Prophetic saying, see Rāzī, *Path of God's Bondsmen*, 156.

24. Q 2:115.

25. Ṭībī, *al-Kāshif*, 6:1788.

26. Q 37:99.

27. Q 21:18.

28. See also the text in *N* I, 335, §560 for a slightly different version that brings in Ḥallāj's famous ecstatic utterance (which we will encounter in later chapters).

29. Mālik, Ṣalāt, 6, no. 177.

30. Q 70:34.

31. Q 70:23.

32. As we will see in later parts of this book, God's Self-prayer is related to Divine Self-knowledge and Self-love. For the manner in which God's Self-praise entails ontological production, see Rustom, *Triumph of Mercy*, chapter 4.

33. Ṣanʿānī, *Muṣannaf*, 2:162.

34. Bazzār, *Baḥr*, 15:391. This is the first part of a popular Prophetic tradition. The second part of it is a citation from Q 26:79: *"He feeds me and gives me drink"*—hence ʿAyn al-Quḍāt's references here to "food" and "drink."

35. Q 4:164.

36. Bukhārī, Tawḥīd, 35, no. 7584.

37. See the discussion in Rosenthal, "Some Minor Problems in the Qur'ân," 72–83.

38. See the commentary on Q 112:2 in *SQ*, 1579–1580.

39. "Howlessness" translates the Persian *bī chūnī*, lit., "without howness." When used alongside the divine Essence, Howlessness and the Howless (P. *bī chūn*) denote Its nondelimited nature.

40. Q 112:1–2.

41. See the paper trail in Khalil, "White Death." For more on Sarrāj, see Karamustafa, *Sufism*, 67–69.

42. Bukhārī, Ṣawm, 57, no. 2014.

43. Q 6:14.

44. For ʿAyn al-Quḍāt's teachings on the heart, see chapter 6, s.v. "The Heart."

45. ʿAjlūnī, *Kashf*, 2:155.

46. Q 6:12 and 54.

47. Q 21:107.

48. Q 48:4.

49. Iṣfahānī, *Ḥilya*, 3:219.

50. In the Islamic tradition, this time or age (*ʿaṣr*) extends from when the Prophet became a Messenger to the moment the world comes to an end.

51. See, for example, *N* II, 191–196, §§284–290; *N* II, 212–219, §§315–327; *N* II, 227, §340; *N* II, 237, §356; *N* II, 244, §369; *T* 194, §251; *T* 198–200, §§257–258.

52. See Chittick, *Divine Love*, 259, and Rūmī, *Signs of the Unseen*, 212–214.

53. *N* II, 244, §369.

54. Muslim, Ṣalāt, 42, no. 1118.

55. *N* II, 237, §356.

56. See, for example, *N* I, 260–262, §§433–435; *N* II, 399–402, §§629–635.

57. *N* I, 451, §752. For indispensable studies on gratitude in Sufism, see Khalil, "On Cultivating Gratitude in Sufi Virtue Ethics"; Khalil, "The Embodiment of Gratitude in Sufi Virtue Ethics"; Lumbard, "The Semantics of Gratitude (*Shukr*) in the Qurʾān."

58. Q 3:37. For the context of this verse, see the commentary in *SQ*, 142. We will devote more attention to ʿAyn al-Quḍāt's understanding of worthiness in later parts of the book, particularly chapters 8 and 10.

59. Q 45:13 (cf. 31:20).

60. *T* 58, §78.

61. Q 34:1.

62. Cf. the statement cited in Samʿānī, *Repose of the Spirits*, 19.

63. That is, *al-shakūr* and *al-ḥamīd* respectively. For the dual meaning of the latter, see Samʿānī, *Repose of the Spirits*, 370ff.

64. Cf. the Sufi glosses on Q 1:2 in Rustom, "Forms of Gnosis," 341–342.

65. This is likely from Dhū'l-Nūn, who is cited on the following line.

66. For this statement, which goes back to Dhū'l-Nūn, see Rustom, "Sufi Teachings of Dhu'l-Nun," 72. Cf. the quote from Basṭāmī translated in Sells, *Early Islamic Mysticism*, 237 (no. 19). ʿAyn al-Quḍāt cites it in *T* 305, §402.

67. Cf. *N* I, 260, §433.

68. For their respective and, on one level, arguably overlapping views on imagination and the imaginal world, see van Lit, *World of Image in Islamic Philosophy*, chapter 3, and Chittick, *SPK*, chapter 7. A comprehensive introduction to the World of Imagination (*ʿālam al-khayāl*) can be found in Corbin, *Spiritual Body and Celestial Earth*.

69. Apart from the present chapter, the only other sustained treatments of ʿAyn al-Quḍāt's understanding of *tamaththul* are Lewisohn, "In Quest of Annihilation," 316–330, and Zargar, *Sufi Aesthetics*, 91–95.

70. For the World of Imagination in Aḥmad Ghazālī, see Chittick, *Divine Love*, 317–318, and Pourjavady, "ʿĀlam-i khayāl az naẓar-i Aḥmad Ghazālī."

71. Q 19:17.

72. ʿĀʾisha was the Prophet's beloved wife who died in 58/678.

73. Cf. Ājurrī, *Sharīʿa*, 3:1510.

74. For this account, see Chittick, *SPK*, 117 and 396, n. 4.

75. Qushayrī, *Risāla*, 289. Cf. Tirmidhī, Tafsīr, 39, no. 3541.

76. Ṭabarānī, *Kabīr*, 12:430.

77. Q 59:24.

78. ʿAyn al-Quḍāt is referring to the standard way of glossing God's name *al-muṣawwir* (Form-Giver) in Persian, namely *ṣūrat-kunanda* (maker of forms). See Samʿānī, *Repose of the Spirits*, 57.

79. Cf. Tirmidhī, Ṣifat al-janna, 15, no. 2747.

80. Abū Bakr Qaḥṭabī (378/986) was a Sufi companion of Junayd (for whom, see chapter 6, n. 4) and a transmitter of the sayings of Ḥallāj. See ʿAyn al-Quḍāt, *Tentations métaphysiques*, 154, n. 2.

81. Q 7:157 (see also 7:158). "Unlettered" translates the Arabic term *ummī*, which is derived from the word "mother" (*umm*).

82. Q 13:39. The "Mother of the Book" (*umm al-kitāb)* is identified with several realities in Islamic teachings, ranging from God's all-comprehensive knowledge to the primordial parchment upon which all of the divine revelations are written. See the commentary in *SQ*, 627.

83. That is, Aḥmad Ghazālī.

84. This passage resolves the problem concerning ʿAyn al-Quḍāt's first name. The biographical literature gives it variously as "Muḥammad" and/or "ʿAbd Allāh."

85. For the two types of imagination being discussed here, see Chittick, *SPK*, 116–117, and Corbin, *Creative Imagination*, 219–224.

86. For whom, see chapter 7.

87. *T* 167, §223. This statement cannot be found in Avicenna's writings. See also Safi, *Politics of Knowledge*, 179–180.

88. *T* 167, §223.

89. Lewisohn, "In Quest of Annihilation," 330.

90. Q 43:85. See also 31:34.

91. We will return to the body in the following chapter.

92. According to Islamic belief, Munkar and Nakīr are the angels who visit people when they are placed in their graves, posing some questions to them about their faith.

93. That is, Avicenna.

94. This statement is not to be found in Avicenna's writings.

95. For a discussion of how the cultivation of these attributes relate to human becoming, see chapter 6, s.v. "Body and Soul."

96. Majlisī, *Biḥār*, 7:314–315.

97. Q 86:9.

98. Q 100:10.

99. Q 89:27–30.

100. Q 76:21.

101. ʿAjlūnī, *Kashf*, 2:346.

102. For their life and teachings, see Gramlich, *Alte Vorbilder des Sufitums*, 2:13–62 (Shaqīq al-Balkhī) and 2:63–93 (Ḥātim al-Aṣamm).

103. Sulamī, *Ṭabaqāt*, 96.

104. This is part of a well-known Hadith: "Whoever dies, his resurrection has happened." See Ibn ʿArabī, *Futūḥāt*, 1:311.

105. See Chittick, *Me and Rumi*, 105. This is a reference to the first Caliph and the Prophet's close Companion Abū Bakr (d. 13/634). In ʿAyn al-Quḍāt's writings, Abū Bakr is the most cited and discussed individual after the Prophet himself, appearing some sixty times in total. ʿAyn al-Quḍāt sees him as the prototype of belief, faith, understanding, scrupulousness, and virtue, and often juxtaposes him with the foremost early enemies of Islam, Abū Jahl and Abū Lahab. For the image of Abū Bakr in Sufi literature, see Renard, "Abū Bakr in Tradition and Early Hagiography."

106. Khotan is a generic reference to Central Asia. See Schimmel, *A Two-Colored Brocade*, general index, s.v. "Khotan." More specifically, Khotan was an ancient Buddhist capital important for its location along the Silk Route. It came under Muslim control in the fourth/eleventh century; today, it is located in Xinjiang, China, and is commonly referred to as Hotan. In classical Persian poetry, Khotan is associated with beauty, a beautiful face, and charm.

107. Q 29:64.

108. This saying is commonly attributed to Jesus in the Islamic tradition and derives from John 3:3.

109. Cf. John 3:5–6. See also *T* 12, §17, where ʿAyn al-Quḍāt offers a more concise explanation of Jesus' words: "Whoever comes out of the world of his mother's stomach sees this world. And whoever comes out of himself sees that world."

110. Q 40:11.

111. Bukhārī, Daʿawāt, 7, no. 6385.

Chapter 6. Wayfarers and Masters

1. To the best of my knowledge, the only detailed treatment of this topic in ʿAyn al-Quḍāt's thought is Ḥasanī, "'ʿĀdat-sitīzī' dar āthār-i ʿAyn al-Quḍāt Hamadānī."

2. Ṭabarānī, *Kabīr*, 3:19. Being "mustered" pertains to the Resurrection, when all people will be gathered together to face God.

3. A *ṣāḥib-i dilī* or "heart-master" is a spiritual guide. See the present chapter, s.v. "The Ripened Master."

4. Uways al-Qaranī (d. 37/657) was a contemporary follower of the Prophet who did not meet him in person, but who legendarily smashed his own teeth when he heard that the Prophet's mouth had been injured in battle. For Uways and his importance in the Sufi tradition, see Schimmel, *Mystical Dimensions of Islam*, 28–29. See also *T* 34–35, §48. Junayd (d. 298/910) was one of the most influential of all early Sufi figures; for more on him, see Ohlander, "al-Junayd al-Baghdādī," and Zaleski, "Sufi Asceticism and the *Sunna* of the Prophet."

5. Cf. Ernst, *Words of Ecstasy*, 74.

6. This statement occurs in the context of ʿAyn al-Quḍāt's treatment of *shāhid-bāzī*, for which, see chapter 10, s.v. "In the I of the Beholder."

7. Q 43:23.

8. Abū Dāwūd, Adab, 80, no. 4974.

9. Muslim, Īmān, 47, no. 303.

10. Q 49:12.

11. Q 49:5.

12. Khiḍr, who appears unnamed in Q 18:65–82 as Moses' teacher, plays an important role in Sufi hagiology, lore, and piety. See the commentary on these verses in *SQ*, 751–756.

13. Q 18:70. A slightly modified version of this passage from *Paving the Path* also appears in *N* II, 102–103, §§145–147 (for a part of it in translation, see chapter 8, s.v. "Vastness and Worthiness").

14. Q 18:15.

15. Cf. Q 12:53.

16. Q 45:23 (cf. the almost identical wording in Q 25:43).

17. We will return to these wimps in chapter 10.

18. Ghazālī, *Iḥyāʾ*, 7:233.

19. Ḥaddād, *Takhrīj*, 2:981. See also *N* III, 441, §287.

20. Q 39:22.

21. Ḥaddād, *Takhrīj*, 4:1535. ʿAyn al-Quḍāt cites this tradition in *T* 14, §20.

22. See also Chittick, *Divine Love*, 129–135, and the commentary on Q 12:53 in *SQ*, 604–605.

23. ʿAjlūnī, *Kashf*, 2:374–375. Cf. the use of this tradition in Rāzī, *Path of God's Bondsmen*, 97.

24. Q 79:40.

25. See the commentary on Q 75:2 in *SQ*, 1446.

26. Q 2:54.

27. Cf. Qushayrī, *Risāla*, 389.

28. A slightly different version of this saying is attributed to the great early Sufi Ruwaym b. Aḥmad (d. 303/915); see Sulamī, *Ṭabaqāt*, 183. For more on Ruwaym, see Gramlich, *Alte Vorbilder des Sufitums*, 1:447–482.

29. See the commentary on Q 89:27 in *SQ*, 1513. A fine example of ʿAyn al-Quḍāt's use of this verse can be found in chapter 5, s.v. "Imaginalization."

30. Overviews of Sufi ethics can be found in Ali, "Classical Sufi Ethics" and Khalil, "Sufism and Qur'ānic Ethics." For an excellent study of the creative ways in which a number of leading premodern Sufis and philosophers wrote on the cultivation of the virtues, see Zargar, *Polished Mirror*.

31. My discussion of the soul's lower and higher possibilities is indebted to the masterful treatment of the topic in Murata, *Tao of Islam*, chapter 9.

32. For the symbolism of the heart in Sufism, see Lings, *What Is Sufism?*, chapter 5, and Nasr, "Heart of the Faithful." See also Murata, *Tao of Islam*, 289–319.

33. Corbin, *Creative Imagination*, 221.

34. Morris, "Imaging Islam," 318.

35. A helpful study of the heart in ʿAyn al-Quḍāt is Shajjārī, "Dil-i ādamī wa-wīzhagī-hā-yi ān az dīdgāh-i ʿAyn al-Quḍāt Hamadānī."

36. Q 94:1.

37. Q 39:22.

38. Q 7:179.

39. Q 22:46.

40. Muslim, Qadr, 3, no. 6921.

41. For his use of this tradition in other texts, see *N* III, 384–385, §196, and *Z* §145.

42. Cf. Qushayrī, *Risāla*, 502.

43. Muslim, Qadr, 3, no. 6921.

44. Saghānī, *Mawḍūʿāt*, 50.

45. See the discussion in Chittick, *Divine Love*, 124–129.

46. For the implications of this point, see Mudarrisī and ʿArab, *Kaʿba-yi dil*, and Rustom, "One Step to God."

47. The wording in Muslim, Birr, 10, no. 6707 comes closest to what ʿAyn al-Quḍāt has here.

48. Q 55:1–2.

49. We will return to the symbolism of the *basmala* and its letters in chapter 8.

50. Q 96:4–5.

51. Q 85:21. The "Preserved Tablet" (*al-lawḥ al-maḥfūẓ*) is often identified by traditional authorities with the Mother of the Book (for which, see chapter 5, n. 82).

52. In Islamic thought, the *qalam* or Pen (derived from Q 68:1) is an active principle, whereas the Tablet is a passive principle. For their function and symbolism, see Murata, *Tao of Islam*, 12–13, 153–158, and 162–167.

53. Abū Dāwūd, Adab, 57, no. 4920.

54. Aḥmad, no. 18019.

55. Tirmidhī, Tafsīr, 3, no. 3256.

56. Q 12:53.

57. Ibn ʿAbbās or ʿAbd Allāh b. ʿAbbās (d. 68/688) was the Prophet's cousin and a major authority on the interpretation of the Quran.

58. That is, Muʿādh b. Jabal (d. ca 18/640), a famous Companion of the Prophet who was placed in charge by him over the Yemen.

59. A most likely context for this saying is the Battle of Ḥunayn, when the Prophet appointed Muʿādh to instruct some new converts to Islam while the Muslim army marched out against the Hawāzin tribe. See Lings, *Muhammad*, 304. In most sources this saying is ascribed to ʿUmar. See Mannūn, *Nibrās al-ʿuqūl*, 93–94.

60. See Tabrīzī, *Minhāj*, 2:704.

61. See Chittick, *SPK*, 159. In its most general application, it simply denotes the very stuff of the varying levels of human personhood as comprised of the spirit, soul, heart, and intellect. For a discussion of this point, see Ghazālī, *Marvels of the Heart*, chapter 1. See also Chittick, *Divine Love*, 106–107 and 110–124.

62. Q 94:1.

63. Q 8:24.

64. Cf. *N* I, 277–278, §461.

65. Vivid accounts of one contemporary author's encounters with such people can be found in Sugich, *Signs on the Horizons*. For the mystical role and significance of the physical body, see Nasr, *Religion and the Order of Nature*, chapter 7.

66. See also Chittick's insightful remark recorded in Lumbard, *Aḥmad al-Ghazālī*, 169.

67. Abū Dāwūd, Adab, 86, no. 4987. Bilāl b. Rabaḥ (d. 20/643) was one of the earliest converts to Islam who became the official caller to the prayer (*mu'adhdhin*) for the Muslim community in Medina. For his conversion story, see Lings, *Muhammad*, 79.

68. Qārī, *Mirqāt*, 3:237. Ḥumayra or "little red one" was a nickname that the Prophet had given to ʿĀʾisha on account of the reddish hue of her cheeks.

69. Mālik, Ḥusn al-khuluq, 1, no. 1643.

70. Cf. the account in Sahlajī, *al-Nūr min kalimāt Abī Ṭayfūr*, 164.

71. Forouzanfar, *Aḥadīth-i Mathnawī*, no. 342. We will return to this famous Prophetic saying in chapter 9.

72. For the sources of this saying, as well as Aḥmad Ghazālī's use of it, see Maghsoudlou, "La pensée de 'Ayn al-Quḍāt al-Hamadānī," 39, n. 97.

73. This text is an expanded version of a passage in *N* II, 56, §74.

74. For whom, see chapter 5, n. 80.

75. *T* 150, §203. *"Be!"* appears in Q 36:82 and passim.

76. Kalābādhī, *Taʿarruf*, 41. Details on Kalābādhī can be found in Karamustafa, *Sufism*, 69–71.

77. The text in Arberry's edition of the *Taʿarruf* does not include a concluding passage that is found in some manuscripts and also noted by Arberry in the notes to his edition. After summarizing the position in question and stating that it means that the spirit does not actually inhere in the body, the variant reading runs as follows: "But this is incorrect. What is correct is that the spirit is an entity in the body and is created like the body." The commentator upon the *Taʿarruf* (for whom, see the next line of the present paragraph) cites these words as a part of the text.

78. See Chittick, *Divine Love*, 288–292.

79. Mustamlī Bukhārī, *Sharḥ*, 2:858–861. For his argument in theological context, see Maghsoudlou, "Status of the Spirit in al-Mustamlī al-Buḫārī's *Šharḥ al-Ta'arruf*," 244ff.

80. Q 17:85.

81. Q 36:82.

82. Q 38:72.

83. Q 42:52.

84. Q 17:85.

85. Q 5:54.

86. Q 36:82.

87. Q 17:85.

88. Q 53:3–4.

89. Q 4:80.

90. Q 48:10.

91. Q 17:85.

92. An expanded version of this passage is in *N* I, 278–279, §463.

93. *T* 37, §52. The litanies are recounted in *T* 36–37, §51.

94. *T* 38, §52. A part of this supplication is translated in chapter 1, n. 29.
95. *T* 38, §53.
96. Q 21:37.
97. Q 65:1.
98. Q 40:82.
99. Q 4:97.
100. Q 4:100.
101. Q 51:55.
102. Ḥaddād, *Takhrīj*, 1:213 and 6:2516.
103. *Z* §176.
104. Q 6:153.
105. Q 51:21.
106. In Islamic cosmology God transcends and is in total control of the entire order of space and time, seated on His Throne (*ʿarsh*) and beneath which is His Footstool or Pedestal (*kursī*). See Murata, *Tao of Islam*, 156, and the commentary on Q 2:256 in *SQ*, 111.
107. Ḥaddād, *Takhrīj*, 4:1541. We encountered a substantially different version of this Hadith earlier in this chapter, s.v. "The Heart."
108. Q 57:4.
109. These famous words are uttered by God in response to Basṭāmī's question as to how he can come near to Him. See Chittick, *SPK*, 319.
110. Q 51:21.
111. Cf. Qushayrī, *Risāla*, 502.
112. Sakkākī, *Miftāḥ*, 430.
113. Bukhārī, Tawḥīd, 50, no. 7630.
114. Cf. this sentence with Maybudī, *Unveiling of the Mysteries*, 135.
115. Cf. the statements on *zuhd* in Kalābādhī, *Doctrine of the Sufis*, 83–84.
116. Q 79:46.
117. Muslim, Janna, 15, no. 7376.
118. Q 56:95 (cf. 69:51).
119. *N* I, 373, §621. See also *N* III, 375, §174. For a useful discussion of the contexts in which ʿAyn al-Quḍāt speaks of this mysterious girl from Baghdad, see Fūlādī, "ʿAyn al-Quḍāt Hamadānī wa-dukhtarak-i Baghdādī."
120. *N* II, 457, §711.
121. *N* III, 375–376, §§174–176.
122. *N* I, 3, §3.
123. *N* III, 376, §178.
124. *N* II, 457, §711.
125. *T* 28, §40; *N* I, 475, §791; *N* II, 124, §182; *N* II, 457, §711.
126. Cf. Q 3:7.
127. Q 29:49.
128. Q 39:22.
129. Q 50:37.

130. Ḥaddād, *Takhrīj*, 1:102–104.

131. Ṭabarānī, *Awsaṭ*, 5:76.

132. See also *T* 9–10, §14.

133. See also ʿAyn al-Quḍāt's critical comments vis-à-vis her shortcomings on the Sufi path in *N* III, 375–376, §§174 and 176–178.

134. Q 8:23.

135. ʿAyn al-Quḍāt also cites this well-known Sufi saying in *T* 28, §40, and *Sh* 10. Cf. the version cited in the following text.

136. Bukhārī, Īmān, 1, no. 8.

137. *Z* §135.

138. A part of *T* 35, §49 is almost identical to this passage.

139. Q 4:80.

140. Q 48:10.

141. Q 4:80.

142. Ibn Māja, Muqaddima, 39, no. 228.

143. Q 49:4.

144. ʿAjlūnī, *Kashf*, 2:237.

145. Abū Dāwūd, Adab, 19, no. 4835.

146. *N* II, 124, §182. This point occurs in the context of ʿAyn al-Quḍāt's refutation of the Ismaili doctrine of instruction from an infallible teacher (*taʿlīm*); for which, see Landolt, "Early Evidence for Nāṣir-i Khusraw's Poetry in Sufism," 372–375.

147. *T* 31, §45.

148. I follow here the much clearer reading in MS Ayasofya 1841, fol. 50v, which has *tamannā-yi maqām-i murīdān* instead of ʿUsayrān's *maqām-i tamannā-yi murīdān*.

149. Q 58:22.

150. Q 16:43.

151. For Abū Bakr's unique status in ʿAyn al-Quḍāt's writings, see chapter 5, n. 105.

152. Q 4:80.

Chapter 7. Knowledge Transcendent

1. Abū Dāwūd, Adab, 57, no. 4920.

2. See Baqlī, *Sharḥ*, 113–114.

3. The first hemistich of a poem that ʿAyn al-Quḍāt explicitly attributes to him in *T* 281, §366; the poem is not in *Incidents*, nor in any of Aḥmad Ghazālī's other writings.

4. Q 59:23.

5. *T* 202–203, §260.

6. See, inter alia, *N* I, 127, §599; *N* II, 92, §127; *N* III, 289, §17; *T* 314–316, §413.

7. For uses of this saying in Sufi literature, see Makkī, *Qūt*, 1:401, and Maybudī, *Unveiling of the Mysteries*, 11–12.

8. *T* 21, §32.

9. Muslim, Birr, 1, no. 6888. ʿAyn al-Quḍāt cites this tradition in *T* 202, §260.

10. ʿAyn al-Quḍāt cites this tradition in *N* II, 91, §128, and on another occasion (see chapter 8). The saying is not found in the standard sources. Cf. the Hadith transmitted on the authority of Abū Hurayra (for whom, see chapter 8, n. 43): "Whoever speaks Arabic is Arab, and whoever understands the two statements of faith in Islam is Arab." See Muḥammad and Jumuʿa, *Jazīrat al-ʿarab*, 1:20, n. 3.

11. *N* II, 91–92, §128.

12. Murata, *Tao of Islam*, 24.

13. Abū'l-ʿAtāhiya, *Dīwān*, 122.

14. Cf. the version cited in Chittick, *SPK*, 178 and passim.

15. Q 24:35.

16. Qushayrī, *Risāla*, 644. See also the relevant discussion of this statement in Chittick, *In Search of the Lost Heart*, 19.

17. *N* I, 86, §115.

18. Q 53:30.

19. For this saying of Ḥallaj in context, see Sells, *Early Islamic Mysticism*, 277.

20. Q 2:2.

21. This maxim goes back to Junayd; see Chittick, *Divine Love*, 250, and Ḥaddād, *Takhrīj*, 4:1758. ʿAyn al-Quḍāt also cites it in *Z* §§76 and 122, and makes use of a slightly different version in *T* 18, §28.

22. Q 56:95 (cf. 69:51).

23. These verses go back to Abū Saʿīd b. Abī'l-Khayr. See Farmanish, *Aḥwāl wa-āthār-i ʿAyn al-Quḍāt*, 292.

24. Q 30:41.

25. Q 55:1–2.

26. Q 2:255.

27. A fine discussion of ʿAyn al-Quḍāt's understanding of this doctrine can be found in Izutsu, "Concept of Perpetual Creation in Islamic Mysticism and Zen Buddhism," 125–133.

28. Q 2:255.

29. Bazzār, *Baḥr*, 1:175.

30. Zurqānī, *Sharḥ*, 7:390.

31. Ḥaddād, *Takhrīj*, 1:207–208.

32. This is a well-known saying of ʿUmar. For an example of its more usual usage, see the commentary on Q 13:10 in *SQ*, 618.

33. Q 57:25.

34. An essential part of this clause is absent in ʿUsayrān's edition. I have included it here, following the reading in MS Ayasofya 1840, fol. 68r.

35. Q 17:35 (this wording is also in Q 26:182).

36. See Ghazālī, *Munqidh*, 111, and Ghazālī, *Niche of Lights*, 36. The most recent discussions on ʿAyn al-Quḍāt's explication of this doctrine can be found Faruque, "ʿAyn al-Quḍāt"; Maghsoudlou, "La pensée de 'Ayn al-Quḍāt al-Hamadānī," 328ff.; Rustom, "Introduction"; Shajjārī, "Maʿrifat az dīdgāh-i ʿAyn al-Quḍāt," 90ff.; Yūsuf-i Thānī and Mahdīpūr, "Tabyīn-i kathrat wa-waḥdat-i wujūd."

37. *Z* §185.

38. *Z* §178.

39. *Z* §§184–185.

40. *Z* §60.

41. *N* I, 378–379, §§630.

42. See the discussion in *N* I, 377–378, §§628–629.

43. *N* I, 378, §629.

44. Cf. the Hadith cited by ʿAyn al-Quḍāt: "God has servants whose hearts are more luminous than the sun and whose actions are those of the Prophets. In the eyes of God, they have the rank of the martyrs" (*T* 44, §60). For a typical usage of this saying, see Chalabī, *Kāshif*, 179.

45. *T* 64, §87. He does not attribute it to any specific person; like many others, he does not deem it a Prophetic utterance and instead refers to it as a report (*khabar*). See *T* 56, §72. For another example of its usage in Sufi literature, see Iṣfahānī, *Ḥilya*, 10:208.

46. See Maqdisī, *Mukhtaṣar*, 116, where this statement is attributed to the famous early Sufi figure al-Ḥasan al-Baṣrī (d. 110/728).

47. Q 25:43 (cf. the almost identical wording in 45:23).

48. Q 6:103.

49. Q 76:28.

50. Q 39:22.

51. Q 7:185.

52. Q 27:34.

53. A saying attributed to ʿUmar. See Ghazālī, *Iḥyāʾ*, 5:54 and 9:297. ʿAyn al-Quḍāt also cites this statement in *T* 12, §17; 202, §260; 279, §365; 299, §392. For its use in Aḥmad Ghazālī, see Lumbard, "Aḥmad al-Ghazālī's *al-Tajrīd fī kalimat al-tawḥīd*."

54. Q 9:128.

55. Aḥmad, no. 11852.

56. Muslim, Ruʾyā, 2, no. 6058.

57. Q 51:21.

58. Q 41:53.

59. Q 9:128.

60. ʿAyn al-Quḍāt understands blessings (*ālā*) in this tradition to refer to God's attributes (*ṣifāt*). See *T* 303, §399.

61. ʿAjlūnī, *Kashf*, 1:356–357.

62. This statement goes back to Abū Bakr. See Qushayrī, *Risāla*, 621, and Sarrāj, *Lumaʿ*, 36.

63. Qushayrī, *Risāla*, 289. Cf. Tirmidhī, Tafsīr, 39, no. 3541.

64. Q 75:22–23.

65. Q 6:91 (this wording is also in Q 22:74 and 39:67).

66. Cf. Ghazālī, *Sawāniḥ*, 26 and 41–42, as well as Ibn ʿArabī's observations translated in Chittick, *SPK*, 112. According to Baqlī, this statement by Abū Bakr is itself an ecstatic utterance. See Baqlī, *Sharḥ*, 86–87. ʿAyn al-Quḍāt also cites it in *Z* §76.

67. Q 42:53.

68. Q 5:54.

69. As noted earlier (chapter 4, n. 29), while the kingdom (*mulk*) refers to the corporeal world and the Dominion (*malakūt*) the spiritual world, when Sufi authors speak of the Invincibility (*jabarūt*), they assign the status of the spiritual world to it and identify the Dominion as a realm between the spiritual and corporeal worlds. See the discussion in Murata, *Tao of Islam*, 150.

70. A study of Bastāmī's ecstatic utterances can be found in Keeler, "Wisdom in Controversy."

71. Q 7:143. The speaker here is Moses. For Moses' encounter with God, see the commentary on this verse in *SQ*, 453–454.

72. Q 7:143.

73. For this saying, see Rustom, "Sufi Teachings of Dhu'l-Nun," 72.

74. Abū'l-Ḥusayn Nūrī (d. 295/907) was a renowned lover of God; see Karamustafa, *Sufism*, 11–15. His treatise *Maqāmāt al-qulūb* (*Stations of the Heart*) was influential upon *The Interior Castle*, a famous sixteenth-century Spanish work of Christian mysticism by St. Teresa of Ávila (d. 1582); see Nasr, *Garden of Truth*, 174–175.

75. Q 6:103.

76. Q 6:103.

Chapter 8. Quranic Origins

1. He mentions this work in *Sh* 41.

2. Boylston, "Writing the Kaleidoscope of Reality," 216–222, situates ʿAyn al-Quḍāt's approach to the Quran against the backdrop of the notion of "unities of plenitude" and the multiple perspective shifts and vantage points

that he assumes in his writings. Surprisingly, neither Mayel Heravi, *Khāṣṣi-yyat-i āyinagī*, 64–119, nor ʿUsayrān, "Muqaddima," discuss ʿAyn al-Quḍāt's understanding of the Quran in their respective surveys of his thought. Some preliminary inquiries are Mudarrisī and ʿArab, "Jāygāh-i Qurʾān wa-taʾwīl-i ān dar *Tamhīdāt*," and Pārsāpūr, "Didgāh-i ʿAyn al-Quḍāt dar bāb-i ḥurūf, ḥurūf-i muqaṭṭaʿa, wa-nuqaṭ."

3. See Aḥmad, no. 11273.

4. *N* II, 486, §761. Incidentally, this same idea is expressed by Sanāʾī. See Schimmel, *Mystical Dimensions of Islam*, 420. For ʿAyn al-Quḍāt's engagement with Sanāʾī's poetry, see the introduction, s.v. "Writings."

5. Q 6:59.

6. Q 59:21.

7. Ṭabarānī, *Kabīr*, 1:255.

8. Q 6:59.

9. Q 15:87.

10. *T* 19, §29.

11. *N* I, 7, §8.

12. Abū Dāwūd, Adab, 80, no. 4973. This passage from the *Letters* is part of a text that largely replicates *T* 12–13, §18 (for a complete translation of which, see chapter 5, s.v. "Habit-Worship").

13. Ibn Māja, Muqaddima, 38, no. 220.

14. Q 47:24.

15. Q 48:26.

16. ʿAjlūnī, *Kashf*, 2:112. Elsewhere, ʿAyn al-Quḍāt likens the Quran to a storehouse of medicine: "The likeness of the Quran is that of a storehouse—the remedy for all sick people is there. This is why God says, *And We send down in the Quran that which is a cure and a mercy for the believers* [Q 17:82]" (*RJ* 1 = *N* II, 483, §758).

17. See also the same point in *N* II, 99, §139.

18. Aḥmad, no. 20753.

19. Q 50:37.

20. Q 25:30.

21. *N* II, 291, §439.

22. *N* III, 325, §77.

23. See also the discussion in chapter 7, s.v. "Brothers and Mirrors."

24. *T* 170–71, §226. It is of interest to note the few instances in which ʿAyn al-Quḍāt discusses a statement that he attributes to ʿUmar: "The Quran does not mention enemies, nor does it address unbelievers." ʿAyn al-Quḍāt understands this to mean that only believers can actually "hear" the Quran, and when it seems to mention enemies like Pharaoh, this is to draw the believers' attention to the negative elements in their own souls. So these "enemies" are all inside the self, which is essentially good and only accidentally bad. On

this logic, the Quran neither mentions "enemies" as such, nor does it address "unbelievers" as such. See *N* II, 75, §88; *N* II, 175, §262; *N* II, 244, §369.

25. Q 16:21.
26. Q 27:80.
27. Q 6:36.
28. Q 8:24.
29. Q 26:212.
30. *T* 178, §236.
31. *T* 178, §236.
32. Ḥaddād, *Takhrīj*, 1:165–167. See also the use of this tradition in *N* I, 89, §121, and *N* III, 371, §163.
33. Cf. *T* 327, §429.
34. Q 1:2.
35. Q 109:1.
36. A part of this text is an expanded version of a passage in *N* II, 57, §75.
37. See *N* II, 368, §573; *N* II, 430, §678; *N* II, 472–473, §737.
38. For a typical usage of this saying, see Chittick, *Me and Rumi*, 152–153.
39. Q 27:80.
40. For an insightful survey of Sufi Quranic exegesis that also takes stock of the existing scholarship on the topic, see Taleb, "Sufi Tafsīr." See also Asghari, "Sufi Interpretation of the Qur'ān," and Dakake, "*Ta'wīl* in the Qur'an and the Islamic Exegetical Tradition."
41. Q 10:3.
42. Ghazālī, *Iḥyā'*, 1:364–365.
43. Abū Hurayra (d. ca. 58/678) was a close Companion of the Prophet and a major transmitter of Hadith.
44. Q 65:12.
45. Makkī, *Qūt*, 2:733. Parts of this passage appear in *N* II, 99, §138.
46. Bazzār, *Baḥr*, 5:423.
47. Q 25:30.
48. This is part of a well-known saying that goes back to Jaʿfar al-Ṣādiq (d. 148/765). See Kāshānī, *Qāmūs*, 305.
49. Q 41:53.
50. Q 56:79.
51. Q 9:28.
52. Bukhārī, Zakāt, 8, no. 1430.
53. Q 24:26.
54. Q 39:73.
55. Q 47:24.
56. Q 110:1.
57. Q 41:53.
58. Q 71:17.

59. Q 6:75.

60. *T* 133, §184.

61. For more on this phenomenon and some of its implications, see the helpful inquiries in Kermani, *God Is Beautiful*, chapter 6, and Sviri, *Perspectives on Early Islamic Mysticism*, chapter 13.

62. For this verse, see the discussion in Lumbard, "Covenant and Covenants," 6–9. Its treatment in Persian Sufi literature is discussed in Chittick, *Divine Love*, 43–53.

63. Q 7:172.

64. Q 9:6.

65. *N* II, 50, §66.

66. *N* II, 51, §66. For the passage in translation, see Shams, "Baraka (Barakat) Hamadānī."

67. That is, "Die before you die" and the one that will be cited in the following text.

68. *N* III, 311, §57.

69. Parts of this passage appear in *N* II, 99, §138. Cf. *N* I, 351, §584.

70. *T* 172, §228.

71. See also *T* 169, §225.

72. Q 59:21.

73. This passage also appears in *N* II, 99, §139, but with some modifications.

74. According to Ghazālī, *Iḥyāʾ*, 2:292, this statement goes back to "one of the recognizers." Mount Qaf is a cosmic mountain atop of which resides the Simorgh, the mythic bird who symbolizes the Divine Presence. Both Mount Qaf and the Simorgh feature most significantly in one of the greatest works of Persian Sufi literature, ʿAṭṭār's *Manṭiq al-ṭayr* or *Speech of the Birds*. See the discussion in Nasr, *Islamic Art and Spirituality*, 109–110; Zargar, *Polished Mirror*, 244ff.; Zargar, *Religion of Love*, passim.

75. For a wide range of representative approaches to the detached letters in the Islamic tradition, see the commentary on Q 2:1 in *SQ*, 13–14; Ibn ʿArabī, "The Science of Letters"; Maybudī, *Unveiling of the Mysteries*, 9–10, 247, 261, 390, and 444; Nguyen, "Exegesis of the *ḥurūf al-muqaṭṭaʿa*"; Rustom, *Triumph of Mercy*, 36 and 152.

76. *N* II, 143, §208.

77. *N* II, 308, §465.

78. *N* II, 143, §208.

79. *N* I, 166, §251.

80. Q 50:37.

81. Burūsawī, *Rūḥ*, s.v. commentary on Q 27:1.

82. To the best of my knowledge, Burūsawī is the only author to draw an explicit connection between the public condemnation of ʿAyn al-Quḍāt and

his understanding of the Quran's detached letters. But this is not a tenable position. See the present book's introduction for ʿAyn al-Quḍāt's charge of heresy in context.

83. Q 20:1.

84. Q 36:1.

85. Q 40:1. See also ʿAyn al-Quḍāt's explanation of "*Ḥā*ʾ, *Mīm*, ʿAyn, Sīn, Qāf" in chapter 1, s.v. "Apparitions."

86. Q 7:1.

87. Q 33:72.

88. Q 16:60.

89. Q 18:109.

90. *N* II, 246, §371.

91. Cf. *T* 337, §443: "These words can only be uttered in a garb that is conjoined. Explicating the conjoined as disconnected can only be done through some images that are inverted by geometric talismans."

92. Q 51:55.

93. Q 2:6.

94. Q 19:1.

95. Q 2:1 (this particular combination of the detached letters is also in Q 3:1, 29:1, 30:1, 31:1, and 32:1).

96. Q 20:1.

97. Q 36:1.

98. Q 96:4.

99. Q 55:1–2.

100. Q 4:113.

101. Sakhāwī, *Maqāṣid*, 73–74.

102. Q 36:1.

103. Q 26:1.

104. Tirmidhī, Faḍāʾil al-Qurʾān, 7, no. 3129.

105. Q 36:1.

106. Aḥmad is another name for the Prophet Muhammad. In chapter 10, we will see how ʿAyn al-Quḍāt associates the highest level of faith with this name.

107. Q 4:164.

108. Q 18:109.

109. Q 31:27.

110. *N* I, 42, §47.

111. Q 28:51.

112. Q 6:97 (the wording is also in Q 6:98 and 126).

113. In chapter 6, we have had occasion to see how ʿAyn al-Quḍāt identifies the Preserved Tablet with the heart. We will reencounter this idea in the present chapter.

114. Q 58:22.

115. Q 54:32. Cf. this passage from *Paving the Path* with *N* I, 368, §614.

116. A thorough study of early Persian Sufi discussions on love (largely informed by Q 5:54) can be found in Chittick, *Divine Love*.

117. Q 5:54.

118. Q 5:54.

119. Although ʿAyn al-Quḍāt cites the clause in Q 5:54 after *He loves them*, namely *and they love him*, his example still only pertains to the Arabic word cluster that spells *He loves them*.

120. Cf. *T* 114, §161, where ʿAyn al-Quḍāt recounts Shiblī's famous answer when asked what he is: "I am the dot under the *bāʾ*." Cf. Ghazālī, *Condemnation of Pride and Self-Admiration*, 21–22, for a report wherein Shiblī interrogates someone who himself claims to be the dot under the *bāʾ* of the *basmala*.

121. Q 5:54.

122. Cf. Q 17:44 and 57:1.

123. Q 13:39.

124. Q 13:39.

125. Q 43:32.

126. Q 16:71.

127. See chapter 9, s.v. "Muhammadan Light."

128. Q 13:39.

129. See the observation in Casewit, *Mystics of al-Andalus*, 231, n. 85.

130. For which, see Saleh, "A Piecemeal Qurʾān."

131. For connections between Sufism and Islamic calligraphy, see Moustafa and Sperl, *Cosmic Script*; Nasr, *Islamic Art and Spirituality*, 17–36; Schimmel, *Calligraphy and Islamic Culture*, 77–114.

Chapter 9. Muhammad and Iblis

1. Shaykh Bustī was a disciple of Ghazālī's first spiritual guide, the famous Abū ʿAlī Fārmadī (d. 477/1084); for the latter, see Gozashteh, "Abū ʿAlī al-Fārmadī." Bustī himself was the master of Muḥammad b. Ḥamūya al-Juwaynī (one of ʿAyn al-Quḍāt's teachers whom we encountered in the introduction) and may have met Aḥmad Ghazālī; see figure 6. For more on Bustī, see Mayel Heravi, "Bustī, Abū al-Ḥasan," and Pourjavady, *Zindagī wa-āthār-i Shaykh Abū'l-Ḥasan Bustī*.

2. See the discussions in Kars, *Unsaying God*, 180–181; Lumbard, *Aḥmad al-Ghazālī*, 87–90; Lumbard, "Aḥmad al-Ghazālī's *al-Tajrīd fī kalimat al-tawḥīd*."

3. Q 8:4.

4. My translation "but God" follows the corresponding correction to ʿUsayrān's reading in Pūrnāmdāryān and Ḥafīẓī, "Nigāhī ba-taṣḥīḥ-i *Tamhīdāt*," 121.

5. An allusion to the famous Prophetic saying, "One of the pulls of the Real equals the work of both the worlds." See Qārī, *Mirqāt*, 3:273 and 9:218.

6. Q 37:173.

7. Ḥaddād, *Takhrīj*, 1:371–373.

8. For Aḥmad Ghazālī's exposition of "No god" as darkness and "but God" as light, see Lumbard, *Aḥmad al-Ghazālī*, 89.

9. Tirmidhī, Īmān, 18, no. 2854.

10. Q 58:22.

11. Q 8:23.

12. Tirmidhī, Īmān, 17, no. 2849.

13. The "great one" here is likely Kharrāz. Cf. the following responses to Kharrāz's statements recorded in Rustom, "Forms of Gnosis," 340–341.

14. It is unclear who the direct object is here.

15. Qushayrī, *Risāla*, 289.

16. Q 39:65.

17. Q 39:65.

18. Ḥaddād, *Takhrīj*, 2:657–658.

19. Q 6:79.

20. Cf. Q 98:5.

21. Sahlajī, *al-Nūr min kalimāt Abī Ṭayfūr*, 104. Basṭāmī goes on to remark that the phrase "No god but God" is uttered with words and expressions, but God is beyond any linguistic confines. Even uttering the words of the Shahada, insofar as the speaker is trying to trap God into some kind of linguistic formula, entails repentance since it implies preoccupation with something other than God. For a helpful discussion of this and related perspectives in early Sufism, see Khalil, *Repentance and the Return to God*, 92 and 167ff.

22. Tirmidhī, Daʿawāt, 139, no. 3934.

23. For the most detailed study of the history of the Muhammadan light doctrine, see Andani, "Metaphysics of Muhammad."

24. See the insightful treatment in Andani, "Metaphysics of Muhammad," 138–143.

25. Q 5:15.

26. Q 7:157.

27. The Tuba tree derives from a phrase (*ṭūbā*) in Q 13:29. See the commentary on this verse in *SQ*, 623.

28. Q 53:14.

29. Q 95:1.

30. Q 95:1.

31. Cf. 28:30.
32. Q 28:30.
33. Q 23:20.
34. Q 7:143.
35. Q 50:1.
36. Q 24:35.
37. Cf. 24:35.
38. Q 24:35.
39. Q 24:35.
40. Cf. *T* 265–266, §349.
41. Q 66:8.
42. Bukhārī, Daʿawāt, 10, no. 6389.
43. Q 93:6.
44. Q 64:6.
45. Q 54:24.
46. Q 18:110.
47. Q 24:35.
48. Muslim, Ruʾyā, 2, no. 6058.
49. We saw a slightly different version of this tradition in a text translated in chapter 5, s.v. "Imaginalization."
50. That is, the early Sufi and theoretician of the Muhammadan light, Sahl al-Tustarī (d. 283/896). For a study of his life and thought, see Böwering, *Mystical Vision of Existence in Classical Islam*. Tustarī's Sufi Quran commentary is available in English translation: *Tafsīr al-Tustarī*.
51. Q 5:15.
52. Q 7:198.
53. In an alternative report, which also accords well with the point ʿAyn al-Quḍāt is making in this passage, we are told that the Prophet did not have a shadow specifically because he was light. See Qāḍī ʿIyāḍ, *Shifāʾ*, 1:522.
54. Q 33:46.
55. See the in-depth study in Ogunnaike, "Annihilation in the Messenger Revisited."
56. Cf. the first text in chapter 1, s.v. "Muhammadan Encounters."
57. Q 48:10.
58. Q 5:3.
59. For different approaches to ʿAyn al-Quḍāt's Satanology, see Awn, *Satan's Tragedy and Redemption*, 134–150; Boylston, "Writing the Kaleidoscope of Reality," 305–335; Moshiri, "Devil's Advocates," chapter 4; Rustom, "Devil's Advocate."
60. For black light in Sufi metaphysics, see Corbin, *Man of Light*, chapter 5.
61. Helpful analyses and complementary diagrams of ʿAyn al-Quḍāt's

treatment of black light framed against the backdrop of his metaphysics can be found in Yūsufī and Ḥaydarī, "Nūr-i siyāh," passim.

62. Q 38:82.

63. Q 21:104.

64. Q 4:164.

65. Q 22:52.

66. Cf. the wording in *N* I 476, §792.

67. Q 2:34.

68. Q 38:82.

69. Q 6:97.

70. Abū Dāwūd, Libās, 5, no. 4033.

71. Q 3:31.

72. Q 38:82.

73. For ʿAzāzīl, see Bodman, *Poetics of Iblīs*, 121, n. 7, and Sells, *Early Islamic Mysticism*, 278–280.

74. ʿUsayrān's edition has a clear error here since it has "ʿAzrāʾīl," which is the name of the angel of death; see also the correction to ʿUsayrān's reading in Pūrnāmdāryān and Ḥafīẓī, "Nigāhī ba-taṣḥīḥ-i *Tamhīdāt*," 124.

75. Cf. Q 59:2.

76. *T* 211, §270. Cf. this statement with the Hadith in Ibn Ḥanbal, *Kitāb al-Sunna*, 1:174: "The Angels were created from the light of exaltedness, and Iblis was created from the fire of exaltedness."

77. *T* 211, §270.

78. Q 25:43.

79. "Ḥusayn" here is of course the first name of Ḥallāj.

80. In *N* III, 279, §4, ʿAyn al-Quḍāt says that the mole can be a reference to Muhammad or to Iblis. If Iblis is conceived as the mole, then Muhammad would correspond to the tresses. Given that both Muhammad and Iblis reveal and conceal "No god but God," such a reading is tenable, although ʿAyn al-Quḍāt only takes up this particular line of interpretation in his writings once in passing (the text is cited later in this chapter).

81. This passage also appears in *N* II, 449, §699.

82. My translation of this sentence and the one before it follows the corresponding corrections to ʿUsayrān's reading in Pūrnāmdāryān and Ḥafīẓī, "Nigāhī ba-taṣḥīḥ-i *Tamhīdāt*," 129.

83. ʿAyn al-Quḍāt seems to be employing the legal term *wājib* or "mandatory" more for rhetorical affect, since reciting the *istiʿādha* formula is not a mandatory (*wājib*/*farḍ*) precondition for the prayer in any school of Islamic jurisprudence.

84. Q 7:12 (the wording is also in 38:76).

85. Q 21:107.

86. Q 38:78 (cf. 15:35).
87. Q 59:22.
88. Q 59:23.
89. See also the last translated text in chapter 3 for a related discussion.
90. Cf. Bayhaqī, *Kitāb al-Asmāʾ wa'l-ṣifāt*, 1:401–403.
91. Q 6:115.
92. Lālikāʾī, *Sharḥ*, 2:606.
93. Q 6:115.
94. Q 33:62 (this wording is also in Q 48:23; cf. 35:43).
95. Muslim, Jumuʿa, 14, no. 2044. Cf. Q 39:36–37.
96. Q 36:1–2.
97. Q 6:75.
98. Q 6:76.
99. Kaʿb the "Rabbi" (d. ca. 32/652) was a major early Muslim scholar and teacher who was formerly a Jewish Rabbi; he converted to Islam during the Caliphate of ʿUmar.
100. Q 6:77.
101. Q 6:78. Cf. *N* I, 391, §653.
102. For a detailed treatment of this point, see Rustom, "Devil's Advocate," 84–89.
103. Cf. this Arabic proverb with Kharrāz's famous answer when asked how he knows God: "Through the fact that He brings opposites together" (see Chittick, *SPK*, 115). Cf. Sells, *Early Islamic Mysticism*, 276, for Ḥallāj's related statement in the *Ṭawāsīn*.
104. Q 59:24.
105. Q 59:23.
106. Q 12:39.
107. Ibn al-Aʿrābī, *Muʿjam*, 1:301–302.
108. See Bodman, *Poetics of Iblīs*, part 2.
109. See Awn, *Satan's Tragedy and Redemption*, and Moshiri, "Devil's Advocates." A very interesting defense of Iblis' salvation in thirteenth/nineteenth-century West African Sufism can be found in Ogunnaike, "Philosophical Sufism in the Sokoto Caliphate," 163–164.
110. For the pioneering scholarship on Ḥallāj's Satanology, see Awn, *Satan's Tragedy and Redemption*, 123–131; Massignon, *Passion of al-Hallāj*, 3:270–327; Sells, *Early Islamic Mysticism*, 266–280. Analyses of Aḥmad Ghazālī's view of the positive role of Satan can be found in Lumbard, *Aḥmad al-Ghazālī*, 109–112, and Pourjavady, "Ḥallāj dar *Sawāniḥ*-i Aḥmad Ghazālī."
111. Cited, with modifications, from Schimmel, *Mystical Dimensions*, 195.
112. We will draw attention to a relevant example later. For a sustained exposition of this point, see Rustom, "Devil's Advocate," 79–96.
113. See the point in *N* II, 69, §94.

114. For Iblis as the teacher of the angels, see *N* II, 417, §658, in addition to the texts that will be cited in this chapter.

115. Cf. Q 4:164.

116. See *T* 316–318, §415. For a discussion of ʿAyn al-Quḍāt's treatment of that other aspect of jealousy, namely God's jealousy, see chapter 2, s.v. "Divine Jealousy."

117. Q 7:12 (the wording is also in 38:76).

118. Q 2:34 (see also Q 7:11, 17:61, 18:50, and 20:116).

119. Q 17:61. This paragraph in which this passage occurs is also to be found, with some adjustments, in *N* II, 187, §280, and 412, §650. See also Sells, *Early Islamic Mysticism*, 278, where in the *Ṭawāsīn* Ḥallāj has Iblis tell God that his disobeying Him is itself a manifestation of His choice.

120. For this important archangel who is mentioned in Q 2:98, see Murata, "Angels," 327–328, and *SQ*, 46.

121. Q 2:34

122. Cf. Q 17:61.

123. Q 38:78 (cf. 15:35).

124. For which, see Chittick, *SPK*, 291–294. See also Chittick, *Divine Love*, 8–9, where he explains how the engendering command is related to the first part of the Shahada and the prescriptive command to the second.

125. Cf. Samʿānī, *Repose of the Spirits*, 51–52.

126. For the multifaceted Maḥmūd-Ayāz trope in Persian Sufi literature, see Schimmel, *A Two-Colored Brocade*, 130–131.

127. Q 2:34.

128. For more on this point, see Rustom, "Devil's Advocate," 84–89.

129. These verses go back to Ḥallāj. See Farmanish, *Aḥwāl wa-āthār-i ʿAyn al-Quḍāt*, 315. Cf. Samʿānī, *Repose of the Spirits*, 389.

130. Q 2:34.

131. For a summary and beautiful partial translation of this work, see Sells, *Early Islamic Mysticism*, 269–280.

132. A slightly different version of this saying is cited in *T* 223, §288. Cf. Ḥallāj's words in Sells, *Early Islamic Mysticism*, 273. Ridgeon, *Morals and Mysticism*, 28–29, notes that Ḥallāj viewed himself, Iblis, and Pharaoh as chevaliers (cf. Sells, *Early Islamic Mysticism*, 277). For the three dimensions of chivalry (*futuwwa*) in ʿAyn al-Quḍāt's writings (the last being in reference to Iblis), see Rustom, "ʿAyn al-Quḍāt on Chivalry."

133. Q 15:21.

134. That is, one must act in accordance with what is demanded by the face, mole, and tresses respectively.

135. For Iblis viewed as the mole, see n. 80.

136. Shaykh Abū'l-Qāsim Gurgānī (d. 465/1073) was a great spiritual guide from Khurasan who was the second master of Abū ʿAlī Fārmadī—Fārmadī's

first master being none other than Abū'l-Qāsim al-Qushayrī (d. 465/1072). Incidentally, ʿAyn al-Quḍāt discusses Gurgānī and Fārmadī in an interesting story in *N* I, 274, §454, and in this same passage notes that Gurgānī is said to have been a spiritual guide for both the Jinn and humans (for the Jinn in Islam, see *SQ*, 1427 and passim). For more on Gurgānī, see Shams, "Abū al-Qāsim Kurragānī," and Maybudī, *Unveiling of the Mysteries*, 102 and 116.

137. For the poverty in question, see chapter 10, s.v. "Levels of Unbelief."

138. For Shaykh Baraka, see the introduction, s.v. "Life."

139. Cf. *T* 224, §289.

140. This passage also appears in *N* II, 449, §699.

141. Q 38:82.

142. That is, *ṣalawāt*, which are to be reserved for the Prophet, since that is his nourishment.

143. Cf. Q 2:199.

144. Cf. Q 2:221.

145. Q 39:74.

146. Q 53:17. See also Ḥallāj's explanation of this Quranic verse in Sells, *Early Islamic Mysticism*, 273.

147. See also the pertinent remarks in Ghazālī, *Sawāniḥ*, 49.

148. See *N* I, 315, §525.

149. For an extended inquiry into this and related points, see Rustom, "Devil's Advocate," 89–96.

150. This seems to be a paraphrase of a statement by Dhū'l-Nun. See Rustom, "Sufi Teachings of Dhu'l-Nun," 78–79.

151. Q 15:35.

152. *T* 224–226 corresponds, with some minor differences, to *N* II, 410–412, §§647–650.

153. The type of carpet ʿAyn al-Quḍāt is referring to is the *gilīm*, which is commonly known in English by its Turkish name *kilim*. The kilim is a type of plain-weave carpet that can take on several different forms. See Sherrill, "Carpets V."

Chapter 10. Love Transcendent

1. *T* 140, §191.

2. Cf. Ghazālī, *Sawāniḥ*, 53.

3. Bukhārī, Maghāzī, 9, no. 4032.

4. *T* 127, §176.

5. *T* 64, §87.

6. Q 75:20–21.

7. Q 34:54.

8. Q 2:4.
9. Q 41:53.
10. Q 17:14.
11. Q 50:22.
12. Q 30:7.
13. Q 34:54.
14. Q 41:44.
15. Ḥaddād, *Takhrīj*, 4:1590–1591.
16. Bazzār, *Baḥr*, 13:32.
17. Q 5:54.
18. Cf. Q 41:37.
19. For this famous Hadith, see Chittick, *SPK*, 396, n. 7. ʿAyn al-Quḍāt also cites it in *Z* §99.
20. Q 27:34.
21. *T* 245, §321. For more on ʿAyn al-Quḍāt's treatment of patience, see *T* 318–319, §416.
22. Q 17:70.
23. Q 65:2.
24. Q 10:93.
25. Q 65:3.
26. Q 26:79.
27. For inquiries into the imagery of wine in Persian Sufi poetry, see Chittick, *SPL*, 311ff.; Pourjavady, "Love and the Metaphors of Wine and Drunkenness," 132–135; Schimmel, *A Two-Colored Brocade*, passim.
28. For Majnun's love for Layla and its various levels of meaning in Sufi literature, see Schimmel, *A Two-Colored Brocade*, 131–133, and Schimmel, *Mystical Dimensions of Islam*, 431–432. For Majnun in ʿAyn al-Quḍāt's writings, see Rustom, "*Theo-Fānī*."
29. *T* 102, §144.
30. *T* 237, §307.
31. Cf. Ghazālī, *Sawāniḥ*, 53–54.
32. "Tavern" (P. *kharābāt*) is a reference to the famous Persian Sufi image of the wine tavern. It is meant to symbolize the Sufi lodge wherein the self becomes annihilated through the wine of divine remembrance that is administered by none other than the divine Wine-Pourer (*sāqī*).
33. The "tavern-dweller" (P. *kharābātī*) denotes the Sufi who has given up everything for God.
34. Schimmel, *Mystical Dimensions of Islam*, 296.
35. *T* 216, §277.
36. *T* 216, §277.
37. Cf. Kubrā, *Taʾwīlāt*, 3:348.
38. See Schimmel, *Mystical Dimensions of Islam*, 294.

39. *T* 101, §142.
40. *T* 101, §142.
41. *T* 101, §142.
42. Q 29:69.
43. Q 22:78.
44. Q 24:35.
45. Q 13:17.
46. Q 21:18.
47. *T* 105, §149.
48. See chapter 4, n. 23.
49. *T* 304–305, §401.
50. *T* 305, §401.
51. Q 9:30.
52. This point occurs in the context of ʿAyn al-Quḍāt's discussion of the Hadith, "God created Adam in the form of the All-Merciful."
53. Q 3:79.
54. Q 10:36 (cf. 53:28).
55. See the analysis on this and related points in Boylston, "Islam from Inside Out," 190–194.
56. Q 109:6.
57. Muslim, Aqḍiya, 6, no. 4584.
58. See also *N* I 91, §124, where ʿAyn al-Quḍāt identifies the black light of Iblis with Yazdan and Ahriman.
59. Q 64:2.
60. Cf. Q 30:22.
61. ʿAyn al-Quḍāt is alluding to his aesthetic theory, to which we will return later in this chapter.
62. This sentence represents ʿAyn al-Quḍāt's gloss on the Arabic saying of a certain Sufi master who identifies love with the path to God, the vision of God with Paradise, and separation from God with Hell.
63. Massignon, *Passion of al-Hallāj*, 2:169.
64. For a subtle discussion of this notion and its implications, see Boylston, "Islam from Inside Out," 182–185.
65. See Ernst, *Words of Ecstasy*, 63–72, and Lewisohn, *Beyond Faith and Infidelity*, 281ff.
66. Cf. Dabashi, *Truth and Narrative*, 224; Ernst, *Words of Ecstasy*, 81–82; Safi, *Politics of Knowledge*, 254, n. 102.
67. The *Risāla al-aḍḥawiyya* is a well-known work on eschatology by Avicenna, but the conversation that is reported by ʿAyn al-Quḍāt is not to be found in it. For the spurious ascription of this passage, see Reisman, *Making of the Avicennan Tradition*, 140–141. According to Yahya Michot, the passage

comes from another work of questionable attribution to Avicenna. See Michot, "A Mamlūk Theologian's Commentary on Avicenna's *Risāla Aḍḥawiyya*," 153–154.

68. *Lamps* (*Maṣābīḥ*) and the quotation from it are not by Abū Saʿīd. See Reisman, *Making of the Avicennan Tradition*, 140–141.

69. See Chittick, *Divine Love*, 236.

70. Q 25:43.

71. Q 14:35.

72. For the true Muslim having to be an "unbeliever," see Maybudī, *Unveiling of the Mysteries*, 245.

73. Q 55:27.

74. Muslim, Ruʾyā, 2, no. 6058.

75. Q 12:106.

76. Q 4:136.

77. Q 64:11.

78. Q 16:93.

79. Q 39:65.

80. Q 12:106.

81. Q 12:106.

82. Q 6:79.

83. That is, the third level of unbelief.

84. Q 6:79.

85. For a discussion of which, see Lewisohn, *Beyond Faith and Infidelity*, 68 and 91.

86. Mutanabbī, *Dīwān*, 1:91.

87. Bukhārī, Jihād, 149, no. 3054.

88. Q 3:85.

89. See the astute observation in Ernst, *Words of Ecstasy*, 75.

90. Kāshānī, *Laṭāʾif*, 353. This statement also appears in *N* II 210, §320, although (as we will see) ʿAyn al-Quḍāt's most sustained engagement with it is in *Paving the Path*. For Shams-i Tabrīzī's explanation of this saying, see Chittick, *Me and Rumi*, 129–130. See also the discussion in Schimmel, *Mystical Dimensions of Islam*, 123.

91. Qushayrī, *Risāla*, 578. ʿAyn al-Quḍāt also cites this saying in *N* II 210, §320. For some Persian Sufi authors' explanations of this tradition, see Chittick, *Divine Love*, 386 and 393.

92. Ḥallāj, *Akhbār*, 99. For the context of these words, see Ḥallāj, *Poems of a Sufi Martyr*, 102.

93. See Massignon's note in Ḥallāj, *Ṭawāsīn*, 198, n. 4.

94. See Ghazālī, *Sawāniḥ*, 20 (version one); *T* 119, §166, and *T* 249, §326 (version two); *N* II, 255, §384 (version three).

95. As noted in chapter 9, black light most commonly refers to the divine Essence. In this poem by Shaykh Bustī, he speaks of It insofar as It can be expressed in words and by relational concepts.

96. Ghazālī, *Sawāniḥ*, 20; cited, with slight modifications, from Chittick, *Divine Love*, 421. For Aḥmad Ghazālī's understanding of black light, see Lumbard, *Aḥmad al-Ghazālī*, 183–184.

97. Cf. Kalābādhī, *Doctrine of the Sufis*, 5 and 7–10.

98. ʿAyn al-Quḍāt likely has in mind the statement by Bastāmī that appears at the end of this passage.

99. Forouzanfar, *Aḥadīth-i Mathnawī*, no. 54.

100. That is, Abū Bakr al-Nassāj (d. 487/1094) (for whom, see Lumbard, *Aḥmad al-Ghazālī*, 60–62).

101. Cf. Chittick, *Divine Love*, 18–19.

102. In *T* 262, §344, ʿAyn al-Quḍāt attributes this saying to the early Sufi master Abū Bakr al-Warrāq (d. 280/893). See also Shīrāzī, *Sharḥ Khuṭbat al-bayān*, 12 and 32.

103. Q 51:56.

104. See the observation recorded in Samʿānī, *Repose of the Spirits*, 123.

105. For a discussion of this point, see Rustom, "Everything Muhammad," 38–39.

106. Q 48:2.

107. Abū Dāwūd, Adab, 126, no. 5132.

108. Cf. the tradition reported in Baqlī, *ʿAbhar*, 138, §276.

109. Cf. *N* II, 403–404, §637.

110. *T* 272, §356.

111. Some helpful investigations into the relationship between beauty and love in the Sufi tradition can be found in Lumbard, "Love and Beauty in Sufism," and Zargar, *Sufi Aesthetics*. For an excellent study of beauty in the Persian Sufi tradition with reference to one of its major representatives who came after ʿAyn al-Quḍāt, see Murata, *Beauty in Sufism*.

112. A recent treatment of *shāhid-bāzī* can be found in Ridgeon, *Awhad al-Dīn Kirmānī and the Controversy of the Sufi Gaze*. For a discussion of *shāhid-bāzī* in ʿAyn al-Quḍāt, see Zargar, *Sufi Aesthetics*, 91–95.

113. Aḥmad, no. 1876 and 2486.

114. See the extensive inquiry in Pourjavady, "Stories of Aḥmad al-Ghazālī 'Playing the Witness' in Tabrīz."

115. Q 17:85.

116. Bukhārī, Daʿawāt, 7, no. 6385.

117. See Ritter, *Ocean of the Soul*, 459–460. ʿAyn al-Quḍāt also cites this tradition and the following one in *T* 321, §420.

118. ʿAjlūnī, *Kashf*, 1:495–496. Elsewhere (*N* I, 156, §230), ʿAyn al-Quḍāt notes that there are some people who have become worshippers of beauty on account of this tradition.

119. For another version that is sometimes cited in place of this saying, see Hujwīrī, *The Kashf al-Maḥjūb*, 311.

120. Q 6:91.

121. Ghazālī, *Iḥyā'*, 8:405. See also the use of this tradition in *N* I, 89, §121.

122. ʿAbd Allāh Anṣārī (d. 481/1089) was a major saint whose Arabic and Persian writings have been very influential upon the Sufi tradition. For his life and teachings, see Farhadi, *'Abdullāh Anṣārī of Herāt*.

123. Q 5:54.

124. Q 5:54.

125. Q 42:11.

126. See the observation in Nasr, *Garden of Truth*, 73.

Bibliography

Works by ʿAyn al-Quḍāt (Editions, Manuscripts, Translations)

Muṣannafāt-i ʿAyn al-Quḍāt [also *Zubdat al-ḥaqāʾiq*]. Edited by ʿAfīf ʿUsayrān. Tehran: Intishārāt-i Dānishgāh-i Tihrān, 1962. Contains editions of *Sh*, *T*, and *Z*.

N = *Nāma-hā*. Edited by ʿAlī Naqī Munzawī (vols. 1–3) and ʿAfīf ʿUsayrān (vols. 1–2). Tehran: Intishārāt-i Asāṭīr, 1998; originally published in Tehran: Bunyād-i Farhang, 1969–1972. Select English translation by Omid Safi as "The Letters" in Nasr and Aminrazavi, eds., *An Anthology of Philosophy in Persia*, 4:412.

NU = *Nuzhat al-ʿushshāq wa-nuhzat al-mushtāq*. Marʿashī Library, MS 4047.

RJ = *Risāla-yi Jamālī*. In *N* II, 483–488, §§756–766 (*Letter* 127).

Sh = *Shakwā'l-gharīb*. In part 3 of *Muṣannafāt*, 1–47 (text) and 49–51 (indexes). Arabic edition and French translation by Mohammed Ben Abd El-Jalil as "La *Šakwā*." *Journal Asiatique* 216, no. 1 (1930): 1–76 (introduction and text); no. 2 (1930): 193–297 (translation, indexes, etc.). Arabic edition by Ahmet Kamil Cihan; Turkish translation by Ahmet Kamil Cihan, Salih Yalın, Mesut Sandıkçı, and Arsan Taher as *Garibin Şikâyeti* in *Zübdetü'l-Hakâik / Şekva'l-Garîb*, 228–315. Istanbul: Türkiye Yazma Eserler Kurumu Başkanlığı, 2016. English translation by A. J. Arberry as *A Sufi Martyr: The 'Apologia' of 'Ain al-Quḍāt al-Hamadhānī*. London: Keagan and Paul, 1969.

T = *Tamhīdāt*. Edited by ʿAfīf ʿUsayrān. Tehran: Intishārāt-i Manūchihrī, 1994; reprinted from part 2 of *Muṣannafāt*, 1–354 (text) and 418–526 (indexes); manuscripts consulted: Cambridge University Library, MS Or. 1564 (selections); Kitābkhāna-yi Dānishgāh-i Tihrān, MS 1237; Kitābkhāna-yi Majlis-i Shūrā-yi Millī, MS 2108; Manisa Genel Kitaplik, MS 1086; Süleymaniye Kütüphanesi, MSS Ayasofya 1839, 1840, 1841, 1842, and 2069. English translation by Omid Safi as *The Tamhidat of 'Ayn al-Qudat*

Hamadani. Mahwah: Paulist Press, forthcoming. French translation by Christiane Tortel as *Les Tentations métaphysiques*. Paris: Les Deux Océans, 1992. Turkish translation by Halil Baltacı as *Temhîdât: Aşk ve Hakikat Üzerine Konuşmalar*. Istanbul: Dergâh Yayınları, 2015. English translation of chapter 1 by Omid Safi as "Dispositions" in Nasr and Aminrazavi, eds., *An Anthology of Philosophy in Persia*, 4:401–411. English translation of chapter 4 by Leonard Lewisohn in Lewisohn, ed. and trans., *Esoteric Traditions in Islamic Thought: An Anthology of Texts on Esoteric Knowledge and Gnosis in Islam*, chapter 5. London: I. B. Tauris in association with The Institute of Ismaili Studies, forthcoming. Italian translation of chapter 6 by Chiara Gabrielli as *Natura dell'Amore*. Padua: Centro Essad Bey, 2013. Select English translations by Leonard Lewisohn in Lewisohn, ed. and trans., *The Wisdom of Sufism*, passim. Oxford: Oneworld, 2001. Select English translations by Omid Safi in Safi, ed. and trans., *Radical Love: Teachings from the Islamic Mystical Tradition*, passim. New Haven: Yale University Press, 2018. Select German translations by Richard Gramlich in Gramlich, ed. and trans., *Islamische Mystik: Sufische Texte aus zehn Jahrhunderten*, 117–130. Stuttgart: Kohlhammer, 1992.

W = [*Wāqiʿa-hā*]. In *N* III, 401–402, §§224–226 (*Letter* 148); also in Aḥmad Ghazālī, *Mukātabāt*, 1–3.

Z = *Zubdat al-ḥaqāʾiq*. New Arabic edition and English translation by Mohammed Rustom as *The Essence of Reality: A Defense of Philosophical Sufism*. Library of Arabic Literature. New York: New York University Press, 2022; English-only edition: New York: New York University Press, 2023. Arabic edition in part 1 of *Muṣannafāt*, 1–102 (text) and 103–131 (indexes). Arabic edition by Ahmet Kamil Cihan; Turkish translation by Ahmet Kamil Cihan, Salih Yalın, Mesut Sandıkçı, and Arsan Taher as *Hakikatlerin Özü* in *Zübdetü'l-Hakâik/Şekva'l-Garîb*, 38–225. English translation by Omar Jah as *The Zubdat al-Ḥaqā'iq of 'Ayn al-Quḍāh* [*sic*] *al-Hamadānī*. Kuala Lumpur: ISTAC, 2000. French translation by Salimeh Maghsoudlou as "La quintessence des vérités." In Maghsoudlou, "La pensée de 'Ayn al-Quḍāt al-Hamadānī," 367–444. Persian translation by Mahdī Tadayyun as *Zubdat al-ḥaqāʾiq*. Tehran: Markaz-i Nashr-i Dānishgāhī, 2000.

Works Misattributed to ʿAyn al-Quḍāt

Ghāyat al-imkān fī dirāyat al-makān. Edited by Raḥīm Farmanish. Tehran: Chāp-i Āftāb, 1960. By Tāj al-Dīn Ushnuhī.

Lawāʾiḥ. Edited by Raḥīm Farmanish. Tehran: Hunar, 1958. By Ḥamīd al-Dīn Nāgawrī.

Risāla-yi Yazdān-shinākht. Edited by Bahman Karīmī. Tehran: ʿAlī Akbar ʿIlmī, 1948. By Shihāb al-Dīn Suhrawardī.

Rāz-nāma. MS Ayasofya 4824. By Shams al-Dīn Hamadānī.

Sharḥ Kalimāt Bābā Ṭāhir ʿUryān. In Jawād Maqṣūd, *Sharḥ-i aḥwāl wa-āthār wa-dūbaytī-hā-yi Bābā Ṭāhir ʿUryān*, part 4. Tehran: Intishārāt-i Anjuman-i Āthār-i Millī, 1975.

Scholarship on ʿAyn al-Quḍāt Cited or Consulted

'Abdul Haq, Muhammad. "'Ayn al-Qudāt Hamdānī's [*sic*] Concept of Time and Space in the Perspective of Sūfism." *The Islamic Quarterly* 31, no. 1 (1987): 5–37. A study of *Ghāyat al-imkān* (see "Works Misattributed to ʿAyn al-Quḍāt").

Adhkāʾī, Parwīz. "Ḥakīm-i ilāhī-yi Hamadān." In Adhkāʾī, ed., *Mātīkān*, 159–192.

———. "Ḥaqīqat yā riwāyat?" In Adhkāʾī, ed., *Mātīkān*, 193–240. A review of Dabashi, *Truth and Narrative*.

———, ed. *Mātīkān-i ʿAyn al-Quḍāt Hamadānī*. Hamadan: Nashr-i Mādistān, 2002.

Afrāsiyābī, Ghulām Riḍā. *Sulṭān-i ʿushshāq*. Shiraz: Intishārāt-i Dānishgāh-i Shīrāz, 1993.

———. "Zindānī-yi Baghdād." *Gawhar* 23–24 (1975): 1074–1079; 26 (1975): 141–145.

Akramī, Mūsā. "Tamhīdātī dar kalām-i sukrān." *Kitāb-i māh-i adabiyyāt wa-falsafa* 28 (2000): 54–63.

ʿAlawī Muqaddam, Mahyār, and Saḥar Saʿādatī. "Naqd wa-taḥlīl-i nigarish-i hirminūtīkī-yi ʿAyn al-Quḍāt Hamadānī." *Faṣl-nāma-yi pizhūhish-hā-yi adabī* 7, no. 27 (2010): 59–76.

Algar, Hamid. *EIr*, s.v. "Eblīs" (passim).

Aladdin, Bakri. "Aspects of Mystical Hermeneutics and the Theory of the Oneness of Being (*waḥdat al-wujūd*) in the Work of ʿAbd al-Ghanī al-Nābulusī (1143/1731)." Translated by Gwendolin Goldbloom in *The Spirit and the Letter: Approaches to the Esoteric Interpretation of the Qur'an*, edited by Annabel Keeler and Sajjad Rizvi, 395–413 (p. 405). Oxford: Oxford University Press in association with The Institute of Ismaili Studies, 2016.

Aminrazavi, Mehdi. "ʿAyn al-Quḍāt Hamadānī." In Nasr and Aminrazavi, eds., *An Anthology of Philosophy in Persia*, 4:398–400.

———. *The Wine of Wisdom: The Life, Poetry and Philosophy of Omar Khayyam*, 22–23 and 349, n. 14. Oxford: Oneworld, 2005.

Andani, Khalil. "Metaphysics of Muhammad: The *Nur* Muhammad from Imam Ja'far al-Sadiq (d. 148/765) to Nasir al-Din al-Tusi (d. 672/1274)." *Journal of Sufi Studies* 8, no. 2 (2019): 99–175 (pp. 138–143).

Anwār, Sayyid ʿAbd-i Ilāh. "*Nāma-hā*-yi ʿAyn al-Quḍāt Hamadānī: jild-i siwum wa-muqaddima-yi āqā-yi duktur Munzawī bar īn nāma-hā." *Chīstā* 171 (2000): 119–122.

Ariankhoo, Masoud, and Mohammed Rustom. "ʿAyn al-Quḍāt's *Tamhīdāt*: An Ocean of Sufi Metaphysics in Persian." In *Islamic Thought and the Art of Translation: Texts and Studies in Honor of William C. Chittick and Sachiko Murata*, edited by Mohammed Rustom, 3–17. Leiden: Brill, 2023.

Asad Allāhī, Khudābakhsh. "Andīsha-hā-yi ʿirfānī-yi ʿAyn al-Quḍāt dar bāb-i Iblīs." *Faṣl-nāma-yi adabiyyāt-i ʿirfānī wa-usṭūra-shinākhtī* 5, no. 14 (2009): 9–26.

———. "Andīsha-hā-yi ʿirfānī-yi ʿAyn al-Quḍāt dar mawḍūʿ-i ʿishq." *Pizhūhish-hā-yi zabān wa-adabiyyāt-i fārsī* 1 (2009): 31–44.

Asadpūr, Riḍā. *Az shūr wa-shikiftan*. Tehran: Ahl-i Qalam, 2001.

———. "'ʿIshq chīzī dīgar ast': gudharī bar sharḥ-i Sayyid Muḥammad Gīsūdarāz bar *Tamhīdāt*-i ʿAyn al-Quḍāt Hamadānī." *Iṭṭilāʿāt-i ḥikmat wa-maʿrifat* 10 (2007): 53–57.

Ateş, Ahmed. "Review of *Risale-i yazdān-şināxt*, edited by Bahman Karīmī" [Turkish]. *Oriens* 3, no. 2 (1950): 332–333. See "Works Misattributed to ʿAyn al-Quḍāt."

Awn, Peter. *Satan's Tragedy and Redemption: Iblīs in Sufi Psychology*, 134–150. Leiden: Brill, 1983.

Behmardi, Vahid. "The *Wajdiyyāt* of 'Ayn al-Quḍāt al-Hamadānī: Youthful Passions of a Sufi in the Making." In *Ghazal as World Literature II*, edited by Angelika Neuwirth, Michael Hess, Judith Pfeiffer, and Börte Sagaster, 39–46. Istanbul: Orient-Institute, 2016.

Bināʾpūr, Hāshim. *ʿAyn al-Quḍāt Hamadānī*. Tehran: Daftar-i Pizhūhish-hā-yi Farhangī, 2004.

Bin Ramli, Harith. *Sufism and Scripture: A Historical Survey of Approaches to the Qur'an in the Sufi Tradition*, chapter 5. Sheffield: Equinox, forthcoming.

Boylston, Nicholas. "Islam from the Inside Out: ʿAyn al-Quḍāt Hamadānī's Reconception of Islam as Vector." *Oxford Journal of Islamic Studies* 32, no. 2 (2021): 161–202.

———. "Writing the Kaleidoscope of Reality, the Significance of Diversity in 6th/12th Century Persian Metaphysical Literature: Sanāʾī, ʿAyn al-Quḍāt and ʿAṭṭār," chapters 5–8. PhD diss., Georgetown University, 2017.

Böwering, Gerhard. *EIr*, s.v. "ʿAyn-al-Qożāt Hamadānī."

Chittick, William C. "Divine and Human Love in Islam." In *Divine Love: Perspectives from the World's Religious Traditions*, edited by Jeff Levin and Stephen Post, 163–200 (pp. 182, 185, and 193). West Conshohocken: Templeton Press, 2010.

Dabashi, Hamid. "'Ayn al-Quḍāt Hamadānī and the Intellectual Climate of His Times." In *History of Islamic Philosophy*, edited by Seyyed Hossein Nasr and Oliver Leaman, 2:374–433. New York: Routledge, 1996.

———. "ʿAyn al-Quḍāt Hamadānī wa-*Risāla-yi Shakwā al-gharīb*-i ū." *Īrān-nāma* 41 (1992): 57–74.

———. "Historical Conditions of Persian Sufism during the Seljuk Period." In Lewisohn, ed., *Heritage of Sufism, Vol. 1*, 137–174 (pp. 144–153).

———. *Truth and Narrative: The Untimely Thoughts of ʿAyn al-Quḍāt al-Hamadhānī*. Richmond: Curzon, 1999.

———. *The World of Persian Literary Humanism*, 120–121. Cambridge, MA: Harvard University Press, 2012.

Dānishfar, Ḥasan. "Guzīnahʾī az *Nāma-hā*-yi ʿAyn al-Quḍāt." In Adhkāʾī, ed., *Mātīkān*, 141–158.

Ernst, Carl. *Words of Ecstasy in Sufism*, 72–84 and 110–115. Albany: State University of New York Press, 1985.

Farhādī Nīk, Laylā. "Nigāhī ijmālī ba-mawḍūʿāt-i *Nāma-hā*-yi ʿAyn al-Quḍāt Hamadānī." *Nāma-yi pārsī* 52 (2010): 47–69.

Farmanish, Raḥīm. *Aḥwāl wa-āthār-i ʿAyn al-Quḍāt*. Tehran: Chāp-i Āftāb, 1959.

Faruque, Muhammad. *SEP*, s.v. "ʿAyn al-Quḍāt," forthcoming.

Fatḥī, Zahrā. "Maḍāmīn-i mushtarak-i ʿirfānī-yi shaykh Shihāb al-Dīn Suhrawardī wa-ʿAyn al-Quḍāt Hamadānī." *Adyān wa-ʿirfān* 8 (2006): 133–149.

———. *Pizhūhishī dar andīsha-hā-yi ʿirfānī-yi ʿAyn al-Quḍāt Hamadānī*. Tehran: Tarfand, 2005.

Fujii, Morio. "ʿAyn al-Quḍāt Hamadānī (d. 1131) and Persian Literature" [Japanese]. *Oriento* 44, no. 1 (2001): 161–164.

Fūlādī, ʿAlī Riḍā. "ʿAyn al-Quḍāt Hamadānī wa-dukhtarak-i Baghdādī." In *Bā qāfila-yi shawq: arjnāma-yi duktur Muḥammad ʿAlī Muwaḥḥid*, edited by Muḥammad Ṭāhirī Khusrawshāhī, 843–855. Tabriz: Intishārāt-i Dānishgāh-i Tabrīz, 2014.

Griffel, Frank. *The Formation of Post-Classical Philosophy in Islam*, 127–138. New York: Oxford University Press, 2021.

———. *Al-Ghazālī's Philosophical Theology*, 81–87. New York: Oxford University Press, 2009.

Gurjī, Muṣṭafā, and Akram Amānī. "Gawhar-i ḥayāt-i maʿnawī dar nigāh-i ʿAyn al-Quḍāt Hamadānī." *Muṭālaʿāt-i ʿirfānī* 6 (2007): 107–130.

Ḥājiyānnizhād, ʿAlī Riḍā. "Maʿrifat az naẓar-i ʿAyn al-Quḍāt Hamadānī." *Dānishkada-yi adabiyyāt wa-ʿulūm-i insānī-yi dānishgāh-i Tihrān* 168–169 (2003): 41–60.

Ḥasanī, Ḥusayn, and Majīd Manṣūrī. "Taʾammulī dar *Nāma-hā*-yi ʿAyn al-Quḍāt Hamadānī." *Kuhan-nāma-yi adab-i pārsī* 4, no. 1 (2013): 1–10.

Ḥasanī, Nargis. "ʿĀdat-sitīzī' dar āthār-i ʿAyn al-Quḍāt Hamadānī." *ʿUlūm-i insānī-yi dānishgāh-i al-Zahrā* 16–17, nos. 61–62 (2007): 71–100.

———. "Sīmā-yi Iblīs dar āthār-i ʿAyn al-Quḍāt Hamadānī." *Muṭālaʿāt-i ʿirfānī* 6 (2007): 5–34.

———. "Sīmā-yi Muḥammad dar āthār-i ʿAyn al-Quḍāt Hamadānī." *Adabiyyāt-i ʿirfānī* 1, no. 2 (2010): 25–47.

Ḥujjat, Muḥammad. "Taṭbīq-i zabān-i ʿirfānī wa-shīwa-yi nigārish-i ʿAyn al-Quḍāt Hamadānī wa-Muḥyī al-Dīn ʿArabī [*sic*]." *Adabiyyāt-i taṭbīqī* 3, no. 5 (2012): 101–122.

Ibrāhīmī Dīnānī, Ghulām Ḥusayn. *ʿAql-i mast: Tamhīdāt-i ʿAyn al-Quḍāt Hamadānī*. Edited by Iḥsān Ibrāhīmī Dīnānī. Isfahan: Mīrāth-i Kuhan, 2021.

Imāmī Jumuʿa, Sayyid Mahdī. "ʿAyn al-Quḍāt dar āyina-yi hirminūtīk-i mudirn." *Dānishkada-yi adabiyyāt wa-ʿulūm-i insānī-yi dānishgāh-i Iṣfahān* 2, no. 39 (2004): 21–34.

ʿIrfānī Mazdak, Farhād. "Ghurūb-i ākharīn sipīda: dāstān-i qatl-i ʿAyn al-Quḍāt Hamadānī." *Chīstā* 220 (2005): 762–769.

Ismāʿīlpūr, Walī Allāh. "Mafhūm-i ʿishq wa-muqāyasa-yi ān dar dastgāh-i fikrī-yi Aḥmad Ghazālī wa-ʿAyn al-Quḍāt Hamadānī." *Zabān wa-adab-i fārsī* 3, no. 9 (2012): 25–46.

Izutsu, Toshihiko. "The Concept of Perpetual Creation in Islamic Mysticism and Zen Buddhism." In *Mélanges offerts à Henry Corbin*, edited by Seyyed Hossein Nasr, 115–148 (pp. 125–133). Tehran: Imperial Iranian Academy of Philosophy, 1977.

———. "Creation and the Timeless Order of Things: A Study in the Mystical Philosophy of 'Ayn al-Quḍāt." *The Philosophical Forum* 4, no. 1 (1972): 124–140.

———. "Mysticism and the Linguistic Problem of Equivocation in the Thought of 'Ayn al-Quḍāt Hamadānī." *Studia Islamica* 31 (1970): 153–170.

Jahanbakhsh, Forugh. "The Pīr-Murīd Relationship in the Thought of 'Ayn al-Quḍāt Hamadānī." In Āshtiyānī et al., eds., *Consciousness and Reality*, 129–147.

Jones, Alan. "Review of Dabashi, *Truth and Narrative*." *Medium Aevum* 69, no. 2 (2000): 333–334.

Kamālīzāda, Ṭāhira. "Maʿrifat-i ʿirfānī dar ārā-yi ʿAyn al-Quḍāt Hamadānī." *Adyān wa-ʿirfān* 44, no. 2 (2011): 61–84.

Kars, Aydogan. *Unsaying God: Negative Theology in Medieval Islam*, 136–137 and 181. New York: Oxford University Press, 2019.

Khātamīpūr, Ḥāmid. "Az Khurāsān tā Hamadān: barrasī-yi taʾthīr-i Aḥmad Ghazālī bar ʿAyn al-Quḍāt Hamadānī." *Pizhūhish-hā-yi adabī wa-balāghī* 1, no. 1 (2013): 88–102.

Khawālidiyya, Asmāʾ. *Ṣarʿā al-taṣawwuf: al-Ḥallāj wa-ʿAyn al-Quḍāh* [*sic*] *al-Hamadhānī wa'l-Suhrawardī namādhij*, 135–172. Beirut: Manshūrāt Ḍifāf, 2014.

Khudāyārī, Zahrā, and Raḥmān Mushtāq Mihr. "Diyāliktīk-i jamāl wa-jalāl dar andīsha-yi ʿirfānī-yi ʿAyn al-Quḍāt Hamadānī." *Adyān wa-ʿirfān* 48, no. 1 (2015): 1–17.

Khurāsānī, Majd al-ʿAlī. "ʿAyn al-Quḍāt." *Armaghān* [old] 8, no. 1 (1927): 31–41.

Kīmīyāʾī, Masʿūd. *Ḥasad: bar zindagī-yi ʿAyn al-Quḍāt*. Tehran: Nashr-i Thālith, 2009.

Kiyāʾī, Fāṭima. "Bāṭinī-garī: ittihām-i ʿAyn al-Quḍāt Hamadānī." *Pizhūhish-nāma-yi adyān* 12 (2012): 127–156.

Kumpānī Zāriʿ, Mahdī. "'Gar ḥijāb az jān-hā bar khāstī . . .': sayrī dar fahm-i Qurʾān-i karīm az manẓar-i ʿAyn al-Quḍāt Hamadānī." *Kitāb-i māh-i dīn* 178 (2012): 31–36.

———. "'ʿIshq farḍ-i rāh ast': nigāhī gudharā ba-āmūza-yi ʿishq dar āthār-i ʿAyn al-Quḍāt Hamadānī." *Kitāb-i māh-i dīn* 178 (2012): 63–69.

Kūshish, Raḥīm, ʿAbd Allāh Ṭulūʿī Ādhar, Bahman Nuzhat, and Ṭāhir Lāwzha. "Taḥlīl-i wajhī az zībāʾī-shināsī-yi sukhan-i ʿirfānī: muṭālaʿa-yi mawridī-yi sajʿ dar *Nāma-hā*-yi ʿAyn al-Quḍāt." *Matn-pizhūhī-yi adabī* 52 (2012): 65–88.

Landolt, Hermann. *EI3*, s.v. "ʿAyn al-Quḍāt al-Hamadhānī 1: Life and Work."

———. "Early Evidence for Nāṣir-i Khusraw's Poetry in Sufism: ʿAyn al-Quḍāt's Letter on the Taʿlīmīs." In *Fortresses of the Intellect: Ismaili and Other Islamic Studies in Honour of Farhad Daftary*, edited by Omar Alí-de-Unzaga, 369–386. London: I. B. Tauris in association with The Institute of Ismaili Studies, 2011.

———. "Ghazālī and '*Religionswissenschaft*'." *Asiatische Studien* 45, no. 1 (1991): 19–72 (pp. 56–58).

———. "Mystique iranienne: Suhravardī *Shaykh al-Ishrāq* (549/1155–587/1191) et 'Ayn al-Quẓāt-i Hamadānī (492/1098–535/1131)." In *Iranian Civilization and Culture*, edited by Charles Adams, 23–37. Montreal: McGill University Press, 1972.

———. "Review of ʿAyn al-Quḍāt, *Tentations métaphysiques*" [French]. *Bulletin critique des Annales islamologiques* 11 (1994): 86–87.

Lashkarī, Sārā. "Nigāhī ba-kitāb-i *ʿAyn al-Quḍāt wa-ustādān-i ū*." *Kitāb-i māh-i dīn* 178 (2012): 20–24.

Leaman, Oliver. *BEIP*, s.v. "Al-Hamadhani, 'Ayn al-Qudat."

Lewisohn, Leonard. *Beyond Faith and Infidelity: The Sufi Poetry and Teachings of Mahmud Shabistari*, passim. Richmond: Curzon, 1995.

———. "In Quest of Annihilation: Imaginalization and Mystical Death in the *Tamhīdāt* of ʿAyn al-Quḍāt Hamadhānī." In Lewisohn, ed., *Heritage of Sufism, Vol. 1*, 285–336.

Lory, Pierre. "Review of Dabashi, *Truth and Narrative*" [French]. *Bulletin critique des Annales islamologiques* 18 (2003): 25.

Lumbard, Joseph. "Review of Dabashi, *Truth and Narrative*." *The Muslim World* 96, no. 3 (2006): 532–534.

Maghsoudlou, Salimeh. *DZAF*, s.v. "ʿAyn al-Quḍāt Hamadānī."

———. "Étude des doctrines du nom dans *al-Maqṣad al-asnā* d'al-Ghazālī et de leur origine théologique et grammaticale." *Studia Islamica* 112, no. 1 (2017): 29–75 (pp. 31–33).

———. "La pensée de ʿAyn al-Quḍāt al-Hamadānī (m. 525/1131), entre avicennisme et héritage ġazālien." PhD diss., École Pratique des Hautes Études, 2016.

———. "Popularization of Philosophy in the Sufi Milieu: The Reception of Avicenna's Doctrine of the Origination of the Human Soul in ʿAyn al-Quḍāt al-Hamadānī's Writings." In *The Popularization of Philosophy in Medieval Islam, Judaism, and Christianity*, edited by Marieke Abram, Steven Harvey, and Lukas Muehlethaler, chapter 13. Turnhout: Brepols, 2022.

Maḥabbatī, Mahdī. "Taʾwīl-i bī khwīsh-niwīsī: taḥlīlī tāzah az nagarah-hā-yi adabī-yi ʿAyn al-Quḍāt Hamadānī." *Naqd-i adabī* 2, no. 8 (2010): 53–72.

Mayel Heravi, Najib. *Khāṣṣiyyat-i āyinagī*. Tehran: Nashr-i Nay, 1995.

Meier, Fritz. "Stambuler Handschriften dreier persischer Mystiker: ʿAin al-quḍāt al-Hamaḏānī, Naǧm ad-dīn al-Kubrā, Naǧm ad-dīn ad-Dāja [*sic*]." *Der Islam* 24 (1937): 1–42 (pp. 1–9).

Meisami, Julie Scott. "Review of Dabashi, *Truth and Narrative*." *Oxford Journal of Islamic Studies* 11, no. 3 (2000): 372–376.

Michot, Yahya. "A Mamlūk Theologian's Commentary on Avicenna's *Risāla Aḍḥawiyya*: Being a Translation of a Part of the *Darʾ al-Taʿāruḍ* of Ibn Taymiyya, with Introduction, Annotation, and Appendices: Part I." *Oxford Journal of Islamic Studies* 14, no. 2 (2003): 149–203 (pp. 153–154).

Mīrbāqirī Fard, ʿAlī Aṣghar, and Maʿṣūma Muḥammadī. "Barrasī wa-taḥlīl-i naqsh-i pursish dar āthār-i fārsī-yi ʿAyn al-Quḍāt Hamadānī." *Faṣl-nāma-yi pizhūhish-hā-yi adabī* 8, nos. 29–30 (2011): 149–166.

———. "Naqsh-i inshā dar zabān-i ʿirfānī: barrasī wa-taḥlīl-i nasqh-i inshā dār āthār-i fārsī-yi ʿAyn al-Quḍāt Hamadānī." *Būstān-i adab* 2, no. 2 (2010): 185–208.

Mīrbāqirī Fard, ʿAlī Aṣghar, and Shahrzād Niyāzī. "Barrasī wa-taḥlīl-i zabān-i ʿirfānī dar āthār-i ʿAyn al-Quḍāt Hamadānī." *Philosophical-Theological Research* 12, nos. 1–2 (2011): 267–286.

Moazzen, Maryam. "A Garden beyond the Garden: ʿAyn al-Quḍāt Hamadānī's Perspective on Paradise." In *Roads to Paradise: Eschatology and Concepts of the Hereafter in Islam*, edited by Sebastian Günther and Todd Lawson, with the assistance of Christian Mauder, 1:566–578. Leiden: Brill, 2017.

Moshiri, Abolfazl. "The Devil's Advocates: The Exoneration of Iblīs in Persian Mysticism," chapter 4. PhD diss., University of Toronto, 2021.

Mudarrisī, Fāṭima, and Maryam ʿArab. "Balāghat-i nathr-i ṣūfiyyāna-khiṭābī dar *Tamhīdāt*-i ʿAyn al-Quḍāt." *Kāwush-nāma-yi zabān wa-adabiyyāt-i fārsī* 25 (2012): 293–322.

———. "Jāygāh-i Qur'ān wa-ta'wīl-i ān dar *Tamhīdāt*-i ʿAyn al-Quḍāt Hamadānī." *Maʿrifat* 20, no. 161 (2011): 97–112.

———. *Kaʿba-yi dil: zabān-i ṣūfiyyāna-yi ʿAyn al-Quḍāt dar Tamhīdāt*. Tehran: Intishārāt-i Chāpār, 2015.

———. "Nigāhī ba-ʿawāmil-i mūsīqīsāz dar *Tamhīdāt*-i ʿAyn al-Quḍāt." *Funūn-i adabī* 5, no. 2 (2013): 35–48.

———. "Shaṭḥiyyāt-i ʿAyn al-Quḍāt Hamadānī." *Faṣl-nāma-yi adabiyyāt-i ʿirfānī wa-usṭūra-shinākhtī* 7, no. 25 (2012): 167–192.

Muḥammadī, Maʿṣūma. "Barrasī wa-taḥlīl-i naqsh-i amr wa-nahy dar āthār-i fārsī-yi ʿAyn al-Quḍāt Hamadānī." *Funūn-i adabī* 3, no. 2 (2011): 139–150.

Muḥammadī Fishārakī, Muḥsin, and Suʿād Sādāt Mūsawī. "Kitāb-shināsī-yi ʿAyn al-Quḍāt Hamadānī dar Īrān." *Āyina-yi pizhūhish* 26, no. 6 (2016): 107–121.

Mumtaḥan, Mahdī. "Āmīkhtagī-yi adabiyyāt-i taʿlīmī bā adabiyyāt-i ʿirfānī dar *Tamhīdāt*-i ʿAyn al-Quḍāt Hamadānī." *Pizhūhish-nāma-yi adabiyyāt-i taʿlīmī* 8, no. 24 (2015): 131–148.

Munzawī, ʿAlī Naqī. "Khudā-shināsī wa-irtibāṭ-i ādamī bā khudā az dīdgāh-i ʿAyn al-Quḍāt Hamadānī wa-dīgar ginūsīst-hā-yi islāmī." *Chīstā* 108–109 (1994): 736–750.

———. "Murūrī bar āthār-i ʿAyn al-Quḍāt." In Adhkā'ī, ed., *Mātīkān*, 1–38.

———. "Zamāna wa-aḥwāl-i ʿAyn al-Quḍāt Hamadānī: nigāhī ba-*Khāṣṣiyyat-i āyinagī*." *Chīstā* 138–139 (1997): 614–630.

Munzawī, Parwīn. "ʿAyn al-Quḍāt Hamadānī." *Waḥīd* 6, no. 6 (1969): 515–529.

Mūsawī, Muṣṭafā. "ʿAyn al-Quḍāt Hamadānī: shigiftī-yi ʿālam-i insānī." *Īrān-shinākht* 10 (1998): 74–135.

Mustaʿlī Pārsā, Ghulām Riḍā. *Naẓar-i ʿAyn al-Quḍāt dar mawrid-i Iblīs wa-irtibāṭ-i ān bā niẓām-i aḥsan*. Tehran: Nashr-i ʿIlm, 2010.

Nanji, Shamas. *Explorations with Ayn al-Qudah* [sic] *in the Third Proximity*. Edmonton: printed by the author, 2011.

Nāṣir Allāhī, Yad Allāh, and Mahnāz Zādfarīd. "Dil wa-bāztāb-i ān dar āthār-i ʿAyn al-Quḍāt Hamadānī." *Adabiyyāt wa-ʿulūm-i insānī* 26 (2012): 111–130.

Nawā'ī, ʿAbd al-Ḥusayn. "ʿAyn al-Quḍāt Hamadānī." *Yādgār* 3, no. 2 (1946–1947): 63–70.

Nguyen, Martin. "Sufi Theological Thought." In *The Oxford Handbook of Islamic Theology*, edited by Sabine Schmidtke, 325–343 (passim). Oxford: Oxford University Press, 2016.

Ogunnaike, Oludamini. "Annihilation in the Messenger Revisited: Clarifications on a Contemporary Sufi Practice and Its Precedents." *Journal of Islamic and Muslim Studies* 1, no. 2 (2016): 13–34 (pp. 21–22 and 26–29).

Papan-Matin, Firoozeh. "'Ayn al-Qudat al-Hamadhani, His Work, and His Connection with the Early Chishti Mystics." *Comparative Studies of South Asia, Africa and the Middle East* 30, no. 3 (2010): 341–355.

———. *Beyond Death: Mystical Teachings of ʿAyn al-Quḍāt Hamadhānī*. Leiden: Brill, 2010.

Pārsāpūr, Zahrā. "Didgāh-i ʿAyn al-Quḍāt dar bāb-i ḥurūf, ḥurūf-i muqaṭṭaʿa, wa-nuqaṭ." *Lisān-i mubīn* 3, no. 6 (2012): 31–47.

Pourjavady, Nasrollah. *ʿAyn al-Quḍāt wa-ustādān-i ū*. Tehran: Intishārāt-i Asāṭīr, 1995.

———. "Introduction." In Pourjavady, ed., *Majmūʿa-yi falsafī-yi Marāgha*, iii–xii.

———. *Sulṭān-i ṭarīqat*, passim. Tehran: Intishārāt-i Āgāh, 1979.

———. *Zabān-i ḥāl*, 173–177. Tehran: Intishārāt-i Hirmis, 2006.

Pūrnāmdāryān, Taqī. "Qāḍī-yi Hamadānī wa-ʿAṭṭār-i Nīshāpūrī." In Adhkāʾī, ed., *Mātīkān*, 39–84.

Pūrnāmdāryān, Taqī, and Mīnā Ḥafīẓī. "Nigāhī ba-taṣḥīḥ-i *Tamhīdāt* pas az nīm qarn." *Nāma-yi farhangistān* 16, no. 2 (2010): 118–132.

Radtke, Bernd. "Review of Papan-Matin, *Beyond Death*." *Oriens* 41, nos. 1–2 (2013): 194–205.

Reisman, David. *The Making of the Avicennan Tradition: The Transmission, Contents, and Structure of Ibn Sīnā's al-Mubāḥaṯāt* (*The Discussions*), 140–141. Leiden: Brill, 2002.

Renard, John. *Knowledge of God in Classical Sufism*, 52–54. Mahwah: Paulist Press, 2004.

Riḍāyī, Laylā, and Abū'l-Faḍl Maḥmūdī. "Fanāy az khwūd wa-marg-i khwūd-khwāsta dar andīsha-yi ʿAyn al-Quḍāt wa-Yūḥannā Ṣalībī." *Adyān wa-ʿirfān* 46, no. 1 (2013): 51–62.

Riḍāyiyyān, Muḥammad Riḍā. "Ramzīna-hā-yi andāmī-yi insān dar rubāʿiyyāt-i ʿAyn al-Quḍāt Hamadānī bā takya bar adabiyyāt-i taʿlīmī, ghināʾī, ʿirfānī." *Taḥqīqāt-i taʿlīmī wa-ghināʾī-yi zabān wa-adab-i pārsī* 14 (2013): 119–138.

Rusek, Renata. "The Defence of Eblis by 'Eyno-l-Qozāt-e Hamadānī (1096/98–1131)." *Folia Orientalia* 40 (2004): 259–266.

———. *Letters by the Pearl of Qadis as an Example of Twelfth-Century Persian Mystical Epistolography* [Polish]. Kraków: Wydawnictwo Uniwersytetu Jagiellońskiego, 2009.

———. "Listen to the Reed, or on the Self-Revealing Powers of Writing." *Folia Orientalia* 42/43 (2007): 251–259.

———. "The Relation between a Spiritual Master and His Disciple According to 'Eyno-l-Qozāt-e Hamadāni (1096/98–1131)." In *In the Orient Where the Gracious Light* [*sic*] *. . . : Satura Orientalis in Honorem Andrzej Pisowicz*, edited by Anna Krasnowolska, Kinga Maciuszak, and Barbara Mękarska, 89–96. Kraków: Księgarnia Akademicka, 2006.

Rustom, Mohammed. "ʿAyn al-Quḍāt between Divine Jealousy and Political Intrigue." *Journal of Sufi Studies* 7, nos. 1–2 (2018): 47–73.

———. "ʿAyn al-Quḍāt on Chivalry." *Journal of Islamic Ethics* 4, nos. 1–2 (2020): 25–37.

———. "ʿAyn al-Quḍāt Hamadānī (d. 525/1131)." In *The I. B. Tauris Biographical Dictionary of Islamic Civilization*, edited by Mustafa Shah. London: I. B. Tauris, in press.

———. "'Ayn al-Quḍāt's Qur'anic Vision: From Black Words to White Parchment." In Ridgeon, ed., *Routledge Handbook on Sufism*, 75–88.

———. "La crise de coeur." Translated by Samir Abada. *Le Miroir d'Isis* 29 (2021): 85–91.

———. "Devil's Advocate: ʿAyn al-Quḍāt's Defence of Iblis in Context." *Studia Islamica* 115, no. 1 (2020): 65–100.

———. "Everything Muhammad: The Image of the Prophet in the Writings of 'Ayn al-Qudat." *Sacred Web* 39 (2017): 33–40.

———. "Introduction." In ʿAyn al-Quḍāt, *Essence of Reality*, xv–xxiii.

———. "One Step to God: 'Ayn al-Qozat on the Journey of the Heart." *Sufi* 101 (2021): 1–6.

———. "Review of *EIs, Vol. 3*." *Iranian Studies* 49, no. 6 (2016): 1103–1105 (pp. 1104–1105). Contains an assessment of Zekavati Gharagozlou, "ʿAyn al-Quḍāt Hamadānī."

———. "Review of Papan-Matin, *Beyond Death*." *Journal of Sufi Studies* 2, no. 2 (2013): 213–216.

———. "*Theo-Fānī*: ʿAyn al-Quḍāt and the Fire of Love." In *Mysticism and Ethics in Islam*, edited by Bilal Orfali, Atif Khalil, and Mohammed Rustom, 123–132. Beirut: American University of Beirut Press, 2022.

Sādāt Mūsawī Jahānābādī, Sīma, and Nāṣir Gudhashta. "Siphir-i dīn-i Kihyirkigūr wa-ṭawr-i warā-yi ʿaql-i ʿAyn al-Quḍāt." *Adyān wa-ʿirfān* 44, no. 1 (2011): 129–148.

Ṣafāʾī, Ibrāhīm. "Ārāmgāh-i Bābā Ṭāhir wa-ʿAyn al-Quḍāt." *Armaghān* [new] 28, nos. 10–11 (1959): 433–438.

Safi, Omid. *EI3*, s.v. "ʿAyn al-Quḍāt al-Hamadhānī 2: Intellectual Legacy and Posthumous Image."

———. *The Politics of Knowledge in Premodern Islam: Negotiating Ideology and Religious Inquiry*, chapter 6. Chapel Hill: University of North Carolina Press, 2006.

———. "The Sufi Path of Love in Iran and India." In *A Pearl in Wine: Essays on the Life, Music and Sufism of Hazrat Inayat Khan*, edited by Pirzade Zia Inayat Khan, 221–266 (passim). New Lebanon: Omega, 2001.

Sākit, Salmān. "ʿIshq az dīdgāh-i ʿAyn al-Quḍāt Hamadānī." *Nāma-yi anjuman* 6, no. 3 (2003): 92–112.

Schimmel, Annemarie. *Mystical Dimensions of Islam*, 295–296, 348, 351, and 370. Chapel Hill: University of North Carolina Press, 1975.

Seyed-Gohrab, Ali Asghar. "Satan as the Lover of God in Islamic Mystical Writings." In *The Beloved in Middle East Literature*, edited by Alireza Korangy, Hanadi Al-Samman, and Michael Beard, 85–101 (pp. 94–98). London: I. B. Tauris, 2017.

Shajjārī, Murtaḍā. "Dil-i ādamī wa-wīzhagī-hā-yi ān az dīdgāh-i ʿAyn al-Quḍāt Hamadānī." *Muṭālaʿāt-i ʿirfānī* 15 (2012): 77–102.

———. "Ḥaqīqat-i īmān az dīdgāh-i ʿAyn al-Quḍāt." *Falsafa-yi dīn* 10, no. 2 (2013): 77–103.

———. "Maʿrifat az dīdgāh-i ʿAyn al-Quḍāt." *Faṣl-nāma-yi adabiyyāt-i ʿirfānī wa-usṭūra-shinākhtī* 6, no. 20 (2010): 85–112.

Ṭabāṭabāʾī, Hādī. "Barrasī-yi kitāb-i *Pizhūhishī dar andīsha-hā-yi ʿirfānī-yi ʿAyn al-Quḍāt Hamadānī*." *Kitāb-i māh-i dīn* 178 (2012): 58–62.

———. "Iblīs miyān-i takfīr wa-taqdīs: barrasī-yi kitāb-i *Naẓar-i ʿAyn al-Quḍāt Hamadānī dar mawrid-i Iblīs wa-irtibāṭ-i ān bā niẓām-i aḥsan*." *Kitāb-i māh-i dīn* 178 (2012): 47–52.

Tanındı, Zeren. "Preliminary List of Manuscripts Stamped with Bayezid II's Seal and Transferred from the Topkapı Palace Inner Treasury to Other Library Collections." In *Treasures of Knowledge: An Inventory of the Ottoman Palace Library (1502/3–1503/4)*, edited by Gülru Necipoğlu, Cemal Kafadar, and Cornell Fleischer, 983–1009 (p. 993). Leiden: Brill, 2019.

Teubner, J. K. *EI2*, s.v. "Al-Hamadānī, ʿAyn al-Quḍāt."

Unknown. "ʿAyn al-Quḍāt." *Armaghān* [old] 12, no. 7 (1931): 471–472.

———. "*Nāma-hā*-yi ʿAyn al-Quḍāt Hamadānī." *Kāwih* 47–48 (1973): 16–21.

ʿUsayrān, ʿAfīf. "Muqaddima-yi muṣaḥḥiḥ," 1–192. In ʿAyn al-Quḍāt, *Tamhīdāt*.

———. "Muqaddimat al-muṣaḥḥiḥ," 1–73. In ʿAyn al-Quḍāt, *Zubdat* (part 1 of *Muṣannafāt*).

Wafāʾī Baṣīr, Aḥmad. "Jāygāh wa-sayr-i tārīkhī-yi sitāyish-i Iblīs dar adab-i fārsī." *Zabān wa-adabiyyāt-i fārsī* 9 (2007): 153–184 (pp. 167–172).

Wāʿiẓ, Saʿīd. "Abyāt-i ʿarabī-yi *Nāma-hā*-yi ʿAyn al-Quḍāt Hamadānī." *Zabān wa-adab* 41 (2004): 1–27; 42 (2005): 52–60; 43 (2006): 33–46.

Wazīn, M. "Murūrī bar āthār-i ʿAyn al-Quḍāt Hamadānī." *Nāma-yi farhangistān* 2, no. 1 (1996): 104–127.

Yamazaki, Mitsuko. "How to Tell Something Impossible to Tell: The Example of ʿAyn al-Quḍāt Hamadhānī" [Japanese]. *Oriento* 45, no. 2 (2002): 148–164.

Yazdānī, Najaf. "Nigāh-i taqrībī-yi ʿAyn al-Quḍāt Hamadānī ba-makātib-i mukhtalif." *Muṭālaʿāt-i taqrībī-yi madhāhib-i islāmī* 9, no. 34 (2014): 30–46.

Yūsufī, Muḥammad Riḍā, and Ilāha Ḥaydarī. "Nūr-i siyāh: pārādūks-i zibā-yi ʿirfānī." *Adyān wa-ʿirfān* 45, no. 2 (2012–2013): 171–191 (passim).

Yūsufīpūr Kirmānī, Pūrān. "Taʾammulī dar andīsha-hā-yi ʿAyn al-Quḍāt Hamadānī." *Faṣl-nāma-yi adabiyyāt-i fārsī* 5, no. 13 (2009): 1–23.

Yūsuf-i Thānī, Maḥmūd, and Ḥasan Mahdīpūr. "Tabyīn-i kathrat wa-waḥdat-i wujūd dar andīsha-yi ʿAyn al-Quḍāt Hamadānī bar asās-i ṭawr-i ʿaql wa-ṭawr-i warā-yi ʿaql." *Jāwīdān-khirad* 21, no. 4 (2012): 135–164.

Zargar, Cyrus Ali. *Sufi Aesthetics: Beauty, Love, and the Human Form in the Writings of Ibn ʿArabī and ʿIrāqī*, 91–95. Columbia: University of South Carolina Press, 2011.

Zāriʿī, Asad Allāh. *Būryā bar ātish: ʿAyn al-Quḍāt Hamadānī*. Tehran: Intishārāt-i Iʿlām, 2006.

Zekavati Gharagozlou, Alireza. *EIs*, s.v. "ʿAyn al-Quḍāt Hamadānī." Translated by Matthew Melvin-Koushki.

———. *ʿIrfāniyyāt: majmūʿa-yi maqālāt-i ʿirfānī*, 59–76. Tehran: Intishārāt-i Ḥaqīqat, 2001.

———. "Nukāt-i intiqādī dar kitābguzārī." In Adhkāʾī, ed., *Mātīkān*, 109–140. Partly a review of Mayel Heravi, *Khāṣṣiyyat-i āyinagī*.

Zibāyīnizhād, Maryam. "*Nāma-hā*-yi ʿAyn al-Quḍāt." *Kitāb-i māh-i tārīkh wa-jughrāfiyā* 32 (2000): 22–26. A review of the edition of the *Nāma-hā*.

Other Primary Sources

Abū'l-ʿAtāhiya. *Dīwān*. Edited by Karam al-Bustānī. Beirut: Dār Bayrūt, 1986.

Abū Dāwūd. *Sunan*. In *Jamʿ jawāmiʿ al-aḥādīth*, vol. 5.

Aḥmad b. Ḥanbal. *Musnad*. In *Jamʿ jawāmiʿ al-aḥādīth*, vol. 12.

Ājurrī, Muḥammad b. al-Ḥusayn al-. *al-Sharīʿa*. Edited by ʿAbd Allāh Dumayjī. Riyadh: Dār al-Waṭan, 1999.

ʿAjlūnī, Ismāʿīl b. Muḥammad al-. *Kashf al-khafāʾ*. Edited by Yūsuf b. Maḥmūd Aḥmad. Cairo: Maktabat ʿIlm al-Ḥadīth, 2000.

ʿAlī b. Abī Ṭālib. *Nahj al-balāgha*. Edited by Muḥammad ʿAbduh. Reprint. Beirut: Dār al-Maʿrifa, 1996.

Āmulī, Ḥaydar. *Tafsīr al-muḥīṭ al-aʿẓam*. Edited by Muḥsin Mūsawī Tabrīzī. Qum: Nūr ʿAlā Nūr, 2002–2006.

Attridge, Harold W., ed. *The HarperCollins Study Bible*. Rev. ed. New York: HarperOne, 2006.

Avicenna. *The Metaphysics of The Healing*. Translated by Michael Marmura. Provo: Brigham Young University Press, 2005.

Baqlī, Ruzbihān. *ʿAbhar al-ʿāshiqīn*. Edited by Henry Corbin and Mohammad Moin. Tehran: Département d'iranologie de l'Institut franco-iranien, 1958.

———. *Sharḥ-i shaṭḥiyyāt*. Edited by Henry Corbin. Reprint. Tehran: Intishārāt-i Ṭahūrī, 2010.

Bayhaqī, Abū Bakr Aḥmad al-. *Kitāb al-Asmāʾ wa'l-ṣifāt*. Edited by ʿAbd Allāh b. Muḥammad al-Ḥāshidī. Jeddah: Maktabat al-Sawādī, 1993.

Bazzār, Abū Bakr al-. *al-Baḥr al-zakhkhār*. Edited by Maḥfūẓ al-Raḥmān Zayn al-Dīn et al. Madina: Maktabat al-ʿUlūm wa'l-Ḥikam, 2006.

Bukhārī. *Ṣaḥīḥ*. In *Jamʿ jawāmiʿ al-aḥādīth*, vol. 2.

Bukhārī, Abū Ibrāhīm Mustamlī. *Sharḥ al-Taʿarruf*. Edited by Muḥammad Rawshan. Tehran: Intishārāt-i Asāṭīr, 1984.

Burūsawī, Ismāʿīl Ḥaqqī. *Rūḥ al-bayān fī tafsīr al-Qurʾān*. Edited by ʿAbd al-Laṭīf Ḥasan ʿAbd al-Raḥmān. Beirut: Dār al-Kutub al-ʿIlmiyya, 2003.

Dīnawarī, Aḥmad b. Marwān al-. *al-Mujālasa wa-jawāhir al-ʿIlm*. Edited by Abū ʿUbayda Mashhūr Āl Salmān. Beirut: Dār Ibn Ḥazm, 1998.

Forouzanfar, Badiozzaman, ed. *Aḥadīth-i Mathnawī*. Tehran: Intishārāt-i Dānishgāh-i Tihrān, 1955.

Ghazālī, Abū Ḥāmid Muḥammad al-. *The Condemnation of Pride and Self-Admiration*. Translated by Mohammed Rustom. Cambridge: Islamic Texts Society, 2018.

———. *Iḥyāʾ ʿulūm al-dīn*. Jeddah: Dār al-Minhāj, 2011.

———. *The Marvels of the Heart*. Translated by Walter Skellie. Louisville: Fons Vitae, 2010.

———. *Maqāṣid al-falāsifa*. Edited by Muḥyī al-Dīn al-Kurdī. Cairo: al-Maṭbaʿa al-Maḥmūdiyya, 1936.

———. *al-Munqidh min al-ḍalāl*. Edited by Kāmil ʿAyyād and Jamīl Ṣalībā. Beirut: Dār al-Andalus, 1967.

———. *The Niche of Lights*. Translated by David Buchman. Provo: Brigham Young University Press, 1998.

Ghazālī, Aḥmad (al-). *Mukātabāt-i Khwāja Aḥmad Ghazālī bā ʿAyn al-Quḍāt Hamadānī*. Edited by Nasrollah Pourjavady. Tehran: Khānaqāh-i Niʿmatullāhī, 1977.

———. *Sawāniḥ*. Edited by Nasrollah Pourjavady. Tehran: Intishārāt-i Bunyād-i Farhang-i Īrān, 1980.

Ḥaddād, Muḥammad b. Muḥammad al-. *Takhrīj aḥādīth Iḥyāʾ ʿulūm al-dīn li'l-ʿIrāqī wa-Ibn al-Subkī wa'l-Zabīdī*. Riyadh: Dār al-ʿĀṣima, 1987.

Ḥallāj, Ḥusayn b. Manṣūr al-. *Akhbār al-Ḥallāj*. Edited by Paul Krause and Louis Massignon. Paris: Paul Geuthner, 1936.

———. *Hallaj: Poems of a Sufi Martyr*. Translated by Carl Ernst. Evanston: Northwestern University Press, 2018.

———. *Kitāb al-Ṭawāsīn*. Edited by Louis Massignon. Paris: Paul Geuthner, 1913.

Hujwīrī, ʿAlī b. ʿUthmān. *The Kashf al-Maḥjūb: The Oldest Persian Treatise on Ṣūfiism*. Translated by R. A. Nicholson. Leiden: Brill, 1911.

Ibn al-Muʿtazz. *Dīwān*. Edited by Karam al-Bustānī. Beirut: Dār Ṣādir, 1961.

Ibn al-Aʿrābī. *Muʿjam Ibn al-Aʿrābī*. Edited by ʿAbd al-Muḥsin Ḥusaynī. Riyadh: Dār Ibn al-Jawzī, 1997.

Ibn ʿArabī. *al-Futūḥāt al-Makkiyya*. Beirut: Dār Ṣādir, 1968.

———. "The Science of Letters." Translated by Denis Gril in Ibn ʿArabī, *The Meccan Revelations*, edited by Michel Chodkiewicz. New York: Pir Press, 2002–2004, 2:161–175.

———. *Sharḥ Khalʿ al-naʿlayn*. Edited by Muḥammad al-Amrānī. Marrakesh: Muʾassasat al-Āfāq, 2013.

Ibn Ḥamdūn. *al-Tadhkira al-Ḥamdūniyya*. Edited by Iḥsān ʿAbbās and Bakr ʿAbbās. Beirut: Dār Ṣādir, 1996.

Ibn Ḥanbal, ʿAbd Allāh b. Aḥmad. *Kitāb al-Sunna*. Edited by Muḥammad b. Saʿīd al-Qaḥṭānī. Dammam: Dār Ibn al-Qayyim, 1986.

Ibn Māja. *Sunan*. In *Jamʿ jawāmiʿ al-aḥādīth*, vol. 8.

Iṣfahānī, Abū Nuʿaym al-. *Ḥilyat al-awliyā'*. Beirut: Dār al-Fikr, 1996.

Jāmī, ʿAbd al-Raḥmān. *Nafaḥāt al-uns*. Edited by Mahdī Tawḥīdīpūr. Tehran: Kitābfurūshī-yi Saʿdī, 1958.

———. *The Precious Pearl*. Translated by Nicholas Heer. Albany: State University of New York Press, 1979.

Jamʿ jawāmiʿ al-aḥādīth wa'l-asānīd wa-maknaz al-ṣiḥāḥ wa'l-sunan wa'l-masānīd. Vaduz: Jamʿiyyat al-Maknaz al-Islāmī, 2000.

Kalābādhī, Abū Bakr al-. *al-Taʿarruf li-madhhab al-taṣawwuf*. Edited by A. J. Arberry. Cairo: Maktabat al-Khānjī, 1933. English translation by Arberry as *The Doctrine of the Sufis*. Cambridge: Cambridge University Press, 1935.

Kāshānī, ʿAbd al-Razzāq. *Laṭā'if al-iʿlām*. Edited by Majīd Hādīzāda. Beirut: Manshūrāt al-Jamal, 2011.

———. *al-Qāmūs al-ṣūfī*. Edited by ʿĀṣim Ibrāhīm al-Kayyālī. Beirut: Kitāb Nāshirūn, 2011.

Kubrā, Najm al-Dīn. *Ta'wīlāt*. Edited by Aḥmad Farīd al-Mizyadī. Beirut: Dār al-Kutub al-ʿIlmiyya, 2015.

Lālikā'ī, Hibat Allāh b. al-Ḥasan al-. *Sharḥ uṣūl iʿtiqād ahl al-sunna wa'l-jamāʿa*. Edited by Abū Yaʿqūb b. Kamāl. Riyadh: Ministry of Islamic Affairs, 2001.

Makkī, Abū Ṭālib al-. *Qūt al-qulūb*. Edited by Maḥmūd Ibrāhīm Muḥammad al-Riḍwānī. Cairo: Dār al-Turāth, 2001.

Mālik. *Muwaṭṭa'*. In *Jamʿ jawāmiʿ al-aḥādīth*, vol. 9.

Maneri, Sharafuddin. *A Mine of Meaning*. Translated by Paul Jackson. Louisville: Fons Vitae, 2012.

Mannūn, ʿĪsā. *Nibrās al-ʿuqūl*. Edited by Yaḥyā Murād. Beirut: Dār al-Kutub al-ʿIlmiyya, 2003.

Maqdisī, Naṣr b. Ibrāhīm al-. *Mukhtaṣar al-ḥujja ʿalā tārik al-maḥajja*. Edited by Muḥammad al-ʿAzādhī. Beirut: Dār al-Kutub al-ʿIlmiyya, 2017.

Majlisī, ʿAllāma Muḥammad Bāqir. *Biḥār al-anwār*. Qum, 1956–1972.

Maybudī, Rashīd al-Dīn. *The Unveiling of the Mysteries and the Provision of the Pious*. Partial English translation by William C. Chittick. Louisville: Fons Vitae, 2015.

Muslim. *Ṣaḥīḥ*. In *Jamʿ jawāmiʿ al-aḥādīth*, vol. 4.

Mutanabbī, Abū'l-Ṭayyib al-. *Dīwān Abī'l-Ṭayyib al-Mutanabbī bi-sharḥ Abī'l-Baqā' al-ʿUkbarī*. Edited by Muṣṭafā Saqā, Ibrāhīm al-Ibyārī, and ʿAbd al-Ḥafīẓ al-Shalabī. Beirut: Dār al-Maʿrifa, 2007.

Nasafī, ʿAzīz al-Dīn. *al-Insān al-kāmil*. Edited by Marijan Molé. Tehran: Département d'iranologie de l'Institut franco-iranien, 1962.

———. *Kashf al-ḥaqā'iq*. Edited by ʿAlī Aṣghar Mīrbāqirī Fard. Tehran: Intishārāt-i Sukhan, 2012.

Nasr, Seyyed Hossein, and Mehdi Aminrazavi, eds. *An Anthology of Philosophy in Persia*. London: I. B. Tauris in association with The Institute of Ismaili Studies, 2008–2015.

Nasr, Seyyed Hossein, Caner Dagli, Maria Dakake, Joseph Lumbard, and Mohammed Rustom, eds. *The Study Quran: A New Translation and Commentary*. New York: HarperOne, 2015.

Nūrī, Abū'l-Ḥusayn. *Maqāmāt al-qulūb*. Edited by Paul Nwyia in Nwyia, "Textes mystiques inédits." *Mélanges de l'Université Saint-Joseph* 44, no. 9 (1968): 117–154 (pp. 130–143).

Pourjavady, Nasrollah, ed. *Majmūʿa-yi falsafī-yi Marāgha*. Tehran: Markaz-i Nashr-i Dānishgāhī, 2002.

Qāḍī ʿIyāḍ. *al-Shifāʾ*. Edited by ʿAlī Muḥammad al-Bajāwī. Beirut: Dār al-Kitāb al-ʿArabī, 1984.

Qārī, Mullā ʿAlī al-. *Mirqāt al-mafātīḥ*. Edited by Jamāl ʿĪtānī. Beirut: Dār al-Kutub al-ʿIlmiyya, 2007.

Qushayrī, Abū'l-Qāsim al-. *al-Risāla*. Edited by Anas Muḥammad ʿAdnān al-Sharafāwī. Jeddah: Dār al-Minhāj, 2017.

Rāzī, Najm al-Dīn. *The Path of God's Bondsmen*. Translated by Hamid Algar. Delmar: Caravan Books, 1982.

Rūmī, Jalāl al-Dīn. *Signs of the Unseen*. Translated by Wheeler Thackston. Boston: Shambhala, 1994.

Saghānī, Ḥasan b. Muḥammad al-. *Mawḍūʿāt al-Saghānī*. Edited by Najm ʿAbd al-Raḥmān Khalaf. Damascus: Dār al-Maʾmūn li'l-Turāth, 1985.

Sahlajī, Abū'l-Faḍl Muḥammad b. ʿAlī al-. *al-Nūr min kalimāt Abī Ṭayfūr*. In part 2 of *Shaṭaḥāt al-ṣūfiyya*, edited by ʿAbd al-Raḥmān Badawī. Cairo: Maktabat al-Nahḍa al-Miṣriyya, 1949.

Sakhāwī, Muḥammad b. ʿAbd al-Raḥmān al-. *al-Maqāṣid al-ḥasana*. Edited by ʿAbd Allāh Muḥammad al-Ṣiddīq. Beirut: Dār al-Kitāb al-ʿArabī, 1985.

Sakkākī, Yūsuf b. Abī Bakr. *Miftāḥ al-ʿulūm*. Edited by Naʿīm Zarzūr. Beirut: Dar al-Kutub al-ʿIlmiyya, 1987.

Samʿānī, Aḥmad. *Rawḥ al-arwāḥ*. Edited by Najib Mayel Heravi. Tehran: Shirkat-i Intishārāt-i ʿIlmī wa-Farhangī, 1989. English translation by William C. Chittick as *The Repose of the Spirits: A Sufi Commentary on the Divine Names*. Albany: State University of New York Press, 2019.

Ṣanʿānī, ʿAbd al-Razzāq al-. *al-Muṣannaf*. Edited by Ḥabīb al-Raḥmān al-Aʿẓamī. Johannesburg: al-Majils al-ʿIlmī, 1970.

Sarrāj, Abū Naṣr al-. *Kitāb al-Lumaʿ*. Edited by R. A. Nicholson. Leiden: Brill, 1914.

Shīrāzī, Maʿṣūm ʿAlī Shāh. *Ṭarāʾiq al-ḥaqāʾiq*. Edited by Muḥammad Jaʿfar Maḥjūb. Tehran: Kitābkhāna-yi Bārānī, 1966.

Shīrāzī, Muḥammad Dihdār. *Sharḥ Khuṭbat al-bayān*. Edited by Muḥammad Ḥusayn Akbarī Sāwī. Tehran: Ṣāyib, 2006.

Shushtarī, Nūr Allāh. *Majālis al-muʾminīn*. Edited by Ibrāhīm ʿArabpūr. Mashhad: Bunyād-i Pizhūhish-hā-yi Islāmī, 2013–2014.

Sulamī, ʿAbd al-Raḥmān al-. *Ṭabaqāt al-ṣūfiyya*. Edited by Nūr al-Dīn Shurayba. Aleppo: Dār al-Kitāb al-Nafīs, 1986.

Ṭabarānī, Sulaymān b. Aḥmad al-. *al-Muʿjam al-awsaṭ*. Edited by Maḥmūd Ṭaḥḥān. Cairo: Dār al-Ḥaramayn, 1995.

———. *al-Muʿjam al-kabīr*. Edited by ʿAbd al-Majīd al-Salafī. Cairo: Maktabat Ibn Taymiyya, 1994.

Tabrīzī, Mullā ʿAbd al-Bāqī Ṣūfī. *Minhāj al-wilāya fī Sharḥ Nahj al-balāgha*. Edited by Ḥabīb Allāh ʿAẓīmī. Tehran: Daftar-i Nashr-i Mīrāth-i Maktūb, 1999.

Ṭībī, Sharaf al-Dīn al-. *al-Kāshif ʿan ḥaqāʾiq al-sunan*. Edited by ʿAbd al-Ḥamīd Hindāwī. Riyadh: Nizār Muṣṭafā al-Bāz, 1997.

Tirmidhī. *Sunan*. In *Jamʿ jawāmiʿ al-aḥādīth*, vol. 6.

Tustarī, Sahl b. ʿAbd Allāh. *Tafsīr al-Tustarī*. Translated by Annabel and Ali Keeler. Louisville: Fons Vitae, 2011.

Ẓarīfī Chalabī, Ḥasan. *Kāshif al-asrār*. Edited by ʿAlī Riḍā Qūjazāda. Tehran: Sazmān-i Tablīghāt-i Islāmī, 2010.

Zurqānī, Muḥammad b. ʿAbd al-Bāqī al-. *Sharḥ al-Zurqānī ʿalā al-Mawāhib al-laduniyya bi'l-minaḥ al-Muḥammadiyya*. Edited by Muḥammad ʿAbd al-ʿAzīz al-Khālidī. Beirut: Dār al-Kutub al-ʿIlmiyya, 1996.

Other Secondary Sources

Abuali, Eyad. "Words Clothed in Light: *Dhikr* (Recollection), Colour and Synaesthesia in Early Kubrawi Sufism." *Iran: Journal of the British Institute of Persian Studies* 58, no. 2 (2020): 279–292.

Adamson, Peter. "From the Necessary Existent to God." In *Interpreting Avicenna*, edited by Peter Adamson, 170–189. Cambridge: Cambridge University Press, 2013.

Addas, Claude. *La Maison muhammadienne: Aperçus de la dévotion au Prophète en mystique musulmane*. Paris: Gallimard, 2015.

Adhkāʾī, Parwīz. *EIr*, s.v. "Hamadān vi. History, Islamic Period."

Ahmed, Asad, and Jon McGinnis. "Faḍl-i Ḥaqq Khayrābādī (d. 1861), *al-Hadiyya al-saʿīdiyya*." In *The Oxford Handbook of Islamic Philosophy*, edited by Khaled El-Rouayheb and Sabine Schmidtke, 535–559. New York: Oxford University Press, 2017.

Ahmed, Shahab. *What Is Islam?* Princeton: Princeton University Press, 2016.

Ali, Mukhtar H. "Sufi Ethics: Synthesis and Legacy." In *The Oxford Handbook of Islamic Ethics*, edited by Mustafa Shah. Oxford: Oxford University Press, forthcoming.

———. *Philosophical Sufism: An Introduction to the School of Ibn al-ʿArabī*. London: Routledge, 2022.

al-Khatib, Mutaz. "Consult Your Heart: The Self as a Source of Moral Judgment." In *Ḥadīth and Ethics through the Lens of Interdisciplinarity*, edited by Mutaz al-Khatib, 268–305. Leiden: Brill, 2023.

Arif, Hassan. "Defending Sufi Metaphysics in British India: Faḍl-i Ḥaqq Khayrābādī's (d. 1277/1861) Treatise on *waḥdat al-wujūd*." PhD diss., McGill University, Institute of Islamic Studies, in progress.

Asghari, Seyed Amir Hossein. "Sufi Interpretation of the Qurʾān." *Burhan Journal of Qur'anic Studies* 1, no. 1 (2016): 28–45.

Āshtiyānī, Jalāl al-Dīn, Hideicho Matsubura, Takashi Iwami, and Akiro Matsumoto, eds. *Consciousness and Reality: Studies in Memory of Toshihiko Izutsu*. Leiden: Brill, 1998.

Avery, Kenneth. *Shiblī: His Life and Thought in the Sufi Tradition*. Albany: State University of New York Press, 2014.

Bin Tyeer, Sarah, and Claire Gallien, eds. *Islam and New Directions in World Literature*. Edinburgh: Edinburgh University Press, 2022.

Bodman, Whitney. *The Poetics of Iblīs: Narrative Theology in the Qur'ān*. Cambridge, MA: Harvard University Press, 2011.

Böwering, Gerhard. *The Mystical Vision of Existence in Classical Islam: The Qurʾānic Hermeneutics of the Ṣūfī Sahl At-Tustarī (d. 283/896)*. Berlin: de Gruyter, 1980.

de Bruijn, J. T. P. *Of Piety and Poetry: The Interaction of Religion and Literature in the Life and Works of Ḥakīm Sanāʾī of Ghazna*. Leiden: Brill, 1983.

Casewit, Yousef. *The Mystics of al-Andalus: Ibn Barrajān and Islamic Thought in the Twelfth Century*. Cambridge: Cambridge University Press, 2017.

Chittick, William C. *Divine Love: Islamic Literature and the Path to God*. New Haven: Yale University Press, 2013.

———. *In Search of the Lost Heart: Explorations in Islamic Thought*. Edited by Mohammed Rustom, Atif Khalil, and Kazuyo Murata. Albany: State University of New York Press, 2012.

———. "Love as the Way to Truth." *Sacred Web* 15 (2005): 15–27.

———. *Me and Rumi: The Autobiography of Shams-i Tabrizi*. Louisville: Fons Vitae, 2004.

———. "Review of de Bruijn, *Of Piety and Poetry*." *Journal of the American Oriental Society* 105, no. 2 (1985): 347–350.

———. *The Sufi Path of Knowledge: Ibn al-'Arabī's Metaphysics of Imagination*. Albany: State University of New York Press, 1989.

———. *The Sufi Path of Love: The Spiritual Teachings of Rumi*. Albany: State University of New York Press, 1983.

Corbin, Henry. *Creative Imagination in the Ṣūfism of Ibn 'Arabī*. Translated by Ralph Manheim. Princeton: Princeton University Press, 1969.

———. *The Man of Light in Iranian Sufism*. Translated by Nancy Pearson. Boulder: Shambhala, 1978.

———. *Spiritual Body and Celestial Earth*. Translated by Nancy Pearson. Princeton: Princeton University Press, 1977.

Cornell, Rkia. *Rabi'a from Narrative to Myth*. London: Oneworld, 2019.

Cornell, Vincent, and Bruce Lawrence, eds. *The Wiley Blackwell Companion to Islamic Spirituality*. Hoboken: Wiley Blackwell, 2023.

Dagli, Caner. *Ibn al-ʿArabī and Islamic Intellectual Culture: From Mysticism to Philosophy*. New York: Routledge, 2016.

Dakake, Maria. "'Guest of the Inmost Heart': Conceptions of the Divine Beloved among Early Sufi Women." *Comparative Islamic Studies* 3, no. 1 (2007): 72–97.

———. "*Ta'wīl* in the Qur'an and the Islamic Exegetical Tradition: The Past and the Future of the Qur'an." In *The Enigma of Divine Revelation: Between Phenomenology and Comparative Theology*, edited by Jean-Luc Marion and Christiaan Jacobs-Vandegeer, 237–259. Cham: Springer, 2020.

———. *Toward an Islamic Theory of Religion*. London: Oneworld, 2023.

Ebrahim, Alireza. *EIs*, s.v. "Dhū al-Nūn al-Miṣrī." Translated by Farzin Negahban.

Farhadi, Rawan. *'Abdullāh Anṣārī of Herāt (1006–1089 C.E.)*. Richmond, Surrey: Curzon, 1996.

Farrell, Jeremy. "Review of Salamah-Qudsi, *Sufism and Early Islamic Piety*." *Journal of the American Oriental Society* 141, no. 3 (2021): 719–723.

Faruque, Muhammad. *Sculpting the Self: Islam, Selfhood, and Human Flourishing*. Ann Arbor: University of Michigan Press, 2021.

———. "Sufi Metaphysical Literature." In *Handbook of Sufi Studies: Sufi Literature*, edited by Alexander Knysh and Bilal Orfali. Leiden: Brill, forthcoming.

Frawley, John. *The Real Astrology*. London: Apprentice Books, 2001.

Galadari, Abdulla. *Spiritual Meanings of the Ḥajj Rituals: A Philological Approach*. Louisville: Fons Vitae, 2021.

Geoffroy, Éric. *Allah au féminin*. Paris: Albin Michel, 2020.

Gozashteh, Naser. *EIs*, s.v. "Abū ʿAlī al-Fārmadī." Translated by Farzin Negahban.

Graham, William. *Divine Word and Prophetic Word in Early Islam*. The Hague: Mouton, 1977.

Gramlich, Richard. *Alte Vorbilder des Sufitums*. Wiesbaden: Harrassowitz, 1995–1996.

Gril, Denis, Stefan Reichmuth, and Dilek Sarmis, eds. *The Presence of the Prophet in Early Modern and Contemporary Islam, Vol. 1: The Prophet between Doctrine, Literature and Arts: Historical Legacies and Their Unfolding*. Leiden: Brill, 2022.

Gruendler, Beatrice. "Longing for Home: *al-ḥanīn ilā l-awṭān* and Its Alternatives in Classical Arabic Literature." In *Representations and Visions of Homeland in Modern Arabic Literature*, edited by Sebastian Günther and Stephan Milich, 1–41. Hildesheim: Olms Verlag, 2016.

Ha'iri Yazdi, Mahdi. *Universal Science: An Introduction to Islamic Metaphysics*. Translated by John Cooper, edited by Saiyad Nizamuddin Ahmad. Leiden: Brill, 2017.

Harb, Lara. *Arabic Poetics: Aesthetic Experience in Classical Arabic Literature*. Cambridge: Cambridge University Press, 2020.

Hinz, Walther. *Islamische Maße und Gewichte*. Leiden: Brill, 1955.

Hirtenstein, Stephen. *EIs*, s.v. "*Dhawq*."

Homerin, Th. Emil. *Passion Before Me, My Fate Behind: Ibn al-Farid and the Poetry of Recollection*. Albany: State University of New York Press, 2011.

Izutsu, Toshihiko. *The Concept and Reality of Existence*. Tokyo: Keio Institute of Cultural and Linguistic Studies, 1971.

Judd, Steven. "Were the Umayyad-Era Qadarites Kāfirs?" In *Accusations of Unbelief in Islam*, edited by Camilla Adang, Hassan Ansari, Maribel Fierro, and Sabine Schmidtke, 42–55. Brill: Leiden, 2016.

Karamustafa, Ahmet. *Sufism: The Formative Period*. Edinburgh: Edinburgh University Press, 2007.

Keeler, Annabel. *Ṣūfī Hermeneutics: The Qurʾān Commentary of Rashīd al-Dīn Maybudī*. Oxford: Oxford University Press in association with The Institute of Ismaili Studies, 2007.

———. "Wisdom in Controversy: Paradox and the Paradoxical in Sayings of Abū Yazīd al-Bisṭāmī (d. 234/848 or 261/875)." *Journal of Sufi Studies* 7, no. 1–2 (2018): 1–26.

Kermani, Navid. *God Is Beautiful: The Aesthetic Experience of the Quran*. Translated by Tony Crawford. Cambridge: Polity Press, 2015.

Key, Alexander. *Language between God and the Poets: Maʿnā in the Eleventh Century*. Oakland: University of California Press, 2018.

Khalil, Atif. "The Embodiment of Gratitude in Sufi Virtue Ethics." *Studia Islamica* 111, no. 2 (2016): 159–178.

———. "On Cultivating Gratitude in Sufi Virtue Ethics." *Journal of Sufi Studies* 4, nos. 1–2 (2015): 1–26.

———. *Repentance and the Return to God: Tawba in Early Sufism*. Albany: State University of New York Press, 2018.

———. "Sufism and Qur'ānic Ethics." In Ridgeon, ed., *Routledge Handbook on Sufism*, 159–171.

———. "White Death: Ibn al-ʿArabī on the Trials and Virtues of Hunger and Fasting." *Journal of the American Oriental Society* 141, no. 3 (2021): 577–586.

Koca, Özgür. *Islam, Causality, and Freedom: From the Medieval to the Modern Era*. New York: Cambridge University Press, 2020.

Lajevardi, Fatemeh. *EIs*, s.v. "Bāyazīd Basṭāmī." Translated by Muhammad Isa Waley.

Lange, Christian. "The Death of Dargazini." In *Fruit of Knowledge, Wheel of Learning: Essays in Honour of Professor Carole Hillenbrand*, edited by Ali Ansari, 90–106. London: Gingko Library, 2022.

———. *Justice, Punishment and the Medieval Muslim Imagination*. Cambridge: Cambridge University Press, 2008.

Lange, Christian, and Alexander Knysh, eds. *Handbook of Sufi Studies, Vol. 2: Sufi Cosmology*. Leiden: Brill, 2023.

Lawrence, Bruce. "The *Lawa'ih* of Qazi Hamid Ud-Din *Naguri*." *Indo-Iranica* 28, no. 1 (1975): 34–53.

Lawson, Todd. *The Crucifixion and the Qur'an*. Oxford: Oneworld, 2009.

Lewisohn, Leonard, ed. *The Heritage of Sufism, Vol. 1: Classical Persian Sufism from Its Origins to Rumi (700–1300)*. Oxford: Oneworld, 1999.

———. "Sufism's Religion of Love, from Rābiʿa to Ibn ʿArabī." In *The Cambridge Companion to Sufism*, edited by Lloyd Ridgeon, 150–180. Cambridge: Cambridge University Press, 2015.

Lings, Martin. *Muhammad*. Reprint. Cambridge: Islamic Texts Society, 1991.

———. *What Is Sufism?* London: George Allen and Unwin, 1975.

Lory, Pierre. "La transgression des normes du discours religieux: remarques sur les *shaṭaḥāt* de Abū Bakr al-Shiblī." In *Unity in Diversity: Mysticism, Messianism and the Construction of Religious Authority in Islam*, edited by Orkhan Mir-Kasimov, 23–37. Leiden: Brill, 2013.

Lumbard, Joseph. *Aḥmad al-Ghazālī, Remembrance, and the Metaphysics of Love*. Albany: State University of New York Press, 2016.

———. "Aḥmad al-Ghazālī's *al-Tajrīd fī kalimat al-tawḥīd* (*A Primer on the Statement of Tawhid*)." *Journal of Sufi Studies*, forthcoming.

———. "Covenant and Covenants in the Qur'an." *Journal of Qur'anic Studies* 17, no. 2 (2015): 1–23.

———. "Love and Beauty in Sufism." In Ridgeon, ed., *Routledge Handbook on Sufism*, 172–186.

———. "The Semantics of Gratitude (*Shukr*) in the Qurʾān." *Journal of Islamic Ethics* 5, nos. 1–2 (2021): 173–193.

Maghsoudlou, Salimeh. "The Status of the Spirit in al-Mustamlī al-Buḫārī's *Šharḥ al-Ta'arruf*: Case Study [*sic*] of the Interrelationships of Ḥanafite Sufism, Sunnī *kalām* and Avicennism in the [*sic*] Fifth / Eleventh Century Transoxiana." *Arabic Sciences and Philosophy* 28 (2018): 225–255.

Malik, Jamal. *EI3*, s.v. "Faḍl-i Ḥaqq Khayrābādī."

Massignon, Louis. *The Passion of al-Hallāj*. Translated by Herbert Mason. Princeton: Princeton University Press, 1982.

Mayel Heravi, Najib. *EIs*, s.v. "Bustī, Abū al-Ḥasan." Translated by Farzin Negahban.

———. "Muqaddima-yi muṣaḥḥiḥ," 9–119. In Samʿānī, *Rawḥ*.

Meftah, Abdel Baki. *Lumière soufie*. Translated by Éric Geoffroy et al. Algiers: Librairie de Philosophie et de Soufisme, 2017.

Meier, Fritz. *Abu Saʿīd-i Abū l-Ḫayr (357–440/967–1049): Wirklichkeit und Legende*. Leiden: Brill, 1976.

———. *Nachgelassene Schriften, Vol. 1: Bemerkungen zur Mohammedverehrung (part 1: Die Segenssprechung über Mohammed; part 2: Die taṣliya in sufischen*

Zusammenhängen). Edited by Bernd Radtke (parts 1–2) and Gudrun Schubert (part 2). Leiden: Brill, 2002–2005.

Meisami, Sayeh. *Naṣīr al-Dīn Ṭūsī: A Philosopher for All Seasons*. Cambridge: Islamic Texts Society, 2019.

Minorsky, Vladimir. *EI2*, s.v. "Ushnū."

Morris, James. "Imaging Islam: Intellect and Imagination in Islamic Philosophy, Poetry, and Painting." In *Traversing the Heart: Journeys of the Inter-religious Imagination*, edited by Richard Kearney and Eileen Rizo-Patron, 303–327. Leiden: Brill, 2010.

Moustafa, Ahmed, and Stefan Sperl. *The Cosmic Script: Sacred Geometry and the Science of Arabic Penmanship*. Rochester, VT: Inner Traditions, 2014.

Muḥammad, Jamāl, and Wafāʾ Jumuʿa. *Jazīrat al-ʿarab*. Mansoura: Dār al-Wafāʾ, 1984–1986.

Murata, Kazuyo. *Beauty in Sufism: The Teachings of Rūzbihān Baqlī*. Albany: State University of New York Press, 2017.

Murata, Sachiko. "The Angels." In Nasr, ed., *Islamic Spirituality*, 1:324–344.

———. *The Tao of Islam*. Albany: State University of New York Press, 1992.

Nasr, Seyyed Hossein. *The Garden of Truth*. New York: HarperOne, 2007.

———. "The Heart of the Faithful Is the Throne of the All-Merciful." In *Paths to the Heart: Sufism and the Christian East*, edited by James Cutsinger, 32–45. Bloomington: World Wisdom, 2002.

———. *Islamic Art and Spirituality*. Albany: State University of New York Press, 1987.

———, ed. *Islamic Spirituality*. New York: Crossroad, 1987–1991.

———. *Religion and the Order of Nature*. New York: Oxford University Press, 1996.

———. *REP*, s.v. "Mystical Philosophy in Islam."

———. "Spiritual Chivalry." In Nasr, ed., *Islamic Spirituality*, 2:304–318.

Nguyen, Martin. "Exegesis of the *ḥurūf al-muqaṭṭaʿa*: Polyvalency in Sunnī Traditions of Qur'anic Interpretation." *Journal of Qur'anic Studies* 14, no. 2 (2012): 1–28.

Ogunnaike, Oludamini. "Philosophical Sufism in the Sokoto Caliphate: The Case of Shaykh Dan Tafa." In *Islamic Scholarship in Africa: New Directions and Global Contexts*, edited by Ousmane Kane, 136–168. London: James Currey, 2021.

———. *Poetry in Praise of Prophetic Perfection: A Study of West African Arabic Madīḥ Poetry and Its Precedents*. Cambridge: Islamic Texts Society, 2020.

Ohlander, Erik. "al-Junayd al-Baghdādī: Chief of the Sect." In Ridgeon, ed., *Routledge Handbook on Sufism*, 32–45.

Ormsby, Eric. "The Taste of Truth: The Structure of Experience in al-Ghazālī's *al-Munqidh min al-ḍalāl*." In *Islamic Studies Presented to Charles J. Adams*, edited by Wael Hallaq and Donald Little, 133–152. Leiden: Brill, 1991.

———. *Theodicy in Islamic Thought: The Dispute Over al-Ghazālī's "Best of All Possible Worlds."* Princeton: Princeton University Press, 1984.

Papan-Matin, Firoozeh. "Gisudaraz, an Early Chishti Leader of the Deccan, and His Relationship with Twelfth-Century Mystics of Iran." *Journal for Deccan Studies* 7, no. 2 (2009): 112–132.

Pourjavady, Nasrollah. "ʿĀlam-i khayāl az naẓar-i Aḥmad Ghazālī." *Maʿārif* 8 (1986): 3–54.

———. *Bābā Ṭāhir*. Tehran: Farhang-i Muʿāṣir, 2015.

———. "Ḥallāj dar *Sawāniḥ*-i Aḥmad Ghazālī." In Āshtiyānī et al., eds., *Consciousness and Reality*, 286–294.

———. "Love and the Metaphors of Wine and Drunkenness in Persian Sufi Poetry." In *Metaphor and Imagery in Persian Poetry*, edited by Ali Asghar Seyed-Gohrab, 125–136. Leiden: Brill, 2012.

———. "Stories of Aḥmad al-Ghazālī 'Playing the Witness' in Tabrīz (Shams-i Tabrīzī's Interest in *shāhid bāzī*)." Translated by Scott Kugle. In *Reason and Inspiration in Islam: Theology, Philosophy and Mysticism in Muslim Thought: Essays in Honour of Hermann Landolt*, edited by Todd Lawson, 200–220. London: I. B. Tauris in association with The Institute of Ismaili Studies, 2005.

———. *Zindagī wa-āthār-i Shaykh Abū'l-Ḥasan Bustī*. Tehran: Muʾassasa-yi Muṭālaʿāt wa-Taḥqīqāt-i Farhangī, 1985.

Renard, John. "Abū Bakr in Tradition and Early Hagiography." In *Tales of God's Friends*, edited by John Renard, 15–29. Berkeley: University of California Press, 2009.

———. *Friends of God: Images of Piety, Commitment, and Servanthood*. Berkeley: University of California Press, 2008.

Ridgeon, Lloyd. *Awhad al-Dīn Kirmānī and the Controversy of the Sufi Gaze*. London: Routledge, 2017.

———. *Morals and Mysticism in Persian Sufism*. Abingdon: Routledge, 2010.

———, ed. *Routledge Handbook on Sufism*. London: Routledge, 2021.

Ritter, Hellmut. *The Ocean of the Soul: Man, the World and God in the Stories of Farīd al-Dīn ʿAṭṭār*. Translated by John O'Kane with the editorial assistance of Bernd Radtke. Leiden: Brill, 2003.

———. "Philologika VII." *Der Islam* 21, no. 1 (1933): 84–109.

Rosenthal, Franz. "Some Minor Problems in the Qur'ân." In *The Joshua Starr Memorial Volume: Studies in History and Philology*, 67–84. New York: Conference on Jewish Relations, 1953.

Rustom, Mohammed. "Forms of Gnosis in Sulamī's Sufi Exegesis of the *Fātiḥa*." *Islam and Christian-Muslim Relations* 16, no. 4 (2005): 327–344.

———. "Philosophical Sufism." In *The Routledge Companion to Islamic Philosophy*, edited by Richard Taylor and Luis Xavier López-Farjeat, 399–411. New York: Routledge, 2016.

———. "Storytelling as Philosophical Pedagogy: The Case of Suhrawardī." In *Knowledge and Education in Classical Islam: Religious Learning between*

Continuity and Change, edited by Sebastian Günther, 1:404–416. Leiden: Brill, 2020.

———. "The Sufi Teachings of Dhu'l-Nun." *Sacred Web* 24 (2009): 69–79.

———. *The Triumph of Mercy: Philosophy and Scripture in Mullā Ṣadrā*. Albany: State University of New York Press, 2012.

Salamah-Qudsi, Arin. "The Exchange of Letters in Early Sufism: A Preliminary Study." *Bulletin of the School of Oriental and African Studies* 83, no. 3 (2020): 391–413.

———. *Sufism and Early Islamic Piety: Personal and Communal Dynamics*. Cambridge: Cambridge University Press, 2019.

Saleh, Walid. "A Piecemeal Qurʾān: *furqān* and Its Meaning in Classical Islam and Modern Qurʾānic Studies." *Jerusalem Studies in Arabic and Islam* 42 (2015): 31–71.

Sarshar, Houman. *EIr*, s.v. "Hamadān viii. Jewish Community."

Schimmel, Annemarie. *Calligraphy and Islamic Culture*. New York: New York University Press, 1984.

———. *And Muhammad Is His Messenger: The Veneration of the Prophet in Islamic Piety*. Chapel Hill: University of North Carolina Press, 1985.

———. *A Two-Colored Brocade: The Imagery of Persian Poetry*. Chapel Hill: University of North Carolina Press, 1992.

Sells, Michael. *Early Islamic Mysticism*. Mahwah: Paulist Press, 1996.

Shādruymanish, Muḥammad. "*Lawāʾiḥ* az kīst?" *Muṭālaʿāt-i ʿirfānī* 10 (2009): 203–224.

Shams, Mohammad Javad. *EIs*, s.v. "Baraka (Barakat) Hamadānī." Translated by Farzin Negahban.

———. *EIs*, s.v. "Abū al-Qāsim Kurragānī." Translated by Maryam Rezaee.

Sherrill, Sarah. *EIr*, s.v. "Carpets V: Flat-Woven Carpets."

Shoarian-Sattari, Naser. *EIs*, s.v. "Abū al-Qāsim al-Dargazīnī." Translated by Maryam Rezaee and Farzin Negahban.

Sugich, Michael. *Signs on the Horizons*. San Bernardino: printed by the author, 2013.

Sviri, Sara. *Perspectives on Early Islamic Mysticism: The World of al-Ḥakīm al-Tirmidhī and His Contemporaries*. Abingdon: Routledge, 2020.

Taleb, Lahouari R. "Sufi Tafsīr." In *The Routledge Companion to the Qur'an*, edited by George Archer, Maria Dakake, and Daniel Madigan, 291–302. New York: Routledge, 2021.

Tor, Deborah. "'Sovereign and Pious': The Religious Life of the Great Seljuq Sultans." In *The Seljuqs: Politics, Society and Culture*, edited by Christian Lange and Songül Mecit, 39–62. Edinburgh: Edinburgh University Press, 2011.

van Lit, L. W. C. *The World of Image in Islamic Philosophy: Ibn Sīnā, Suhrawardī, Shahrazūrī and Beyond*. Edinburgh: Edinburgh University Press, 2017.

Zaleski, John. "Sufi Asceticism and the *Sunna* of the Prophet in al-Junayd's *Adab al-muftaqir ilā Allāh*." *Oxford Journal of Islamic Studies* 32, no. 1 (2021): 1–26.

Zargar, Cyrus Ali. *The Polished Mirror: Storytelling and the Pursuit of Virtue in Islamic Philosophy and Sufism*. London: Oneworld, 2017.

———. *Religion of Love: Sufism and Self-Transformation in the Poetic Imagination of ʿAṭṭār*. Albany: State University of New York Press, forthcoming.

———. "Sober in Mecca, Drunk in Byzantium: Antinomian Space in the Poetry of ʿAṭṭār." *Journal of the American Academy of Religion* 89, no. 1 (2021): 272–297.

Index of Translated Texts

ʿAyn al-Quḍāt's works are listed in accordance with the number of times they have been cited, from most to least.

Tamhīdāt (T)

1, §1: 9
2, §2: 195
3, §4: 169
3, §4: 165
3–4, §4: 183
4, §5: 145
5, §6: 133
5–6, §7: 147
6, §8: 168
7, §9: 168
7, §10: 169
7, §11: 174
8, §11: 146
8–9, §12: 121
9, §12: 138
9, §13: 137
9, §13: 138
9, §13: 138
10, §15: 134
10–11, §15: 134
11, §15: 137
11–12, §16: 171
12, §17: 285n109
12–13, §18: 114
13, §19: 128
14, §20: 234
14–15, §21: 117
15, §22: 27
16, §24: 122
17, §26: 127
19, §29: 128
19, §29: 130
19, §30: 130
20, §31: 72
20, §31: 131
21, §32: 142
21, §33: 111
21, §33: 236
22, §33: 127
22, §33: 239
22, §33: 239
22–23, §34: 239
23, §35: 130
24, §36: 119
24, §36: 119
24, §36: 129
24, §36: 130
25–26, §38: 114
29, §41: 202
29, §42: 204

***Tamhīdāt* (*T*)** *(continued)*
29, §42: 205
30, §43: 200
30, §43: 203
30, §43: 217
30, §44: 132
30, §44: 138
31–32, §45: 133
32–33, §45: 136
32, §46: 132
34, §48: 138
35, §49: 134
36, §50: 182
38, §52: 272n29
38, §53: 127
42, §59: 51
45, §62: 152
49, §67: 198
49, §68: 207
50, §68: 229
53, §72: 183
55, §75: 182
55, §75: 182
56, §75: 143
56–57, §77: 155
57, §77: 198
58, §78: 157
58, §78: 101
58–59, §79: 156
59, §80: 156
60, §81: 155
62, §84: 158
62–63, §85: 154
63, §85: 154
63, §85: 157
64, §87: 38
64, §87: 224–225
65, §88: 118
66, §91: 238
68, §94: 113
68, §94: 114
68, §94: 114
70, §97: 128
70, §98: 93
70–71, §98: 93
71, §98: 94
72, §99: 132
72, §99: 145
73, §101: 189
73, §101: 206
74, §102: 188
74, §102: 188
74, §102: 189
74, §102: 200
74, §103: 200
75, §104: 188
76, §106: 190
76, §106: 192
76, §107: 191
76–77, §107: 193
77, §108: 188
77, §108: 192
77, §108: 193
78, §109: 190
79, §112: 94
80, §114: 96
81, §116: 96
81, §116: 96
82, §118: 96
83, §119: 95
83, §119: 257
84, §121: 95
90–91, §128: 100
91, §129: 97
92, §130: 98
92, §131: 129
92–93, §131: 119
94, §133: 99
94, §134: 123
95, §135: 98
95, §135: 99
96, §136: 223
96, §136: 232
96, §137: 222

96–97, §137: 223
97, §137: 234
97, §138: 222
98, §139: 228
98, §140: 233
98, §140: 233
99, §141: 235
100, §141: 235
101, §142: 234
101, §142: 234
101, §142: 234
101, §143: 252
102, §143: 252
102, §144: 232
103, §145: 144
104, §148: 229
105, §149: 235
106, §150: 172
106, §150: 228
107, §151: 226
108, §152: 228
108, §153: 224
110, §156: 231
110, §157: 225
111, §157: 227
111, §158: 225
111, §158: 226
113, §160: 224
115, §162: 253
115, §162: 257
115–116, §163: 238
117, §164: 203
117, §164: 204
118, §165: 242
118–119, §166: 201
119, §168: 200
119, §168: 202
121, §169: 203
121, §169: 204
122, §170: 68
122, §170: 79
122–123, §171: 244
123, §172: 253
123–124, §172: 258
124, §172: 260
124–125, §173: 258
125, §174: 224
126, §175: 201
127, §176: 224
128, §177: 227
129, §180: 246
130, §181: 246
132, §182: 38
133, §184: 172
135–136, §187: 91
139, §190: 222
140, §191: 223
140, §191: 222
142–143, §193: 122
143, §194: 122
146, §198: 118
146, §198: 119
146, §198: 122
148–149, §201: 125
148, §201: 124
148, §201: 129
149–150, §202: 125
150, §203: 125
150, §203: 126
151, §204: 123
155, §209: 123
155–156, §209: 120
156, §210: 126
157, §211: 120
157–158, §212: 124
164–165, §220: 196
165–166, §221: 105
167, §223: 105
167, §223: 105
168, §224: 162
168, §224: 163
168, §224: 165
168–169, §224: 177
169, §225: 162

***Tamhīdāt* (*T*)** *(continued)*
169, §225: 162
169, §225: 173
172, §228: 174
172, §228: 174
173, §229: 174
175, §232: 177
175, §232: 178
175, §233: 179
175–176, §233: 181
176, §233: 180
176–177, §234: 164
177, §234: 165
177, §234: 173
177, §234: 179
177–178, §235: 170
178, §236: 153
179–180, §237: 230
180–181, §238: 71
181, §238: 71
181–182, §239: 238
184, §242: 167
185, §242: 72
185–186, §243: 73
186, §244: 208
186–187, §245: 210
187–188, §245: 207
188–189, §246: 87
189, §247: 84
189, §247: 208
190, §247: 84
195, §252: 115
196, §254: 27
197–198, §256: 121
198–199, §257: 92
199–200, §258: 100
204, §263: 233
204, §263: 242
204–205, §263: 256
205–206, §265: 52
206–207, §265: 245
207, §266: 41
207, §266: 232
208, §267: 245
209, §268: 241
209, §268: 244
209, §269: 240
209, §269: 241
211, §270: 201
211–212, §271: 242
211–212, §271: 244
212–213, §272: 209
214–215, §275: 243
215, §275: 246
216, §277: 233
216, §277: 233
217, §277: 207
217, §278: 251
217, §278: 251
218, §279: 250
219, §281: 117
220–221, §282: 251
221, §283: 230
221–222, §284: 216
222, §285: 231
223, §288: 214
224, §289: 216
224, §289: 218
227, §293: 212
227, §294: 206
229, §297: 250
229, §297: 250
230, §299: 50
231–232, §301: 53
233, §302: 209
233–234, §303: 116
234, §304: 34
235, §305: 28
235, §305: 50
235–236, §306: 53
236, §306: 50
237, §307: 233
237, §307: 232
238, §308: 233

238, §309: 234
240, §313: 233
242, §315: 137
242, §316: 92
242, §316: 235
243, §318: 230
244, §318: 229
244–245, §318: 218
245, §320: 229
246, §322: 102
246–247, §323: 101
247, §324: 42
247–248, §325: 31
248, §326: 197
248, §326: 197
248, §326: 199
249, §326: 199
249, §327: 27
249, §327: 196
250, §327: 29
250–251, §328: 30
251, §329: 50
252, §330: 115
255, §335: 69
255–256, §336: 70
257, §338: 68
257, §339: 70
258, §340: 202
263, §346: 62–63
263–264, §347: 195
264, §347: 73
265, §347: 247
266, §349: 196
266, §350: 51
268, §351: 98
268, §351: 194
268, §352: 194
269, §352: 56
269, §352: 97
269, §353: 51
271, §355: 142
271–272, §355: 142
272, §356: 249
273, §357: 154
273, §357: 154
273, §357: 154
274, §359: 142
275, §360: 249–250
279–280, §375: 251
280–281, §366: 32
281, §366: 141
283, §367: 158
283, §367: 235
283, §368: 223
284, §368: 223
284, §368: 252
284, §369: 237
285, §370: 236
286, §372: 238
286, §372: 254
286–287, §373: 129
287, §373: 129
287, §374: 106
287–288, §374: 108
288, §374: 109
288, §375: 106
288–289, §376: 106
289, §377: 107
289–290, §378: 129
290, §379: 148
291, §381: 226
291, §382: 226
292, §383: 107
292, §384: 239
293, §385: 102
293, §385: 105
293–294, §385: 103
294, §385: 255
294, §386: 102
295, §387: 253
295, §387: 255
295, §387: 255
295, §387: 258
295–296, §387: 255

***Tamhīdāt* (*T*)** *(continued)*
296, §388: 103
296–297, §388: 103
297, §389: 104
297, §389: 253
297, §389: 254
298, §390: 104
299–300, §393: 257
300, §394: 29
300, §394: 257
300–301, §394: 53
301, §395: 71
301–302, §395: 196
303, §397: 33
303, §398: 198
303–304, §399: 159
304, §399: 62
304, §399: 64
304, §400: 64
304–305, §401: 236
305, §401: 80
305–306, §402: 159
307, §404: 109
309, §406: 10
310, §407: 26
310, §408: 72
311, §409: 131
312, §410: 131
312, §410: 132
312–313, §410: 132
313–314, §412: 247
316, §414: 212
319, §417: 154
319–320, §418: 109
320, §418: 109
320, §419: 113
320, §419: 254
321, §420: 254
321, §420: 255
322, §421: 108
322, §422: 33
323, §422: 195
323, §423: 196
323, §423: 197
323, §423: 236
323–324, §424: 26
324, §424: 69
324, §424: 70
324–325, §425: 243
326, §427: 107
327, §428: 245
327, §429: 255
327–328, §430: 73
328, §431: 256
332–333, §439: 133
333, §439: 135
336, §443: 62
337, §443: 297n91
337, §445: 56
338, §448: 58
339, §449: 237
339, §449: 237
340, §451: 246
340–341, §452: 115
341, §452: 233
341, §452: 244
341, §452: 254
341–342, §453: 231
342–343, §454: 201
343, §454: 71
347, §459: 32
348, §461: 191
348–349, §462: 31
349–350, §463: 240
353, §468: 146
353–354, §469: 34
354, §470: 10

***Nāma-hā* (*N*)**

I 5, §7: 164
I 7, §8: 163–164
I 16, §17: 12
I 21–22, §24: 171

I 22, §24: 161
I 22, §24: 162
I 22, §24: 225
I 24, §25: 90
I 25, §27: 163
I 25–26, §27: 91
I 42, §47: 167
I 42, §47: 178
I 42, §47: 178
I 43, §49: 163
I 43, §49: 163
I 44, §50: 112
I 46–47, §54: 44
I 47, §54: 135
I 52, §62: 42
I 54, §67: 112
I 64, §80: 223
I 65, §83: 226
I 65–66, §83: 112
I 69, §88: 112
I 73, §93: 16
I 74, §95: 62
I 74, §96: 134
I 75, §98: 213
I 82, §107: 111
I 84, §112: 170
I 86, §115: 144
I 86, §117: 127
I 87, §117: 127
I 88, §120: 31
I 91, §124: 166
I 91, §124: 199
I 92, §126: 144
I 92, §126: 144
I 96, §132: 213
I 96, §132: 218
I 96, §133: 199
I 97, §133: 215
I 97, §134: 216
I 97, §134: 217
I 97–98, §135: 219
I 106, §149: 39
I 111, §159: 95
I 113, §163: 145
I 113, §163: 145
I 114, §164: 41
I 114, §165: 39
I 114–115, §166: 43
I 123, §178: 225
I 126, §181: 175
I 126, §182: 178–179
I 132–133, §§190–191: 69
I 133, §191: 67
I 134, §192: 67
I 134, §192: 67
I 134, §192: 67
I 138, §200: 67
I 144, §209: 65
I 149, §217: 171
I 149, §218: 12
I 156, §230: 245
I 157, §232: 46
I 158, §234: 82
I 164, §248: 26
I 166, §251: 163
I 166, §251: 165
I 173, §264: 64
I 173, §264: 66
I 178, §273: 63
I 180, §279: 206
I 182, §281: 43
I 209, §335: 42
I 213–214, §344: 157
I 214, §344: 157
I 225, §370: 114
I 225, §371: 127
I 232–233, §383: 66
I 233–234, §385: 45
I 242, §400: 166
I 253, §421: 201
I 269, §446: 138
I 269, §446: 138
I 270, §448: 27
I 270, §448: 133

***Nāma-hā* (N)** *(continued)*
I 270–271, §449: 42
I 273, §453: 12
I 274, §454: 37
I 274, §454: 128
I 279, §465: 192
I 279, §465: 193
I 280, §466: 27
I 280, §466: 190
I 280, §466: 192
I 280, §466: 192
I 280, §466: 193
I 304, §509: 208
I 314, §524: 211
I 315, §525: 217
I 333, §558: 163
I 334, §559: 177
I 343, §573: 78
I 345, §576: 79
I 349, §582: 163
I 349, §582: 165
I 351, §584: 165
I 351, §584: 167
I 370, §617: 26
I 373, §621: 132
I 378, §629: 152
I 390, §652: 173
I 390, §653: 182
I 401, §667: 78
I 401, §668: 78
I 401, §668: 79
I 402, §670: 80
I 415, §695: 203
I 415, §695: 217
I 451, §752: 101

II 7, §9: 86
II 25, §34: 29
II 28, §40: 252
II 47–48, §63: 166
II 54, §70: 124
II 69, §94: 217
II 76–77, §105: 166
II 92, §128: 113
II 92, §128: 118
II 92, §129: 112
II 95, §133: 101
II 98, §136: 175
II 98, §137: 180
II 99, §138: 181
II 99, §139: 182
II 99, §139: 183
II 102, §145: 164
II 111, §160: 26
II 128, §188: 223
II 143, §208: 175
II 143, §208: 175
II 143, §208: 175
II 153, §224: 228
II 153, §225: 38
II 153, §225: 38
II 160, §237: 216
II 187, §280: 212
II 187, §281: 214
II 187, §281: 216
II 187, §281: 217
II 199, §293: 27
II 206, §304: 12
II 211, §314: 39
II 219, §327: 232
II 219, §327: 232
II 219, §328: 232
II 232, §349: 207
II 246, §371: 176
II 252, §379: 111
II 254, §382: 62
II 262, §395: 238
II 268, §401: 84
II 268, §401: 86
II 269, §402: 81
II 269, §402: 82
II 269, §402: 83
II 269, §402: 83
II 281, §423: 81

II 292–293, §441: 76
II 294, §444: 76
II 294, §444: 77
II 307, §463: 237
II 307, §464: 83
II 308, §465: 26
II 308, §465: 28
II 308, §465: 82
II 308, §465: 176
II 344, §528: 26
II 357, §554: 48
II 358, §555: 48
II 360, §557: 49
II 361, §561: 49
II 368, §573: 134
II 370, §577: 118
II 374–375, §583: 42
II 375, §584: 46
II 375, §584: 47
II 388–389, §609: 47
II 412, §650: 212
II 412, §650: 214
II 416, §657: 215
II 416, §657: 216
II 417, §658: 215
II 418, §660: 214
II 422, §666: 112
II 433, §683: 38
II 433, §683: 41
II 433–434, §683: 41
II 438, §689: 40
II 438, §689: 40
II 438, §689: 40
II 469, §730: 38
II 478, §747: 113
II 482, §754: 12
II 482, §755: 12

III 278, §3: 28
III 279, §4: 203
III 290, §18: 12
III 302, §42: 44
III 311, §57: 173
III 336, §95: 85
III 337, §99: 85
III 338, §100: 85
III 364, §150: 91
III 378, §182: 215
III 397, §219: 66
III 397, §219: 127
III 397, §219: 158
III 398, §221: 67
III 398, §221: 158
III 406, §234: 43
III 410, §238: 43
III 412, §242: 45
III 412, §243: 45
III 413, §245: 46
III 433, §272: 37
III 434, §274: 135
III 434, §274: 135

***Zubdat al-ḥaqāʾiq* (Z)**

§2: 15
§§13–14: 24
§14: 24
§28: 16
§31: 59
§31: 59
§33: 56
§33: 57
§34: 57
§34: 57
§34: 58
§46: 249
§47: 58
§47: 58
§50: 58
§54: 149
§58: 148
§58: 149
§60: 151
§65: 150

Zubdat al-ḥaqāʾiq (Z) *(continued)*
§65: 150
§67: 153
§67: 153
§71: 151
§72: 227
§81: 65
§81: 66
§81: 66
§95: 67
§107: 67
§116: 60
§121: 147
§122: 145
§132: 136
§133: 136
§134: 25
§137: 136
§137: 136
§141: 60
§141: 61
§142: 61
§142: 61
§160: 25
§160: 25
§176: 150
§179: 106
§181: 106
§183: 106
§184: 151
§184: 151
§186: 148
§187: 148
§188: 150
§191: 234

Shakwā'l-gharīb (Sh)

1: 47
5: 48
31: 17

[Wāqiʿa-hā] (W)

2 (= N III 402, §§225–226): 31
2 (= N III 402, §§225–226): 31

Risāla-yi Jamālī (RJ)

1 (= N II 483, §758): 294n16

Nuzhat al-ʿushshāq (NU)

243.1: 18

Index of Quranic Passages

1:2 Praise be to God, Lord of the worlds, 168
2:1 *Alif, Lām, Mīm*, 178
2:2 in which there is no doubt, 145
2:3 and they spend from that which We have provided them, 39
2:4 and who are certain of the next world, 225
2:6 Surely it is the same for them whether thou warnest them or warnest them not. . . . , 177
2:21 Worship your Lord, who created you, 45
2:34 "Prostrate unto Adam!" ; he was among the unbelievers, 212, 213
2:54 "Slay your souls!," 117
2:115 Wheresoever you turn, there is the face of God, 95
2:151 he teaches you what you knew not, 72
2:152 Remember Me, 38
2:189 Come into houses by their doors, 31
2:255 the Living, the Self-Abiding . . . they encompass nothing of His knowledge, 67, 147
3:7 firmly rooted in knowledge, 32, 133
3:31 Say, "If you love God, follow me, and God will love you," 200
3:37 Thus her Lord accepted her in a beautiful way, 101
3:79 "Be lordly people," 236
3:85 Whosoever seeks a religion other than submission. . . . , 245
3:103 on the brink of a pit of fire, 23
3:173 Those to whom the people say. . . . "an excellent guardian is He!," 40
3:196 Let it not delude thee that those who disbelieve are free to come and go in the land, 41
4:77 "Paltry is the enjoyment of this world," 41
4:80 Whosoever obeys the Messenger has obeyed God, 72, 135, 138
4:97 "Was not God's earth vast enough that you might have migrated therein?," 128

4:100 Whosoever emigrates in the way of God. . . . ; whosoever forsakes. . . . , 41, 128
4:113 He taught thee what thou knewest not; God's bounty toward thee is tremendous, 72, 178
4:136 O you who believe! Believe in God and His Messenger, 243
4:143 Wavering between this [and that], being neither for one group nor for the other, 44
4:157 And they did not slay him, nor did they crucify him. . . . , 30
4:158 But God raised him up to Himself, 31
4:164 and unto Moses God spoke directly, 97
5:3 This day I have perfected for you your religion, 198
5:15 There has come unto you, from God, a light and a clear Book, 194, 197
5:54 He loves them, and they love Him, 72, 158, 180, 227, 258, 298n119
5:75 And his mother was truthful, 49
6:1 Praise be to God, who created the heavens and the earth. . . . , 79
6:12 has prescribed mercy for Himself, 100
6:14 "And He feeds and is not fed," 98
6:36 Only those who hear will respond. As for the dead, God will resurrect them, 167
6:59 nor is there anything moist or dry, but that it is in a clear Book, 162, 163
6:75 Thus did We show Abraham the dominion of the heavens and the earth, 171, 208
6:76 When the night grew dark upon him, he saw a star. He said, "This is my Lord!," 208
6:77 When he saw the moon rising he said, "This is my Lord!," 209
6:78 When he saw the sun rising . . . "This is my Lord!," 209
6:79 "Surely I have turned my face toward the one who created. . . . ," 193, 244
6:91 They did not measure God with His true measure. ; Say, "God!," then leave them, 156
6:97 the darknesses of land and ocean. ; We have separated the signs, 179, 200
6:103 Sight grasps Him not, but He grasps sight, 154, 159
6:115 The Word of thy Lord is fulfilled in truth and justice. None alters His Words, 208
6:153 "This indeed is My path made straight; so follow it," 128
7:1 *Alif, Mīm, Ṣād*, 176
7:12 "Thou hast created me from fire, while Thou hast

created him from clay," 204, 212
7:143 He came. ; "show me!" ; "Thou shalt not see Me; but look upon the mountain," 72, 158, 195
7:151 "The most merciful of the merciful," 78
7:155 "It is naught but Thy trial. . . . ," 87
7:157 the unlettered Prophet. ; and those who follow the light. . . . , 103
7:172 "Am I not your Lord?," 172
7:179 It is they who are heedless, 118
7:180 Unto God belong the most beautiful names; so call Him by them. . . . , 50
7:185 Or have they not contemplated the dominion of the heavens and the earth?, 154
7:194 Surely those whom you call upon apart from God are servants like you, 45
7:198 Thou seest them looking upon thee, but they see not, 197
7:204 And when the Quran is recited, hearken unto it, and listen. . . . , 172
8:4 It is they who truly are believers, 188
8:23 Had God known of any good in them, He would have made them to hear, 190
8:24 Respond to God and the Messenger. . . . ; God comes between a man and his heart, 122, 167
9:6 And if any of the idolaters seek asylum with thee. . . . , 172
9:28 The idolaters are surely unclean, 170
9:30 the Christians say that the Messiah is the son of God, 236
9:128 A Messenger has indeed come to you from yourselves, 155
10:3 Surely your Lord is God, who created the heavens and the earth in six days. . . . , 169
10:36 And most of them follow naught but conjecture. . . . , 237
10:93 and We provided them with good things, 230
11:6 There is no creature that crawls upon the earth but that its provision lies with God, 45
11:45 "the most just of judges," 78
12:39 the One, the Paramount, 58, 210
12:53 "Surely the soul commands to ugliness," 116, 120
12:106 And most of them believe not in God, save that they are associators, 45, 242, 243
13:16 "They have no power over what benefit or harm may come. . . . ," 45
13:17 Thus does God set forth the real and the unreal, 234

13:39 God obliterates what He will. . . . ; and with Him is the Mother of the Book, 183, 184
14:7 If you are grateful, I shall surely increase you, 101
14:34 And were you to count the blessings of God, you could not number them, 101
14:35 "And keep me and my children from worshipping idols," 241
14:48 on that Day the earth shall be changed into other than the earth, 93
15:21 And We do not send it down, save in a known measure, 215
15:72 By thy life, 72
15:87 We have indeed given thee the seven oft-repeated, and the tremendous Quran, 163
16:21 dead, not living, 167
16:43 Ask the people of the Reminder if you know not, 138
16:60 And unto God belongs the loftiest similitude, 57, 177
16:71 And God has favored some of you above others in provision, 183
16:93 He leads astray whomsoever He will and guides whomsoever He will, 86, 243
17:1 He carried, 72
17:14 "On this day, your soul suffices as a reckoner against you," 226
17:35 straight scale, 148
17:61 "Shall I prostrate unto one whom Thou hast created of clay?," 212
17:70 And We carry them over land and ocean, 230
17:82 And We send down in the Quran that which is a cure and a mercy. . . . , 294n16
17:85 they ask thee about the spirit. . . . , 125, 126
18:15 "These, our people, have taken gods apart from Him," 114
18:65 and We taught him knowledge from Our Presence, 53
18:70 "Question me not about anything. . . . ," 114
18:107 Those who believe and perform righteous deeds, theirs shall be the Gardens. . . . , 90–91
18:109 "If the ocean were ink for the Words of my Lord. . . . thereof to replenish it," 177–178
18:110 "I am only a mortal man like you"; Whosoever hopes for the meeting with his Lord. . . . , 91, 196
19:1 *Kāf, Hāʾ, Yāʾ, ʿAyn, Ṣād*, 178
19:17 He imaginalized himself to her as a mortal man, well-proportioned, 102
19:23 "Would that I had died before this and was utterly forgotten!," 49
19:83 We unleash the satans on the unbelievers, to incite them cunningly, 86
20:1 *Ṭāʾ, Hāʾ*, 176, 178

21:18 Nay, but We cast the real against the unreal, and it crushes it, 234
21:37 Soon shall I show you My signs; so seek not to hasten Me!, 128
21:104 that Day We shall roll up the sky like the rolling of scrolls used for writing, 199
21:107 And We sent thee not, save as a mercy unto the worlds, 71, 73, 100, 206
22:46 Have they not . . . ? ; Surely it is not the eyes that go blind. . . . , 118
22:52 And no Messenger or Prophet did We send before thee. . . . , 199
22:78 Strive in God as He should be striven in, 234
23:20 a tree issuing forth from Mount Sinai, 195
23:71 Were the Real to follow their caprices . . . would have been corrupted, 78
24:26 good women are for good men, 171
24:35 God is the light of the heavens and the earth. ; kindled from a blessed olive tree. ; even if no fire had touched it . . . ; Light upon light. . . . , 69, 195, 234
25:23 And We shall turn to whatever work they have done and make it scattered dust, 90
25:30 And the Messenger will say, "O my Lord! . . . ," 166, 170
25:43 Hast thou considered the one who takes his caprice as his god?, 201, 241
25:45 Hast thou not considered thy Lord, how He spreads out the shade?, 72
26:1 *Ṭā᾽, Sīn, Mīm*, 178
26:79 "He feeds me and gives me drink," 230, 281n34
26:212 they are debarred from hearing, 167
27:34 "Surely kings, when they enter a town, corrupt it," 229
27:80 Surely thou dost not make the dead hear, 167, 169
28:30 "O Moses!," 158
28:51 We have joined the Word for them, 179
28:68 And thy Lord creates what He will, and chooses; no choice have they, 78
29:6 Surely God is beyond need of the worlds, 46
29:17 "Surely those whom you worship apart from God . . . seek your provision with God," 45
29:49 Nay, it is but clear signs in the breasts of those who have been given knowledge, 133
29:64 And surely the abode of the next world is life indeed, 109
29:69 Those who strive in Us, We shall surely guide them in Our ways, 93, 234
30:7 They know an outward aspect of the life of this world . . . , 226

30:41 Corruption has appeared on land and in the ocean, 146
31:27 And if all the trees on earth were pens. . . . , 178
32:11 Say, "The angel of death will take you," 86
33:4 God has not placed two hearts in the breast of any man, 73
33:41 frequent invocation, 38
33:46 a luminous lamp, 197
33:62 and you will never find alteration in the custom of God, 208
33:72 Surely We offered the Trust unto the heavens and the earth. . . . , 176–177
34:1 Praise be to God unto whom belongs whatsoever is in the heavens. . . . , 101
34:54 And a barrier is set between them . . . they were in confounding doubt, 225
35:3 Is there a creator other than God who provides for you?, 86
36:1 *Yāʾ, Sīn*, 178, 208
36:2 By the Wise Quran, 208
36:82 His command when He desires a thing is only to say to it "Be!," and it is, 213
37:96 "God created you and what you do," 86
37:99 "Surely I am going unto my Lord," 95
37:173 Our host will surely be victorious, 188
38:72 I breathed into him of My Spirit, 125
38:78 "And surely My curse shall be upon thee until the Day of Judgment," 206, 212
38:82 "By Thy exaltedness, I shall certainly cause them to err, altogether!," 200, 217
39:10 "God's earth is vast," 41
39:22 What of one . . . a light from his Lord . . . ? Woe to those whose hearts are hardened!, 133
39:42 God takes souls at the moment of their death, 86
39:65 if thou dost associate, thy work will surely come to naught, 192
39:73 "Well done! Now enter it, abiding," 171
39:74 How excellent is the wage of the workers!, 217
40:1 *Ḥāʾ, Mīm*, 180
40:11 They will say, "Our Lord, Thou hast caused us to die twice over. . . . ," 109
40:82 Have they not journeyed upon the earth and observed?, 118, 128
41:44 "They are called from a place far off," 226
41:53 We shall show them Our signs . . . He is the Real, 170, 225
42:11 There is nothing like Him, 258
42:52 thus have We revealed unto thee a spirit of Our command, 125
42:53 Truly affairs are journeying unto God, 157
43:23 "We found our fathers upon a creed, and we

surely follow in their footsteps," 113
43:32 We have divided their livelihood among them, 183
43:85 And with Him lies knowledge of the Hour, 106
45:13 for you whatsoever is in the heavens . . . altogether, 101
45:23 So hast thou considered the one who takes his caprice as his god?, 114, 154, 201, 241
47:12 They enjoy themselves and eat as cattle eat, 45
47:24 Do they not contemplate the Quran, or do their hearts have locks upon them?, 164
48:2 That God may forgive thee thy sins that went before, and those that are to come, 250
48:4 He it is who sends down tranquility into the hearts of the believers, 100
48:6 ugly thoughts about God; upon them is an ugly turn!, 57
48:10 Surely those who pledge allegiance unto thee. . . . , 126
48:26 they are more worthy of it and deserving of it, 164
49:4 Surely those who call thee from behind the apartments, most of them understand not, 135
49:5 Had they been patient until thou camest out unto them. . . . , 114
49:12 And do not spy, 113
50:1 *Qāf*. By the glorious Quran, 195
50:22 "You were indeed in heedlessness of this . . . today your sight is piercing!," 226
50:37 Surely in that is a reminder for whosoever has a heart, 133, 165, 175
51:21 and within yourselves—do you not see?, 130, 155
51:55 And remind, for surely the reminder benefits the believers, 128, 177
51:56 I did not create jinn and mankind, save to worship Me, 249–250
53:3–4 he does not speak out of caprice. . . . , 126
53:14 the lote tree of the boundary, 195
53:17 The gaze swerved not, nor did it transgress, 218
53:30 That is the extent of their knowledge, 144
53:42 the ultimate end is unto thy Lord, 70
54:24 "Shall we follow a single mortal man from amongst us? . . . ," 196
54:32 We have indeed made the Quran easy to remember; but is there anyone to remember?, 180
55:1–2 The All-Merciful taught the Quran, 119, 146, 178
55:26–27 All that is upon it is perishing . . . possessor of majesty and bounty, 242
56:79 None touch it, save those made pure, 170

56:95 the truth of certainty, 132, 145
57:4 He is with you wheresoever you are, 129
57:25 We have indeed sent Our Messengers with clear proofs . . . and the scale, 148
58:22 God has inscribed faith in their hearts, 180
59:13 Surely you incite more intense dread in their breasts than God. . . . , 44
59:21 Had We made this Quran descend upon a mountain. . . . , 163
59:22 the All-Merciful, the Ever-Merciful, 206
59:23 Peace, the Believer, the Protector. ; the Compeller, the Proud, 142, 206
59:24 He is God, the Creator, the Maker, the Form-Giver, 103, 210
64:2 He it is who created you; among you are unbelievers and among you are believers, 238
64:6 They say, "Will a mortal man guide us?" So they disbelieved, 196
64:11 And whosoever believes in God, He guides his heart, 243
65:1 Perhaps God will bring something new to pass thereafter, 128
65:2 And whosoever is wary of God, He will appoint a way out for him, 230
65:3 He will provide for him whence he reckons not, 230
65:12 God it is who created the seven heavens, and from the earth the like thereof. . . . , 169
66:8 "Our Lord, complete our light for us," 70, 195
66:11 "My Lord, build for me a house near unto Thee in the Garden," 91
67:3–4 who created seven heavens one upon another . . . will return to thee, humbled, wearied, 79–80
70:23 Those who are constant in their prayers, 96
70:34 Those who are mindful of their prayers, 96
71:17 And God made you grow forth from the earth like plants, 171
75:2 the blaming soul, 116
75:20 love the ephemeral, 225
75:21 and forsake the next world, 225
75:22 Faces that Day shall be radiant, 156
75:23 gazing upon their Lord, 156
76:21 a wine most pure, 107
76:28 and whensoever We will, We shall entirely change their likenesses, 154
79:40 As for one who fears standing before his Lord. . . . , 116
79:46 The day they see it, it will be as if they had tarried but an evening. . . . , 131
85:21 Preserved Tablet, 120
86:9 secrets are laid bare, 107
89:27–30 O tranquil soul! Return to thy Lord, content, contenting. . . . , 107

93:1–2 By the morning brightness, and by the night when still, 72
93:6 Did He not find thee an orphan and shelter thee?, 196
94:1 Did We not expand for thee thy breast?, 118, 121
95:1 the olive, 195
96:4–5 He taught by the Pen. ; taught man that which he knew not, 120, 178
100:10 And what lies within breasts is made known, 107
102:5 the knowledge of certainty, 15
109:1 Say, "O unbelievers!," 168
109:6 "Unto you is your religion, and unto me is my religion," 237
110:1 When God's help and victory comes, 171
112:1–2 Say, "He, God, is One; God, the Self-Sufficient," 98

Index of Hadiths, Proverbs, and Sayings

A pleasant word is charity, 39
A man follows the religion of his intimate friend, 135
A man is abundant with his brother, 135
A man is with the one he loves, 143
A vile guide for man is his conjecture, 113, 164
Ablution is disconnection and prayer is union. . . . (Shiblī), 94
Affability with people is charity, 39
Beware of glancing at beardless youths. . . . (Sufi saying), 255
Blessed be the one who sees me and believes in me, 155
Caprice is the most hated god that is worshipped on the earth, 114
Children are throwing stones at him. (Arabic expression), 31
Chivalry is not fitting for anyone except Iblis and Aḥmad. (Ḥallāj), 214
Consult your heart, even if the muftis give you a fatwa, 120
Cursed be the servant of the dirham! . . . , 114
Deeds are by intentions. . . . , 90
Die before you die, 296n67
Disclosing the secret of lordship is unbelief. (Sufi saying), 50, 51
Do as you please, for I have forgiven you. (*ḥadīth qudsī*), 223
Every striver is correct, 237
Faith and unbelief are two stations beyond the Throne. . . . (Sufi saying), 243
Follow the religion of old women, 226
Everything has a heart, and the heart of the Quran is *Yā'*, *Sīn*, 178
Glory be to Me! (Basṭāmī), 158
Glory to the one who has not given people a way to recognize Him. . . . (Abū Bakr), 156
God created Adam in the form of the All-Merciful, 197, 306n52
God created Adam and his offspring in the form of the All-Merciful, 103
God created people in darkness. Then He sprinkled some of His light upon them, 189
God has a Garden in which there are neither Houris, nor palaces, nor milk, nor honey, 91
God has disclosed Himself to His servants in the Quran. (Jaʿfar al-Ṣādiq), 170
God has fallen in love with Himself so much that He has no care for anybody. . . . (Sufi saying), 250

God has placed the truth upon the tongue of ʿUmar, and in his heart, 271n17
God has servants whose hearts are more luminous than the sun. . . . , 292n44
God is goodly, and He only accepts the goodly, 170–171
God is the Source of existents. (Ḥallāj), 68
God looks at neither your forms nor your actions, but He looks at your hearts, 119
God purifies the Sufis from their attributes and makes them pure. . . . (Basṭāmī), 247
Guide of the bewildered. (Shiblī), 24
Have mercy on those below you, and the One above you will have mercy on you, 39
He is God. (Basṭāmī), 247
He is the one who is poor . . . the Sufi is God. (Basṭāmī), 247
He praises Himself through Himself. (Sufi saying), 101
He used to walk, but he had no shadow, 197
He who does not delight in the striking of the Beloved. . . . (Dhū'l-Nūn), 218
He who does not taste, does not know. (proverb), 28
He who does not taste, does not recognize. (proverb), 134
He who draws near to Me a hand's span. . . . I come to him running. (*ḥadīth qudsī*), 130
He who has no master has no religion. (Sufi saying), 134
He who resembles a people is one of them, 200
He who recognizes himself recognizes his Lord. (Sufi saying), 153, 251
He who sees me has seen the Real, 155, 197, 198, 242
He who works for the next world. . . . (similar saying attributed to ʿAlī), 40
His prayer is laudation for Himself, 96
How strange are a people who are led to Paradise in chains but are unwilling to go!, 91
I am the dot under the *bāʾ*. (Shiblī), 298n120
I am the Real! (Ḥallāj), 145, 158, 246
I cannot enumerate Your laudation. You are as You have lauded Yourself, 100, 258
I created the world for you, and I created you for Myself. (*ḥadīth qudsī*), 71
I do not look at anything except that I see God in it. (Abū Bakr), 143
I follow the religion of my Lord (Ḥallāj), 145, 158, 202, 246
If only the Lord of Muhammad had not created Muhammad!, 100
I have a moment with God, 94
I have been sent as a caller, but guidance does not come from me in any way. . . . , 208
I have been sent to perfect noble character traits, 122
I have seen Muṣṭafā seven hundred times . . . I have been seeing myself! (Aḥmad Ghazālī), 104
I praised the Lord through the Lord. (likely Dhū'l-Nūn), 102
I recognized my Lord through my Lord. (Dhū'l-Nūn), 102

I saw my Lord on the night of the Ascension in the form of a beardless youth. . . . , 255
I saw my Lord on the night of the Ascension in the most beautiful form, 103, 156, 191
I saw my Lord through my Lord. . . . (Dhū'l-Nūn), 159
I saw the Lord of exaltedness in the form of my mother. (Abū Bakr Qaḥṭabī), 103
I seek refuge in You from associationism and doubt, 192
I spend the night with my Lord. . . . , 195
I saw the makeup of the universe . . . neither this nor that remained. (Abū'l-Ḥasan Bustī), 247
I was a Hidden Treasure and I loved to be recognized. (*ḥadīth qudsī*), 99, 249, 250
I will eat death. . . . (Ḥātim al-Aṣamm), 108
If I explain the verse . . . you would declare me an unbeliever." (Abū Hurayra), 169
If I were to interpret the verse . . . you would stone me. (Ibn ʿAbbās), 169
If Iblis' light appeared to people, he would be worshipped as a god. (al-Ḥasan al-Baṣrī), 201
If you can sacrifice your spirit, then come! . . . (Dhū'l-Nūn), 117
In everything there is a sign indicating that He is one. (Abū'l-ʿAtāhiya), 143
In the cloak of a mortal man, Muṣṭafā appeared with a body. . . . (Sahl al-Tustarī), 197
In the hearts of His believing servants, 119
Islam is built upon five, 134
Leave yourself and come! (Basṭāmī), 129
Love for one's homeland is a part of faith, 48
Love is a fire in the heart—it burns away everything other than the Beloved. (Shiblī), 234
Love is God's greatest punishment. (Sufi saying), 234
Many a reciter of the Quran is there whom the Quran curses. (Mālik b. Anas), 169
Modesty is a part of faith, 46
Most of the people in the Garden are foolish. . . . , 226
Munkar is one's ugly works, and Nakīr is one's wholesome works. (ascribed to Avicenna), 107
My Friends are under My robe—none knows them but Me. (*ḥadīth qudsī*), 51
My God! For how long will You kill the lovers? (Shiblī), 52
My heart saw my Lord. (ʿUmar), 154
My Lord has neither night nor day, 95
My Lord taught me etiquette, 178
Neither the heavens nor the earth embrace Me. . . . (*ḥadīth qudsī*), 118
"No god but God" is My fortress. . . . (*ḥadīth qudsī*), 189
No one other than my Lord has seen my Lord. (Nūrī), 159
None knows God but God. (Kharrāz), 56
O Bilāl! Relieve us!, 122
O David! Come close to Me through enmity with your soul. (*ḥadīth qudsī*), 121

O God! Everyone seeks You for gentleness and comfort, but I seek You for tribulation. (Shiblī), 230
O God! For whom were You? . . . For whom will You be? (Shiblī), 251
O God! Give me a light in my face, a light in my body, a light in my heart. . . . , 195–196
O God! I live through You and die through You, 255
O God! Whiten my face with the light of Your noble face, 73
O how I long to meet my Brothers!, 73
O Ḥumayra! Speak with me!, 122
O Light of light!, 70
O Lord, He was a servant of Yours, a man of faith. . . . (Shiblī), 52
O my Lord! You are a mirror for me and I am a mirror for You! (Basṭāmī), 141
One night, I was with ʿAlī b. Abī Ṭālib. . . . a pitcher next to a tremendous ocean. (Ibn ʿAbbās), 174
One of the pulls of the Real equals the work of both the worlds, 299n5
Only like can know like. (Presocratic saying), 156
Part of a man's felicity is in resembling his father. (proverb), 236
People are asleep; when they die, they awaken, 228
Poverty is almost unbelief, 246
Poverty is my pride, 247
Pursue matters using your own opinion, 121
Reflect on God's blessings, but do not reflect on God's Essence, 155, 159
Seek bounty from the merciful ones of my community, living under their shelter, 133
Seek knowledge, even to China, 147
Speak to people in accordance with their intelligence, 168
Take on the character traits of God, 257
Take yourselves to account before you are taken to account. (ʿUmar), 148
That is, look at the light of Muhammad. (Ibn ʿAbbās), 195
The angel has a suggestion and the devil has a suggestion, 120
The angels were created from the light of exaltedness. . . . , 301
The believer is a mirror of the believer, 120, 141, 142
The believer takes his religion from God. . . . (possibly al-Ḥasan al-Baṣrī), 154
The best of what I and the Prophets before me have said is, "No god but God," 193
The entire world has known God, yet they have not recognized Him. . . . (Sufi saying), 251
The fast is Mine, and I recompense for it. (*ḥadīth qudsī*), 97
The first thing that God created was my light, 123, 196, 204
The Garden is a prison for the recognizers. . . . (Yaḥyā Muʿādh-i Rāzī), 91
The heart is the house of God. (Sufi saying), 130

The heart of the believer is between the two fingers of the All-Merciful, 119
The heart of the believer is the house of God. (Sufi saying), 119
The heart of the believer is the Throne of the All-Merciful, 119
The incapacity to perceive perception is perception. (Abū Bakr), 156, 157
The knowers are the heirs of the Prophets, 135
The knowers of my community are like the Israelite Prophets, 147
The light of Iblis is from the fire of exaltedness. . . . (al-Ḥasan al-Baṣrī), 201
The Messenger of God was perpetually in reflection, always in sorrow. (ʿĀʾisha), 102
The one who is not born twice shall not enter the Dominion of the heavens. (Jesus), 109
The parts of numbers are one in oneness. (Ḥallāj), 255
The prayer-performer is whispering to his Lord, 96
The Qadariyya are the Zoroastrians of this community, 81
The Quran does not mention enemies. . . . (ascribed to ʿUmar), 294n24
The Quran is God's banquet on earth, 170
The Quran is richness, with no poverty after it and no richness apart from it, 163
The Quran is the medicine, 165
The Quran was sent down in seven readings, each of which is clear and sufficient, 165
The Real speaks on the tongue of ʿUmar, 29
The recognizer is above what he says, but the knower is below what he says. (Sufi saying), 144
The repentance of people is from their sins. . . . (Basṭāmī), 193
The search for knowledge is an obligation upon every Muslim. . . . , 46
The sincere ones are in tremendous danger, 116
The soul is the greatest idol. (Sufi saying), 241
The spirit does not enter under the lowliness of "*Be!*" (Abū Bakr Qaḥṭabī), 124
The tale-bearer shall not enter the Garden, 113
The tongue of the state is more articulate . . . than the tongue of speech. (proverb), 271n13
The witness sees what the absent one does not see, 73
The world is a prison for the believer and a garden for the unbeliever, 280n6
The worst of men is one who eats alone, 100
There are no flaws in reports apart from their transmitters. (al-Sharīf al-Raḍī), 82
There is a kind of hidden knowledge that is not known to knowers. . . . , 133
There is a market in the Garden in which forms are sold, 103
There is a meaning in wine that is not in grapes. (al-Mutanabbī), 244

There is no repose for the believer apart from the encounter with God, 128
There is no difference between me and Him except that. . . . (Abū Bakr al-Warrāq), 249
There is no difference between me and my Lord except for two attributes. . . . (Ḥallāj), 246
There is no good for you in keeping the company of someone . . . as sinless. (Dhū'l-Nūn), 42
There is no master more penetrating than love. (Aḥmad Ghazālī), 223
There is no one in the Garden other than God. (Shiblī), 91
There is no Prophet but that he has a counterpart in his community, 210
There is no religion for one who has no master. (Sufi saying), 134
There is no report like seeing, 254
They are merely your works brought back to you, 107
Those worthy of the Quran are worthy of God, and are His chosen ones. 164, 165
Things are distinguished through their opposites. (proverb), 210
This world with respect to the next world . . . what it is that the finger returns with, 131
Through the fact that He brings opposites together. (Kharrāz), 302n103
We enter compelled, subsist in bewilderment, and exit unwillingly. (ascribed to a Greek sage), 124
Were it not for you, I would not have created the two worlds. (*ḥadīth qudsī*), 71
Were the cover to be lifted, I would not increase in certainty. (ʿAlī), 93
what no eye has seen and no ear has heard, and what has never occurred to a mortal man, 91
When destiny is mentioned, restrain yourselves!, 75
Where do you come from? He said, "He.". . . . (likely Kharrāz), 191
When poverty is perfected, he is God. (Sufi saying), 246, 247
Who is your master? He said, "God.". . . . (likely Kharrāz), 191
Whoever acts in accordance with what he knows . . . what he does not know, 147
Whoever changes his religion, slay him, 245
Whoever dies, his resurrection has happened, 284n104
Whoever fasts endlessly does not have a fast, 98
Whoever God guides, none shall lead him astray. . . . , 208
Whoever loves a people shall be mustered with them, 112
Whoever recognizes God becomes speechless. (Junayd), 145
Whoever says "No god but God" enters the Garden, 190
Whoever sees the Prophet's beauty will become an unbeliever. . . . (Abū Saʿīd b. Abī'l-Khayr), 242
Whoever seeks and perseveres shall find. (proverb), 130
Whoever speaks Arabic is Arab. . . . (Abū Hurayra), 291n10
Whoever submits is Arab, and the believer's heart is Arab, 143

Whoever wants to see a dead man walking . . . let him look at Ibn Abī Quḥāfa, 108
You must have done a lot of good for him. (ʿAlī), 39
Your greatest enemy is the soul between your two sides, 116
Your love for something makes you blind and deaf, 251

Index of Names and Terms

abjad-i ʿishq, 179, *see also* love, alphabet of
Abraham, 71–72, 171, 208–209, 241
Abū Bakr, 138, 142–143, 156–157, 168, 210, 284n105, *see also* Ibn Abī Quḥāfa
Abū Ḥanīfa, 92, 121, 238
Abū Hurayra, 169, 291n10, 295n43
Abū Jahl, 73, 167–169, 207, 210
Abū Lahab, 73, 210
Abū Saʿīd b. Abī'l-Khayr, 94, 236, 240, 242
accident, 70, 202, 210, 224
Adam, 103, 197, 210–213
ʿādat, 111, *see also* habit
affirmation, 95, 188, 190, 199
ʿĀʾisha, 102, 122
ʿālam al-khayāl, 283n68
ʿālām-i rūḥ, 105
ʿālam-i sirr, 179, *see also* world of mystery
ʿālam-i yaqīn, 183, *see also* world of certainty
alchemy, 107, 126, 154, 195, 230, 238
ʿAlī b. Abī Ṭālib, 39, 47, 93, 121, 174
alms tax, 98, 99, 100, 118
Āmulī, Abū ʿAlī, 34
amr, 212; *al-taklīfī*, 212; *al-takwīnī*, 212, *see also* command
angel(s), 57, 96, 107, 120, 210–211, 213, 215; of death, 43, 86, *see also* ʿAzrāʾīl; Gabriel; Michael; Munkar and Nakīr
annihilation, 100, 107–108, 182, 209; in God, 197; in the Messenger, 197
apparition(s), 29, 31–33, 132
ʿaql, 58, 148, *see also* intellect
ʿārif, 144, *see also* recognizer(s)
ʿarsh, 289n106, *see also* Throne
Aṣamm, Ḥātim al-, 108
Ascension, 96, 103, 156, 191, 255
Ashʿarism, 1, 63, 277n16
Āsiya, 91
asmāʾ, 61, *see also* name(s), divine
assent, 91, 93, 166
associationism, 45, 112, 188, 191–192, 242, 259
ʿAṭṭār, Farīd al-Dīn, 20
attributes, 13, 16, 61–65, 68, 72, 98, 124–125, 141, 148–149, 155–156, 194, 205–207, 224–225, 246, 248
Avicenna (Abū/Bū ʿAlī Sīnā), 16, 64, 74, 76–77, 84, 105, 107, 239–240
awliyāʾ Allāh, 5, *see also* Friends of God
āyāt, 143, *see also* sign(s)

Ayāz, 213
azal/azalī 25, 275n5, *see also* Beginningless, the/ Beginninglessness
ʿAzāzīl (Azazel), 201
ʿAzīz al-Dīn, 6–7
ʿAzrāʾīl, 301n74

bad transmitters, 81–83
Baghdad, 1, 4, 7, 12, 47, 238
Baghdad, little girl from, 132–133
Balkhī, Shaqīq al-, 108
baqāʾ, 63, 184, *see also* subsistence
Baqillānī, Abū Bakr al-, 277n16
Baqlī, Ruzbihān, 19–20
basmala, 120, 173–174, 181
Baṣrī, al-Ḥasan al-, 201
Basṭāmī, Abū Yazīd (Bā Yazīd), 5, 123, 141, 158, 193, 202, 247, 289n109, 299n21
bāṭin, 169, *see also* esoteric
beauty, 11, 25, 53, 77, 79, 92, 99, 108, 113–114, 124–125, 144, 150, 164–165, 171–172, 176, 178–180, 183, 187, 190–192, 195, 202–209, 215, 217, 219, 221, 231, 235, 238, 241–242, 249, 252, 257–258, 260
Beginningless, the/ Beginninglessness, 25, 31–32, 58, 67, 126, 148, 163, 171, 177–178, 201, 215–216, 224, 247, 271n5
Beloved, the, 18, 49, 51, 53, 109, 202–205, 208, 211–213, 216–219, 221, 223–230, 232, 234–235, 238, 250–254
Bible, 36
Bilāl b. Rabaḥ, 122
brothers, 47–48, 141–142
Bukhārī, Abū Ibrāhīm Mustamlī, 125
bulbul, 231, *see also* nightingale
Burūsawī, Ismāʿīl Ḥaqqī, 19, 20, 175–176, 296n82
Bustī, Abū'l-Ḥasan, 187, 246, 298n1

candle, 235, 254
caprice(s), 42, 78, 114, 115, 116, 126, 145, 154, 200–201; -worship, 241
charismatic gifts, 29–30, 152
charity, 6, 38–39, 112, 135
cheek, 202–204
chevalier, 31, 42, 44, 45, 48, 82, 127, 144, 145, 157, 163, 174, 176, 178, 182, 199, 203, 213, 214, 215, 216, 225, 245, 246
China, 46, 147, 284n106
Chishtī, Muʿīn al-Dīn, 8
Chishtī order, 20–21
Chittick, William, xiv, 21, 51
chivalry, 214–215
Christian(s), 236, 293n75
coextensivity, 60
command, of God, 125–127, 134–135, 169, 213, 254; engendering, 212–213; prescriptive, 212–213
compelled, 84–85, 124, 213–214
compulsory return, 108
Corbin, Henry, 117

Dargazīnī, Abū'l-Qāsim, 6–8
David, 121, 249
death, 16, 37, 43, 47, 50, 68, 86, 95, 105–109, 111, 151, 208, 228, 254
determination, divine, 80–81
detached letters, the, 19, 175–182, 185
dhawq, 15, 28, *see also* tasting
dhikr, 38, 272n31
Dhū'l-Nūn al-Miṣrī, 41–42, 158–159
dil, 94, 99, 117, 136, 147, 225, 285n3
disciple(s), 2–3, 6–8, 11–14, 33, 37, 42–44, 46, 49, 108, 126, 147, 233

discipleship, 128, 138, 192
Dihlawī, Naṣīr al-Dīn Chirāgh, 21
Dominion, 84, 95, 106, 108–109, 154, 171, 177, 187, 191, 199, 201, 208, 280n29, 293n69
dot(s), 19, 175, 181–185, 246
dreams, 32–34, 52, 103–104
dualism, 80–81, 243

ecstatic utterances, 281n9, 293n71
elements, four, 28, 104–105
eschatology, 15, 106, 148–149, 306n67
esoteric, 11, 159, 169
Essence (of God), 13, 16, 55–58, 62–66, 97, 155–156, 159, 194, 198, 206, 224, 237, 244
Eternal, the, 58–59, 69
evil, 73, 75–83, 209
execution, 4–5, 7–8, 47, 50
exoteric, 92, 214

faith, 15, 40, 42–43, 46, 48, 52, 80, 137, 148–150, 153, 163, 175–176, 180, 190, 198, 205–210, 230, 238, 240, 242–243, 254, 256, 259; true, 244, 248
fanāʾ, 182, 197, *see also* annihilation
faqīr, 246, 248, *see also* poor one; poverty
Farghānī, Saʿīd al-Dīn, 20
fasting, 96–98, 112, 118
Fāṭima b. Abī Bakr al-Kattānī, 17
fikr, 38, *see also* meditation
fire, 28, 47, 76–78, 85, 95, 105, 195, 201, 204, 210–212, 214, 226, 230, 233–235, 239
fire-worship, 82, 242, 245
Footstool, 289n106
freedom, human, 80–81, 84–86, 211
Friends of God, 5, 77, 142, 152, 193, 231, 272n27
friendship, 135, 152–153, 189
futuwwa, 272n26, *see also* chivalry

Gabriel (Archangel), 86, 102–103, 212, 280n39
ghayrat, 51, 211, *see also* jealousy, divine
Ghazālī, Abū Ḥāmid al-, 2–3, 5, 15–16, 23–24, 28, 32, 68–69, 77, 149, 170, 265n52, 270–271n1, 276n11, 296n74
Ghazālī, Aḥmad, 3, 7, 10, 14, 24, 29–30, 32, 102, 141, 160, 187, 198, 211, 216, 246, 248, 254, 273n32, 298n1
Gīsūdarāz, Sayyid Muḥammad, 21
gratitude, 100–101
Greek sage, 124
guidance, 24, 32, 73, 86, 93, 111, 179, 205–209, 216–217, 243
gul, 231, *see also* rose
Gurgānī, Abū'l-Qāsim, 215–216, 303n136

habit, 43, 63, 111–114, 164, 175
habit-worship, 111–117, 164–165, 214, 225, 241
ḥadīth qudsī, 51, 71, 118
Hajj, 98–99, 118, *see also* pilgrimage
ḥāl, 16, 25, 27, *see also* spiritual state
Ḥallāj, 4–5, 10, 18, 50, 52, 68, 211, 214, 239, 246, 255, 265n34, 275n68, 276n11, 283n80, 301n79, 302n103, 302n110, 303n119, 303n129, 303n132, 304n146
Hamadānī, Shaykh Baraka, 2–3, 172–173, 216
ḥaqīqat-warzī, 113
hawāʾ, 78; *-parastī*, 241, *see also* caprice(s)
Heravi, Najib Mayel, 1–2

Hidden Treasure, 99, 249–250
Hülegü Khan, 20
ḥulūlī, yi-majāzī, 256, 259; *yi-maʿnawī*, 256, 259; *see also* incarnationist
ḥurūf al-muqaṭṭaʿa, al-, 175, *see also* detached letters, the
huwiyya, 271n6, *see also* identity
hypocrite(s), 44, 154

Iblis, 10, 86, 187, 206–208, 210–218, 237–238, 241, 248, 250; black light of, 198–203, 205, 207–209; as chevalier, 214–216, 225, 303n132; leader of the abandoned ones, 216, 219; teacher of the angels, 211, 213, 215; tresses of, 203–205, 301n80, *see also* ʿAzāzīl; devil(s); Satan; satan(s); Satanology
Ibn ʿAbbās, 121, 128, 166, 174, 195
Ibn Abī Quḥāfa, 108
Ibn ʿArabī, 20, 64, 66, 102
Ibn al-Fāriḍ, 19
Ibn al-Fuwaṭī, 7
Ibn al-Muʿtazz, 25–26
Identity, 25, 271n6
idol(s), 113–114, 228, 241, 256
idol-worship, 82, 113–114, 164, 236–237, 242, 245, 256, 259
ikhlāṣ, 90, *see also* sincerity
imaginalization, 102–106, 197, 214, 257–259
imagination, 102–106, 145
īmān, 148, 259; *-i ḥaqīqī*, 244, 248, *see also* faith
incarnationist, metaphorical, 256, 259; of meaning, 256, 259
inrushes, 27–28, 127
intellect, 16, 24–25, 57–58, 60–61, 67, 79, 107, 145, 147–149, 150–153, 158, 232; eye of, 61; scale of, 147–148; stage beyond, 16, 149–153, 158
intention, 13, 89–91, 112
Invincibility, 158, 293n69
Iqbal, Muhammad, 72
irādat, 128, *see also* discipleship
ʿIrāqī, Fakhr al-Dīn, 20
ʿĪsawī, 18, 20, 30, *see also* Jesus-like
islām-i majāzi (*al-islām al-majāzī*), 239-240, 248, *see also* metaphorical Islam
Ismailism, 5, 7, 13, 276n11, 290n146
ithbāt, 184, 188, *see also* affirmation
Izutsu, Toshihiko, 55

jabarūt, 293n69, *see also* Invincibility
jaʿd, 202, *see also* tress(es)
Jāmī, ʿAbd al-Raḥmān, 19, 20
jān, 123, 126
jawānmardī, 272n26, *see also* chivalry
jawhar, 56, *see also* substance
jealousy, divine, 49–53, 123, 158, 211–212
Jesus, 29–30, 109, 236, 284n108, 285n109
Jesus-like, 30
Jew(s), 236, 302n99
Jewish 273n40
Jinn, 210, 249, 303n136
Junayd, al-, 112
Juwaynī, Muḥammad b, Ḥamūya al-, 2, 298n1

Kaʿb the "Rabbi," 208
kabāʾir, 40–41, *see also* major sins
Kalābādhī, Abū Bakr al-, 124–125
kalām (divine attribute), 63, 194
kalām (rational theology), 1, *see also* theology
Kalbī, Diḥya al-, 103
Kāmil al-Dawla, 4, 49–50
Kāshānī, Rukn al-Dīn, 21
khadd, 202, *see also* cheek
khāl, 202, *see also* mole

kashf, 46, 171, *see also* unveiling
kernel, 170, 245
kharābāt, 305n32, *see also* tavern
kharābātī, 305n33
Kharrāz, Abū Saʿīd al-, 56
khayāl, 102–104, *see also* imagination
Khayrābādī, Faḍl-i Ḥaqq, 20
Khayyām, ʿUmar, 1–2
khidmat, 46
khidmat-i kafshī, 46, *see also* sandal-service
Khiḍr, 114, 285n12
Khotan, 108, 284n106
Khudānamā, Mīrān Jī Ḥusayn, 21
Khurasan, 108, 238, 303n136
Khwārazmī, Ḥusayn-i, 20
kingdom, 84, 95, 108, 171, 177, 187, 191, 280n29, 293n69
Kubrā, Najm al-Dīn, 19
Kubrawī order, 18–19
kufr, 239–240, 259; *-i ḥaqīqī*, 243–245, 248, 259; *-i ilāhī*, 243; levels of, 239; *-i Muḥammadī*, 241, 259; *-i nafs*, 241, 248; *-i qalb*, 241, 248, 259; *-i ẓāhir*, 240–241, 248; *zunnār-i*, 244
khwud-shināsī, 9, *see also* self-recognition

Layla, 222, 231
Lawāʾiḥ (*Flashes*), 7
letters, 173, 229; black, 184, 214; conjoined, 177, 179, 181, 183; detached, 19, 175–182, 185; garb of, 177, 202; imprint of/without, 173, 175, 181
Lewisohn, Leonard, xv, 9
light, 70, 101, 122, 150, 171, 184–185, 206, 251; black, 198–203, 205, 207–209, 247; chains of, 91; and darkness, 121, 187, 189, 191; of God, 68–70, 73, 79, 86, 115, 118, 133, 142, 144, 154, 189, 193, 204, 208–209, 214, 234; of the Kaaba, 99, 123; levels of, 55, 68, 71; of lights, 68; Muhammadan, 32–33, 190–199, 201–204, 207; Source of, 68; in Zoroastrianism, 80–81
love, 10, 13, 17, 72, 112, 151, 158, 176, 200, 215–219, 221–234, 237–239, 249–260; alphabet of, 179–180; doctrine of, 10–11; heart-, 253; for one's homeland, 48–49; path of, 228–229, 231, 236; poetry, 18; of the Prophet, 34, 142–143, 250–251; religion of, 236–238; School of, 8, 10; self-, 232, 248, 250–251, 253, 259; taste of, 233, *see also* lover(s); Beloved, the
lover(s), 18–19, 34, 44, 51–53, 112, 119, 151, 154, 175, 177–178, 198, 203–204, 212, 214, 218–219, 221–226, 228–235, 238–239, 250–253, 257–258, 260

maʿād, 15, 148, *see also* eschatology
Madrasa Mujāhidiyya, 20
maʿdūm, 77, *see also* nonexistent
maghz, 170, *see also* kernel
Maḥmūd (Ghaznavid Sultan), 253
Maḥmūd II (Seljuq Sultan), 6–7
maḥw, 182, *see also* obliteration
maʿiyya, 16, 60, *See also* withness
Majnun, 222, 231
major sins, 40–41
malakūt, 280n29, 293n69, *see also* Dominion
Manīrī, Sharaf al-Dīn, 21
maʿrifat-i nafs, 9, *see also* self-recognition
Mary, 48–49, 101–102, 280n39
maṣdar al-anwār, 68, *see also* light, Source of
Masʿūd Bakk, 21

Maybudī, Rashīd al-Dīn, 18, 52
meditation, 38, 173
Meier, Fritz, 9
mercy, 38–41, 44, 73, 77, 99–100, 172, 206–207, 212, 214, 217, 219
Messengers, 5, 148, 152
metaphorical Islam, 240–241
Michael (Archangel), 212
miracles, 4, 29, 152
miʿrāj, 96, *see also* Ascension
mirror, 67, 107, 120, 138, 141–145, 154, 156, 191, 218, 230, 248–250, 252, 255, 259
misguidance, 14, 15, 73, 86, 115, 199, 205, 207–209, 211, 213, 216–217
mole, 202–205, 215, 249, 301n80
Morris, James, xiii, 117
Moses, 33, 71–72, 86, 97, 158, 178, 195, 199, 236
moth, 235
Muʿādh b. Jabal (Muʿādh-i Jabal), 121, 287n58
muḍṭarr, 84, see also compelled; subjugation/subjugated
Muhammad, 32–35, 46, 55, 70–73, 79–80, 86, 90, 93, 96, 99–100, 103, 109, 114, 116, 119, 121–122, 126–127, 129–130, 138, 142, 143–144, 155–156, 165, 167–168, 178, 187, 190–211, 214, 222, 225, 233, 238, 241–242, 248–251, 254–256, 258
Muhammadan eyes, 79–80
mulk, 280n29, 293n69, *see also* kingdom
Mullā Ṣadrā, 19, 185
Munkar and Nakīr, 106
Murata, Sachiko, 143
musakhkhar 84, see also compelled; subjugation/subjugated
musāwiq al-wujūd, 60, *see also* coextensivity
Muʿtazila, 80–81, 84
muwaḥḥid, 275n69, *see also* unity-voicer

Nābulusī, ʿAbd al-Ghanī al-, 20
Nāgawrī, Ḥamīd al-Dīn, 8
Nāma-hā (*The Letters*), 3, 6, 11–14, 26, 28–29, 37, 43–44, 80, 94, 126, 152, 159, 170, 262
name(s), divine, 13, 16, 50, 61–65, 69, 97–98, 101, 103, 141–142, 194, 205–207, 229, 248
nāqilān-i bad, 83, *see also* bad transmitters
Nasafī, ʿAzīz al-Dīn, 19
Nasr, Seyyed Hossein, xiii
Necessary Existent, 58–59, 64–65, 68
nightingale, 231–232
niyya, 13, 89, *see also* intention
Niẓām al-Dīn Awliyāʾ, 21
niẓām al-khayr, 77, see also order of the good
nonexistent, 69, 70, 76–77, 182, 196–197
nubuwwa, 148, *see also* prophecy
nuqaṭ, 181, *see also* dot(s)
nūr, 70, *see also* light
nūr al-anwār, 68, *see also* light, of lights
Nurī, Abū'l-Ḥusayn, 159, 293n75
nūr-i siyāh, 198, *see also* light, black
Nuzhat al-ʿushshāq (*The Lovers' Excursion*), 17–18

obedient deeds, 41, 80, 90, 93, 223
obliteration, 95, 182–184
oneness of existence, 66–67
order of the good, 77
Ottoman(s), 19

Paradise, 90–91, 101, 116, 129, 145, 161–162, 210–211, 225–226

parwāna, 235
Persian, xix–xx, xxiii, 3, 4, 8, 12, 14, 18, 19, 20, 21, 62, 125, 162, 171, 198, 235, 253, 254, 284n106, 296n74
Pharaoh, 91, 294n24, 303n132
pilgrimage, 2–3, 7, 98, 119, 135
pillars, of practice/faith, 11, 13, 92–93, 105, 148
pīr-i pukhta, 132, *see also* ripened master
poor one, 246–248
Pourjavady, Nasrollah, 8
poverty, 79, 163, 216, 246–247
prayer, 12, 65, 89, 95–96, 98, 112, 117, 172, 204, 217
Preserved Tablet, 120, 127, 174, 229
prophecy, 15, 16, 28, 48, 148–149, 152–153, 233
Prophets, 5, 14–15, 33, 57, 71–72, 77, 135, 144, 152, 167, 193, 195, 199
purity, 94–95, 170, 227
pust, 170, *see also* shell

qadar, 80, *see also* determination, divine
Qadariyya, 80–81, 84
qadīm, al-, 16, 58, *see also* Eternal, the
Qaḥṭabī, Abū Bakr, 103, 124
qalb, 117, 241, see also *dil*
Qaranī, Uways al-, 112, 285n4
qiyāma, 33, *see also* Resurrection
qiyās burhānī¸ 59
Quran, 13–15, 19, 28, 30, 32, 41, 44–45, 49, 66, 68, 78, 82–83, 86, 90, 96–97, 103, 116, 119, 143, 145–146, 159, 161–180, 183–185, 194–195, 208, 210, 214, 242
Quranic interpretation, 13, 166–167, 169

Rābiʿa al-ʿAdawiyya, 17
Rāzī, Fakhr al-Dīn al-, 20
Rāzī, Najm al-Dīn, 18–19
Rāzī, Yaḥyā Muʿādh-i, 91
recognizer(s), 45, 52, 60–61, 67, 91, 136, 144–147, 149, 151, 155–157, 249
reflection, 66, 102, 129, 143, 170, 172
renunciants, 90, 131–132, 145, 247, 257
Resurrection, 33, 99, 106–108, 173
revealed religions, 167
ripened master, 132–133
Risāla-yi ʿAyniyya (*Treatise Dedicated to ʿAyn al-Quḍāt*), 264n27
Risāla-yi Jamālī (*Treatise Dedicated to Jamāl al-Dawla*), 14–15
Ritter, Hellmut, 8
rose, 73, 100, 231–232
rūḥ, 101, 105, 123, 127
rujūʿ al-iḍṭirārī, al-, 108
rujūʿ al-ikhtiyārī, al-, 108
Rūmī, Jalāl al-Dīn, 20
ruwāt-i bad, 83, *see also* bad transmitters

ṣadaqa, 38, *see also* charity
Safavids, 7, 19
sage, 33, 170, 198
ṣalāt, 96, *see also* prayer
Samʿānī, Aḥmad, 18, 52
Sanāʾī, 8, 18
sandal-service, 44–47
sāqī, 305n32
Sarrāj, Abū Naṣr al-, 98
Satan, 5, 10–11, 86, 115, 198–200, 204, 211, *see also* ʿAzāzīl; devil(s); Iblis; satan(s); Satanology
satan(s), 46, 86, 94, 111, 115, 120
Satanology, 10–11, 198, 205, 210
Sawāniḥ al-ʿushshāq (*Incidents of the Lovers*), 7–8, 10
Schimmel, Annemarie, 233
sects, 82, 236

self-disclosure(s), 62, 249
self-recognition, 9, 153, 155–158, 168, 228
selfhood, 93, 115–116, 122, 137, 158, 214, 246
selflessness, 107, 116–117, 137
Seljuqs, 6, 44, 46–47, 265n52
Shabistarī, Maḥmūd, 20
Shādruymanish, Muḥammad, 81
Shāfiʿī, al-, 92, 121, 238
Shahada, 93, 127, 187, 190–191, 199, 205, 299n21
shāhid, 253, *see also* witness
shāhid-bāzī, 253–254, 256, 259
Shakwā'l-gharīb (*The Exile's Complaint*), 5–7, 16–18, 47–49
shamʿ, 235, *see also* candle
Sharaf al-Dawla, Jamāl al-Dīn, 14
Sharia, 92–94, 97–99, 113, 124, 129, 159, 212, 233, 240, 248, 254, 256
sharīʿat-warzī, 113
shaṭaḥāt, 281n9, *see also* ecstatic utterances
Shaykh Fatḥa, 2–3, 218
shell, 47, 170
Shiblī, Abū Bakr al-, 52, 91, 94, 112, 230, 234, 251, 298n120
Shīrāzī, Maʿṣūm ʿAlī Shāh, 18, 20
shirk, 45, 191, 242, 259, *see also* associationism
shukr, 101, *see also* gratitude
ṣifāt, 61, 194, *see also* attributes
sign(s), 57, 128, 133, 143, 155, 171, 179, 227, 238
sincerity, 90–91, 127, 230, 239
Siyāwish, Shaykh, 33–34
spiritual state, 16, 24–25, 27
St. Teresa of Ávila, 293n75
subjugation/subjugated, 84–85, 124, 193, 213, 280n30
subsistence, 63, 184, 209, 231
substance, 56, 70, 202, 207–208, 210, 224, 238
Suhrawardī, Shihāb al-Dīn al-, 20, 68, 102
Sumnūn al-Muḥibb, 187

ṭāʿāt, 41, *see also* obedient deeds
Tabrīzī, Shams al-Dīn, 19, 254
tafsīr, 166, *see also* Quranic interpretation
ṭahārat, 94, *see also* purity
taḥrīf, 13, 81, *see also* alteration
tajalliyyāt, 62, *see also* self-disclosure(s)
tajdīd al-khalq, 16, 146
tamaththul, 102, *see also* imaginalization
Tamhīdāt (*Paving the Path*), 4, 8–12, 19–22, 29, 34, 52, 56, 101, 115, 153, 174, 224
taṣdīq, 93, *see also* assent
tasting, 15, 28–29, 72, 82–83, 136, 145, 175, 178
tavern, 233, 254, 305n32
Ṭawāsīn, Kitāb al-, 10, 214
tawḥīd, 15, *see also* oneness of God
theology, 1, 13–14, 63, 81, 185; mystical, 5, 11, 13, 55; philosophical, 20; rational, 1–2, 7, 13, 15–16, 23–24, 80
thorns, 231
Throne, 119, 129, 169, 174, 182, 211, 215, 243, 289n106
Tirmidhī, Abū Saʿīd, 30
Torah, 33, 208
tress(es), 202–205, 301n80
trial and tribulation, 52, 228–231
Turkish, 19, 304n153
Ṭūsī, Muḥammad Maʿshūq-i, 94
Ṭūsī, Naṣīr al-Dīn, 20
Tustarī, Sahl b. ʿAbd Allāh, 197

ʿUmar, 29, 142, 168, 210, 271n17, 287n59, 294n24
unity-voicer, 52, 237, 257
unveiling, 46–47, 171

ʿUryān, Bābā Ṭāhir, 3
ʿUsayrān, ʿAfīf, 9–10, 21

voluntary return, 108

waḥdat al-wujūd, 66, *see also* oneness of existence
wājib al-wujūd, 58, *see also* Necessary Existent
walāya, 152, *see also* friendship
Wāqiʿa-hā (*Apparitions*), 14
wāridāt, 27, *see also* inrushes
wayfaring, 33, 43, 82, 93, 101, 127, 130–131, 134, 136, 180
wine, 107, 155, 228, 231, 244, 305n32
withness, 16, 60–61
witness, 16, 24, 73, 93, 133, 136, 145–147, 150–152, 174, 184, 248, 252–257
world of certainty, 183, 226
world of mystery, 179
worthiness, 120, 138, 162, 165

ẓāhir, 169, *see also* exoteric
zakāt, 99, *see also* alms tax
Zoroastrians, 80–82, 236–237, 242
Zubdat al-ḥaqāʾiq (*The Essence of Reality*), 2, 5, 9, 15–17, 20, 110
zuhhād, 90, *see also* renunciants